VOODOO
in Haiti

VOODOO
IN HAITI

ALFRED MÉTRAUX

Translated by
HUGO CHARTERIS

NEW INTRODUCTION BY
SIDNEY W. MINTZ

SCHOCKEN BOOKS · NEW YORK

To the memory of
LORGINA DELORGE
mambo of La Salines
whose sacred name was 'Dieu devant'
and to
MADAME ODETTE MENNESSON-RIGAUD
'certified' *mambo*
without whose help
this book could never have been written

CONTENTS

CONTENTS

PLATES

ILLUSTRATIONS IN THE TEXT

VOODOO
in Haiti

Introduction to the
Second English Edition

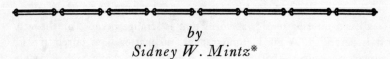

by
*Sidney W. Mintz**

In 1948–49, while Alfred Métraux was engaged in anthropological fieldwork in the Republic of Haiti, some of Professor Julian Steward's students (this writer included) were making a series of community studies in nearby Puerto Rico. It was our good fortune that Professor John V. Murra, then of the University of Puerto Rico and an intimate friend of Métraux's, should have received all of us one night in his apartment, while Métraux was visiting. During the day Métraux had visited one of us—Eric Wolf—in the field and had displayed the energy, single-mindedness, and enthusiasm for which he was so justly famous. After an exhausting trip to and from that community (where, to everyone's amazement, including Wolf's, he had sprung from his horse in order to begin eliciting data, matter-of-factly and in excellent Spanish, on house types and house construction, from some of Wolf's startled informants), he received us on Murra's terrace, beneath a brilliant Antillean sky. Sitting at ease in a lounge chair, drink in hand, Métraux began to talk about anthropology and about what it meant to be an anthropologist.

Tributes to Métraux have been written by the score, and by those close to him; this writer has no proper part in adding to what has already been said. But that starlit evening had its impact on those of us for whom anthropology possessed a magic it is now rapidly losing. We who were its students might not only look forward to living among strange and remote peoples someday but might also learn in the presence of those whose lives were given over to doing just that. Can one borrow a more contemporary image? Moonwalkers fill us

* Dr. Simone Dreyfus-Gamelon and Professors John V. Murra and Richard Price kindly read and criticized very usefully an early draft of this introduction. I am grateful to them all, but they do not share my responsibility for interpretations I have made here.

I

with awe because they have been brave, and they have experienced somewhere alien and distant. Anthropology finds its beginnings in a related awe, the wonder of unknown worlds, and the educated wonder of our teachers, who have seen and continue to question.

But the anthropologist's unknown world, unlike the astronaut's, is really an interior world, a world that is strange because of the way it is perceived. A good ethnographer, no matter how unrelativistic, always recognizes that reality is, among other things, what people have learned to see. And while the outer world may seem bizarre, exotic, and remote, it is to the relationship between that outer world and the perceptions and intents of men that anthropology directs its attention. Métraux exemplified that concern and the puzzlement that all good ethnographers are commonly prey to. What he had seen had become part of what he saw with, but only after the lenses provided by his own culture had themselves been clearly seen.

Métraux apparently viewed each society in terms of its uniqueness, its special character; Haiti was such a society, though he talked relatively little about it that night. He was not—it seemed—interested in problems of the evolutionary succession of societies, in their ecological fit, in their range of variation. In fact, Métraux's concern with "grand theory" was faint. Progression, retardation, the study of society on a cosmic scale, these did not appear to be matters in which he was much interested. The sometime student of Nordenskiöld and Rivet, Métraux had become a field anthropologist *par excellence*. But he did not follow closely or with great interest the theoretical advances of his British and North American colleagues. Inevitably, then, it was for his ethnography that he was known. Such an assertion, however, is neither defense nor criticism: it merely suggests that Métraux was as Métraux did, a fieldworker's fieldworker, an ethnographer's ethnographer, who left most of the theorizing to others. Herein, perhaps, one perceives the poignance of Claude Tardits' piercing posthumous evaluation of him: "One might almost say that Métraux, after having been the student of his Indians, wanted nothing more than to be the Indian of his students" (Tardits 1964: 18–19).

Métraux's ethnographic skill was famous among anthropologists, and it rested on diverse talents: a great gift for languages, the strength and endurance of two ordinary men, an ability (doubtless sometimes distressing and perhaps even an obstacle) to forget all else while pursuing the slightest snippet of data, and a genuine consecration to the field. Until he began his work in Haiti, Métraux had usually worked among peoples better described as "primitive" than as "peasant," to use two of the descriptive terms anthropologists are fond of. Though he had a very substantial familiarity with Andean Indians—among his other accomplishments, Métraux had written on the Uru-Chipaya (e.g., Métraux 1934, 1935) and other Andean peoples—the bulk of his publications before Haiti concerned South American Indians of the tropical lowland. Even this much-qualified assertion is imprecise; yet it is probably correct to claim that the Haitian people represented a different—and doubtless far more western—cultural variant than any that had concerned Métraux previously.

In 1941, while Métraux was visiting the Ile à Tortue off Haiti's north coast in the company of Jacques Roumain, the idea of creating a Bureau of Ethnology for that country was born—an idea that Roumain was later able to convert into a proud reality. Métraux's awareness of Haiti's cultural richness was stimulated—as he tells us in *Voodoo*—by an intense campaign by the Church against the local religion, during which untold artistic riches were savagely destroyed in the name of a higher faith. Once awakened, Métraux's interest in Haiti never ceased; in an article in *Afroamérica* (Métraux 1945), long before he began his Haitian fieldwork, he wrote glowingly of the Bureau d'Ethnologie and its collections, taking justifiable pride in his part in the Bureau's creation. Between that time and his death, he published scores of articles and several books on Haiti, of which this, originally *Le vaudou haïtien,* is the best known.

Métraux had worked on Easter Island before becoming a specialist on Haiti (e.g., Métraux 1940). In later years, when he found himself fascinated by Haiti's folk religion, he wondered out loud whether he had been consecrated to the study of insular enigmas. Yet he had not gone to Haiti for this purpose, and his genuine interest in *vaudou* matured only after he had developed a commanding knowledge of Haitian culture in general. He had begun his investigations in Marbial Valley in 1948 at the behest of UNESCO, to provide "educators, doctors, agronomists who made up the team charged with the completion of the project, with concrete data on the life and beliefs of the peasantry." And he continues, "It was hence during the course of a general sociological study treating nutrition, life circumstances, social organization, in short all the aspects of social life, that I found myself in the presence of *vaudou*. Thus I was able to take account of what it meant for these people" (Bing 1964).*

Without a serious reading of Métraux's Haitian ethnography, written as his interest in *vaudou* grew, however, it is not easy to see the skill with which his study of Haitian religion was invested. For instance, *Making a Living in the Marbial Valley, Haiti,* which he wrote with some of the Haitian scholars who made up his Marbial team and which is still little known today, even to many Haiti enthusiasts, was published in 1951; it remains one of the most useful single sources available on Haitian peasant culture (Métraux 1951a). Also in 1951, Métraux published the best paper ever done on Haitian rural house-types (Métraux 1951b) in a relatively unknown French geographical journal; and yet another, on inheritance, in a Belgian africanist review (Métraux 1951c). In 1953, again, Métraux was able to help Robert Hall in his preparation of the linguistic monograph *Haitian Creole* (Hall 1953). Thus Métraux came to *vaudou* while steeping himself in the study of Haitian culture generally—and toward the end of an intensely active field career that had given him an ethnographic breadth and perspective rarely equalled.

"Vaudou," he told Madame Fernande Bing in a 1961 interview,

is an extremely vast universe, an African religion indeed, but also a European religion: in a word, a syncretic religion that has blended together not only different African cults but also certain beliefs from European folklore. One finds here Norman and Breton traditions, carried by the French colonists and adopted by the Blacks; one even finds masonic rites. In short, this is a sort of conglomeration of elements of all kinds, dominated by African traditions. This religion is practiced by ninety per cent of the Haitian people. . . . At the same time these people consider them-

---

* A close co-worker believes that Métraux hoped—at least in the beginning —that his work for UNESCO would ultimately benefit the Haitian people themselves, though he had no such optimism in the case of primitive peoples, whom he felt were doomed. Dreyfus-Gamelon, *in lit.,* November 25, 1971.

selves Catholic, and while I affirm that nine-tenths of the population practice *vaudou,* I do not mean that they are not Christian. All *vaudou* believers are in effect excellent Catholics, extremely pious. In their belief, there is no sharp break between the religion that they practice and in which they believe, and the Catholicism to which they are bound. Thus *vaudou* does not reveal itself as a religion opposed to Catholicism. Haitian peasants all, I repeat, are good Catholics, and really perceive no contradiction, no opposition, between the official religion of their country and the particular faith that they have inherited from their ancestors. *Vaudou* took on its character in Haiti in the absence of a Church. The slaves, imported from Africa in the eighteenth century, were baptized, forced to go to church, but they received no religious education. Thus they remained faithful to the one possession they had been able to bring with them, that is, their beliefs. They remained even more attached since they were thus able to guard some hope and, in spite of the reality, to give to their lives some meaning, thanks to certain values that these beliefs preserved. The life of the slaves was horrible, abominable—and *vaudou* brought to them that which it brings to Haiti's poor today: the grounds for hope, for confidence, and above all, a way of distracting oneself, of escaping from reality.

(Bing 1964: 28–29)

The interview from which this passage is taken was taped in 1961, three years after the first publication of *Voodoo* in French. In it, Métraux talked at greater length about the mysteries of *vaudou*— which is to say, those aspects of this complex religious system that were not, and are not, understood. The interview itself revealed him once again as an ethnographer who never stopped asking *himself,* as well as his informants, what things mean. In Haiti as elsewhere, he was consumed with a desire to determine what, indeed, was true, and his discussion of the priestess Lorgina Delorge shows well how carefully he sought to disentangle the loose ends of truth. More, perhaps—because Métraux found Haitians strange, it seems, in ways that the Indians of the forest were not strange—and his friendship with the Haitians apparently achieved a warmth and mutual sympathy that had not always been possible in the jungle (Dreyfus-Gamelon, *in lit.,* November 25, 1971).

This book gives us what is surely the most authoritative general account of that complex of belief and practice called *vaudou* available in the literature. Yet Métraux himself is careful to warn us that *vaudou* is difficult to study; that he was able to deal with only a part of it; that it is a cluster of different ceremonies, beliefs, practices, all changing and changeable. Métraux had been a fieldworker too long, had too much respect for human complexity, to suppose that cheerful positivism, careful work, and bounding energy were enough to guarantee the documentation of more than one segment of *vaudou*'s reality. What is more, his unwillingness to handle "high-level theory" led him to discuss his subject piece by piece, and to devote relatively little attention to the wider (and more interior) perspectives from which *vaudou* might be viewed. This must surely be the major weakness of *Voodoo*. On the one hand, Métraux contributes relatively little to any comparative theory of religion, restricting himself largely to "the facts." On the other hand, he shows little ease with the elements of ecstasy and of mystery that contribute so much to the character of *vaudou* as a religious system. His approach is, in fact, empirical, rationalistic, and conservatively ethnographic. At the same time, it bears stressing that no other observer of *vaudou* has contributed to its study the exquisite documentation of detail that marks the works of Alfred Métraux.

Though anthropologists are often said to be driven by their liking for the bizarre and exotic, this assertion probably misses the point. Georges Condominas has suggested (Condominas 1965) how the exotic becomes everyday, once it is experienced that way; and some anthropologists might say that what excites them most is the process by which the apparently bizarre becomes ordinary. Therein the matter-of-factness of modern life finds its other nature, in the view of strangers: for is there doubt that the character of modern life is as bizarre and exotic as any other man has invented? Yet we who inhabit today's societies, while obediently living up to the value of social self-criticism so typical of that modernity, find our own societies far less bizarre (and far more agreeable in fact) than we care to admit. More—we rush about the globe, encouraging our children to do likewise, in search of something "truly different," even while we relentlessly turn it all into something that is "the same"; that is, more like our own.

In its savage and repeated thrusts into the world outside, the West has gone very far in replacing difference with sameness, in supplanting other, contrasting modes of thought and act, in changing what had once been exotic for westerners into pale and tawdry reflections of itself. It may be that the day when the total history of European hegemony is finally written, the indictment that we made many societies resemble ours will count as heavily as that we destroyed many others altogether. Yet during the five centuries that we have been steamrolling others into poky simulacra of ourselves, we have been alternately amused and enraged by the consequences. Both those who imitate us too well and those who imitate us not quite well enough are threatening; perhaps we would like most a perfect mimicry of the flesh accompanied by a total emptiness of the spirit.

If ever there were a society that ought to have ended up totally annihilated, materially and spiritually, by the trials of "modernization," it is Haiti. After the destruction of the aboriginal population and the early experiments in plantation production, Española (as the Spaniards called it), like its sister islands, was eclipsed in importance by the mainland from Mexico to the Andes, where a seemingly inexhaustible supply of mineral resources and of subjugated labor became the conquerors' special obsession. Between the Discovery, so-called, and the first quarter of the seventeenth century, the Caribbean was a Spanish sea; but the conquest of the highlands reduced it to a highway for the galleons.

Before the middle of the seventeenth century, however, the Ile à Tortue, off Española's north coast, and the northwest tip of Española itself, had become havens for anti-Spanish vagabonds, religious and political refugees, deserters, and runaways. Repeated Spanish attempts to dislodge these interlopers were never entirely successful; such buccaneers represented the first serious territorial challenge to Spain in the Greater Antilles. When the Treaty of Ryswick (1697) made the western third of Española formally French, the groundwork was already laid for what would become for a time the single most lucrative colony in western colonial history: Saint Domingue.

No mystery here, since it had become perfectly clear that the plantation production of newly established proletarian and urban commodities—sugar, tobacco, coffee, rum, etc.—for the European markets would be good business for centuries to come. The capital to buy slaves, to furnish the plantations and to create a flourishing economy founded on human flesh as property was readily forthcoming. Curtin (1969: 84) in a careful estimate, probably conservative, supposes that Saint Domingue received slightly fewer than 900,000 slaves during its history as a plantation colony. Between 1739 and 1788, 317,300 slaves were imported; between 1779 and 1790— *twelve years*—313,200 slaves were imported (Curtin 1969:79). To grasp fully the scale of this commerce in human beings, one need imagine what transatlantic transportation was like, before the start of the nineteenth century.

In 1681, sixteen years before the Treaty of Ryswick, Española had 2000 slaves. In 1739, 42 years after that Treaty, French Saint Domingue had 117,400 slaves; in 1791, on the eve of the Haitian Revolution, there were an estimated 480,000 slaves. Such figures, of course, tell us nothing by themselves about life expectancy on the plantations. But the record of cruelty in this most profitable of slave-based plantation colonies is very clear. One need only examine any of the exquisitely detailed studies of individual plantations by Gabriel Debien (1962) to grasp as much—at Sucrerie Cottineau, for instance, almost the entire slave contingent was replaced by "new stock" between 1766 and 1775, three-quarters freshly imported from Africa (Debien 1962: 50). Clear, too, is the way the ever-heightened importation of enslaved Africans limited the creolization of the slave population, keeping alive African traditions and an active resistance to *enslavement,* and not simply to *slavery.* When the Revolution began, only an estimated 36,000 Europeans and 28,000 freemen of mixed ancestry lived in the colony; indeed, it was the struggle between these groups that opened the way for a servile revolt. More than ten years of war followed; by any reasonable measure of the time, the Haitian Revolution was more important than the upheaval that had preceded it by only a few years in the thirteen British colonies to the north.

In 1804, when the Haitian Revolution ended, substantially all those who had held power in Saint Domingue were gone. The second independent republic of the New World had been born, and it was a black republic. What is little remembered by outsiders today is the hostile world within which the republic had to survive. If an independent white United States, even with its built-in slave economy, was once threatening to Europe, one may well imagine what an independent black Haiti must have meant to the powerful, in the United States as elsewhere. "Our policy with regard to Hayti is plain," intoned Sen. Robert Y. Hayne of South Carolina in 1824, two decades after Haiti became free. "We never can acknowledge her independence ... which the peace and safety of a large portion of our union forbids us even to discuss" (Schmidt 1971: 28).

At the same time that Haiti's leaders were justifiably suspicious of outsiders interested in establishing businesses or in acquiring land in Haiti, those same outsiders avoided the establishment of diplomatic relations on the basis of equality between nations. The behavior of the United States toward Castro's Cuba and Mao's China thus merely proves that there is not, after all, that much new under the sun, at least in American foreign policy: the United States did not recognize Haiti until 1862!

The period following the declaration of Haitian independence in 1804 was immensely important for the shaping of Haitian culture and character, and the isolation of the people from the world outside, both by the world and by the majority of the country's leaders, helps to explain the highly distinctive quality of Haitian life today. Whereas the period before 1804 was marked by almost constant flux, due to the rapid economic growth of the colony and the incredibly massive importations of African slaves after 1697, the period following 1804 was typified by an almost total stasis of the society with relation to the outside world, particularly after the death of Christophe in the north, and the reconsolidation of Haiti as a single country.

The plantation system upon which Saint Domingue's immense profitability to France had rested began to deteriorate, first slowly, then with great rapidity. The national institutions of the colony—particularly the Church—withdrew; the hinterland became truly Haitian, for the first time. But this is merely a summary account of a large number of different processes, all occurring at once: the breakdown of a system of ownership of men by men, and of all of the means by which slavery was perpetuated; the dissolution of the master classes, and their substantial replacement, both by a different structure for the wielding of power and by largely different personnel; the breakup of the large estates, and of the system of control wielded over those who had manned them—not merely slavery, but the network of paternalism and the mass of custom in which it was embedded; the retreat of Catholicism and of its representatives from the countryside (the schism lasted from 1805 until 1860); the decline of the export economy and, accordingly, of the import economy as well; the rise of the small family property, its control vested in a senior male; and the concordant development of new religious forms and institutions, some either forbidden, or at best hidden, before the Revolution. Such a list barely suggests some of the ways by which Haiti stopped being what it had been, in order to become something else. The writer has attempted elsewhere (Mintz 1966a, 1966b) to suggest what some of the end-products of these processes have been, in a country which is today the most rural and agrarian, the most thoroughly peasant, and the poorest, in the New World. In terms of the substance of this book, however, only a few points require elaboration here.

The fundamental substance of the convulsion of 1791–1804 was the transformation of a lucrative slave-based plantation colony, dedicated to the creation of profit for European capitalist investors, and to the production of market commodities for European consumers, into a nominally independent country where men were no longer slaves, where the capitalistic system continued to function only on a much-simplified basis, where production for subsistence supplanted in good measure production for the market, and where the small agricultural enterprise based on family labor replaced the large plantation with its massed and coerced labor. Political and economic changes were at the base of the Revolution, but the Revolution expressed the genuine quality of the life of the Haitian people in every other sphere as well. *"1804 est issu du Vodou,"* the Haitian savant Dr. Jean Price-Mars once wrote (Schmidt 1971: 23), and even the Haitian guerrillas who waged a valiant but doomed struggle against the North American invaders 125 years later are said to have worn *vaudou* amulets into battle (*ibid.*). The Haitian Revolution was in no sense a "religious war," but a revolution against an inhuman system. Its ideological overtones were not those of Africa against Europe, nor even entirely or consistently of black against white—certainly not of African religion against European religion. Yet *vaudou* surely played a critical role in the creation of viable armed resistance by the slaves against the master classes—and against the armies of other powers besides France, interested in resubjugating the once immensely profitable colony. Thus the ideological elements of slave life and of slave resistance formed part of the war the slaves fought for themselves and, inevitably, part of the life of the Haitian freeman, once the war was won. *Vaudou* cannot be interpreted apart from its significance for the Haitian people, and for Haitian history. Correspondingly, Haiti cannot be understood if, on the other hand, one chooses to ignore *vaudou*. But since it is with *vaudou* that Alfred Métraux's book is concerned, we need do little more than set his penetrating study into a slightly broader context.

The Haitian Revolution freed not only the slaves but also their creative capacities: it was through modes of symbolic expression, including the religious, that this new-found freedom was able to manifest itself. The new religious forms which grew up or were built upon during the nineteenth century found their roots principally in Africa, but these forms were not simple transfers, nor were they modified in any single (or clear-cut) fashion. Haitian horticulture is not African horticulture; Haitian domestic organization is not African domestic organization; and Haitian religion is not African religion. In fact, to ask whether some feature of Afro-American life is or is not "African" in origin is somehow to beg the question, since this circumvents the complex tribal heterogeneity of African peoples who played a role in the development of New World cultures (Mintz 1970a, 1970b, 1971). What holds for Haitian horticulture and Haitian domestic organization holds as well as for Haitian religion; to ask whether *vaudou* is "African" is to ignore serious questions of tribal-specific origins for particular features of that religion, as well as the important related questions of how that religion, *as system,* took on its characteristic modern form. These latter questions are of great theoretical significance, since they have to do with the very nature of culture itself, and with the ways culture changes.

Throughout the history of African enslavement in prerevolutionary Saint Domingue, we suppose that the slaves sought to create religious traditions, building both upon their diverse pasts and upon the conditions of their enslavement. Knowing as we do that *vaudou* not only survived the Revolution but played a part in it, we also know that the changed conditions of life after freedom must have been reflected in the religion itself. That is, the character of this religious system must have accorded—and accords—intelligibly with the specific sociology of Haitian life, whether in rural or in urban settings, and in the past as in the present. But this is certainly not to say that *vaudou* is merely a reflection or a projection of other aspects of life. Now, as before, it remains a fundamental part of life for a very great many Haitians, and still plays an important role in the lives of many others.

Yet we properly expect an ideological subsystem to be highly responsive to changes in the sociology of local life, to economic pressures of all kinds, and even—at times—to fads, vogues, and new customer demands. For example, the family cult-practices that apparently typified *vaudou* a century ago have diminished sharply over time, to judge by all that we know, as the family compounds themselves have dissolved, under demographic, economic, and political pressure. Thus one expects to find a delicate interdigitation of belief and belief system, on the one hand, and of the specific character of social life, on the other. Though *vaudou* flourishes in the city, as Métraux points out, largely in response to tourism, more traditional cult centers continue to function there as well—each variant serving some purpose; in one case, the traditional sociological, psychological, and economic utility of the system persists, while in the other, economic considerations, perhaps, prevail over others. Yet this is not a matter of "genuineness" or "authenticity," so much as evidence of the plasticity of a complex institution, its manifold utility, and the very blurred line between the sacred and the secular. That believers can be possessed—as the writer has witnessed—in the midst of a secular dance in a deserted country marketplace attests to the vitality of *vaudou,* not to its feebleness.

Which is to say that *vaudou,* like any other complex of belief and practice, is a vital, living body of ideas and behaviors, carried in time by its practitioners, and responsive to the changing character of social life. This must have been true from its very beginning as a transatlantic system of faith, when African slaves from a score of different societies first attempted to implant their symbolic pasts in the hearts and minds of their children. It followed almost inevitably that *vaudou* would come to be associated with the endless struggles of the Haitian people against their condition; as we have seen, there is good evidence that the stirrings of revolt before 1791 were intermeshed with *vaudou* and its power. After the Revolution, *vaudou* must have grown like all else in the tropics—swiftly, and wildly. There is no national church, there never has been; there is no association of priesthood, no written dogma, no code, no missionization. In stark contrast to the proselytizing religions implanted in Haiti, *vaudou* has never had to fight for its own even when attacked (which has, indeed, been often enough), precisely because it *is* the popular religion of Haiti. And yet, beneath the apparent absence of any unified social or ideological super-structure, there is a body of basic beliefs and practices that typify *vaudou* throughout Haiti: the twin cult, the *loa* and their specific per-sonifications, the phenomenon of possession, the role of the dead, the relationship between gods and the land, and much else, provide a core of belief—one might almost say a series of philosophical postu-lates about reality—that make a national church (complete with bingo, rock records, and basement ping-pong tables) unnecessary and irrelevant. While outsiders may say that the trouble with Haiti is that its people are so superstitious, the man who recognizes that one man's religion is another man's superstition might be more inclined to say that the trouble with Haiti is that its people are so religious.

There is no doubt that *vaudou* has lost ground among the Haitian people in the course of the last half-century. Quite aside from the powerful campaigns launched against it and its practitioners by the Church, the work of missionizing Protestant churches since the North American invasion has also made inroads. A deepening poverty in the countryside has reduced the richness of ritual there (though not the intensity of belief), while the movement to the cities has much modified the nature of *vaudou* practice. Yet it has also been contended that the personal politico-religious ideology of the late President Duvalier, who was in power from 1957 until 1971, effected a renascence of *vaudou,* while charms and amulets entered as never before into the prosecution of political objectives. There is a naive chauvinism in such simplification. While it may be contended fairly that the Duvalier regime did nothing to weaken the meaning of *vaudou* for the Haitian masses, it is at least as important that it was Duvalier *père* who supplanted a foreign Catholic clergy with a Haitian Catholic clergy and got the Church to cooperate in the process. It is at least conceivable that a Haitian clergy will do more to wean the masses away from certain elements of *vaudou* belief than their Belgian, French-Canadian, and French predecessors ever did— though this was probably not in the late President's mind. If *vaudou* has received a new lease on life in the last two decades, it is probably as much the result of a deepening rural economic crisis, as of any emotional, political, or ideological predispositions of the regime in power. Assertions that treat *vaudou* as some kind of undifferentiated and homogeneous system of belief cannot possibly explain very much in any case, since it is *vaudou*'s peculiar strength to lack entirely any centralization of practice, priesthood, or power. This problem, among others, is dealt with by Métraux's analysis.

It is Métraux, in fact, more than any other student of Haiti's folk religion, who perceived its remarkable resiliency, the continuous input of new symbolic materials by those who practice and preach it, and the great degree to which it is a westernized religion, in spite of the massive African contributions to its form and contents. That the peoples and cultures of the Caribbean region should be among the most western of the modern world is not, in fact, mysterious: after all, they were among the first victims of the West. In the case of Haiti, they were also among the first to fight back successfully. That struggle was ideological as well as physical; *vaudou* was part of it. But let Alfred Métraux tell us.

Yale University
December 1971

BIBLIOGRAPHY

Bing, Fernande
  1964 Entretiens avec Alfred Métraux. *L'homme*, IV (2):20–32.
Condominas, Georges
  1965 *L'exotique est quotidien*. Plon, Paris.
Curtin, Philip
  1969 *The Atlantic Slave Trade: A Census*. The University of
    Wisconsin Press, Madison.
Debien, Gabriel
  1962 Plantations et esclaves à Saint Domingue: Sucrerie Cottineau.
    Notes d'Histoire Coloniale, No. 66:9–82.
Hall, Robert
  1953 *Haitian Creole*. Memoirs of the American Folklore Society,
    Vol. 43. Philadelphia.
Métraux, Alfred
  1934 L'organisation sociale et les survivances religieuses des Indiens
    Uru Cipaya de Carangas (Bolivie). *Actas y Trabajos Cien-
    tíficos del 25 Congreso Internacional de Americanistas*
    (La Plata, 1932), t.1:191–213.
  1935 La religión secreta y la mitología de los Indios Uru-Chipaya
    de Carangas. *Revista del Instituto de Etnología de la Uni-
    versidad Nacional de Tucumán*, t.3,1a:7–84.
  1940 *Ethnology of Easter Island*. Bulletin 160 of the Bernice P.
    Bishop Museum. Honolulu.
  1945 Le Bureau d'Ethnologie de la République d'Haïti. *Afro-
    américa*, I (1–2):81–84.
  1951a *Making a Living in the Marbial Valley (Haiti)*. UNESCO
    Occasional Papers in Education, No. 10. Paris.
  1951b L'habitation paysanne en Haïti. *Bulletin de la Société Neu-
    châteloise de Géographie*, LV (1) (1949–51):3–14.
  1951c Droit et coutume en matière successorale dans la paysan-
    nerie haïtienne. *Zaïre*, 5(4):339–49.
Mintz, Sidney W.
  1966a The Caribbean as a Socio-cultural Area. *Cahiers d'Histoire
    Mondiale*, IX (4):912–37.
  1966b Foreword to Leyburn, James G., *The Haitian People*. Yale
    University Press, New Haven.
  1970a Foreword to Whitten, N., and Szwed, J. (eds.), *Afro-
    American Anthropology*. Free Press, New York.
  1970b Creating Culture in the Americas, *Columbia University
    Forum*, XIII:4–11.
  1971 Toward an Afro-American History. *Cahiers d'Histoire
    Mondiale*, 13 (2):317–32.
Schmidt, Hans
  1971 *The United States Occupation of Haiti, 1915–1934*. Rutgers
    University Press, New Brunswick, N.J.
Tardits, Claude
  1964 Hommage à Alfred Métraux. *L'homme*, IV (2):15–19.

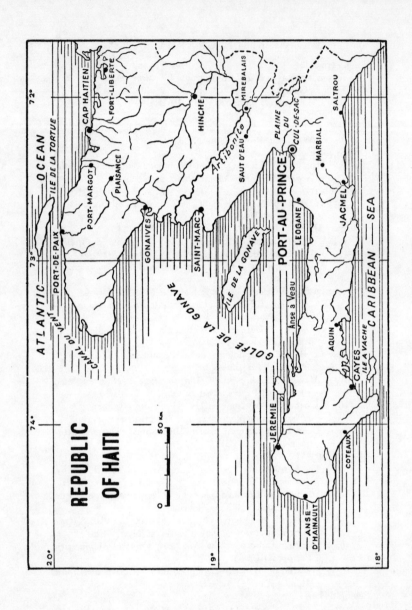

REPUBLIC OF HAITI

Foreword

Certain exotic words are charged with evocative power. Voodoo
is one. It usually conjures up visions of mysterious deaths, secret
rites—or dark saturnalia celebrated by 'blood-maddened, sex-
maddened, god-maddened' negroes. The picture of Voodoo
which this book will give may seem pale beside such images.

In fact—what is Voodoo? Nothing more than a conglomeration of beliefs and rites of African origin, which, having been
closely mixed with Catholic practice, has come to be the religion
of the greater part of the peasants and the urban proletariat of
the black republic of Haiti. Its devotees ask of it what men have
always asked of religion: remedy for ills, satisfaction for needs
and the hope of survival.

Seen from close, Voodoo has not got the morbid and halluci-
natory character which books have given it. A talented but rather
fanciful American writer, W. H. Seabrook, has given the most
complete account of the black legend of Voodoo. But that legend
belongs to the past. It belongs to the colonial period when it was
the fruit of hatred and fear. Man is never cruel and unjust with
impunity: the anxiety which grows in the minds of those who
abuse power often takes the form of imaginary terrors and
demented obsessions. The master maltreated his slave, but feared
his hatred. He treated him like a beast of burden but dreaded the
occult powers which he imputed to him. And the greater the
subjugation of the Black, the more he inspired fear; that ubiqui-
tous fear which shows in the records of the period and which
solidified in that obsession with poison which, throughout the
eighteenth century, was the cause of so many atrocities. Perhaps
certain slaves did revenge themselves on their tyrants in this
way—such a thing is possible and even probable—but the fear
which reigned in the plantations had its source in deeper re-
cesses of the soul: it was the witchcraft of remote and mysterious
Africa which troubled the sleep of the people in 'the big
house'.

Torture and branding were not merely reserved for 'poisoners'

15

but also for anyone suspected of belonging to the dreaded sect called 'The Voodoos'.

Even so, the few allusions to Voodoo which may be found in documents and books little known to the general public, could not have raised this rural paganism into the legendary terror it became, had not a British Consul, Spencer St John, written a book, *Haiti or the Black Republic* (published in 1884), in which he described the most blood-curdling crimes committed by the Voodoo sect. This work was widely read and for long has been regarded as the main authority. The degree of its influence may be judged from the fact that it inspired Gustave Aymard to write his adventure story *Les Vaudoux*—a book in which the sect is described as a lot of fanatics thirsting for blood and power.

Spencer St John's revelations of alleged cannibalism in Haiti provoked, according to his own admission, very strong feeling in Europe and the United States. Although faced with an outcry in Haiti he nevertheless thought good to repeat his allegations in the second edition (1886), and even to add new details. As a result several writers denounced Voodoo as a cannibal religion and from their writings Haiti came to be regarded as a savage country where, every year, children were sacrificed and devoured by the monstrous worshippers of the Serpent.

The occupation of Haiti by American Marines resulted, amongst other things, in a renewal of interest in this African religion which the White world saw in such a dark light. The rhythm of drums which echoed peacefully in the hills to stimulate the effort of workers became, for the occupying forces, the voice of Africa, barbaric and inhuman, asserting itself over a country which had been seized from the Whites and from their civilization.

I intend in this book to discuss Voodoo from the point of view of an anthropologist—that is to say with method and prudence. If I have been chary of the enthusiasm of those who, at first whiff of an exotic religion, are seized with a sort of sacred vertigo and end by sharing the gullibility of its devotees, I have also taken pains to avoid the attitude of those smalltime, niggardly Voltairians who never stop talking about pious fraud—with a good wink, of course.

My first encounter with Voodoo was in 1941. I had scarcely disembarked in Port-au-Prince before I heard of the campaign being waged by the Catholic Church 'against superstition'. Having once read several papers on the suppression of idolatry in the Spanish colonies I took some interest in the methods used by the Haitian clergy in the twentieth century, and soon had to admit, with a certain amount of surprise, that the Dominicans and Augustans who hunted down demons with such zeal in Peru, would not have been ashamed of their French successors. It was at Croix-des-Bouquets, near Port-au-Prince, that I was given a glimpse of the vigour with which African cults had spread in Haiti: an enormous pyramid of drums and 'superstitious objects' towered high in the court of the presbytery, waiting for the date on which there was to be a solemn *auto-de-fé*. I pleaded for certain pieces, which for scientific or aesthetic reasons, deserved to be spared; but in vain: the *curé* explained to me that the honour of Haiti was at stake and all must be destroyed.

The scale of this offensive against Voodoo, and the brutality of the measures taken against its devotees, suggested that its days were numbered; and so I conceived the desire to study it before it was too late. The Haitian writer Jacques Roumain, who went with me to La Tortue, was equally convinced of the need to put on record the story of Voodoo which seemed so gravely threatened. To this end, and out of our discussions, was born the idea of a 'Bureau of Ethnology' for Haiti.

When I returned to Haiti in 1944 the Bureau of Ethnology, founded meanwhile by Jacques Roumain, had managed to save important collections from the flames and had undertaken various researches into little-known aspects of Voodoo. Thanks to M. Lorimer Denis and other members of the Bureau (Jacques Roumain had now been dead for several months) I was able to get in touch with several Voodoo priests who had become friends and collaborators. It was during this period that I had the rare luck of meeting Mme Odette Mennesson-Rigaud. Few Whites have ever succeeded in getting to know Voodoo as intimately as this French woman who became Haitian by marriage. There is not a single sanctuary where she is not received as a friend—more—as an initiate. Once in the course of a Voodoo ceremony I heard her 'valiant' name mentioned among those of other priestesses of Port-au-Prince. The dedication of this book to her is but a small token of my gratitude.

Mme Odette Mennesson-Rigaud introduced me to Lorgina Delorge whose sanctuary lay in the popular quarter of La Salines, not far from the place called Tête de Boeuf. *Maman* Lorgina was a well-known priestess who, in spite of money troubles, 'respected' her *loa* (spirits) and conducted her rites according to the tradition learnt from her masters.

Although she was often carried away and looked terrible when in trance, she was an excellent woman, benevolent and hospitable. I frequented her sanctuary in preference to any other and was thus able to take part intimately in the domestic life of a Voodoo temple.

Lorgina's welcome won me the sympathy and confidence of the whole fraternity. Although remaining very discreet about certain ceremonies and the initiation rites, Lorgina and the people in her house went to great pains to satisfy my indiscreet curiosity and always took care to let me know if a ceremony was due to take place in her sanctuary. My information therefore derives to a great extent from what I learnt from Lorgina during my numerous visits to Haiti. Lorgina died in 1953. I shall not forget that she gave me the title *pititt caye*—child of the house—and that I called her *maman*.

My relations with the Voodoo societies were not, however, limited to the Lorgina sanctuary. I knew several *hungan*—in particular Abraham who was one of the main sources of information for Jacques Roumain when he wrote his celebrated monograph *The Sacrifice of the Assoto Drum*. I was also present at many Port-au-Prince ceremonies, at Croix-des-Bouquets; and in 1947 I was able to spend Christmas in a family sanctuary in the neighbourhood of Léogane.

Some of the stories in the chapter on magic I got from M. Thoby-Marcelin; but it would be impossible to list here the names of all who generously provided me with accounts of magic, metamorphosis and encounters with evil spirits. I regret the dimensions of this work have limited me to the use of only a few.

As head of a sociological survey of the Marbial valley I stayed in Haiti from 1948 to 1950. Unfortunately the region where I had to work was the least fruitful for research into Voodoo. The anti-superstition campaign had there enjoyed an almost complete success. Those who in their heart of hearts remained faithful to the ancestral spirits did not dare mention it aloud, still less celebrate public ceremonies. However, the talks I had with voodooists *sub rosa* taught me a lot about the attitude of peasants towards Voodoo and about the colourful history of that religion. A recent trip gave me the opportunity of checking my information and of working in the archives of the Library of Les Frères de l'Institution St Louis de Gonzague where there are real documentary treasures. Let me here extend to Frère Lucien my warmest thanks for his help.

Nor should I forget the young Haitians—Remy Bastien, Lamartinière Honorat, Michelson Hyppolite, R. Mortel, Jeanne G. Sylvain—who went with me to Marbial and took part in research. Some of their observations, and some stories which they picked up at my request, have been included in the text. I do not forget their efforts or goodwill.

The presentation of the material, collected in the course of different periods of residence in Haiti, has not been easy. It was impossible to describe, short of making this work quite unreadable, even a small fraction of the ceremonies I attended. The need to prune so many details will result, I fear, in the surprised indignation of many Haitian specialists who will search in vain through these pages for points of ritual which they perhaps consider vital. Again, certain descriptions will seem to differ from what they themselves have witnessed. May I remind them that Voodoo is a religion which is practised by autonomous cult groups of which each often has its own peculiar custom and tradition. Whatever anyone may say to the contrary, there is no Voodoo liturgy and doctrine to which priests and priestesses are obliged to conform. Such an idea is a widespread illusion which we must avoid.

Just as the Creole language in the north of the republic differs in many particulars from the language used in the south and centre, so Voodoo practised at the Cap Haitian and at Port-de-

Paix is not exactly the same as that which I studied at Port-au-Prince and at Jacmel. It is therefore Voodoo of the capital and the surrounding area which forms the material of this book.

There is no literature on Haitian Voodoo to compare, in scope and quality, with that which deals with the African cults of Brazil and Cuba. Nevertheless, books and articles on Voodoo keep coming out and it seemed to me worth taking stock. This work is merely an attempted synthesis in which I have tried to include at least some part of all the documents to which I have had access. Naturally, I gave preference to my own observations and I never had recourse to the work of my predecessors except when it contained information which for one reason or another I was not able to collect for myself.

The great path-finder in Voodoo research is Moreau de Saint-Méry who, in a celebrated passage, written at the end of the eighteenth century, gave a summary but valuable description. Among the authors of former times who have written seriously of the religion let us mention d'Aubin whose work on Haiti, published at the beginning of the century, is too often forgotten.

To Dr Jean Price-Mars, today Haitian Ambassador in France, belongs the credit for making Voodoo respectable and even endearing to Haitian public opinion; he has exorcized the bogy with which the cult had become identified. *Ainsi parla l'Oncle* will therefore remain a great Haitian classic, less perhaps for its rather too timid pages on Voodoo than for the influence it had on a whole generation. It would be unjust not to mention the name of Dr Dorsainvil who, a few years earlier, tried to interpret Voodoo scientifically and explain away mystical possession as neurosis.

The work of Jean Price-Mars provoked a series of articles in local newspapers and reviews. The Bulletin of the Bureau of Ethnology offered a platform for the intellectuals of Haiti—men like François Duvalier (now President of Haiti), Lorimer Denis, Emmanuel Paul, Lamartinière Honorat and Michel Aubourg who devoted themselves to the study of Voodoo and certain aspects of folklore.

Major Louis Maximilien's work *Le Voudou Haïtien* may be consulted with profit even if one is not always in agreement with

the speculations of the author. Although Milo Rigaud's book
La Tradition vaudoo et le vaudoo haïtien is dominated by occultist
preoccupations and thus remains outside the anthropologist's
scope, it nevertheless contains excellent descriptions of ceremonies and copious, very exact information not to be found
elsewhere.

Certainly Voodoo is still waiting for its Homer, or more
modestly a good folklorist who will take the trouble to record the
rich oral tradition of its pantheon. But an effort has been made in
this direction by M. Milo Marcelin who has devoted two books
to some of the outstanding Voodoo gods.

Among the foreign anthropologists who have concerned themselves with Voodoo, Melville T. Herskovits appears in his rightful place as a pioneer. His book *Life in an Haïtian Valley*, written
in 1936, is still the best source of information on Voodoo, and if
subsequent works—notably those of Mme Odette Mennesson-
Rigaud—have completed it on several points, they have nevertheless revealed no mistaken observation or false interpretation.

The American musicologist, Harold Courlander, starting
from study of Voodoo songs and rhythms, went on to draw up a
list of gods and dances. The sociologist E. Simpson, also
American, undertook the study of the Plaisance region. He is the
author of many articles on Voodoo rites as they were celebrated
in the north. In this very brief catalogue of our principal sources
a very particular place must be reserved for a book written by the
American film camerawoman, Maya Deren, who in *Divine
Horsemen* proved herself to be an excellent observer, though her
book is burdened with pseudo-scientific considerations which
reduce its value.

Voodoo today is less frightening than it was. The Haitians
look upon it more and more as 'folklore'—which seems to dispel
the harm those practices do to the reputation of their country.
Has not every country its 'folklore'? It is therefore normal and
desirable that Haiti should also have its own. People in other
countries who say to their friends 'Don't go to Haiti: Voodoo is
something diabolic, it is the worship of snakes and black magic'
are becoming rare. Distrust and disgust are giving way to
curiosity which itself is gradually turning into indulgent sym-

pathy. But prejudice is tenacious. Only anthropology, in explaining the true nature of Voodoo and in throwing cold light on the facts, can make this religion emerge from its cloaking shadows and free it of the nightmares which it still inspires in many honest but misinformed people.

Certain Haitians will no doubt be saddened that a foreigner whom they welcomed so warmly has, like so many before him, felt the need to write a book on Voodoo which they look upon as one of the most embarrassing aspects of their national culture. Let them understand that I have not given way to a wish to exploit a subject of which the mere mention is sufficient to stimulate the curiosity of the public; nor have I wished to obtain personal notoriety at the expense of their country. Throughout the vast domain of anthropology I have always been interested by religious phenomena and in the formation of syncretic cults. Voodoo in this respect proved a particularly fertile field. I am not its apologist and I know that sooner or later it must disappear. My purpose has been to describe Voodoo as it appeared to me. It remains for other anthropologists to decide if I was mistaken or not. I shall feel satisfied if, in approaching the study of Voodoo seriously and with patience, I have helped to make known the ordinary people of the Haitian towns and countryside, whom I learnt to love and respect.

LANGUAGE

The language of Voodoo is Creole which in Haiti is spoken by everyone except the haute bourgeoisie. It is not a coarse patois, as has often been said, but a comparatively recent language derived from French, just as French is derived from Latin. It has preserved phonetic habits and grammatical structures which, in origin, are clearly African. Most writers who have concerned themselves with Voodoo transcribe Creole according to French spelling. In so doing they make it easier to understand terms which are not too remote from the original, or which, intrinsically, have even maintained their French form. The disadvantage of this system is that it conveys the sound of Creole only very imperfectly and it tyrannizes over the language wherever it has in fact evolved to a state of independence from the parent stem. It might, therefore, have been logical to use some kind of simpler and more exact phonetic spelling for Creole. If I have followed in the track of those who have gone before me it is because this work is meant for non-specialists. It was important not to put readers off with renderings which would keep them from recognizing a French word. Who would suspect that '*pwè*' is merely a way of writing '*point*' and '*balâsé*' of '*balancer*'? In giving Creole words an exotic appearance I would have been reproached with pedantry.

It is a different matter with the Creole texts which are quoted out of regard for scientific accuracy. For these the use of a phonetic spelling was essential. I have employed the one which was introduced to Haiti by the Protestant missionaries and which has been recommended by linguists. It follows the principles of all phonetic transcription. For every sound there is a single symbol. The rule has only one exception: the sound corresponding to the French *ch* (*sh* in English) has been rendered by two letters simply to avoid a diacritical sign on *s*. Nasalization is conveyed by a circumflex accent on the vowel (*â*: French *an*, *en*) (*ê*: French *ein*, *ain*, *in*). The accent grave (`) indicates an open vowel; the accent aigu (´) a closed vowel. The vowel *u* is pronounced like the French *ou*. We have thus simplified the so-called Laubach orthography which maintains the *ou* and the *gn* for the palatalized *n* which in this work is represented as in Spanish (*ñ*). Fragments of African languages, which have survived in Voodoo liturgy under the name of *langage*, have been transcribed according to this same system.

I

The History of Voodoo

ORIGINS AND HISTORY OF THE VOODOO CULTS

The history of Voodoo[1] begins with the arrival of the first batches of slaves at Saint-Domingue in the second half of the seventeenth century.

Writers such as Moreau de Saint-Méry, who described the social and economic conditions of Saint-Domingue at the end of the colonial age, took pleasure in listing the numerous African tribes represented on the plantations: Senegalese, Wolofs, Foulbe, Bambara, Quiambas, Aradas, Minas, Caplaus, Fons, Mahi, Nago, Mayombe, Mondongues, Angolese etc.[2] Looking at these lists one might believe that the whole of Africa had contributed to the population of Haiti, but, in company with Herskovits,[3] I very much doubt if the tribes of the interior had much share in this forced migration. And Voodoo is not, in fact, a hotch-potch of mystic displays and ritual practice borrowed from all parts of Africa.

The available censuses of slave population do not give much indication of the relative proportions of the various black nations represented in the colony. It would be possible to make precise estimates only by a meticulous breakdown of slavers' bills-of-lading, of deeds of sale and of notices in the local press. Such research would demand a lot of patient effort, but it would result in more than the mere satisfaction of a scholarly curiosity. In fact until it has been done, it will remain impossible to reconstruct the history of Voodoo without wasting attention on regions and cultures which have never contributed to the formation of the people and civilization of Haiti.

But, until such an inquiry has been undertaken, we may deduce from the historical evidence available and from the many surviving African characteristics to be found in Haiti, that most of

25

the slaves came from the region of the Gulf of Benin, known till quite recently as the 'Slave Coast'. Certainly Congo and Angola were forced to contribute by the French slavers of Saint-Domingue, and so too were Senegal and Guinea but the annual intake from the African coast consisted mainly of Blacks from Dahomey and Nigeria. The whole of the Gulf of Benin area had advantages of which slavers were well aware. The native population was very dense, as it still is today, and it seemed to offer an inexhaustible supply of men. Transactions were mainly with princelings who had long-standing trade-relations with the Whites and who were thirsting for European products—arms, glass beads, cotton materials, metal implements and brandy. To take the best known example, in the kingdom of Dahomey the slave trade had become a national industry. The economy of the whole country was based on annual expeditions against neighbouring peoples. The king kept a monopoly of the many thousand prisoners and sold them to the Whites, keeping back only those due to be sacrificed to the ancestors or those who as agricultural labourers had to fill the gaps in the Dahomean population caused by annual war. In 1727 the king of Dahomey 'smashed' the little kingdom of Whydah (the 'Juda' of the old travel accounts) and turned its capital into a huge slave emporium which was frequented by slavers right up to the second half of the last century. It has been reckoned that 10,000 slaves were sold annually at Whydah. To cross the few miles of dune and marsh which divides this town from the coast, is to fall prey to a vision of those long caravans of men, women and children who here took their last steps on the continent of their birth. The beach of Whydah is today deserted; there is nothing to recall the brutal scenes which took place whenever a slaver embarked its pitiful cargo to the sound of whips and screams. But surely the sadness which emanates from this desolate landscape has something to do with the memory of so much anonymous suffering.

The Mahi and Nago (Western Yoruba) were the traditional opponents of the Dahomeans. The raids of which they were the victims are today the reason why in Haiti the *rada* (Dahomean) rite is never celebrated without the performance of Mahi dances and without honouring and invocation of Nago gods.

The Dahomeans of today have not forgotten their cousins, taken away, over the seas. When they offer up sacrifices on behalf of their royal ancestors, they do not forget those who once were sold to the Whites. Melville T. Herskovits[4] writes that as soon as the blood of the sacrificial victim flows, a voice from behind a curtain may be heard singing: 'Oh, ancestors, do all in your power that princes and nobles who today rule never be sent away from here as slaves to Ame'ika, to Togbomé, to Gbulu, to Kankanu, to Gbuluvia, to Garira. We pray you to do all in your power to punish the people who bought our kinsmen, whom we shall never see again. Send their vessels to Whydah harbour. When they come, drown their crews, and make all the wealth of their ships come back to Dahomey.'

As this was said, an old man called out, 'And is that not a just payment for what they have taken?' To this the reply, in which all joined, was: 'Yes, yes, yes! And it is not enough. The English must bring guns. The Portuguese must bring powder. The Spaniards must bring the small stones which give fire to our fire-sticks. The Americans must bring the cloths and the rum made by our kinsmen who are there, for these will permit us to smell their presence. Long live Dahomey! You have not succumbed to slavery here, act so that those three . . . who died for the cause of our country in Brazil be kept in the memory of all Dahomeans, nd give us news of them by White strangers to come to Abomey.'

Philology helps to confirm the data of history and tradition. The very word 'Voodoo' puts us on the track. Some people, in their anxiety to whitewash the Voodoo cults, saw it as a corruption of 'Vaudois' (the name of a sect founded in the twelfth century by Father Valdesius), but which had finally become a term applied vaguely to heretics and sorcerers. However, in Dahomey and Togo, among tribes belonging to the Fon language-group, a 'Voodoo' is a 'god', a 'spirit', a 'sacred object', in short, all those things which the European understands by the word 'fetish'. The servants of the divinity are '*hunsis*' (from the Fon *hu*—a divinity, and *si*—a spouse); the priest is the *hungan*, that is to say the 'master of the god'. Objects used in ritual are still known by their Dahomean names: *govi*—pitchers, *zin*—a pot, *asson*—sacred rattle, *azein*—holy emblems, *hunto*—drum, etc.[5]

If, turning for a moment from liturgy, we look at the list of Voodoo divinities, we find that the most important of them belong to the Fon and the Yoruba. Legba, Damballah-wèdo, the Aida-wèdo his wife, Hevieso, Agassu, Ezili, Agwé-taroyo, Zaka, Ogu, Shango, and many others, still have their shrines in the towns and villages of Togo, Dahomey, and Nigeria.

It is true that in the catalogue of Haitian *loa* one may also find the names of deities from the Congo and other parts of Africa, but most of these rank far lower in popular piety than the great *loa* of 'African Guinea' (*L'Afrique Guinin*).

Moreover, as we shall see when we study the Voodoo pantheon, the main divinities are still classified according to the tribe or region from which they originate. Thus we have Nago gods, Siniga (Senegalese), Anmine (Minas), Ibo, Congo and Wangol (Angolese) gods. Some gods even carry as an epithet the name of their African place of origin: for instance Ogu-Badagri (Badagri is a town in Nigeria) and Ezili-Freda-Dahomey (Ezili of Whydah-Dahomey).

Haitians and Dahomeans look very alike which is the more remarkable that for one hundred and fifty years their lot has been very different and no contact has been maintained between them; the Haitian peasant thinks of Guinea and Dahomey as mythical countries and virtually looks upon himself as an original inhabitant of Haiti. Yet the culture of Dahomey survives not only in the domains of religion and aesthetics, and in certain aspects of economic life, but also in such subtle forms of behaviour as gestures or facial expressions. And although the vocabulary of Haitian Creole, with the exception of a few African and Spanish words, is entirely French, the phonetics and grammar have much in common with those of the Dahomean and Nigerian languages.

But what has become of the other African tribal groups in Haiti? Documents and oral tradition witness the one-time presence of Congolese, Senegalese, Minas; but these must have been merged in the main mass of Fon and Yoruba, enriching the Voodoo pantheon with a few gods and adding to the liturgy their own peculiar dances and rhythms. Such additions have not appreciably altered the nature of Voodoo which in structure and spirit has remained essentially Dahomean. Moreau de Saint-Méry[6], speaking of Voodoo in the last years of the eighteenth century, records that 'it is the Aradas Negroes (that is to say the Blacks from Dahomey) who are the real devotees of Voodoo, keeping up its spirit and rules.'

The various ethnic groups of the Gulf of Guinea have basically a common culture in spite of linguistic differences and deep antagonisms. Resemblances were increased by reciprocal influence and frequent contact. All the slaves who came from that culture area had no difficulty in combining their respective traditions to build up a new syncretic religion.

The religious systems of West Africa, of which Voodoo is often merely an impoverished example, could hardly be described as primitive. They have kept alive beliefs and rituals inherited from the ancient religions of the classical East and of the Aegean world. Witness the part played by the *labrys*—the Cretan double-axe—in the worship of the god Shango.

Dahomean religion is full of subtleties. The Geomancy of Fa (divination by palm nuts) is so complex and so refined in its symbolism that it could only have been evolved by a learned priesthood with leisure for theological speculations. If we try to analyse, generally speaking, the idea Dahomeans formed of the supernatural world, then we find a supreme god, of uncertain sex, Mawu, and other gods related to him, grouped in pantheons and sometimes in hierarchies. A special place in this mythology is held by Fa, the personification of Fate. In addition to the major gods of nature there is also a multitude of divine beings: ancestors of clans, gods of vassal tribes, monsters and aborted royal foeti. Music and dance are so closely woven into the cults that one could almost speak of 'danced religions'. Dance is itself linked with divine possession—the normal mechanism by which a divinity communicates with the faithful. Gods are represented by 'fetishes'—stones, plants, vases, bits of iron and other symbols. In Dahomey the representation of the divinity by an anthropomorphic image is much less common than in Nigeria and this it is which surely explains the rarity of idols in Haiti, though in Brazil, where the Yoruba are numerous, anthropomorphic

representations of gods are quite common. The cult of which the
vodû are the object is celebrated by priests, many of whom profess to be the descendants of the divinity itself, or of a line of
priests who have been in its service since the beginning of time.
Each divinity is also 'served' by its *vodû-si* (consorts of the
Voodoo) that is to say by people, generally women, who have been
consecrated to that divinity and initiated in a 'convent'. They
dance for the *vodû*, are possessed by him, wear his colours and
look after his sanctuary.

As far as can be deduced from ancient documents, the Dahomean religion of today is not substantially different from that of
the seventeenth and eighteenth centuries except of course in the
matter of human sacrifice which was then practised on a large
scale.

The transplanting of the cult of the *vodû*, from Dahomey to
Haiti, raises many problems which have usually been disposed
of in summary fashion. For a long time the apologists of the slave
trade tried to establish a theory that slave cargoes were made up
merely of the dregs of Africa which was then all the healthier
for being rid of them. In fact most slaves were prisoners of war,
or people guilty of some 'crime'—a word which covered *lèse-
majesté* and sorcery, as well as common wrong-doing. Consequently the holds of the slavers contained representatives of all
classes of Dahomean society. The formation of Voodoo in Haiti
can only be explained by the presence, in the labour gangs, of
priests or 'servants of the gods', who knew the rites. Otherwise
the religious systems of Dahomey and Nigeria would have
deteriorated into incoherent practices or simple rites of black
and white magic. Instead, what do we find in Haiti? Temples,
organized clergy, a rather complicated ritual, sophisticated
dances and rhythms. In spite of brutal uprooting from their own
social milieu, the slaves contrived to resurrect, in exile, the
religious framework in which they had been brought up.
Bokono (magicians) and *vodû-no* (priests), trained in Africa,
taught the following generations, born in slavery, the names and
characteristics of the gods and the sacrifices required.

One of the peculiarities of West African religions is their
domestic quality. Each sib has its own hereditary gods, which it

honours to gain favours and avoid wrath. It is a striking fact that
of the *vodû* still invoked in the temples of Haiti, quite a number
belong to the royal family of Abomey: for instance in Haiti today
people still worship the god Agassu who, when he possesses a
devotee, obliges him to crook and stiffen his hands like claws. In
Dahomey, Agassu, the result of the union of a panther and a
woman, is the founder of the royal line of Abomey. In Haiti, he
is associated with water deities and sometimes takes the form of
a crab, one of the mythical creatures who once gave assistance to
the Ancestor (and thus became taboo). Another god worshipped
in Haiti is Three-horned-Bosu: Justin Aho, *chef de canton* in
Dahomey and grandson of King Gléglé, to whom I mentioned
this god, told me that Bosu was a *toxosu*, that is to say a sacred
monster of the royal family, a deformed child or an aborted
foetus, shaped like a tortoise with three protuberances sticking
up from his shell. All these survivals suggest that members of the
royal family, reduced to slavery, carried their own gods with them
to Haiti, since no one else would have been qualified to establish
their worship. The hazards of war and the exportation of slaves
on a huge scale thus succeeded in planting in America gods
whose cult in Africa has either vanished or lost importance.

Although some Moslem Negroes must have been imported to
Haiti from the markets of Senegal, Mohammedan influence on
Voodoo is imperceptible. It should be noted, however, that
when a Siniga (Senegalese) spirit possesses one of his adherents
he obliges him to go through a strange salutation—to move his
right hand first to his forehead then to his left shoulder, then to
the right shoulder, then to his chest and finally to put his thumb
to his mouth, saying '*ânâdiz sâdrivo—hibi wadhau—minâ âlahim
—kalabudu*', or '*Salama Salay gêmbo*', or '*Salam, salam malekum,
salay salam ma salay*', which seem to be corruptions of Moslem
salutations.

In West African society religion is so closely bound up with
every detail of daily life that we can hardly be surprised at its
survival in the New World—even in the face of all those factors
which ought logically to have destroyed it.

For the slave the cult of spirits and gods, and of magic too,
amounted to an escape; more, it was an aspect of the resistance

which he sustained against his oppressive lot. The degree of his attachment to his gods may be measured by the amount of energy he spent in honouring them—and this at risk of the terrible punishment meted out to those who took part in pagan ceremonies in which the colonists saw nothing but sorcery. Slavery could have demoralized them completely and sunk them into that gloomy apathy which goes with servitude. Mere physical exhaustion should have prevented them from dancing and singing as Voodoo ritual requires. Apart from the cruelties of which they were the helpless victims, slaves were made to work, even by good owners, to the limit of human capacity. 'For the Negroes work starts before dawn'—wrote Girod-Chantrans[7] in 1782. 'At eight o'clock they get their dinner; they go back to work till midday. At two o'clock they start again and carry on till nightfall; sometimes right up to ten or eleven p.m.' The two hours allowed in the middle of the day, and all holidays, were given over to the cultivation of their own foodstuffs. This account is confirmed by many other travellers of the same period. The over-exertion was so crushing that the life of a Negro sold to a plantation in Saint-Domingue was reckoned at never more than ten years. We can but admire the devotion of those slaves who sacrificed their rest and their sleep to resurrect the religions of their tribes—this under the very eyes of the Whites, and in the most precarious conditions. Think what energy, what courage it took to enable the songs and rites due to each god to be handed down across the generations! Writers who have described for us the Saint-Domingue of the eighteenth century often refer to the nocturnal escapades of the Blacks. The French owners, in that *siècle galant*, regarded them as love trysts. They were surely right, in many cases, but how often too must these dangerous nocturnal expeditions have led to some glade where everyone danced 'Voodoo'? An Ordinance of 1704 specifically prohibited slaves from 'gathering at night under the pretext of holding collective dances'. It can hardly have been very effective for the police soon had to issue further decrees to prevent 'gatherings of Blacks'. Night dances or *calenda* were forbidden to coloured men and Negro freedmen after nine o'clock in the evening and in addition they had to have a Judge's licence. A planter was fined 300 *livres* for having 'allowed a gathering of Negroes and a *calenda*' on his property. When, in 1765, a body of light troops was formed and named The First Legion of Saint-Domingue, it was assigned the role of 'breaking up Negro gatherings and *calendas*'. The word *calenda*, which is no longer used, must certainly have meant Voodoo. It was already suspect with the authorities. The Blacks cocked a snook at all these regulations and danced the *calenda* up to the Revolution. Moreover, in certain circumstances the owners allowed it, notably on the arrival of a mailboat from France.[8]

Officially all these Blacks who showed such loyalty to their 'fetishes' were Christians. A police decree issued in 1664 by M. de Tracy, 'lieutenant-general for the king of the French Islands of America' compelled owners to baptize their slaves. Article 2 of the *Code Noir* (March 10, 1685) states:

'All slaves who come to our islands will be baptized and instructed in the Catholic, Apostolic and Roman religion. Residents who buy newly-arrived slaves must inform the governors and intendants of the said islands within eight days at latest under penalty of immediate fine. The Governors will give the necessary orders for the baptism and instruction of the slaves within a suitable period.'

Royal authority set great store by these decrees since the only moral justification of the slave trade was the conversion of the Negroes. But in practice colonists did not care. The only article of the Negro Code which was properly observed was the one relating to baptism. The newly arrived Negroes wanted it because the sprinkling of holy water was part of their initiation to life in the colony and saved them from the disdain of the Creole Blacks, whose companions in misfortune they became.

After this ceremony the owner felt acquitted of his duty to God and king. No religious instruction was given to the slaves. Few planters would allow priests on their land, fearing censure of their immorality and of their cruel treatment of the slaves. They were also dimly aware of the revolutionary implications of the tenets of the Gospel. 'The owners of Saint-Domingue'— states a document of the time—'far from being concerned at seeing their Negroes live without religion, were, on the contrary, delighted, for in Catholic religion they saw nothing but the teaching of an equality which it would be dangerous to put in the minds of slaves'. [9]

Similarly the owners were not the least anxious that slaves should fulfil their religious observances. Saints' days and religious processions were largely considered a waste of time. The planters even asked the king to obtain a decree from the court of Rome reducing the numbers of saints' days without work to ten. Others cast a disapproving eye on religious ceremonies simply because they gave the Blacks 'increased opportunity to see and understand each other which is to be avoided for fear of revolts and mutinies.' [10]

Supported by the royal Government, the clergy rehearsed to the owners the advantages of religious education for slaves . . . in terms which owners might appreciate. They described it as the only brake strong enough to contain a slave's desire for freedom since 'only by fulfilling the duties of the condition and situation to which Providence has called him, can a man achieve sanctity'. Religion, said they, would be the best way of preventing 'all running away, poisoning and abortion'. [11]

What requires explanation, is not so much the persistence of African cults, but their rapid intermingling with so many Catholic elements which were greedily adopted by slaves who were forbidden the means and opportunity of becoming familiar with Christian doctrine and practice.

The only Blacks in a position to acquire even a veneer of Christianity were the house slaves who lived in the bosom of the Whites' family life, went to Mass with them and took part in family prayers every evening. Freedmen, too, had opportunities of getting to know Christian doctrine and practice.

A statute of the *Conseil du Cap* (1761) [12] tells us that a Jesuit lived in that town for no other purpose than to teach the Negroes. Instead of shutting himself up in catechism, sermons and prayer this priest took on all priestly functions single-handed. The result was the Blacks were formed under his guidance into a corps of adherents, different and distinct from others; some of them became cantors, churchwardens and vergers and 'pretended to copy the practices of a Church Council'. This solicitude for the Black soul was considered irregular. It figured among the crimes of which the Jesuits were accused at the time of their expulsion in 1762.

We are quite justified in labelling as 'Voodoo' all those gatherings which the slaves of the Cape 'covered with the veil of obscurity and orthodox religion'. These took place in churches which 'had become the refuge of runaway slaves and, often, hotbeds of prostitution'.

All doubt is removed when one reads in the Decree that members of these gatherings 'often mingled the Holy utensils of our religion with profane and idolatrous objects'. It seems, too, that wherever there was a shortage of priests, some Blacks took it upon themselves to catechize or preach to the others and thus 'the truths and dogmas of religion were altered'. Here, straight away, we hit upon the root of that 'blending' which, two centuries later, was to provoke the indignant wrath of the Catholic clergy of Haiti against Voodoo.

The police decrees forbidding Blacks to gather at funerals, and prohibiting the sale of charms and *macandals* (amulets), suggest the existence of the very pattern of beliefs and practices from which Voodoo would be born.

That excellent observer Father Labat[13] had already pointed out a fusion of Christianity with fetishism among the slaves of the Antilles: 'The Negroes,' he wrote, 'do without a qualm, what the Philistines did; they put Dagon with the Ark and secretly preserve all the superstitions of their ancient idolatrous cult alongside the ceremonies of Christianity.'

Essay on Slavery, a manuscript work of 1760, contains a very precise reference to the phenomenon of 'possession': 'The dance known in Surinam as *Water Maman*, and in our colonies as *La mère de l'eau*, is strictly forbidden. They build it into a great mystery, and the only thing known about it is that it greatly heats their imagination. They work themselves up to a frenzy whenever they contemplate some mischief. The ringleader goes into a trance of ecstasy. When he comes to himself, he says his god has spoken to him and told him what to do; but since they none of them have the same god they fall out and spy on each other, and this kind of project is nearly always betrayed.' In 1777, in a letter quoted by de Vaissière,[14] a certain Monsieur de Blaru records that 'the slaves danced in silence' all round him to get their gods to grant him a cure.

But it was not until the monumental work of Moreau de Saint-Méry,[15] *Description of the French part of Saint-Domingue*, written in the last years of the colonial period, that a detailed description of Voodoo became available. Since it has often been quoted, I shall only touch on it here.

Having translated, very exactly, the word *vaudou* as 'an all powerful and supernatural being', Moreau de Saint-Méry identifies it as 'the snake under whose auspices gather all who share the faith'. The Voodoo—that is to say the snake—will not give of its power or make known its will, except through a high priest and priestess, known as 'king and queen, master or mistress or even *papa* or *maman*'. In them we may recognize the *hungan* and the *mambo*, 'leaders of the great Voodoo family' which must pay them unlimited respect. It is they who decide whether the snake approves the admission of a candidate to the society, who set out his duties, the tasks he must fulfil; it is they who receive the tribute and presents which the god expects as his due. To disobey or resist them is to resist the god himself and run the risk of dire misfortune.

Voodoo gatherings take place secretly, at night, in 'a cloistered place shut off from the eyes of the profane'. The priest and priestess take up their positions near an altar containing a snake in a cage. After various ceremonies and a long address from the 'Voodoo king and queen', all initiates approach, in order of seniority, and entreat the Voodoo, telling him what they most desire. The 'queen' gets on to the box in which lies the snake and—'modern Pythoness—she is penetrated by the god; she writhes; her whole body is convulsed and the oracle speaks from her mouth'. The snake is then put back on the altar and everyone brings it an offering. A goat is sacrificed and the blood, collected in a jar, is used 'to seal the lips of all present with a vow to suffer death rather than reveal anything, and even to inflict it on whoever might prove forgetful of such a momentous pledge'.

Then begins what is, strictly speaking, the *danse vaudou*. This is the moment when new initiates are received into the sect.

Possessed by a spirit, the novices do not come out of their trance till a priest hits them 'on the head with his hand, wooden spoon or, if he thinks necessary, ox-hide whip'.

FIG. 1. The symbol (*vèvè*) of the snake god, Damballah-wèdo, drawn by the *hungan* Abraham

The ceremony ends with a collective delirium which Saint-Méry believed to be the result of magnetic emanations. As proof he cites the paroxysms of Whites who had merely come as spectators. He gives quite a good description of the trance: 'Some are subject to fainting fits, others to a sort of fury; but with all there is a nervous trembling which apparently cannot be controlled. They turn round and round. And while there are some who tear their clothes in this bacchanal and even bite their own flesh, others merely lose consciousness and falling down are carried into a neighbouring room where in the darkness a disgusting form of prostitution holds hideous sway.'

Analysed in the light of our present knowledge, the words of Moreau de Saint-Méry allow no room for doubt that there existed in Saint-Domingue, towards the end of the eighteenth century, rites and practices which have scarcely changed up to modern times. The authority of the priest, his dress, the importance of trance, signs drawn on the ground are familiar now as then. Moreau de Saint-Méry, however, was wrong in setting down this religion as a simple ophiolatry. Today also, the devotees of Voodoo worship Damballah-wèdo, the serpent-god, one of the divinities of the Dahomey mythology, but he is far from being the only great 'Voodoo'. Moreau de Saint-Méry allowed himself to be influenced by the prejudice of his milieu and by the main anthropological theories of his time. Although it is not normal practice now to represent Damballah-wèdo by living serpents, it must have been otherwise in the time of Moreau de Saint-Méry since his contemporary Descourtilz[16] talks of having been taken to a gathering of slaves where he saw a snake worshipped in front of a huge *mapou* tree in which it was living.

Between prayers the priests served him victuals in the shape of meat, fish, calalu and particularly milk. Descourtilz tells how he sacrilegiously killed this snake without provoking much emotion among its worshippers. Moreau de Saint-Méry points out that the presence of living snakes in the old Voodoo temples was not surprising since many of the slaves came from Whydah where there was, and is still, a big temple of snakes. But this is as maybe, snake-worship died out in the nineteenth century during which there is no further mention of it.

The following passage from Saint-Méry[17] has posed a problem in the history of Voodoo which has never yet been resolved: 'In

1768 a Negro of Le Petit-Goave, a Spaniard by birth, abused the credulity of the Negroes with superstitious tricks and gave them the idea of a dance, similar to the Voodoo dance, but more hectic in its movements. To give it an extra filip they added well crushed gunpowder to the rum which they drank while dancing. Sometimes this dance, called the *Danse à Don Pèdre* or The Don Pedro, inflicted fatal casualties on the Negroes; and sometimes the very spectators, electrified by the convulsive movements, shared the madness of the dancers, and drove them on, with their chanting and hurrying rhythm to a crisis which, to a certain extent, they shared. The Don Pedro was forbidden under threat of direst penalty—sometimes without avail.'

Now, as we shall see later, most Voodoo gods are divided into two groups: *rada* and *petro*. The origin of the word *rada* is easily found. It comes from the town Arada (in Dahomey)—a name which in the eighteenth century covered all Dahomeans.

On the other hand in the word *petro* we recognize the Pedro discussed above. Only a very naïve person could believe that the complicated liturgy, which is inseparable from the worship of the *petro* divinities, could have been introduced by one man, however inspired. Furthermore the *petro* rites as well as the *petro* music, although not Dahomean, are none the less African in origin. In contemporary Voodoo Dompèdre is a powerful god who is normally greeted by the detonation of gunpowder. And so it seems certain there must have once been a *hungan* whose impact was so profound that his name took the place of African 'nations' who today worship gods bearing his name, *petro*, and not theirs. But unless we can discover documents telling us about the role of this Don Pedro, his deification and powerful effect on Voodoo will remain a mystery.

Descourtilz,[18] who assembled his information at the beginning of the last century, also refers to 'Dompète,' describing him as the all-powerful chief of the teeming fanatics of Voodoo, a man who could reputedly 'see with his own eyes everything that was happening—anywhere, no matter how far away or how secluded'. Clairvoyance is one of the usual attributes of a *hungan*.

We can see then that Voodoo, on the eve of the French Revolution, was an organized religion different from the Voodoo of today only in that it bore a much more African character. Were not many of its adherents men and women who had actually been born and bred in Africa? It was, of course, beginning to become Christianized but at this stage the ritual had not been invaded, as it is today, by the Catholic liturgy. The number of slaves from the markets of the Congo and Angola was still increasing and after 1785 arrivals from these regions exceeded the totals from Guinea. These new-comers introduced rites and divinities which were absorbed, for better or worse, in the system which the Guinea Blacks had recreated after their own fashion.

With the Revolution and the Wars of Independence a new chapter in the history of Voodoo opens. Gone are the ties with Africa, the Catholic clergy is scattered and official control of religious activity is no longer so strict. Voodoo can evolve freely, sealed off hermetically, receiving contributions only from Catholicism and this all the more easily as the successors of the colonial priests proved lax and superstitious.

For the sake of clarity it might be worth recalling a few landmarks in the history of events with which Voodoo was more or less directly involved.

In 1789 Saint-Domingue was the richest jewel in the French crown. The slave population was about 500,000 Blacks. In addition there were 40,000 Mulattos and 30,000 Whites. The Revolution created a profound disturbance among the White population, who wanted a greater measure of independence, and among the Mulattos, who insisted on their rights of equality as citizens. The fever which possessed free men soon spread to the slaves. In 1791 there was a slave revolt. It would have proved nothing but a mad, blind peasant rising, quickly put down, had there not emerged from the armed bands war-leaders like Toussaint-Louverture, Dessalines and Christophe, who knew how to command and organize. Toussaint-Louverture, imprisoned by Napoleon, was destined to die in France, but his generals Dessalines and Christophe, aided by the Mulatto, Pétion, were to annihilate the French troops of Leclerc. On January 1, 1804, Dessalines proclaimed the Independence of Haiti. A savage massacre put paid to White supremacy.

After the short reign of Dessalines, who assumed the title of Emperor (1804–6), the country split in two. Christophe, having become king of the north, reigned till 1820. The south, under Pétion, maintained a republican constitution. After the long dictatorship of Boyer (1820–33), who extended his power over the whole island, the Republic went through a difficult time until the dictatorship of Soulouque (1847–67), who achieved fame by his parody of imperial forms and behaviour.

Haiti freed itself from Soulouque only to make way for a string of presidents who reached power by *coups d'états* or revolutions. Trouble was still rife in the opening years of the twentieth century. In 1915, after the assassination of President Sam, American Marines landed at Port-au-Prince. This American occupation was to last till 1933. The nation's economy was much improved thereby and since then the country has developed a great deal without, however, achieving political stability. Fresh disturbances and political acts of violence have been added to the long list of past revolutions. Even as I write these lines, Haiti is once more prey to political dissension.

The rôle of Voodoo, in the social history of Haiti, may be glimpsed from brief allusions in the writings of the nineteenth century. Without these we would have lost all record, not only of popular religion, but also of peasant life. The Haitian nationalists, who set themselves to reinstate Voodoo, claimed that its influence had been all-important on the men who had won independence for the country. Although they might find it difficult to support such an opinion with facts, they were certainly not wrong in thinking that the African cults were a unifying force, and that the exhortations of the Voodoo priests must have helped inflame the hearts of the black soldiers. One historian, Dantes Bellegarde,[19] who on this point is above suspicion since he has never concealed his distaste for the African traditions of Haiti, did not hesitate to write, in his *Histoire du peuple haïtien*, that 'the slaves found in Voodoo the ideal stimulus for their energy—since Voodoo had become less a religion than a political association—a sort of "black carbonaro" dedicated to the destruction of the Whites and the deliverance of the Negroes'. M. Bellegarde does wrong to deny the religious nature of Voodoo, though it is true that the circumstances in which the Oath of Bois Caiman, the signal for the Black revolt, took place, do provide a case for those who believe that Voodoo helped directly towards the liberation of the slaves and the independence of Haiti. Here is the account of that memorable night—of August 14, 1791—as it is told to the school children of Haiti:[20]

'To put an end to all holding-back and to obtain absolute devotion, he [Boukman] brought together a great number of slaves in a glade of Bois Caiman, near the Red Mountain. When all were assembled a storm broke. Lightning scribbles the low dark clouds with brief radiance. In a few minutes torrential rain begins to turn the ground into a marsh while a savage wind twists the moaning trees till even the thickest branches are wrenched off and crash to the earth.

'In the middle of this impressive scene, motionless, petrified in sacred awe, the assembled slaves behold an old Negress rise up, her body shaking from head to foot. She sings, she pirouettes and over her head she brandishes a huge cutlass. Now, in the great congregation an ever more pronounced stillness, more bated breath, eyes ever more burning fixed on the Negress, show how the crowd is rapt. At this moment a black pig is produced. The din of the storm drowns his grunts. With one vivid thrust the inspired priestess plunges her cutlass into the animal's throat. The blood spurts—and is gathered smoking to be distributed in turn, to the slaves; all drink, all swear to obey Boukman.'

The Bois Caiman ceremony which has been passed down to tradition only in a confused form, was certainly one of those blood pacts 'by means of which the Dahomeans, in a dangerous undertaking, bound themselves to their comrades. Three things are sure to emerge from such pacts: a spirit of solidarity (for better or for worse), unlimited confidence on the part of all who have been "blooded", and finally complete discretion as regards all secrets imparted under the seal of the blood pact and unfailing punishment of anyone who breaks them.' The rites which produce these emotions are very complex but they include the sacrifice of a pig (symbol of discretion, since he proves himself not inquisitive by seldom looking at the sky) and then the licking-up of the pig's blood after it has been mixed with other in-gredients. Once the oath has been taken—woe to him who breaks it. Magic powers have been set up which will return against those who have voluntarily submitted to them. On the eve of a revolt, of which the outcome was still uncertain, what more natural than that the conspirators should seal their agree-ment by drinking a mystic potion and invoking the Voodoos of their distant homeland.[21]

A few days after the Bois Caiman ceremony the White masters were massacred in their plantations and the cane fields reduced to ashes. A thick cloud of smoke hung over Saint-Domingue. So began the merciless war which was to last twelve years. The bands of insurgent slaves, who fought under the command of Jean François, of Biassou and other less famous guerilla leaders, were made up of Africans who still practised ancestral cults and of Creole Negroes who were mostly Voodooists. They included in their ranks priests and priestesses who by prayers, sacrifices and charms did their utmost to ensure victory.

The historian Madiou has gathered stories on this subject which although warped and exaggerated, are certainly related to fact. 'Biassou's tent,' he writes, 'was full of little, variously coloured cats, snakes, dead-men's bones and every sort of object typical of African superstition. At night huge fires were lit in his camp; naked women carried out hideous dances round these fires, singing words only understood in the deserts of Africa and twisting their bodies into frightening shapes. When exaltation reached its peak, Biassou, followed by his sorcerers, showed him-self to the crowd and announced that he was inspired by God; he told them that if they were killed in battle they would go back to Africa and live again in their native tribes. Then came the sound of long terrible cries far away in the forest; singing and sombre drumming began again. Biassou would use just such a peak of exaltation as the moment to move his bands against the enemy, taking all by surprise, in the dead of night.'

Madiou tells us of another guerilla leader, Lamour Derance, who was 'sunk in crude delusions, joined faith to sorcery and to the prophecies of the fetish priests and *papas* from whom he drew his counsellors. His system was barbarous; his followers, grouped by tribes, were never organized as regular troops. When he went into battle he was preceded by bands of Congos, Aradas, Ibos, Nagos, Mandingoes, Hausas who hurled themselves against the French battalions with fabulous courage, shouting that bullets were merely dust. But this spirit, fanned by superstition, smashed itself on the fire and steel walls of European squares.'[22]

The presence of Voodoo priests and priestesses is also recorded by Colonel Malenfant[23] in his account of an expedition, in February 1792, against a rebel camp in the Fonds Parisiens, in the Plaine du Cul-de-Sac: 'As we drew near the camp we were amazed to see huge poles stuck at the side of the road each crowned with a different dead bird, arranged in a different position. Some had herons, some white chickens, others black chickens. In the roadway birds had been chopped up, thrown down at intervals and surrounded by stones artistically arranged; finally we came across seven or eight broken eggs circled by zig-zag lines.

'In spite of these marvels I pushed on with fifty dragoons. After a quarter of an hour I saw a camp covered over with *ajoupas* arranged like soldiers' tents. Imagine my astonishment when we perceived all the Blacks leaping about and more than two hundred Negresses dancing and singing without a care in the world. We rode full tilt at the camp and the dance was soon finished. The Negroes fled. We chased them right into Spanish territory, killing about twenty. They killed three of our dragoons . . .

'When I got back I found that the dragoons who had stayed with the infantry had chased the Negresses: two hundred were taken without any harm being done to them. The Voodoo High Priestess had not fled: she was taken prisoner: instead of listening to her and finding out her plans they cut her down with their sabres. She was a very fine Negress, well dressed. If I hadn't been away at the time, chasing the Blacks, I would not have let her be massacred, not, at least, without having first made a thorough inquiry into what she was up to.

'I singled out a few Negresses for special questioning; some, from the little Gouraud settlement at the Fonds Parisien, knew me; they couldn't understand how we had managed to get past the obstacles which the expert Voodoo priestess had scattered across our path. It was faith in these—the devices of their priestess—which had given them confidence to dance. Since I had stayed, for a time, on a small hill, to watch them, they thought we were stuck there by magic. This priestess was a lovely Creole Negress from the Boynes settlement and I believe at other times an excellent subject.

'In the year 4 we captured an Arrada Negress in the Saint-Suzanne mountains. She was of the Voodoo sect. This woman was taken to Le Cap; she was questioned but she spoke very little Creole. She was tried by the black Telemaque, and taken into the great square before a huge crowd of all colours. Negroes and Negresses were saying openly that no human power could affect her. Telemaque made a passionate speech; he was not afraid to say it made him ashamed to be black when he saw how easily fooled his fellow Blacks could be. "The hairs of this Negress," said he, "which are so beautifully curled, so well matted with resin and gum and which you think are so powerful are going to fall." He then addressed a few words to the sorceress, who, like the Pythoness, was put before a little brazier on a tripod. She was sad and calmly disdainful. Then he ordered a Black executioner to cut off her hair which, to the great astonishment of the credulous crowd, then fell from the scissors' edge. They were no less surprised to see the sacred hairs consumed by the flames. This Negress was taken back to prison, and a few days later she was sent to a plantation where she became the laughing-stock of the Blacks.

'Let it not be thought in France that all the Blacks are like this: the Creoles and those who have been "Creolised" laugh at and make fun of all this hocus-pocus.'

In many places where the white man has imposed his law and religion on so-called 'primitive' societies, prophets have risen, calling the people to revolt and announcing the dawn of a new era in which the Whites are to be cast down and the native traditions restored in all their former glory. These revivalistic movements, called 'Messianic', usually spring from the reaction of a social group which feels itself at bay—the impotent spectator of the slow death of its own culture and values. In a last desperate lashing-out it tries to escape its destiny. Time and again, ever since the sixteenth century, the Indian or half-caste masses of Brazil have lent a willing ear to prophets who have promised them the return of the Culture Hero and the beginning of a new Golden Age. The Blacks, on the other hand, have taken part in such movements but they have never instigated them. Indeed the absence of such movements among the Blacks of Brazil puzzled the French sociologist Roger Bastide.[24] He wondered what could be the cause of such a falling-short—when everything seemed favourable to the blossoming of messianic urges amongst the slave population. According to him it was the lack of a mythology from which they could have developed a revolutionary mystique with religious overtones that prevented them, even in their brutal subjugation to European civilization and bitter resentment of it, from throwing up a truly prophetic movement. Their rebellions have been weakened by the lack of precise and real objectives.

And it is a fact: the slave rebellions in Haiti do not seem to have taken a typically messianic form. Certain chiefs did, none the less, assume the role of prophets or miracle-workers. The best known of these was Macandal who was one of the forerunners of Haitian independence. His attempt took place in 1757. He was an African from Guinea who, having been maimed on a plantation, ran away and took command of a band of fugitive slaves whom he soon turned into fanatics, persuading them 'that he was immortal and inspiring them with such fear and respect that they thought it an honour to serve him on bended knee and to worship him as they normally worshipped the god of whom he professed to be the mouthpiece. The most beautiful Negresses fought for the honour of sharing his bed.'[25] He seems to have been possessed by a determination to drive the Whites from Saint-Domingue and to turn it into an independent kingdom. His weapon was poison. He exhorted his supporters to do away with the people in the big houses, to wreck workshops and annihilate cattle. Having imprudently attended a dance on a plantation he was recognized and arrested. Condemned to be burnt alive, he put about a rumour that he would escape from the flames by turning into a fly. The crowd, assembled for his torture, experienced a moment when his prophecy looked as if it would come true. Driven by the agony of the flames into violent writhing he tore up the stake to which he was bound and finally pitched out, over the logs. A cry went up 'Macandal saved'. Panic broke out; but Macandal tied to a plank was once again given to the flames. Although his body was reduced to ashes many Blacks refused to believe that he had perished.

Today the name 'Macandal' still lives in popular memory—but it has come to mean 'poison' or 'poisoner'.

There were imitators of Macandal during the revolutionary wars. One guerilla leader, who operated in the west of the country in 1793, signed himself 'Romaine the prophetess' and announced he was the godchild of the Virgin.[26] He insisted that it was on orders from his Holy Godmother that he massacred Whites. In the eyes of his men Romaine was endowed with supernatural powers.

When this prophet became a military commander he is supposed to have promised his followers, if not immortality, then at least immunity against bullets. The Voodoo priests who threw themselves into the revolutionary maelstrom always made a point of giving a similar assurance to the faithful. Hyacinthe, who distinguished himself at the Battle of Croix des Bouquets, convinced his men they had nothing to fear from cannon: they turned up armed with knives, hoes, iron-shod sticks and slings —only to be decimated by artillery. Colonel Malenfant[27] who witnessed this engagement said that some put their arms into the cannon's mouth and shouted to their comrades: '*Veni veni, moi tin bin li*' (Come, come, I am holding it fast). As for Hyacinthe himself, he went through the thickest fire 'in range of the pistols, holding a little whip made of horse-hair, which he whisked about, shouting "Forward! Come on! It's water (coming out of the cannons' mouths). Don't be afraid." ' After the victory Hyacinthe went to the nearest presbytery to get his troops blessed by the priest—first asking absolution for himself. This shows that even in those days a Voodoo priest did not find his vocation incompatible with the duties of a good Catholic.

Although Toussaint-Louverture has never been accused—to my knowledge at least—of having practised Voodoo, Descourtilz[28] tells how on the arrival of the French expeditionary force commanded by Leclerc 'he had his fortune told at the fort of Crête-à-Pierrot by a Voodoo priest, famed for his powers of divination, only to learn that he would be betrayed and handed over to the French by his most trusted and senior general—the ferocious Dessalines'.

As a slave, Toussaint-Louverture had practised the art of healing with herbs. It was as 'herb-doctor' that he began his military career with the guerilla bands of Jean François. 'Herb-doctors' are neither *hungan* (priests) nor *boko* (sorcerers) but when treating people they make use of many magic prescriptions; and Toussaint-Louverture will have been no exception. Nevertheless his zeal for the Catholic Church proves that he had little time for the gods of Africa and served them not at all. He did however believe in magic and if what Madiou[29] relates is true he used often to say that if he did not speak through his nose it was only because the Voodoos had cast an evil spell on him. It is to this that Toussaint's horror of Voodoo is attributed by the Haitian historian.

In a commendable attempt to glorify the name of Voodoo, several contemporary nationalist writers have convinced themselves that Dessalines, the founder of the Haitian State, was a zealous 'servant of the *loa*' and that he had a quite special feeling for Ogu, the Nago god of iron and war. Dessalines, who had been a plantation slave, must have known Voodoo better than Toussaint-Louverture who had always lived in 'the big house'. Descourtilz[30] says he used to consult the *macandals* (magicians) of the country and that from them he learnt to find out a man's intentions by the humidity—or dryness—of the tobacco inside his snuff-box. According to the same writer (who is reporting the gossip of Blacks who stayed faithful to the French), 'the Congo Negroes and other Guineans were so superstitiously affected by the utterances of Dessalines that they even let him persuade them that to die in battle, at the hands of the French, was nothing but a blessing since it meant they were immediately conveyed to Guinea where, once again, they saw Papa Toussaint who was

waiting for them to complete the army with which he proposed
to reconquer Saint-Domingue. This absurd system worked so
well, said the informant, everyone goes into the attack with supernatural dash, singing the traditional songs of Guinea as though
already possessed by hope of seeing old friends once more.'[31]

Dessalines is none the less the only hero of the struggle for
independence who was deified. The Haitian anthropologist,
Lorimer Denis[32] vouches that once, during a Voodoo ceremony,
he saw a priest possessed by the spirit of the terrible emperor:
'It was indeed the man himself,' he writes. 'I saw the ferocious
face, the fanatic cast of countenance and the whole body moulded
in a vengeful attitude.' As soon as the god Dessalines appeared
the choir of the 'servants of the gods' sang as follows:

Apérè Désalin o (bis)	Oh Emperor Dessalines o,
Nu sé vayâ gasô	You're a fine fellow,
Sa u kué yo fè nu	What do you think they did to us,
Péi la nâ mê nu déja	This country is already in our hands.

There is another Voodoo song which mentions Dessalines and
which thrills with the far-off echoes of revolutionary airs:

Pito muri pasé m'kuri	Better to die than run away,
Désalin Désalin démâmbré	Dessalines Dessalines the power-ful,
Viv la libèté	Long live liberty.

In spite of such evidence there is good reason to doubt if the
Liberator had much sympathy with Voodoo. The historian
Madiou[33] tells how Dessalines, when appointed inspector-general
of culture in the western departments, 'relentlessly hunted down
all the secret societies in which African superstitions were
practised'. Hearing that a Voodoo reunion was going on in the
Cul-de-sac plain, under the direction of a *mambo*, he rushed there
with a battalion, set fire to the house where the meeting was
being held, broke it up and having taken fifty Voodooists prisoner
'killed them with bayonets'. Once he became Emperor he
showed the same distrust of Voodoo, prohibited 'services' and
shot its adherents.

The entrenchment of Voodoo in Haiti is largely due to what local historians rather pompously call 'the great Haiti schism'. Throughout the period which stretched from the Proclamation of Independence to the Concordat of 1860, Haiti had, in fact, been separated from Rome and remained outside the framework of the Church. It was only Catholic in the solemn declarations of its various constitutions. Catholic worship had not been suspended, but it had fallen into unworthy hands. Evidence of this may be found in the account of Victor Schoelcher[34] who visited Haiti in 1832. 'He (President Boyer) was pleased to entrust these lofty and delicate functions to the rubbishy rejects of the French and Spanish Churches; he was ready to receive as a priest—without examination, without any system of control, or verification of his standing—the first tramp who laid claim to the office. Haiti has many clerics who were certainly never clerics anywhere else . . . Far from enlightening the people they keep them fixed in the silliest superstitions. One takes ten gourdes for saying prayers to bring rain which some labourer needs, another takes five good piastres for an exorcism which is to bring peace of mind to an old woman accused of being a were-wolf; and when you reproach these pedlars of sanctity they blandly reply: "But monsieur, only faith can help you and unless I had taken that woman's money she would still think she was a were-wolf." To explain the fortunes made quickly in the sale of holy objects, I ought to add that the priests, over and above the celebration of Mass, vie with the makers of *wanga*, *grigris* and charms, and with the soothsayers who make stones talk, and that they sell scapularies and printed prayers to be hung round the necks of children in a locket to keep out cockroaches. And so whichever way the people turn they find nothing but lying and deceit. Is it surprising, in such circumstances, that in the country, as we are assured, there are Haitians who worship snakes?' These adventurers simply fitted themselves in with Voodoo and became the accomplices and associates of the *hungan* and *mambo*. We have proof of this in an ecclesiastical document which denounces the ease with which these priests baptized 'animals, crops, boats, canoes and, in fact, anything which was brought to them'.

Under the famous Emperor Soulouque, Voodoo, for a few

years, became almost the established religion of the State. For it was in a world 'frequented by zombi and omens, by the marvellous and the fearful' that Soulouque was sought out to be raised to the presidency. This obscure soldier, who was so soon to turn into a bloody tyrant, gave a glimpse, even on the day of his investiture, of the superstitious fears which haunted his imagination. During the *Te Deum* he obstinately refused to sit down in the presidential chair which he thought was enchanted. On his behalf let it be pointed out that the fate of those who had preceded him in the chair did not inspire confidence. Soulouque was equally reluctant to settle into the presidential palace; he only resigned himself after consulting a *mambo* of whom Madame Soulouque herself was a client. After a magical consultation the priestess declared that President Boyer, overthrown in 1843, had hidden a charm in the palace garden before he left. The charm prevented any successor from staying in power longer than thirteen months. Soulouque ordered a search which revealed the charm in the place indicated.

Soon after having himself crowned Emperor, Soulouque, now Faustin the First, celebrated Mass for his mother at Le Petit-Goave, where he was born. The day was given over to the rites of the Church but in the dead of night Soulouque went to the cemetery where 'the blood of a lamb, sacrificed by his own hand, was sprinkled on the tomb of the old slavewoman who had given Haiti an Emperor'. The funeral rites lasted a week. The Emperor had 100 bullocks killed to feed the 20,000 guests who had come from all over the country.

To what extent are they true, these anecdotes gleaned from a book by Alaux[35] which was written when Soulouque was still Emperor? The author admits that the Mulattos—who had good reason for hating a man who treated them with the greatest cruelty—spread stories of a kind calculated to make a fool of him. On the other hand it would have been surprising if Soulouque had not shared the beliefs of the Voodoo milieu in which he was brought up and of the great mass of the people who were his main supporters. His precautions against spells, the rites which he celebrated for his mother are still common practice in Haiti today and it is quite possible that he did behave like a zealous servant of the *loa*—which would not have prevented him from remaining the good Catholic who tried, for instance, to achieve a Concordat with Rome.

Finally let us cite an incident, related by Spencer St John, which tells us a lot about the influence of the *hungan* and the *mambo* under the rule of Soulouque.[36] A Voodoo priestess was arrested for having performed a sacrifice too openly. 'When about to be conducted to prison, a foreign bystander remarked aloud that probably she would be shot. She laughed and said, "If I were to beat the sacred drum, and march through the city, there's not one, from the Emperor downwards, but would humbly follow me." She was sent to jail, but no one ever heard that she was punished.'

The famous *affaire de Bizoton*, which took place in 1863 during the presidency of Geffrard, demands our attention only because it achieved a notoriety out of all proportion to its importance, and because it gave, quite unjustifiably, Voodoo—and therefore Haiti too—a bad name. It is told in great detail in the work of Spencer St John, *Haiti or the Black Republic*.[37] Briefly the facts are as follows: a certain Congo Pellé, whose sister was a *mambo*, made plans with two other *papa-loa*, to sacrifice his niece to a Voodoo god. He kidnapped the child who was eventually strangled and cut up at an end-of-the-year ceremony. Her flesh was cooked, with other eatables, and consumed by all who had taken part in the rite. A few days later another little girl was carried off to be sacrificed on the Day of Kings. The police were warned and they found the girl, who was due to have her throat cut, lying bound under a Voodoo altar; and at the same time they discovered the remains of the girl who had been killed earlier. Eight people involved in this affair were arrested and tried. They confessed monstrous crimes but before accepting their confessions as proof, we would do well to remember the disturbing statement made by one of the accused. Asked to confirm her confession in front of the tribunal she said, 'Yes, I did confess what you assert, but remember how cruelly I was beaten before I said a word.'

Seemingly the prisoners were tortured by the police—a custom which has not died out. The confessions therefore are open to doubt. None the less, the remains of the victim, which Spencer St John was able to see, and various other evidence, amounted to a weight of proof which was deemed sufficient to procure the death sentence for all the accused.

Spencer St John gives us other rather doubtful stories about human sacrifice and cannibalism. The terrifying picture which these elements enabled him to paint, struck the popular imagination with such power that people have been addicted, ever since, to thinking of the peaceful Haitian countryside as a sort of jungle where hideous crimes were perpetrated. Echoes of such fantasy are to be found in relatively recent works by Americans—such as *Black Bagdad* by John Craig. These legends, against which the Haitians protest, with good reason, do in fact spring from folklore—and not, as has often been said, from the calumny of Whites. What Haitian is there who has not heard tales far more sinister than those of Spencer St John! The peasants are haunted by the fear of sorcerers whom they look upon as cannibals thirsting for the blood of children. Such folk tales are taken as gospel truth by the Haitian élite and foreign journalists. When we come to the question of sorcery we shall have an opportunity of returning to all these terrors which survive, fed by a tradition which remaining basically the same through the ages, merely adapts itself to fashion. Many presidents of Haiti have been accused of Voodooism. A good many of the stories about them belong to the kind of folklore which Haitians never fail to weave round men in position; but probably several generals, risen from the ranks, brought to the palace, as Soulouque did, the religious ideas and practice of the milieu in which they were brought up.

If we can believe Spencer St John,[38] President Salnave, harassed by enemies, finally gave in to the lure of Voodoo and agreed to take part in a ceremony which entailed the sacrifice of various animals. Considering the popularity enjoyed by Salnave in Voodooist circles, the story seems far from impossible. But the English writer is beginning to overdo things when he accuses the wretched president of having consented to sacrifice a 'goat without horns'—in other words a human being.

Apart from Soulouque, no president of Haiti ever achieved a reputation as Voodooist and sorcerer comparable to that which

is still enjoyed by Antoine Simon. This former rural constable,
a peasant who had but slightly lost his uncouth ways, swept to
power by revolution in 1908, believed in the *loa* and in the power
of witchcraft. His daughter Celestina was reputedly a Voodoo
priestess with marvellous 'knowledge'. She went through various
rituals in the grounds of the presidential palace to counter the
traps laid by those who were plotting against her father; but to
no avail: after two and a half years of dictatorship he was overthrown by another revolution. In all the countless stories still
told about him today, an important part is assigned to a goat
called Simalo. People go as far as to say that once he wanted this
goat to be blessed by the archbishop, specially for some Voodoo
ceremony, and so he substituted it for the mortal remains of a
general whose solemn funeral was to take place in the Cathedral.
The story, out of which W. H. Seabrook makes some amusing
pages,[39] is a good example of the kind of lampoon so dear to the
Haitian heart. But the 'angling' which doesn't spare the all-
powerful head of the state does not always stop at funny stories.
W. H. Seabrook[40] is unpardonable for giving as authentic a
terrible story which he picked up in Port-au-Prince: Celestina,
wanting a human heart for a magic rite, caused a soldier of the
guard to be disembowelled in front of her. She was seen, dressed
in red, walking towards her father's palace carrying the heart on
a silver platter. Faced with this kind of fantasy, which unfortunately Whites are only too ready to believe, we can but share the
justified exasperation of the people of Haiti.

Aubin,[41] who is one of the well-informed and very honest
writers, makes an observation about the *humfo* of La Petite
Plaine, near Port-au-Prince which deserves to be quoted:
'*Papalois* and *hungan* rely less on the local people than on the
inhabitants of Port-au-Prince who though by nature sceptical
and irregular in their offices, are revived now and again by a
resurgence of African atavism. I did not have the good fortune
to meet M. Durolien, at Croix-des-Missions. He was the special,
private *papaloi* to President Hyppolite.'

All presidents during, and since, the American occupation
(1915–33) have belonged to the educated bourgeoisie and are
hardly targets for charges of Voodooism. Public malice has

nevertheless reproached them for having transactions with the *hungan* and has poked fun at their terror of black magic. We must remember that the people of little Haiti are always tempted to establish a chain of cause and effect between sorcery and success. Not many years ago it was said, quite openly, among the people of Port-au-Prince, that the then President owed his office to one of his uncles who was regarded as a powerful magician.

It is impossible to gauge with any accuracy the role which Voodoo plays today in the politics of Haiti. It is said that certain priests and priestesses are prepared to act as police informers and that this co-operation is the price of the immunity they enjoy. Candidates for the Chamber or the Senate take good care not to overlook the support of certain priests or priestesses whose influence is sometimes enormous, to say nothing of the support of the *loa* themselves which is not to be disdained. Some candidates ensure themselves of this support by generous gifts to the Voodoo sanctuaries or by paying for ceremonies out of their private purse.

During the troubles which occurred in 1957 a charge of Voodooism was lodged against Dr François Duvalier, presidential candidate and former director of the Bureau of Ethnology.* This politician was indeed very interested in Voodoo—to the extent of gleaning information for, and publishing, various articles on the subject. This was enough for his rivals to anoint him chief *hungan*.

During the American occupation Voodoo was looked upon as a sign of barbarism and served as a butt for the spite of the military authorities. One of the Marine officers, John Craig, treats it in his book *Black Bagdad* with as much naïveté as horror. In reading some of his accounts, allegedly authentic, you cannot help wondering which is the more gullible and has the greater weakness for marvels—the unsophisticated peasant or the White chief of police. All the same, the persecution of Voodoo, which went on throughout this period, was limited to the arrest of a few *hungan*, the laying waste of a few sanctuaries and the confiscation of drums. Later on it was to experience a more serious ordeal: the Catholic offensive. This action was somewhat un-

* Dr Duvalier is now President of Haiti.

grateful on the part of the Church as Voodoo had in one way
made the task of the Concordat easier: during the so-called
schism, it had kept alive the memory of Catholicism, alongside
its own African rites and beliefs, to such good effect that priests
who came over from France did not find themselves confronted
by a completely pagan population.[42]

After the Concordat of 1860 the Catholic Church did not give
much thought to Voodoo. It deplored its existence, denounced it
from the pulpits, but hoped that with time and patience the
whole population would end up completely Christian. Were
there not touching signs of devotion to the Church on the part
of the people? In 1896 Monseigneur Kersuzan organized an anti-
Voodoo League but his attempt came to nothing. It was not
until 1940, after events which I will speak about later, that
the Church abruptly changed its attitude. The violent campaign
waged at that time by the clergy is known amongst the people
as *la renonce*. It has left its scar on Haiti, and would perhaps have
forced Voodoo 'underground' if the government had not taken
steps to moderate the zeal of the priests.

Today Voodoo is tolerated. In certain parts a police permit is
still required for 'beating the drum'. At Marbial, where I conducted my research, the priest kept a jealous watch to see that
no ceremony was celebrated in his parish. The *chefs de section*
were compelled to keep up a strict supervision. Nevertheless, the
peasants still secretly danced for the *loa*, and defied the priest
and his police.

Although neither Church nor State has succeeded in breaking the hold of Voodooism, tourism, on the other hand, in its
most commercial forms is having a rapidly destructive effect.
For several years now, thanks to the efforts of the government,
Port-au-Prince has been turning into a vast tourist centre. Every
American who disembarks there has but one word on his lips—
'Voodoo'; and one wish—to see ceremonies which he imagines
to be orgiastic and cruel. Many *hungan* and *mambo* who for
several years have been pleased to see parties of Americans turn
up at their *humfo*, have responded with alacrity to the curiosity
of foreign clients. The *humfo* threw wide their doors to the
tourists; link-ups were made between hotel porters and *hungan*,

to such good effect that on Saturday evenings long files of cars may be seen in some wretched back-street near a sanctuary. Some enterprising *hungan* have even put on Voodoo 'shows' which are repeated weekly and designed purely for tourists. They have altered their ancestral rites so as to provide their clientèle with the picturesque which it demands. They take care, it seems, to stage for the ravished eyes of the readers of Seabrook and other titillating works, the goat with lighted candles on the tips of its horns. Sanctuaries have become neon-lighted theatres. Great sums may have been made by the *hungan* and *mambo*, but they have driven away true believers from their temples. It is true that this shameless prostitution of religion, at the hands of its own priests, flourishes only in Port-au-Prince, but it will end by shaking the faith of the country people who are under the influence of the capital. Another formidable enemy is Protestantism which, in the course of gaining many converts, has shown itself inimical to Voodoo, harrying it with relentless hatred and, unlike the Catholic Church, refusing all compromise.

II

The Social Framework of Voodoo

I. THE SOCIAL FRAMEWORK OF VOODOO

Voodoo is essentially a popular religion. The greater part of its adherents are recruited among the peasants who form 97 per cent of the total population of the country. As to the city dwellers —they have remained faithful to it in whatever measure they have kept up their rural roots. The practice of Voodoo, along with the exclusive use of the Creole language, is one of the characteristics which sociologists have kept to distinguish between the masses and the small class of educated people who enjoy a certain material ease and call themselves the 'élite'. The members of this élite, who are mostly Mulattos, adhere with the utmost tenacity to Western modes of life and thought, and hold the country people in the greatest contempt. Between these two classes the cleavage is so pronounced that the élite has been termed a 'caste' and one American sociologist, Leyburn,[1] has gone so far as to describe them as two different nations sharing the same country. In fact the differences have been very much exaggerated. The élite is not a caste since it is open to those who succeed in raising themselves, either by talent, luck or politics from the masses. Even in the subject which concerns us here, the contrasts are not so marked as one might think. Most of the élite children are brought up by servants who come from the *mornes* (mountains) and carry with them the terrors of 'African Guinea'. All Haitians, whatever their social status, have trembled in their youth at stories of *zombi* and werewolves and learnt to dread the power of sorcerers and evil spirits. Most of them, under the influence of school or family, react against such fancies but some give in to them and consult a Voodoo priest in secret.

On this point I will quote the evidence of a bishop who unfortunately must remain anonymous: 'Superstition is so widespread and deep that it could be said to touch everyone. The best,

even those who don't practise it, have to fight against the feelings
they experience when faced with certain facts, certain signs
which recall superstition to them.' Even a Haitian priest once
confessed that he was prone to such feelings: 'The whole of one's
being is impregnated with them, right to the bottom of the soul;
the smallest detail of existence is dominated by them.' And beside this testament we can quote an excerpt from a conference
held by Monseigneur Kersuzan in 1896: 'A *bocor* [sorcerer]
crosses our streets. We know him. Everyone spots him. Where
is he going? You might think to some poor person who cannot
afford doctor or chemist. But no. He is going to a superb house
where he will operate on the father of some family in the highest
rank of society.'

This evidence of superstition among the upper classes, perhaps
slightly exaggerated at source, nevertheless fits in with the
description of Voodoo which we have given so far. The cult is,
before all else, a rural paganism and must be considered in its
true setting—in the *mornes* and villages. The political and social
frameworks peculiar to the African tribes from whom the Haitians
of today are descended, were pulverized by slavery. Even the
family did not survive that dissolution; only in haphazard fashion
was it reconstituted on the fringe of plantation life and in the
first years of the country's independence Toussaint Louverture,
Dessalines and Christophe had all intended to maintain the
system of huge properties on which the peasants would have
lived as serfs. History decided otherwise. It was the peasant
small-holding which triumphed in the end. The families which
divided between them the lands of the State, regrouped along
lines which, though not strictly speaking African, yet recalled
the organizational forms common to Africa and Europe. Not
very long ago, the social unit of the Haitian countryside was the
extended family consisting of the head of the family, his children,
married or unmarried, and his grandchildren. Each *ménage* had
its house and field. The whole group of conjugal families, all
closely related, was called the 'compound' (*laku*), and its houses
and granaries often made up a hamlet. Its members were further
bound together by worship of their common root-*loa* (*loa-
racines*), that is to say of the gods and protecting spirits of the

extended family which were inherited just like property. The compound head kept a little sanctuary or *humfo* for his gods and there, in the presence of his kin, he officiated. A *hungan* (priest) and *mambo* (priestess) were only called upon in the event of serious illness or to 'feed' the family gods.

Today the compound is tending to disintegrate. Families are being dispersed by the carving up of land and weakening of the kinship ties. The cult of ancestral spirits with its attendant obligations continues to assure a measure of cohesion between the members of a scattered kin group: when the gods and spirits demand food the whole family must be present and share the costs. Nevertheless Voodoo as a domestic cult is losing importance daily to the profit of the small autonomous cult-groups which grow up round the sanctuaries.

People who regret that Voodoo is, in fact, the religion of the people of Haiti, forget how hard is the life of the average peasant and worker. Isolation, economic stagnation, administrative fecklessness, ignorance—all help to explain the misery which is to be found among the masses. At the source of that poverty stands the familiar curse of so many under-developed countries: over-population on ever less fertile land. Haiti has the highest density of population in the Western Hemisphere—250 people to the square mile. Beneath a gay and optimistic exterior the peasant conceals a chronic anxiety which is, unfortunately, only too well justified. Seldom does he own enough land to escape the dearth which occurs at the slightest caprice of weather. Usually he is in debt, in possession of doubtful title-deeds and can neither read nor write. Unable to speak French as do the town-folk, he feels an easy prey to their cupidity. And then to all these causes of anxiety is added the dread of illness. Tuberculosis, malaria and hookworm are endemic and their threat is always present in addition to that of the accidents which may ruin him. Voodoo reflects these cares. What the faithful ask of their gods is not so much riches and happiness but more the removal of the miseries which assail them from every quarter. Illness and misfortune seem to them divine judgments which must somehow be mitigated by offerings and sacrifice. It is unjust and naïve to reproach the peasants for wasting much of their meagre resources on pagan ceremonies. As long as medical services are non-existent in the country districts, so long may the Voodoo priests be sure of a large clientele. Voodoo allows its adherents to find their way back to a rudimentary form of collective life, to show their artistic talents and to have the exalted feeling of contact with the supernatural. At Marbial where Voodoo has been more or less suppressed, a wretched depression has settled over the valley, and life for the peasants has lost all point.

We have seen that Voodoo exists in two forms—one domestic, the other public. It is this last which mainly concerns us here. Most of my observations were made at Port-au-Prince where the sanctuaries are numerous and prosperous and where the ritual is full of refinements and subtleties which are lacking in the rural cults. People are prone to suppose that the purest and richest traditions are to be found in the remotest valleys. The little I was able to see of rural Voodoo convinced me that it was poor in its ritual compared to the Voodoo of the capital. Simplicity of rite is not always a guarantee of antiquity. It is often the result of ignorance and neglect. No doubt some African characteristics are better preserved in the backwoods than in the faubourgs of Port-au-Prince, but the purity of the African heritage only moderately concerns us. Voodoo deserves to be studied not only as regards the survival of Dahomean and Congolese beliefs and practices, but also as a religious system born fairly recently from a fusion of many different elements. It is the dynamic aspect of Voodoo always evolving before our eyes which is more to our purpose than the rich material it affords to the erudite, possessed by a craving for the search for origins.

II. VOODOO CLERGY AND CULT-GROUPS

Voodoo has preserved one of the fundamental characteristics of the African religions from which it is derived: worship is sustained by groups of adherents who voluntarily place themselves under the authority of a priest or priestess whose sanctuary or *humfo* they frequent. The faithful who have been initiated in the same sanctuary and who congregate to worship the gods to which it is sacred, form a sort of fraternity called 'the *humfo* society'. The importance of this cult-group depends to a great extent on the personality and influence of the priest and priestess who preside.

This complex religion with its ill-defined frontiers may perhaps be more easily approached through a study of its social and material frameworks. It is the priests and their numerous acolytes who have out of widely different beliefs and rites formed a more or less coherent system.

Spirits incarnate themselves at will in the people they choose. Any devotee can therefore enter into immediate contact with the supernatural world. Such intimacy, however, does not involve communication or dialogue with the god since the person possessed is mere flesh, a receptacle, borrowed by the spirit for the purpose of revealing himself. If you wish to get a hearing from the spirits—particularly when health and fortune are at stake—it is better to have recourse to the skills of a priest or priestess: *hungan* and *mambo*, less commonly called *papa-loa* and *maman-loa*. The word *gangan*, used as a synonym of *hungan*, carries with it a nuance which is respectful or depreciatory, according to the region.[2]

Although *hungan* and *mambo* are often closely linked with each other, they are by no means part of a properly organized corps. They are the heads of autonomous sects or cult-groups, rather than members of a clerical hierarchy. Certainly the prestige of a *hungan* may spread and affect sanctuaries served by his disciples, but there is no subordination, as such, of one *hungan* to another. The profession has its grades which correspond with the various degrees of initiation, but a priest only has authority over those who voluntarily offer themselves as servants of the spirits worshipped in his sanctuary.

There is the greatest variety of types in this profession, ranging from the ignorant, inspired peasant who puts up an altar near his little house and invokes the *loa* on behalf of his neighbours, to the grand *hungan* of the capital, cultivated in his own way, subtle and tinged with occultism, with a sanctuary full of artistic pretensions. Some priests enjoy a reputation which goes no further than the limit of their district and others attract crowds of clients and are known all over the country.

Some *hungan* and *mambo* even cut a figure in the world of fashion. Their *humfo* is frequented by members of the bourgeoisie who are not afraid to rub shoulders with artisans and workmen. Some years ago, a *mambo* of Croix-des-Bouquets who was getting ready to celebrate a grand ceremony for his guardian *loa*, sent out printed invitation cards to his many relations in the town. The evening was a great success. An elegant gathering, which included several high-ranking members of the government, crushed into his peristyle. The *mambo* led them through the rooms of her sanctuary, replying graciously to the naïve questions which were put to her and, while the *hunsi* were possessed by perfectly mannered *loa*, she had refreshments served. Indeed, she was the perfect hostess, and the impresario of an exhibition which convinced the most prejudiced that Voodoo was obviously a wholesome and picturesque entertainment.

All sorts of fantastic stories about the powers of *hungan* may be heard. Atenaïse, a woman in Marbial who claimed to be a *mambo*, often spoke to me about her grandfather, a *hungan* well versed in all the lore of Africa who could 'change people into animals and, what is harder still, into Guinea grass!' The power of remaining several days under water is attributed to many *hungan* and *mambo*. Madame Tisma, who was none the less a well balanced and intelligent woman, told me in the most normal tones that she had spent three years at the bottom of a river where she had received instruction from water spirits.

The gift most prized in a priest is second sight. To some *hungan* it has brought fame which merely increased after their deaths. A certain Nan Gommier acquired such a reputation that even today a soothsayer will say as a boast, 'What I see for you, Antoine Nan Gommier himself would not have seen.' This *hungan* is reputed to have known a long time in advance who was going to come and consult him and if it were a person of importance he sent a horse to meet him. With Nan Gommier questions and explanations were superfluous. He read people's thoughts and replied before being asked.

Voodoo adepts use the word 'knowledge' (*connaissance*)

to describe what we would define as 'supernatural insight and the power which is derived therefrom'. It is in degrees of 'knowledge' that various *hungan* and *mambo* differ from each other. In addition to this power, which depends more or less on supernatural gifts, *hungan* and *mambo* must also acquire a more technical kind of education: they must know the names of the spirits, their attributes, their emblems, their various special tastes and the liturgies appropriate to the different kinds of ceremony. Only those who have mastered this lore deserve the title *hungan* or *mambo*. To do so requires perseverance, a good memory, musical aptitude and a long experience of ritual. A good *hungan* is at one and the same time priest, healer, soothsayer, exorcizer, organizer of public entertainments and choirmaster. His functions are by no means limited to the domain of the sacred. He is an influential political guide, an electoral agent for whose co-operation senators and deputies are prepared to pay handsomely. Frequently his intelligence and reputation make him the accepted counsellor of the community. Those who frequent his *humfo* bring their troubles to him and discuss with him their private affairs and work. He combines in his person the functions of *curé*, mayor and notary. Material profit is not the only attraction of his profession: the social position which goes with it is such as to interest all who feel they have enough talent and application to raise themselves above manual labour. To become a *hungan* or *mambo* is to climb the social ladder and be guaranteed a place in the public eye.

A psychological study of *hungan* and *mambo* would perhaps reveal that most of them shared certain characteristics. My experience in this subject is not wide enough to allow me to generalize. Many *hungan* whom I knew seemed to me to be maladjusted or neurotic. Among them were homosexuals—impressionable, capricious, over-sensitive and prone to sudden transports of emotion. On the other hand Lorgina, with whom I had a long friendship, was a perfectly normal woman. She did occasionally 'go off the deep end'—with the violence of a cyclone—but she calmed down so quickly that these frightening outbursts never struck me as being completely sincere. Madame Andrée, another prominent *mambo*, was remarkable only for her intelligence and cunning. In spite of her peasant origin she became a complete bourgeoise in her tastes and behaviour. Of the *hungan* I knew there was one whose name I shall withhold who acquired a certain reputation among intellectual circles by his intelligence and by his readiness to put himself at the disposal of anthropologists. He was rather a disturbing person, sickly, perhaps a drug-addict and gifted with a rather odd imagination. To strengthen the effect of his services he made innovations which he subsequently justified by bold and naïve theological speculation. Beneath a genial exterior he concealed a morbid vanity and sensitivity. When I refused to pay the costs of a ceremony which he had wanted to organize in my honour, he revenged himself by inviting me to his *humfo* to take part in a fête. Pretending to honour and to doctor me, he in fact made me expiate my crime with all kinds of small cruelties.

Most of those who choose the profession of *hungan* or *mambo*, do so at the impulse of a motive in which faith, ambition, love of power and sheer cupidity are all inextricably mixed. Priestly vocation is none the less interpreted as a call from the supernatural world which cannot be disregarded with impunity. Suspicion and censure weigh heavily on those who are accused of having 'bought' their patron spirits, for if they have indeed done this, then it is because the 'good *loa*' rejected them as unworthy and the mercenary *loa*, to whom they applied in despair, accepted them. Those who have done such a thing can only be *hungan* 'working with both hands' (*travaillant des deux mains*) that is to say the kind of sorcerers known as *boko*. The amount of power put into the hands of a *hungan* lays him open to great temptations, though his profession—like that of medicine, with which it has much in common—has its ethic. Unhappily this is often violated. Have not certain *hungan* been accused of showing themselves to be in no hurry to cure their patients and even of aggravating an illness in order to make it more fruitful of fees? It has even been suggested that they get together with the sorcerers who have cast a spell on their client in order to learn the secret of the spell which caused the disease. The two accomplices then share the profits from the treatment. Against this kind of extortion the faithful are powerless or, more exactly, they have no other refuge than the moral sense of the *loa* themselves. Spirits do not like to see their help abused. Sometimes they punish the guilty *hungan* by withdrawing their patronage and depriving him of his 'knowledge'. Their punishment can even go as far as subjecting him to prison or to some other humiliation.

Spirits who have chosen a man (or a woman) as vessel for supernatural powers and have decided to keep him in their service, make their will known to him either by the utterances of the possessed or by a symbolic dream. Before one man, Tullius, became a *hungan*, he often saw, in dreams, a gourd containing the beads and snake-bones covering the sacred rattle (*asson*), symbol of the priestly profession. To say of someone that he (or she) has 'taken the *asson*'* means that person has become a *hungan* or *mambo*.

Anyone singled out by the *loa* could only avoid the summons at risk to himself. Some time after he had dreamed the dream which we have just mentioned, Tullius became seriously ill. He believed he had been struck down by the *mystères* who had grown tired of his inability to make up his mind. He felt all the more guilty since *loa* had announced, at his birth, by means of various miracles, that he was predestined to serve them: his mother fleeing from a cyclone which had burst on the region, took refuge in a church and was there gripped by the first pangs of childbirth. She then distinctly heard the noise of drums and religious chanting: this was the sound of her guardian spirits Ogu-balindjo, Linglessu, and Mistress-Mambo-Nana, who were coming to her assistance. She had her baby in the porch, to the dismay of the *curé* who would have liked to rush her to hospital. Finally—another omen of an exceptional career—the baby came feet first.

---

* The *asson*, or sacred rattle, is used for summoning the *loa*. It consists of a gourd (*Lagenaria* sp.) dried and emptied of its flesh and pips. It is covered over with a network of china beads which vary in colour and number according to whichever *loa* are 'masters of the *humfo*'. Snake vertebrae are mingled with the china beads. Sometimes the vertebrae predominate. *Asson* are usually furnished with a bell which the priest rings during a ceremony. There are two main types of *asson*: the master-*asson* and the ordinary *asson*. Before they are used in a service these rattles must first be consecrated by baptism. When a person is 'ordained' as *hungan* or *mambo* he or she is put to bed with an *asson*.

The case of a famous *mambo* of Port-au-Prince, Madame L.,
affords another example of a person not daring to resist a supernatural vocation. She was a zealous Catholic, proud of belonging
to the Société du Sacré-Coeur. She was covered with pious
medals and her certificate of baptism was framed on the wall of
her parlour. In spite of her repugnance, the *loa* insisted on her
becoming a *mambo* and she gave way only because she was afraid
of their 'punishment'. In return they helped her to set herself up
and contributed to the success of her treatments. They did not
require her to give up her Christian duties and that is why, on
her altar, a prayer book stands cheek by jowl with the playing
cards and rattle of the seer.

The call of the spirits is sometimes heard by people who seem
in no condition to comply with them. I was told the extraordinary
story of a peasant who became a Protestant after the death of his
son: he wanted to get his own back on the *loa* who had disregarded
his prayers. In fact he bore them such hatred that he had sworn
never again to have anything to do with them. Then, one
evening, when he was returning from a gathering at the church,
he met three mysterious beings on the road. He distinctly heard
one of these say 'No—it is not he . . .' whereupon he lost consciousness. A few days later, waking from a deep sleep, he found
on his chest the emblems of a *hungan*: two 'thunderstones' and
the pack of cards of a soothsayer. Realizing his danger he took
the hint. He gave up Protestantism, went back to the bosom of
the Catholic church and became a *hungan*. It is said that he
brings about remarkable cures and that his predictions always
come true.

The profession of *hungan* can be hereditary. Naturally a father
likes to hand on the secrets of his art to his son, and train him
up to take his place. The mere fact that the sanctuary, and the
spirits which live in it, form part of the inheritance entails a
responsibility for the heir from which he can only escape with
difficulty: on the one hand the *loa* and the clientele of the *humfo*
constitute a sort of capital which a family does not lightly give
up, and on the other the abandoned, famished spirits may turn
on the person whose duty it is to feed them. The struggle which
takes place in the soul of the man who finds the profession of

hungan repugnant and who in spite of this is pushed into it by his family, soon takes on the nature of a personal conflict with the ancestral *loa*. He feels they are threatening him. He attributes every illness, every disappointment to their hostility and so, weakened by fear, he often gives in to what he imagines to be a supernatural appeal. Sometimes the very opposite happens. A son wishes to succeed his father but the spirits are against it and put every obstacle in his path.

Most candidates for the priesthood go through a course of instruction lasting several months or even several years with a *hungan* or *mambo* who wishes to take them on. They learn the technique of their profession by passing through all the 'grades' of the Voodoo hierarchy, serving their master successively as *hunsi*, *hungenikon* (choirmaster), *la-place* and *confiance*. The master's fame is reflected on his pupils and these, when they become *mambo* or *hungan*, talk with pride of their apprenticeship.

Some priests say they got their education directly from the spirits. Among the *loa*, Ogu, Legba, Ayizan and Simbi regard themselves as proper *hungan* and undertake the instruction of certain novices, selected by them. A man who has received his *asson* from the 'mysteries' will pretend to be proud of it—in order to conceal a feeling of inferiority, for he who claims supernatural patronage has never had the advantage of a proper training and so tries to say as little as possible about his 'knowledge'. He is known as a *hungan-macoutte*,* a name which bears a disparaging nuance. Similarly it can happen that priests who want to make innovations in ritual without offending their terrestrial masters, attribute the novelties to the fuller instructions which they say they have got from the *loa*.

The transmission of 'knowledge' can be effected through a magic object. A *hungan* of Port-au-Prince, who had set himself up in Marbial, was gifted—so people said—with such extraordinary powers of second sight that he managed to amass a fortune which was estimated at more than 10,000 gourdes (i.e. $2,000). On his deathbed he gave his *soeur baptême*† a piece of

---

* Straw bag carried by peasants.

† People with the same godfather or godmother call each other 'brother' or 'sister'.

silk which he always wore round his waist. As soon as the girl girdled herself with it she was possessed by a *loa*, and inherited, on the spot, her brother's gifts. She followed in his steps and became a *mambo*.

When a candidate to the priesthood has completed his apprenticeship he must pass through an initiation which is surrounded by the greatest secrecy. If we are to believe what I was told by one *hungan*, the rites observed on this occasion are more or less the same as those of the *kanzo* initiation which we will discuss later. It is simply tougher: 'there are more punishments'. The *hungan*-to-be is shut up in one of the sanctuary rooms for nine days. He lies on a straw mat with his *asson* by his side. His head rests on a stone under which a pack of cards has been placed. He may only sit up for a few minutes. His dreams during his confinement are extremely important: they are the means by which the gods—particularly the local ones—convey him their instructions. The formal enthronement of the *hungan* is called 'lifting' (*haussement*) because the main rite consists of raising the candidate three times in an armchair amid the cheering of all present. 'Lifting' is also practised whenever a community member achieves a new grade in the Voodoo hierarchy.

The gift of clairvoyance which earns a *hungan* the title of *divino* (seer) is obtained at the end of a special ceremony, 'the gripping of the eyes' (*la prise des yeux*) which is looked upon as the highest degree of priestly initiation.

THE DIGNITARIES OF THE 'HUMFO'

Initiates, men or women, who regularly take an active part in ceremonies and who help the priest in his functions, are called *hunsi*, a word of Fon derivation meaning 'the spouse of the god'. Together they make up a little court round the *mambo* or *hungan* or, more exactly, a society sworn to the worship of the *loa* and made up usually of more women than men. Hence we shall speak of the *hunsi* as feminine, although the title is common to both sexes.

There are many different reasons which prompt people to belong to a society. They might join simply because they live in the neighbourhood of a sanctuary or because a member of their family is already part of it. Others attach themselves to a priest (or a priestess) because they have been treated by him or simply because they admire his style or have a high opinion of his 'knowledge'. Equally a devotee might tend to visit a sanctuary where his own *loa* took precedence over others.

Hunsi who agree out of piety to serve the *loa* in some chosen sanctuary, are tied down to many duties. They must be prepared to spend whole nights dancing and singing beneath a peristyle and to be possessed by spirits. A *hunsi* is committed not only to offer sacrifices to the *loa* of the *humfo*, but also to devote herself to the humblest tasks, without hope of any reward beyond the friendship and protection of the *loa*, as well as living in dread of divine punishment should she prove negligent. The singing and dancing can be a satisfaction in themselves but the same could scarcely be said of the down-to-earth chores such as cooking food for the *loa*, cleaning the peristyle, collecting and making ready the sacred objects—in short fulfilling the rôle of 'spouse of the god'. Moreover the *hunsi* can only do their job adequately if details of ritual are familiar to them. The initiation of the *kanzo*, during which they receive proper instruction, rounds off the religious training acquired by assiduous attendance at the *humfo*.

Zeal, devotion to the *hungan* or *mambo*, and obedience are the main qualities expected of a *hunsi*. She must be as deferential to the *mambo*, whom she calls *maman*, and to the *hungan* whom she calls *papa*, as she would be to her own parents. The good name of a sanctuary depends much on the discipline and *esprit de corps* of its *hunsi*.

It is high praise to say of a *hungan* that he keeps his *hunsi* in good order; the negligence or lax behaviour of a *hunsi* upsets the serious atmosphere which should obtain when *loa* are expected. Naturally the occasional mischief and inattentions of the *hunsi* are resented by *hungan* as personal slights. Lorgina, whom illness and old age had made suspicious and touchy, was always complaining of her *hunsi*. She found them idle, irresponsible and above all *radi* (*hardi*—brash and disrespectful). When possessed by a severe *loa* she seized the opportunity of lecturing and some-

times chasing them with a whip. Once I saw her beat an unfortunate *hunsi* in fury and then take her on her knee to comfort
her. Of course *hunsi* punished like this could not complain since
it was the *loa* who had chastized them—without Lorgina knowing anything about it . . .

The misbehaviour of *hunsi* weighed on Tullius too. One day
when he had got Guédé-fatras into his head he lectured his
hunsi at length on the theme of obedience and to edify them told
the story of the young woman who having been whipped for
making some mistake in procedure, not only bore no grudge
against her *maman* but came and sang to her:

Salânyé onaivo	Salânyé onaivo
M'respèté hûngâ mwê	I respect my *hungan*
M'respèté mâmbô mwê	I respect my *mambo*.

For his part the *hungan* has responsibilities towards the
hunsi: he is their counsellor and protector and if they find themselves without means of support, through no fault of their own,
he houses, feeds and clothes them until he has found them a
job. When they are ill, he looks after them as though they were
members of his family.

The *hungan* unloads part of his responsibilities on the most
devoted and zealous of his *hunsi*. She who is promoted to the
rank of *hungenikon* or 'queen chorister' (*reine-chanterelle*) is
mistress of the choir during ceremonies. The standard of the
liturgical singing depends upon her. It is she who with arms
dramatically uplifted, sings out in a full strong voice the first
notes of the hymns, and she who subsequently scolds and chivvies
the *hunsi* if they sing feebly. Finally it is she who shaking her
rattle (*chacha*), breaks the rhythm of the singing which she
wishes to stop. It is she also who identifies each *loa* as it appears,
who chooses the songs to be sung in its honour and stops them
after the approved number of couplets or at the order of the
hungan. During fêtes the *hungenikon* work themselves silly night
after night, all night long, never sparing themselves and without
even seeking the relaxation and rest which is to be found in the
dizziness of trance. For a *hungenikon*, no less than a drummer,
must remain in possession of her faculties and attend to what is

happening; otherwise chaos would bring the ceremony to an end.

The head storekeeper, also called the *hungenikon*-quartermaster, is a man or woman appointed to be in charge of the offerings. The *la-place*—abbreviation of the Commander in chief of the city (*commandant général de la place*)—is the master of ceremonies. His emblem is a sabre or a matchet with which he juggles in an elegant manner. He marches in front of all processions and controls their movements. He is also responsible for keeping order during ceremonies. Last of all the personages of importance we must mention the confidant (*le confiance*)—the right-hand man of the *hungan* and the 'beast of burden' or majordomo who takes care of the administrative chores of a *humfo*.

The staff of a *humfo*—*hunsi, hungenikon, la-place, drummers*, etc. as well as people who have been treated there—*pititt-feuilles* (small leaves), or who have become regular attendants—*pititt-caye* (children of the house), make up what is known as the '*humfo* society'. This sometimes assumes the character of a mutual assistance association. The 'support society' (*société soutien*) is not always the same as the *humfo* society, although it would be difficult to draw a boundary between them. As its name suggests, the *société soutien*, by means of its subscriptions, helps towards the maintenance of the *humfo*, defends its interests if they are threatened, and helps the *hungan* to organize the 'big feastings of the gods' which he is bound to give. These societies have been most aptly compared to the parish councils of the Catholic Church. Hence the *hungan* try and stiffen them with influential politicians or prosperous tradesmen, whose moral or financial support could be of use.

Associations like these, which grow up round a *humfo*, are often modelled on the co-operative work groups which are to be found everywhere in the Haitian countryside. They comprise a whole hierarchy of dignitaries whose rolling titles flatter the vanity of the members. The 'ranks' are conferred in the course of a 'lifting' ceremony, and they turn the little groups into a parody of the State—with a President, a fully fledged Minister, Secretary of State, Senators and Deputies, Generals, Government Commissioners, etc. Women are not left out of this generous distribution of titles and lofty functions. There are the 'flag-queens' (*'reines drapeaux'*), the 'silence queens' (*'reines silence'*) whose job it is to enforce complete silence during ceremonies, the 'empresses of Dahomean youth', the 'directing ladies' and even the *agaceuses* who incite people to drink. The *humfo* society itself always has some fine name like Gold Coast, God First, Polar Star, Who Guides, The Flower of Guinea Society, Remembrance Society, etc., which is written up proudly on the façade of the main *caye-mystère*.

Certain priests do without a society. They content themselves with the appointment of a *père-soutien* or *mère-soutien* to whom they apply in times of financial emergency. The only compensation available to the bearer of such a title—and such a burden—is the honour of 'keeping up' the *humfo*.

THE ECONOMY OF A 'HUMFO'

Becoming a *hungan* or *mambo* can be an expensive business. First of all the ceremony called 'the taking of the *asson*' costs 400 dollars or more, according to the reputation of the initiator chosen. Then, to practise his profession a priest must first get together a *humfo* which means buying a piece of land, and putting up several groups of buildings including a peristyle. Finally, the accessories of worship, fairly cheap in themselves, represent a considerable expense in view of their number. In other words a Port-au-Prince *hungan* must invest at least a thousand dollars before he can practise. Given the standard of living of the average Voodooists this outlay, which is merely a minimum, represents a veritable fortune. To amass such a sum many young men temporarily take up other work which will enable them to save up. One of the best performers in Catherine Dunham's troupe was in fact a young *hungan* who had recently 'taken his *asson*' and was hoping, by touring the world, to save enough to set himself up. Some *hungan* begin by practising their art in small, single rooms, treating the sick and telling people's fortunes; in time they hope to get enough money to build a big *humfo*.

The responsibilities of a *hungan* are usually heavy: we have already seen how he is morally responsible for housing, feeding and clothing those *hunsi* who through no fault of their own have become destitute. In addition, at more or less regular intervals he has to hold a 'general service' for all his *loa*. Even if he is helped by the *humfo* society this ceremony is inevitably a burden. It can go on for two weeks during which time the *hungan* must support the *hunsi* and his guests. I heard of a feast in which four bullocks, fifteen goats and about a hundred chickens were sacrificed: the total cost was more than a thousand dollars.

These expenses are fortunately balanced by considerable profits. Many *hungan* and *mambo* appear comfortably off or even rich compared to their usual customers. The main income of a *hungan* comes from his fees for treating the sick. A 'course of treatment' can bring him in, on average, anything from fifty to a hundred dollars. Although *hungan* only deal with 'supernatural' illnesses, that is to say those caused by *loa* or sorcerers, they nevertheless constitute a serious source of competition for 'medical doctors'. Indeed they like to compare themselves with the town doctors and say their own methods of therapy are as rigorous as those of their colleagues. People in Lorgina's establishment maintained that she had an understanding with a doctor in Port-au-Prince by which he sent her his desperate cases—and, of course, *vice versa*. Thus this doctor sent her a patient whose internal organs were 'inside out' and a tubercular case for whom X-ray 'predicted death in a short time'. She was able to cure these two difficult cases because her 'knowledge' enabled her to diagnose the illnesses as outside the conventional scope of doctors, both being cases of witchcraft against which the bookish science of the Whites could do nothing. Madness, epilepsy and tuberculosis, which are essentially supernatural diseases, are the special province of certain *hungans*. Shortly before his death the *hungan* Abraham had toyed with the idea of turning his house, which adjoined the *humfo*, into a clinic for the insane. He flattered himself that he could cure lunatics by attacking the evil spirits which were tormenting them. This would be easy for him, people said, because he was in constant touch with all sorts of *petro loa*. The *loa* who help *hungan* to carry out such treatment also make sure the patients pay whatever they have promised. If an invalid gets well and then refuses to pay the *hungan*, the matter is placed in the hands of the *loa* who will not only put the person's health back where it started, but—if he continues to turn a deaf ear—will kill him into the bargain. Good *loa* assist the *hungan* who serves them, provided he treats his clientèle honestly. If he exploits people, they abandon him and withhold from him the 'knowledge' he needs.

It is important not to confuse *hungan* and *mambo* with the 'herb-doctors' who treat people with infusions and 'baths' made of medicinal herbs, and who, apart from well-tried recipes, only know a few spells for special occasions.

Treatment of the sick provides the largest and surest source of revenue for a priest, but he also earns money foretelling the future. And then each ceremony brings in, for the priests who organize it, the sort of gain which is difficult to evaluate since even if no fees are collected, there are still various kinds of profit made on the 'eatables', the purchase of animals to be sacrificed and on all the different accessories which priests like to enumerate when they discuss a project with a client. In fact the whole *humfo* staff live for several days on offerings which have not been consumed or destroyed during a fête.

In addition, every initiation to the grade of *kanzo* earns a considerable sum for the *hungan* who conducts it, particularly if his *humfo* enjoys a great prestige.

Finally *hungan* earn a lot of money by selling 'magic powders' and other talismans, much in demand, for ensuring success in business or love affairs, or as protection against evil spells. They also make 'guards' which shelter children from the evil eye, and attacks by werewolves. Joseph Antoine, *hungan* and husband of Lorgina, did a big trade in 'powders'. He got letters which he gave me to read. They were from foreigners, particularly white Americans, and they described ailments to him and asked for an adequate remedy, in return for cash down. Joe, who was illiterate, got friends to reply to each client. He enclosed a few pinches of one of his precious powders and charged as much as fifty dollars.

No doubt this analysis of a priest's income is incomplete; but it gives some idea of the profession's very solid advantages, and explains why it attracts so many ambitious people who have no means of improving their situation other than the exploitation of religion.

Dependence on an undependable clientèle makes *hungan* touchy and irritable. Competition being bitter, even the best are quick to criticize their colleagues and spread embarrassing stories about them. My friends never failed to insinuate that such and such a *hungan* 'worked with both hands' or made of 'bad *loa*'. Whenever a client admitted he had been treated previously by another *hungan*, a very timely *loa* was called in to tell him the people who treated him before were not only ignorant and incompetent, but also had borne him a grudge and fostered his illness instead of curing it. One of the commonest ways for *hungan* to slander each other was to accuse a colleague of casting spells to destroy the good effects of his rivals' treatments. There are even some *hungan* wicked enough to sow *wanga* (charms) round the *humfo* of a colleague who, unless he does something about it, will soon see all his cures brought to nothing. This at least is sometimes how the failure of an expensive treatment is explained away. A *hungan* knows by certain signs when his reputation is on the wane: the sick no longer come to be cured by him, his *hunsi* are undisciplined or desert him and finally, the last straw, initiates take back the 'head pots' (*pots-tête*) with which they entrusted him. The fame of a *hungan* is a fragile thing: it is at the mercy of rumour and gossip. Hence that thirst for advertisement, that boasting and skin-deep vanity which are to be found in even the most honest and sincere *hungan* and *mambo*.

There are men entitled *pères-savane* (bush-priests), but they are no part of the Voodoo hierarchy. On many occasions, none the less, their services are indispensable. They are, as we shall see, people who have succeeded in memorizing a great many prayers and songs in French and Latin, and who fulfil the rôle of *curé* whenever Catholic liturgy is incorporated into Voodoo ritual. To a certain extent they are representatives of the Catholic Church in the heart of paganism.

III. THE SANCTUARIES

To understand the way ceremonies are conducted and religious ideas given material shape, we must first form an exact idea of the sanctuaries, where members of fraternities gather to worship, and where the faithful come separately to consult the *hungan* or *mambo*.

There is hardly any difference between the 'houses of the *mystères*' and ordinary houses. A *humfo* is not a temple in the ordinary sense of the word, but a religious centre comparable in appearance to the old compound which formerly included the households of an extended family. The number, disposition and decoration of the houses which make up a Voodoo sanctuary depend in the first place on the private resources of the priest and priestess concerned, and to a lesser extent on their imagination, taste or the taste attributed to the spirits. There are poor *humfo* reduced to a little hut, others which look like a small village. At Port-au-Prince, where ground and construction is expensive, the space available to the gods is unavoidably cramped: often the *humfo* consists of no more than a covered area and a main building which shelters the *loa* and also the family of the *hungan* or *mambo*. On the other hand sometimes these town sanctuaries show a gimcrack luxury which is seldom seen in the country.

The only feature of a *humfo* which makes it recognizable from the outside is the 'peristyle', a sort of shed, mainly covered over, where dances and ceremonies are held free from the vagaries of the weather.

The roof, either thatched or more often made of corrugated iron, is held up by brilliantly painted posts: one of them, in the middle, is called *poteau-mitan* (the centre post) and forms the pivot for ritual dances. During ceremonies it is the object of various attentions which attest its mainly sacred significance. In ritual its rôle is to act as 'the passage for spirits', that is to say as the ladder by which spirits come down into the peristyle when they are invoked. On one occasion Lorgina, angered by a *hunsi* who showed herself lacking in respect towards this post, cried out, 'Don't you realize there's a spirit inside it?' The *poteau-mitan* is nearly always decorated with brightly-coloured spiral bands or with scattered bright spots on a uniform background. The general effect is entirely decorative and as far as I kno v has no symbolic meaning. The base of the post is usually embed, ed in a conical or cylindrical cement pediment which is used during services as a table for putting things down on.

Apart from the feasts, nothing except the drums har.ging from hooks on the ceiling, or faded paper wreaths, would suggest that such a place is the scene of the most spectacular manifestations of Voodoo. The sick are sometimes housed there for treatment; also, sometimes, visitors from far away, or out-of-work *hunsi* dependent on the head of the society. There too the master of the *humfo* is pleased to receive friends and it is there that the members of the household hang about, iron clothes or shell peas. Nevertheless *mambo* and *hungan* keep their peristyles very clean and tidy. They never forget that for the faithful this building is so important in the cult that it has become the symbol of the *humfo* and that the word 'peristyle' has become synonymous with 'sanctuary'. Some priests in Port-au-Prince, in search of modernity, have lit up their peristyles with luminous tubes, red and blue—the national colours of Haiti—and their dance floors are surrounded by rows of seats in tiers. This sort of innovation makes the sanctuaries look like theatres or *palais de danse*. In *humfo* where respect for tradition is still the first consideration, and where space allows, there is a special arched recess, specially reserved for the Petro *loa* and sometimes even a second recess for the Congo *loa*.

Usually the grand peristyle is adjacent to the building in which are situated the 'chambers of the gods'. The room containing the patron spirits of the *humfo* opens directly on to one of its sides. The façade of the *humfo*, which forms the back of the peristyle, is decorated with paintings of Haiti's national coat-of-arms, the emblems of the principal *loa* and other ornamental motifs. You may also see there, written out, the complete name of that particular '*humfo* society'. Near the door portraits of the President of the Republic and influential senators or deputies are pinned up. Such pictures prove the loyalty of the head of the temple who, threatened by regulations, tries to put himself under the temporal protection of the *'grands nègres'*.

The sanctuary proper which is sometimes referred to as the *caye-mystères*, sometimes as the *bagi, badji* or *sobadji*, is a room

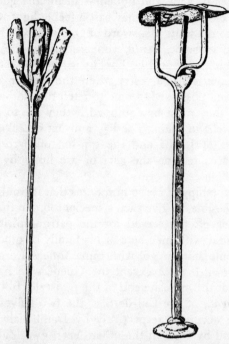

FIG. 2. Two supports for ritual objects. That on the right, of Dahomean origin, would carry a crock or pot containing a spirit (Musée de l'homme, no. 50.66.3); that on the left would serve as a candelabra, planted in front of an altar (Musée de l'homme, no. 50.29.5).

backed by one or more stonework altars (*pè*) in the base of which are one or more arched niches. On the table of certain altars there are sinks prepared for the needs of aquatic spirits. When these spirits are the object of special veneration the water basins are built separately and big enough for a person to bathe in. In some *humfo* the altars are arranged in tiers which makes it easier to arrange things as well as to increase the number of holy objects displayed.

A *bagi* is a veritable junk shop: jars and jugs belonging to the spirits and the dead, platters sacred to twins, carrying-pots belonging to the *hunsi*, 'thunder stones' or stones swimming in oil belonging to the *loa*, playing cards, rattles, holy emblems beside bottles of wine and liqueur—all for the gods. Amid the jumble one or more lamps may cast a feeble light. Colour prints are pinned to the walls, the sword of Ogu is driven into the earth and near it, in some *humfo*, you see *assein*, the curious iron supports which may still be bought in the market of Abomey. The *loa*'s room is also a vestry where the mediums—the people who have been possessed—come to fetch the clothes and objects with which they must be equipped if they are to represent the god who dwells in them. The bag and hat of Zaka hang beside the crutches of Legba and the top-hat of Baron; clusters of *hunsi* necklaces festoon the *govi* or are hung by wires across the room.

The *loa* worshipped are so numerous that it would be difficult, indeed impossible, to give each a special room in the *humfo*; such a privilege is often reserved for the patron spirit, but he too shares his altar with members of his family or other *loa* who by virtue of some affinity 'go' with him. *Mambo* Lorgina had only one *bagi* for all her *loa* except the Guédé who had a house to themselves at the opposite end of the peristyle. In the house of a leading *hungan*, of the Cul-de-Sac, the two halves of the same house were occupied respectively by Damballah-wèdo on the one side, and by Ogu on the other. Yet Agwé, Zaka and Simbi each had their own dwelling. The room devoted to Ezili-Freda-Dahomey was fitted up as a boudoir.

In many *humfo* there is a special part, the *djèvo*, in which the future *kanzo* are confined during their initiation. A separate house is sometimes kept for the sick. The master of the *humfo* and his family often live under the same roof as the 'mysteries', but in separate rooms. In the towns a *mambo* with a certain amount of prestige will have a salon inside the *humfo*, where she can entertain visitors. Such rooms are furnished and decorated like any interior of the Haiti petite bourgeoisie.

Sacred objects are also to be found on the outskirts of the sanctuary: the *pince* (iron bar) of Criminel sticking up out of a brazier, a pool which may vary in size for Damballah, a large black cross often crowned with a bowler hat and clad in a frock-coat, which represents Baron-Samedi, or an imitation concrete tomb on which are placed offerings for the Guédé. Every *humfo* is encircled by 'sacred trees' (*arbres-reposoirs*) which may be recognized by the stone-work edging all round them, by the straw sacks (*macoute*) and by the strips of material and even skulls of animals hung up in their branches. Even when there is no barrier round the sacred precincts, the entrance is none the less called the 'portal'. Guarded by the god Legba, this spot is invested with a religious significance which is expressed in details of ritual.

This brief sketch of a *humfo* incorporates the commonest characteristics of all sanctuaries and leaves out the many differ-ences to be found among them. But the picture would be in-complete without mention of the cocks, hens, pigeons, and guinea-fowl which run about outside and which perch on the sacred trees. They are all waiting for the day of sacrifice, as are the goats whose bleating may be heard from a nearby enclosure. In many *humfo* the difference between sanctuary and farm is hard to discern since the *hungan* combines the functions of both farmer and priest.

III

The Supernatural World

I. GODS AND SPIRITS IN
HAITIAN VOODOO

To construct a Voodoo theology out of the infinitely varied, often
contradictory and fragmentary notions of the supernatural world
held by Voodoo adepts, is no easy task. The confusion which
exists in this field is made worse by the absence of any attempt to
reconcile the traditional African attitudes to gods and spirits
with the teaching of the Catholic Church—a teaching which is
nevertheless 'accepted' without reserve. God, Jesus Christ, the
Virgin and the Saints are more or less relegated to the background of religious life while spirits, great and small, invade
every ceremony and monopolize the attention of the faithful.
Some of these are old gods of Africa who have kept their prestige,
others have rather colourless personalities and merely deserve to
be called spirits and demons. These supernatural beings, the
worship of whom is the essential purpose of Voodoo, are called
loa, 'mysteries', and in the north of Haiti 'saints' or 'angels'. No
one has ever listed all of them because, although it is easy to
catalogue the 'great *loa* of African Guinea', it would be an endless task to do the same for all the minor local spirits. In fact new
loa are always being created by popular faith and fantasy, while
others are forgotten for want of devotees.

The *loa* are not the only supernatural powers which men must
take into account. There are also the Twins, who are extremely
powerful, and the Dead who insist upon sacrifices and offerings
and exert direct influence on the fate of the living.

Adepts of Voodoo are not at all put out by the incompatibility
of a complicated polytheism with belief in one supreme and all-
powerful god. When asked about His power and the power of the
Saints, they repeat what they have heard in church except, unlike Catholics and Protestants, they refuse to see the *loa* as

82

'wicked angels', damned for their revolt against God. 'The *loa*,' a Catholic Voodooist once explained to me, 'are spirits, something like winds. They are like a man who, having received a good education in the town and learnt a trade there thanks to his father, then rebels against him. Even if this ungrateful son is finally driven out of the home, he still possesses much knowledge. Thus it is with the *loa*. God taught them what He taught the angels, but they revolted. Now when they enter into people, they 'possess' them just as the Holy Ghost enters into the *curé* when he sings Mass.'

To those who argue that the *loa* are merely vulgar 'satans', Voodooists reply they could not be that, since the 'Great Master' created them to be of use to mankind. Is there not daily proof of their benevolence and compassion? Certainly there are spirits who are willing to assist villains and who are feared for their violence and cruelty, but these should be called *diab* (devils). Decent people have nothing to do with them and if they fall under their power they try to appease them before sinking to crime. No more than man does God approve the activities of the bad *loa*, the 'bought *loa*', whom sorcerers use for their shady machinations.

The word 'God' is always on the lips of the Haitians but it would be unwise to conclude that they feared Him or even gave Him much thought. '*Le Bon Dieu*' is a *Deus otiosus*, if He is anything. He conjures up no precise image and He is too far away for there to be much point in addressing Him. 'He's a nice easy-going *papa* who wouldn't dream of getting angry or frightening people. With Him it will be easy to come to some arrangement when you have to give an account of your life. There's no point therefore in serving Him too seriously.' (Mgr Robert.)

In Voodoo the idea of God seems to get mixed up with the idea of a vague and impersonal power, superior to that of the *loa*. It would seem to be something like what we understand, in present-day usage, by the word 'fate' or 'nature'. Common illnesses, too usual to be the work of bad spirits or sorcerers, and which we would call 'natural', in Haiti are called 'illnesses of God'. Meteorological phenomena and cataclysms which occur without seeming to be the work of *loa*, are also attributed to the

'Good God'. Whenever a man of the people talks of some plan
for the future, no matter how simple, he adds prudently '*Si Dieu
vlé*' (God willing), less to entrust the matter to God's will, than
to exorcize bad luck.

Too often the words 'God is good', ending the account of
some misfortune, have seemed the proof of the Haitian peasant's
eternal optimism, when in fact they merely expressed his
fatalism under the heel of a crushing destiny.

The word *loa* is usually translated as 'god' but 'spirit' or
better, literally, 'genius', gives a more precise indication of the
nature of these supernatural beings. Here we will keep the title
'god' for those ancient African divinities who, although fallen
from their first glory, have still kept enough prestige and rank to
ensure them a privileged place among the countless multitude of
loa. Lesser 'mysteries' we shall call 'spirits'. The word 'god'
usually evokes feelings which will not suit certain evil spirits or
still less the merely snooping and comic ones whose sole function
is to cheer up ceremonies. Between such minor spirits, with their
often picturesque names—Ti-pété, Ti-wawé, Cinq-jours-mal-
heureux—and the grand *loa* of 'African Guinea', there is such a
huge gulf that one is tempted to talk in terms of an aristocracy and
a proletariat of gods. To the former would belong the *loa* of
African origin venerated in all sanctuaries, and to the second the
greater part of the 'Creole' gods, called 'Creole' because aboriginal and of recent 'birth'. Among these there are a great many
ancestors and also many *hungan* and *mambo*, promoted to the
rank of *loa* after their death. This, as we have already seen, was
what happened to the celebrated Don Pedro who not only became
a *loa* but also split, as did the African gods, into several different
divinities.

The Voodoo pantheon is always enriching itself with new
'mysteries'. Some are revealed and imposed upon members of a
cult-group when a devotee is suddenly possessed by an unknown god, who introduces himself, states his name and demands
worship. Others owe their existence to a dream. A man visited
by a spirit in a dream, hastens to make it the object of a cult. If
he is an influential and well-known *hungan* this will not be
difficult. Sometimes a woman introduces the spirits of her

maiden home, her *habitation*, into her husband's family. One of my informants in Marbial, Janvier, who had been a cane-cutter in Cuba, brought with him from that island an invisible protector who in spite of his very Creole name, Ti-nom (Little Man) was nevertheless a Spanish *loa* belonging, for some unknown reason, to the Nago group of *loa*. Every year Janvier offered him fruit, eggs, oil and *kola** for unlike most Nago, the *loa* Ti-nom did not like rum. Janvier used to fall into a trance and begin singing and talking in Spanish. Sometimes his spirit deigned to speak in Creole. Many *loa* of equally humble beginnings have been promoted from family level to regional level—and even to national level.

An object picked up and kept as a talisman on account of its quaintness or the circumstances in which it was found, sometimes becomes an independent *loa*, quite separate from its original material manifestation.

One story, in which I knew the principal protagonist, gives an excellent example of the vicissitudes of an ordinary fetish. A fisherman from the neighbourhood of Port-au-Prince had taken out of his lobster-pot a stone with two shells sticking to it. Intrigued by his find he kept it at home without, however, giving it much attention. Soon he realized luck had deserted him. Nothing succeeded. Tired of tribulation he consulted a *hungan* who told him his stone was a new *loa* called Capitaine Déba, and advised him to keep it in oil near a *lampe perpétuelle*† and to make sacrifices to it. Our friend did this and found that his luck returned. When he died, his daughter, a shop-keeper of Port-au-Prince, inherited the *loa* and its cult. She attributed to the spirit the likeness and tastes of an officer of the United States Navy, such as they had been described to her by her lover who was a quartermaster on a warship. Every year on a set day she 'fed' Captain Déba. Possessed by him, she wore a peaked cap, sat on a stool, pretended to row and sang sea-shanties in English.

Theologians of Voodoo, rather in the manner of naturalists, have divided *loa* into groups and sub-groups[1]; unfortunately they have not managed to standardize their system which varies

---

* An aerated, non-alcoholic drink.
† Cup or bowl full of oil on which floats a lighted wick.

from one region, from one sanctuary and even from one priest to another. I do not think there exist any two catalogues of *loa* exactly the same. It is true that most of the 'great *loa*' have secure and unquestioned positions, but others and, not necessarily the least important, are placed sometimes in one category and sometimes in another. Where Voodoo is in a state of decay classification tends to be simplified. At Plaisance and Mirebalais, for instance, Voodoo adepts scarcely gave the matter a thought, even in the course of worship.

At the root of this classification of spirits stand two main categories of *loa*: *rada* and *petro*. It will be remembered that this word *rada* is the Haitian version of the town of Arada, in Dahomey. We have also seen how Don Pedro was an historic personality who lived in the middle of the eighteenth century; and how his name, for obscure reasons, took the place of some African tribe whose rites he had exalted to a place of honour. Each *loa* category has its own special drum rhythms, musical instruments, dances and salutations. No one can mistake a *rada* ceremony for a *petro* ceremony. The difference between the two rituals is expressed in many small characteristics and this makes confusion unlikely. For instance in a *rada* ceremony the ritual acclamation, at the end of a song or at the climax of a sacrifice, is '*Abobo*'—a cry which is accompanied by noise made by striking the mouth with the hand. The acclamation of *petro* ritual is '*bilobilo*', and *petro loa* are welcomed by cracks of a whip (*fouette-cache*) which are 'fashioned' in the air. *Petro* are reputed to like gunpowder. Small charges are therefore detonated in their honour to please them. Ritual sprinklings of *kimanga*, a liquid based on rum and various spices, are carried out with very precise movements and are exclusively reserved for *petro loa*.

The term *petro* is not used in the north and north west of Haiti where these spirits go under the name *Lemba*. This—the name of a Congo tribe—covers divinities and a complex of rites which roughly correspond to those covered by the word *petro*.

Within or on the fringe of these two main groups, we find many sub-groups of spirits who bear the names of African tribes or nations—Ibo, Nago, Bambara, Anmine, Hausa, Mondongue etc.—or African regions—Congo, Wangol (Angola), Siniga

(Senegal), Caplau etc. Hence such groups are called *nanchon* (nations). This term is equally applied to all groups of a religious nature, even to a category of spirits as far-flung as that of the *rada* or *petro*, or to a group of devotees whose 'heads were washed' by the same *hungan* (e.g., *nanchon* Dodo, *nanchon* Pierre etc.) Among the minor groups of *loa* there are some important enough to stand as autonomous categories with their own ritual. This is notably the case with the *nanchon* Ibo and Congo. Voodooists make the word *fanmi* (family) synonymous with *nanchon*. Strictly speaking the *fanmi* is a subdivision of the *nanchon* and this term should only be applied to sub-groups of closely related *loa*. However, the meaning of the word *fanmi* in current usage lacks precision. People speak of the *fanmi rada* or the *fanmi petro*. On the other hand it is not said of the numerous Guédé that they form a *nanchon*, but a *fanmi*, since the members of this group 'work' with different rites—*rada*, *petro* and even Congo rites.

What is the good of losing ourselves in the intricacies of this subtle classification? Let us take one sample: the Congo group. It is divided into *Congo-du-bord-de-la-mer* (Congo of the sea-shore) and *Congo-savane* (Savannah Congo). The former, water-side *loa* are said to have fairer skins, to be more intelligent and better mannered than those of the interior. The latter, however, are superior in knowledge of medicinal herbs. The *Congo-savane*, also called *zandor*, are sub-divided into families of which the main members are: the *Kanga*, *Caplau*, *Bumba*, *Mondongue* and *Kita*. There are two sorts of *Kita*: the true *Kita* and the *Kita-secs* (dry-Kita). There are also *Congo-francs*, *Congo-mazone* and *Congo-mussai* whose connections with the other *Congo* it is difficult to establish in view of contradictory assertions by various informants.[2]

Racial origin of *loa* has played a fundamental part in their classification. Most if not all Dahomean or Nigerian *loa* have been placed automatically in the *rada* group. The word 'Dahomey' is often linked with the word *rada* or used as a synonym for it. When a devotee talks of the *loa* of '*Afrique Guinin*' (African Guinea) he means primarily the *rada loa*. The *petro* group also includes many African deities (Agirualinsu, Simbi etc.) but these usually come from some other part of Africa than ancient Dahomey. The majority of the aboriginal spirits, whose Creole names suggest a more or less recent accession to the Voodoo pantheon, are also regarded as *petro*. These are not always deified ancestors, as might be expected; among them are a few African spirits who have been re-christened with, literally, a Christian name, and whose physical appearance has been modified by living in Haiti. Ti-Jean-petro, for instance, is a tree-dwelling spirit who is represented as a dwarf with one foot (the Joazinho of Brazilian folklore). This *loa* with a French name is derived from spirits of the African bush, spirits who are described as having only one leg.

Today the racial and geographical nature of the classification has been forgotten. The difference between *rada* and *petro* is marked more by the characteristics attributed to the *loa* of the two groups. To some extent they bear the same relation to each other as did in Ancient Greece the Olympian and the chtonian gods. Just as beside the Olympian Zeus there was a chtonian Zeus, so Voodoo has a Legba *rada* and a Legba *petro*. These two spirits, although as like each other as brothers, yet have different natures. Legba *petro* is apparently 'stiffer', more violent than his *rada* alter ego. These are nuances rather than radical differences, but they do give a distinctive colouring to the way in which the faithful represent the *loa* of these two groups. The word *petro* inescapably conjures up visions of implacable force, of roughness and even ferocity—qualities which are not *a priori* associations of the word *rada*. Epithets such as 'unyielding' 'bitter' and even 'salty' are applied to the *petro* while the *rada* are 'gentle'. The *petro loa* are, moreover, specialists in magic. All charms come under their control. The frontier which separates white magic from black magic is so vague that spirits who devote themselves to these arts are inevitably slightly suspect. Everything therefore which has to do with *petro* is shadowed with doubt and inspires fear.

A *hungan* who shows too marked a preference for the *petro loa* will soon become suspect and accused of 'serving with two hands', in other words of practising sorcery. My friend Tullius, ill and believing himself bewitched, kept crying out: 'No, no,

I'm not for the *petro*. All my root-*loa* are in African Guinea.'
(That is to say in the *rada*.) By this affirmation he wished to let
it be understood that having done wrong to no man, he had been
afflicted unjustly. No more delicate praise can be paid to a
hungan or a *mambo* than to say his or her *humfo* is set beneath the
sign of the *rada* and that the *loa-Guinin-Dahomey* are evidently
served there.

Petro loa owe their popularity to their skill as supernatural
magicians. They can cure as well as cast spells. When a cure
undertaken with *rada* help fails to give the expected results, a
hungan may advise his patient to have recourse to the *petro* and
to submit to rites which, however frightening, can bring about
an immediate cure. Whoever swears himself to the *petro* feels
protected against witchcraft. He also may expect to become
prosperous because the spirits of that 'family' are 'givers of
money'. But the price they claim for their favours is high: any
transaction with the *petro loa* entails risk. They are pitiless
creditors who never give an inch on the terms of a contract and,
too often, prove insatiable. Woe to him who cannot pay his debts
to a *petro* or fails to keep his promise.

No one calls the *rada* 'eaters of men'. They kill to punish but
never, like certain *petro*, out of sheer spite. Nor will they co-
operate with sorcerers. The *petro* family, on the other hand, includes, along with helpful and decent *loa*, many *diab* (devils),
'eaters of men'. The *petro loa* who bear a *rada* name followed by
a surname (Damballah-flangbo, Ogu-yansan, Ezili-mapyang
etc.) all have a bad reputation. As to the spirits called 'red-eyes'
(*Jé-rouge*) they are without exception evil and cannibal. Remember that redness of the eye is a distinctive sign of werewolves.
In short even were it untrue to say that all *petro loa* are by
definition evil, it could nevertheless be truly said that the most
dreaded *loa* are placed automatically in this category.

The confidence inspired by the *rada loa* and the official nature
of their cult, ensures precedence for them at grand ceremonies,
particularly at those in which 'ranks' in a cult-group are conferred.

Certain *loa* occupy a marginal position between *rada* and
petro and are placed either in one group or the other, according

to circumstances or personal views. The Simbi, of their very nature, belong to the *rada*, but they are served in the *petro* rite since, neglected by their devotees and gnawed by hunger, they tend to turn cruel.

The chief *loa* seem to have been freely multiplied by addition to their names of African or Creole surnames. Thus we have Legba-atibon, Legba-si, Legba-sé, Legba-zinchan, Legba-signangon, Legba-katarulo etc. Azaka-vodu, Azaka-médé, Azaka-si etc. Ezili-wèdo, Ezili-doba etc. In most cases this proliferation of deities has little importance from the religious point of view. They are merely lists of names in liturgical invocation. Probably the surnames themselves are fragments of African liturgical texts, syllables or words which, having become unintelligible, were torn out of context and used as epithets of divinities. The nature of the link between gods of the same name, but different surname, only becomes a problem when the two related gods tend to assume different personalities. For instance Ogu-badagri and Ogu-ferraille can reveal themselves during a ceremony at the same moment—a fact which would suggest that they were not merely 'forms' or 'aspects' of the same god, but different *loa* belonging to the same family. All that can be said on this subject is that sometimes the same god is conceived in different forms as with our Virgins whose surname and attributes often vary from church to church, and at other times gods of the same name have finally taken a separate identity and have been set up as independent deities each with their own worship. The *hungan* Abraham, with whom I discussed this question, said that *loa* with the same family name 'worked' in different directions: in other words that the degree of their supernatural power was not the same. Thus Nago-iki, Nago-oyo, Nago-bolisha, although without distinct separate personality each had their special 'points'. It is an ingenious interpretation but it represents merely the opinion of one subtle *hungan* who was inclined to resolve all difficulties by the theory of 'points' (mystical power).

Most *hungan* and *mambo* scarcely trouble themselves at all with theological speculation. When the surname and the epithet is Creole, and therefore understood by the faithful, that is enough to give the *loa* an obvious identity which the possessed try to express in movements and attitudes. For instance Guédé-z-araignée imitates the movements of a spider. Guédé-ti-wawa weeps like a child. In the same way possessions induced by Legba-atibon are not the same as those provoked by Legba-avarada. The former walks leaning on a crutch, the latter, weighed down with illness and old age, lies stretched on a mat and touches the faithful with closed fists. Ezili-taureau (Ezili-bull) bellows, which may seem strange from a *loa* who bears the name of the most gracious and most *coquette* of all the Haitian divinities. Certain *loa*, of outstanding importance, are associated with others of a lesser rank who 'escort' or 'work' with them. During a possession induced by a great *loa*, one or two of his followers can sometimes reveal themselves at the same time.

The diversity of taste and temperament to be found among members of the same *fanmi* or *nanchon*, is liable to result in troublesome mix-ups and mistakes in ritual. Madame Mennesson-Rigaud told me the following story which she witnessed herself: a family carrying out a ceremony for Ogu, wanted to sacrifice a goat to him; but the *loa*, due to possess a woman who was ready to receive him, did not materialize in spite of the efforts of the officiating priests. The woman was made to dance with the goat in her arms, in the hope that the *loa* would then enter into her. She was then addressed as though she had become the receptacle of the *loa*. It was a waste of time: she merely kept repeating, 'I'm tired—leave me alone.' Finally she shut herself up in the *humfo*. It was then suggested that a mistake had been made: Ogu-badagri was expected but perhaps Ogu-balindjo had been the one who wanted to come down, and he, not finding the kind of welcome hoped for, had taken offence and left immediately. Hadn't he been offered rum—a drink he was known to abhor? Finally they managed to bring down Ogu-badagri and the sacrifices could take place.

The *loa*, or at any rate the most important ones, live in Guinea. This name has for long been without real geographical meaning, for Guinea is a sort of Valhalla, not situated anywhere. The *loa* leave it when they are called to the earth. They are also assigned an entirely mythical city: Ville-au-Camps. Unfortunately the information available about this headquarters of the 'mysteries', near St-Louis-du-Nord, is rather meagre. The *loa* also frequent mountains, rocks, caves, rivers and seas. Many live on river-beds or in the depths of the sea. *Hungan* and *mambo* with great 'knowledge' go and visit them in their watery homes and stay with them for long periods. They come back with new powers and sometimes bring back shells—the concrete proof of their exploit.

The *loa* are also present in the sacred trees which grow round the *humfo* and the country dwellings. Each *loa* has his favourite variety of tree: the *medicinier-béni* (*Tatropha cureas*) is sacred to Legba, the palm-tree to Ayizan and the Twins (*marassa*), the avocado to Zaka, the mango to Ogu and the bougainvillea to Damballah etc. A tree which is a 'resting-place' may be recognized by the candles burning at the foot of it and the offerings left in its roots or hung in its branches. Wherever *loa* may be they hasten to the call of their servants as soon as they hear prayers or the sound of sacred instruments.

Each *loa* has one or two days a week which are sacred to him (e.g., Tuesday and Thursday for Ezili, Thursday for Damballah-wèdo etc.). He also has his own colour (white for Agwé and Damballah, red for Ogu, black for Guédé: white and red for Loco, and rose on white for the Congo).

Of the African myths describing the origin of the gods, their adventures and cosmic rôle, only a few faint traces remain. With difficulty some muddled, and sometimes contradictory, data may be gathered from the mouths of priests about the relationships of the gods, and a few more or less scandalous stories gleaned about their love affairs. Mythology in the narrow sense of the word has been dragged down to the level of village gossip; it is less concerned with the private life of the spirits than with their dealings with the faithful. Voodoo is a practical and utilitarian religion which cares more for earthly than for heavenly goings-on. Its Golden Legend is made up of stories which are of a tedious uniformity. The greater part of them have as theme either the intervention of the *loa* on behalf of their devotees or the punishment they inflict on those who neglect them. This folklore is developed in the sanctuaries, the normal stages of day-to-day

incidents provoked by the *loa*. *Hungan* and *mambo* profit in-
directly from the prestige which such anecdotes confer on the
spirits they serve. They are glad to recount them whenever
opportunity offers, and thus, equipping them with a guarantee of
authenticity, feed them into the stream of local conversation. The
stories end by being known and believed by the whole population
of a region.

Mystical possession exerts a profound influence on this kind
of mythology. Spirits, in the flesh-and-blood form of the persons
in whom they become incarnate, mix with the common crowd;
the public, which frequents the sanctuaries, can therefore see and
hear them. Moreover the possessed, by assuming the qualities of
the *loa* and imitating their general appearance, their walk and
their voice, help to fix a concrete idea of them in popular tradition. Possession to a certain extent takes the place of the statuary
and holy images which are almost certainly lacking in Voodoo. It
is said in Haiti that to learn about the *loa* you must watch the
possessed.

Certain incidents, which obtain during trances, are such as to
engrave themselves on the minds of spectators. At the source of
legends concerning the origin of *loa* there is often an authentic
'event' which took place in the presence of dependable witnesses.
In other words Voodoo mythology is constantly being enriched
by the narration of divine interventions in human affairs, interventions which are in fact 'played' by actors, suddenly inspired.

The liturgies intoned during ceremonies to greet *loa* shed
considerable light on the attributes, adventures and character of
the spirits. Often, when a member of the Voodoo priesthood is
asked about the personality of some *loa* he will answer with a
song or the recitation of a single couplet to prove the reliability
of his information. The songs contain not only epithets and
'sacred names' ('*noms vaillants*') of *loa* but also short judgments
on their behaviour. A satirical vein is not looked upon as irre-
verent.

Such are the sources of Voodoo mythology available to us. To
them should be added the information which *hungan* and
mambo are always ready to give about the tastes and character of
the *loa* they serve.

The way in which gods are worshipped is the responsibility of autonomous religious groups, therefore divergence and contradictions are inevitably numerous. Still less is coherence to be expected in Voodoo beliefs when the heterogeneity of their origins is taken into account. The main gods, common to all sanctuaries, are almost the only ones whose identities stand out with any precision. Variety would be even more pronounced were it not for the fact that certain well known *hungan* educate other priests, whose learning therefore springs from a common source. As long as the general form of ceremonies is not altered, innovations of detail, particularly if they are picturesque, are well received by the public. The idea of tradition, pure or impure, is foreign to Voodoo; it is more a question of a line, often arbitrary, drawn by Haitian intellectuals separating practices which they regard as authentic from those which seem to them to be adulterated. Have I not heard a writer cry out in the middle of a Voodoo ceremony 'But these rites are contrary to Voodoo philosophy!' A *hungan* will pride himself on his 'knowledge' and acquire fame by becoming the successor of such and such a priest; but the idea of a pure Voodoo doctrine is entirely alien to him.

Doubtless much could be gained by making a detailed study of the ritual peculiar to each *loa*. In this way fairly precise outlines of the power and character of the main divinities could be obtained. It would, however, be a long-winded work and the results would not always repay the effort expended. Too often the meaning of ritual has become obscured with the passing of the years. The true nature of Voodoo divinities will become more intelligible if, laying aside these minute details, we are content to recall the main outlines of some of the most representative of the *loa*.

There is little difference between the supernatural society of the *loa* and the Haitian peasantry which imagined it. The spirits distinguish themselves from men solely by the extent of their 'knowledge', or, which is the same thing, their powers. They are all country people who share the tastes, habits and passions of their servants. Like them they are fond of good living, wily, lascivious, sensitive, jealous and subject to violent attacks of rage which are quickly over; they love or they detest each other, they frequent or avoid each other, as do their worshippers. When they show themselves, by means of possession, their behaviour is not always what might be expected of supernatural beings; indeed, they are capable of speaking coarsely, swearing, drinking too much, quarrelling with other *loa*, lying or ganging up against each other in a childish manner. We shall be referring to their weaknesses and fads in the following pages which, be it remembered, constitute a mere sketch of Voodoo mythology.

II. THE POWER OF THE *LOA*

'The *loa* love us, protect us and guard us. They tell us what is happening to our relations who live far away, they suggest to us remedies which bring us relief when we are sick . . . If we are hungry the *loa* appear to us in a dream and say: "Take courage: you will earn money" and the promised money comes.' This profession of faith from the mouth of a Marbial peasant sums up, fairly well, what the devotees of Voodoo expect from the *loa*. To complete it he should have added: 'The *loa* warn us of the machinations of those who wish us harm.'

A regular client of Lorgina's *humfo* once told me all the benefits she had received from the *loa*: she would have been drowned in the sea if Ogu-balindjo had not helped her in time; customs officers would have thrown her into prison if another god had not turned up at 'the moment when the bayonets were crossed in front of her', and finally Guédé himself took the trouble to avenge her on a rival by killing the rival's brother. Such statements, uttered with the emphasis of faith, give some idea of the many forms which the benevolence of the *loa* can take.

A *loa*'s solicitude sometimes goes as far as to procure employment for his *protégé*: a trader or official may be suddenly accosted in the middle of a fête by a *loa*, who demands through the mouth of someone possessed, a post—for the possessed person. The god answers for the zeal and honesty of the candidate and even promises to help him in his work. Believers hesitate to reject such recommendations. This is not all: there are banker *loa*—even usurers—who lend money to devotees in need; though Haitians do not like to have a 'mystery' as creditor. The *loa* are known to be pitiless in money-matters: you take a heavy risk if you fail to meet your *loa* creditors. A taste for speculation will sometimes drive a *loa* to invest money with a merchant from whom good dividends may be expected. For reasons which have just been set down, believers will only accept such sums under duress. Few are they who simply pay no attention. Money, however, which a *loa* gives through the hand of someone possessed, is holy money and brings luck. I heard of a woman who received ten centimes from the hand of a woman possessed by Zaka. She bought a few leaves of tobacco which she re-sold at a profit, and so was able to buy other articles. In this way she earned 35 gourdes. She gave half of them to Zaka but he advised her to use the whole sum to buy goats and then breed from them.

The fees received by a priest for a treatment which he has accomplished with the assistance of a *loa* belong by rights to the latter. They must be employed on the god's behalf although any interest which accrues may be used for personal ends. I was told of a *hungan* who invested the money of Ogu in a haulage business, that of Zaka in the sale of peas and finally that of the Guédé in loans at interest. When a *hungan* negotiates a deal he is possessed by the god who goes into the terms. An animal offered as a sacrifice and spared at the god's request remains the property of that god. The priest scrupulously shares the progeny of the animal which he has taken into his keeping.

The good offices of the *loa* are never obtained for nothing. Whoever is benefited contracts definite 'obligations', the most important being the sacrifices and offerings which have to be carried out at more or less regular intervals; but the 'obligation' can also be a 'promise' (a vow made at a special ceremony), or participation in certain rites or finally compliance with orders which the *loa* transmit by dreams or through the medium of possession.

To resist the will of a supernatural being is an act of 'rebellion'. So, in every Haitian family the rage of parents knows no limits when they suspect their children of 'rebelling', that is to say of disobeying purposely in order to defy.

A *loa*'s book-keeping is as meticulous as that of a wayside stallholder. He enters presents received against favours granted, and never forgets promises made. In the course of an invocation of *loa* I heard most revealing remarks in this respect: spirits had been called by Lorgina who wished to consult them about the illness of Tullius, her adopted son. When Ogu-balindjo heard the young man's name he cried out: 'Who? Tullius? I don't know him. Who are you talking about?' When told the invocation concerned his protégé, who was ill and praying for help, the *loa* said disdainfully: 'That man never gave me anything. Although he earned a lot of money he never gave me a present. He doesn't seem to me to care much for the *loa*.' Then it was Ezili-batala's turn to complain: 'I am root-*loa* of Tullius,' she said, 'he hasn't bought me or even offered me the least little spree. *Sak vid pa kâpé* (an empty sack doesn't stand up).' With this proverb she let it be understood that the *loa*, offended by the negligence of Tullius, had abandoned him and refused to come down 'into his head' to protect him from harmful spells.

Loa become the proprietors of whatever they receive in the way of presents: they alone have the right to make use of them. The following story, about a woman I had met with Lorgina, shows how much they resent their effects being disposed of without their permission. The woman in question had a prosperous business and had offered an evening dress decorated with lace to her patron spirit, Mambo Grande Maîtresse Batala. Before leaving for Cuba where she had important matters to attend to, she was imprudent enough to give this dress to a relation, promising Batala, whose permission she had not asked, to bring her a prettier one. The goddess thought this behaviour cavalier and decided her servant must be punished. The woman, who was a bit of a smuggler, was soon 'sold' to the police and thrown into prison. Her goods were confiscated and she sank into the most dismal poverty. She had not, however, given up hope of reconciliation with Mambo Batala and a return to happier times.

In Haiti the sensitivity of the *loa* is as raw as that of the men. The least little thing offends them. Particularly in matters of ritual are they touchy: if they do not get their allotted number of rounds danced for them, or if they are given food they do not like, or if people pretend to be possessed by them when they are not—that's that: they are angry and ready to behave cruelly. They even object to imprudent words spoken by their devotees in an access of rage. My friend Tullius, having fallen ill, began wondering if he had not been punished by *loa* for having said, in a moment of anger, that he wanted to have done with them and be converted to Protestantism. Lorgina thought it wise to beg forgiveness from the *loa* on his behalf. 'His crime is not great,' she explained to them, 'he only said he would become an adventist. Have mercy on him, take pity! *Loa*, you know well that he doesn't like Protestants.'

Not quite all the *loa* are so sensitive. There are some who put up with teasing and take in good part the not very respectful remarks of their servants, provided these are not intended to hurt. Other *loa*, on the contrary, will not tolerate the least impertinence. Thus a woman who was talking to Ezili (that is to say with another woman possessed by Ezili) and who was having difficulty in understanding her, asked her to speak more clearly and added, 'If you were a man you would speak better.' The goddess replied in French: 'Madam, it seems to me that you are lacking in respect: kindly repeat what you said.' The woman did so and received a bang on the head.

When a person becomes the butt of an angry *loa* the spirit is said to have 'seized' him. Supernatural punishments take many different forms. They vary to a certain extent with the sex, character and type of the offended spirit. These considerations shape justice more than the nature or seriousness of the offence. Some *loa* are more severe than others; what for one is a venial sin, for another is an unforgivable wrong. The great *loa* of African Guinea are regarded as more moderate and just than those which consort with the evil genius of the *petro*. The root-*loa* who are, as it were, members of the families which worship them, are indulgent and show great patience. If a man 'picks up' his root-*loa* and is unable to offer them the feasts to which they are accustomed, they are prepared to wait, sometimes many years, until his financial situation is improved. When they think their servant is in a position to acquit himself of his obligations, then they warn him in a dream, or by the mouth of someone possessed, that the moment has come to 'feed' them. If, even

then, he persists in refusing them satisfaction or invents false
excuses, their demands become more and more pressing until
the moment they decide to strike. According to the code which
governs relations between men and spirits, the *loa*, having been
informed that a fête is to be offered them at a certain date, must
trust their servant and allow him time for preparation. It is only
if he breaks his word knowingly that they have the right to treat
him severely. Supernatural punishments take many different
forms: usually *loa* afflict the culprit with an illness the gravity of
which is not always in proportion to the offence. The spirits are
more passionate than just. True, some of the more moderate *loa*
treat considerately those with whom they have found fault.
They start by sending a man some slight ailment and this only
becomes serious, or even mortal, if he still does not take their
warnings to heart.

Madness is nearly always a supernatural punishment. A
hungan even told me that 'only those who resisted the will of
the "mysteries" go mad'. At Marbial someone pointed out to me
a certain Florilius who, because he had neglected the cult of his
ancestral spirits, had become subject to attacks of madness
during which he tore his clothes, scratched his flesh and accused
himself of having cast spells on his relations, in particular on his
sister.

Loa often visit the sins of parents upon their children. The
death of a little girl who was being treated at the sanctuary of
mambo Lorgina, was attributed to Linglessu. In this way the
god was thought to have punished the girl's mother for some
sacrilegious theft.

Persistent bad luck is nearly always put down to some trans-
gression which has roused the wrath of a *loa*. That is why a
person whose business falls into a bad way is advised to consult a
hungan. The priest with his technique of divination is the only
person in a position to reveal the name of the offended *loa* and
the nature of the offence. On the other hand the hostility of the
'invisible ones' does not necessarily take an active form. A *loa* can
also punish his erring servant simply by showing indifference to
his lot and withdrawing his protection. A man deserted by *loa*
is at the mercy of 'poisons'. Before actually suffering in his flesh

he is weighed down by a feeling of helplessness in face of the various dangers by which he is beset.

The touchy and arbitrary nature attributed to *loa* ensures their punishments will be accepted without too much recrimination. Victims usually appeal not to their justice but to their mercy. It can, however, happen that in times of great misfortune, people do complain of their severity and vindictive spirit. I heard Lorgina accuse the *rada loa* of having abused their power in making one of her clients ill.

III. THE VOODOO PANTHEON

A complete list of all *loa* known and 'served' is, as I have already remarked, out of the question and would anyhow only interest those who are looking for old African divinities in Haiti. My purpose being solely to give a general idea of Voodoo mythology, I will limit myself to describing the principal gods worshipped throughout the sanctuaries of the republic, and who, by general consent, are regarded as the 'great *loa*'. These are, moreover, the gods whose personalities and qualities it is easiest to define. In this inevitably brief presentation of the Voodoo pantheon, it seems to me useless to keep to the various classifications which have been adopted by the faithful, or to enumerate the *loa* in the order in which they are summoned during ceremonies. I prefer to divide them, roughly, into nature gods and functional spirits. This approach, which has no other advantage than classical precedent, is inevitably arbitrary in a syncretic religion in which, in the last resort, one is repeatedly faced with the overlapping of the powers of the various divinities and a chaotic distribution of their attributes and scope. The Voodoo pantheon includes no less than six storm gods. It would be easy to draw up long lists of *loa* fulfilling the same functions or personifying the same natural forces. Moreover the term 'nature gods' must not be taken too literally or be allowed to give the impression that *loa* grouped under this heading are regarded as the exclusive masters of the one aspect of nature or phenomenon with which they are associated. Anthropomorphism is so highly developed in Voodoo that the *character* of the god is far more important than his often tenuous link with nature.

In any catalogue of Voodoo divinities first place must certainly be given to Legba—the god who 'removes the barrier' and who is saluted first of all *loa*.

Atibô-Legba, l'uvri bayè pu mwê, agoé!
Papa-Legba, l'uvri bayè pu mwê
Pu mwê pasé
Lo m'a tunê, m'salié loa-yo
Vodu Legba, l'uvri bayè pu mwê
Pu mwê sa râtré
Lo m'a tunê m'a rémèsyé loa-yo, Abobo.

> Atibon-Legba, remove the barrier for me, agoé!
> Papa Legba remove the barrier
> So I may pass through
> When I come back I will salute the *loa*
> Voodoo Legba, remove the barrier for me
> So that I may come back;
> When I come back, I will thank the *loa*, Abobo.

In Dahomey, Legba acts as interpreter to the gods. Without him they could not communicate with each other nor could human beings communicate with them. A vestige of this function is preserved in Voodoo. No *loa* dares show itself without Legba's permission. Whoever has offended him finds himself unable to address his *loa* and deprived of their protection. Care must therefore be taken not to offend him. He holds the 'key of the spiritual world' and for this reason he has been identified with St Peter.

Master of the mystic 'barrier' which divides men from spirits, Legba is also the guardian of the gates and of the fences which surround houses and, by extension, he is the protector of the home. In this latter rôle he is invoked under the name of Maît'-bitasyon (Master of the habitation). He is also the god of roads and paths. As 'Master of Crossroads' he is the god of every parting of the way—a favourite haunt of evil spirits and propitious to magic devices; and it is at crossroads that he receives the homage of sorcerers and presides over their incantations and spells. Many magic formulae begin with the words: 'By thy power, Master of Crossroads.'

Legba is represented as a feeble old man in rags. Pipe in mouth and haversack slung over his shoulder, he moves painfully, leaning on a crutch. (On most sanctuary walls there is a crutch, the symbol of Legba.) His pitiful appearance has earned him the nickname of Legba-pied-cassé (Legba of the broken foot), but conceals the terrific strength which becomes apparent in the violence of possessions induced by him. Anyone who receives Legba into his body is thrown on the ground and there struggles frantically or lies motionless, as though struck by lightning.

Of the *loa* who preside over the elements, the one whose province is most clearly defined is Agwé or Agwé-taroyo. The sea with all its flora and fauna, as well as the ships which plough its surface and those who live off its produce, all come under his jurisdiction. He is invoked under the names 'Shell of the Sea', 'Eel', and 'Tadpole of the Pond'. His emblems are miniature boats, oars painted blue or green, shells and madrepores, and sometimes small metal fishes. He is represented in the frescoes which decorate *humfo*, by steam-boats with smoking funnels or by warships bristling with guns. This Haitian Neptune also has a trident as part of his insignia but it may well be asked whether this emblem, borrowed from classical antiquity, may not have been adopted quite recently through the influence of the intellectuals whose interest in folklore is positively militant. Like many aquatic spirits the symbolic colour of Agwé-taroyo is white. That is why he is depicted as a mulatto with a fair skin and eyes as green as the sea. He wears the uniform of a naval officer, white gloves and a helmet. He is also every inch a 'president' of Haiti. Agwé likes gunfire. Many people think the salvoes which salute the arrival of warships in the harbour of Port-au-Prince are fired in his honour. Any reference to signalling can only come as a pleasure to this god:

U signalé Agwé-taroyo	You make signals Agwé-taroyo
M'apé signalé Agwé-taroyo	I will make signals Agwé-taroyo,
M'apé signalé kuala zâgi	I will make signals kuala zangui
Signalé duâ uelo	I will make signals duan wèlo

M'ap signalé	I will make signals President
Presidâ Agwé	Agwé.

He is the protector of seafaring men and it is to him they pray in times of danger.

Mèt Agwé kòté u yé?	Maitre Agwé where are you?
U pa wè mwê nâ résif?	Don't you see I'm on the reef?
Agwé taroyo, kòté u yé?	Master Agwé, where are you?
U pa wè mwè su lâ mè	Don't you see, I'm on the reef?
M'gê z'avirô nâ mê mwê	Don't you see I'm on the sea?
M'pa sa tunê déyé	I've a rudder in my hand
M'duvâ déja	I can't go back
M'pa sa tunê déyé	I'm already going forwards
Mèt Agwé-woyo kòté u yé nu	I can't turn back.
U pa wè mwê nâ résif.	Agwé-taroyo, where are you?
	Don't you see I'm on the reef?

'Services' for Agwé take place beside the sea (sometimes on the edge of a lake or river), and his effigy—a miniature boat—is then carried in procession. The dishes of which Agwé is most fond and his favourite drinks (champagne among others) are put on a 'bark' —a float with tiers, painted blue and decorated with marine motifs. Any 'society' wishing to offer a 'great service' to Agwé, hires a boat and sets sail in the direction of the Trois Islets, a well-known reef about three miles from the coast. The boat is festooned with streamers, the flags of the *humfo* crack in the wind, drums beat and the *hunsi* dance as best they may on the bridge or in the hold. When the boat reaches the Islets, one or two white sheep are thrown into the sea. After making a few libations in the water, the faithful make off as quickly as possible, without looking back in case they offend the god when he surfaces to get the offering. The moment the sacrifice is eaten many possessions are induced by Agwé and other sea spirits, such as Ogu-balindjo and Agau, who are part of Agwé's 'escort'. The crew have to take care that people possessed by sea deities do not give in to their sudden marine nature and jump overboard. One of Lorgina's acolytes told me in front of her mistress, without being contradicted, that during her youth, in the course of such voyages she often jumped into the sea 'with Agwé in her head', and swam to the shore without knowing she had done so. On several occasions Lorgina is said to have dived to the bottom of the sea and come back each time with seven fish and seven shells.

Offerings to Agwé are also sometimes loaded on to a little boat which the current is allowed to take to the Trois Islets. If it floats to the shore it means Agwé has refused the sacrifice. He must then be appeased by some other 'service'.

The Siren and the Whale are two marine divinities so closely linked that they are always worshipped together and celebrated in the same songs. Some say the Whale is the mother of the Siren, others that he is her husband; and there are still others who say that these two names are used for one and the same deity. The Siren is represented according to European tradition, but when she turns up in a sanctuary the person possessed by her appears simply in the rôle of a young coquette most careful of her looks. During one Voodoo ceremony the Siren and the Whale were incarnated in two young women who, affecting elegance, began talking French. A Guédé, exasperated by their snobbery, took them off so cruelly that the two poor goddesses fled in shame.

In most Voodoo sanctuaries a sink is installed in a corner of the *péji* or in the altar. This is sacred to one of the most popular of the Voodoo gods, Damballah-wèdo, the serpent god, who is invoked in the following song:

Kulèv, kulèv-o	Serpent, serpent-o
Dâbala-wèdo, papa	Damballah-wèdo papa
U kulèv-o	You are a serpent
Kulèv, kulèv-o	Serpent, serpent-o
M'apé rélé kulèv-o	I will call the serpent
Kulèv pa sa palé,	The serpent does not speak
Dâbala papa u sé kulèv	Damballah papa you are a serpent.
Si nu wè kulèv	If you see a snake
U wè Aida-wèdo	You see Aida-wèdo
Si u wè kulèv	If you see a snake
U we Dâbala	You see Damballah
Aida-wedo sé ñu kulèv-o	Aida-wèdo is a snake.

He and his wife, Aida-wèdo, are often shown on *humfo* murals as two snakes who look as if they were diving into the sink, and by a rainbow. This last being merely a celestial serpent, it is identified with both Damballah and Aida-wèdo. Damballah is also lightning.

People possessed by Damballah-wèdo dart out their tongues, crawl on the ground with sinuous movements and climb trees or the supports of the peristyle. Hanging on to the beams of the roof they let themselves fall head first like a boa. Damballah does not speak but he whistles, and that is why people possessed by him utter a staccato 'tettetetete'. They try to make themselves understood by modulating this sound into a phrase of whatever language obtains. The *loa* Ogu, or failing him the priest of the sanctuary, interprets this god's messages.

'All trees are resting places for Damballah because snakes climb all trees.' Being both snake and aquatic deity, he haunts rivers, springs and marshes. White is his colour and white must be the food and drink which is offered him. Silver is a 'white metal' and so he is in charge of it. Hence it is he who grants riches and allows treasure to be discovered. Between treasure and rainbow there is a mysterious correspondence. Whoever can grasp the diadem of Aida-wèdo will be assured of wealth.

The Simbi, too, are guardians of fountains and marshes. They cannot do without the freshness of water. I remember a woman who, being 'ridden' by Simbi-yan-kita, kept repeating 'water water' until, opening and shutting her mouth like a fish out of its element, she threw herself head first into a pool. Simbi feasts are held near springs and several of their songs mention such places specifically as being their favourite haunts:

Simbi nâ sus o	Simbi in the spring o
Rélé loa yo, o papa Simbi etc.	Call this loa, O papa Simbi
Grâd Simbi wa yo	The great Simbi wa yo
Grâd Simbi sôti lâ sus	The great Simbi is coming out of the spring
Li tut muyé	He is all wet.

Children who go to fetch water at springs run the risk—particularly if they are fair skinned—of being abducted by Simbi who takes them under water to be his servants. After a few years he sends them back to the earth and, as reward for their trouble, bestows upon them the gift of clairvoyance.

Sogbo, brother of Three-horned-Bosu, is the god of lightning. It is he who hurls down polished stones which are piously collected and used as symbols of the *loa*. Badé, his inseparable

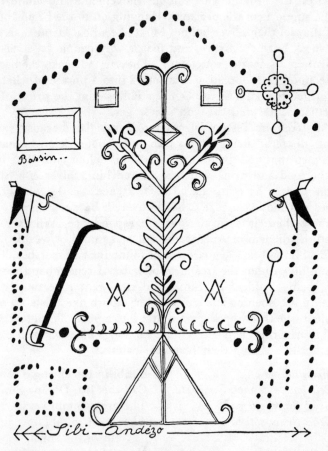

FIG. 3. The symbol (*vèvè*) of the *loa* Simbi-yandezo, drawn by the *hungan* Abraham

companion, is the *loa* of the winds. He shares his functions with
Agau who, as the following song shows, is also a storm spirit:

Agau vâté vâté	Agau blows, blows
Li vâte Nodé	The north-west blows
Li vâté Sirwa	The south-west blows
Agau sé pa mun isit	Agau is not a person who lives here
Agau grôdé, grôdé	Agau roars, roars
Li grôdé, l'oraj	The storm roars
Agau vâté, vâté	Agau blows, blows
Li vâté, vâté	He blows, blows
Agau sòti lâ Guinê	Agau has left for Guinea
Li vâté, li grôdé	He blows, he roars.

When there are earth tremors it is Agau who is angry. Trances
induced by this god are extremely violent. He can cause by his
brutality the death of the people he 'rides'. Those who are strong
enough to harbour him in their bodies try to imitate the grum-
blings of thunder and the moaning of tempest, puffing with all
their strength and spluttering like seals. All the time they keep
repeating 'It is I who am the gunner of God; when I roar the
earth trembles . . .'

Ogu-badagri (of the great family of Nago *loa*) delights in the
din of battle and probably that is why a Voodoo hymn makes him
the master of lightning and storm, a rôle which by Nago tradition
devolves upon Shango, a *loa* of the same group.

Badagri-o, jénéral sâglâ	Badagri oh! ferocious general sanglant
Badagri ki kêbé l'oraj	Badagri who keeps the storm
U sé jénéral sâglâ	You are a ferocious general
Zèklè fè kataoo	The lightning goes kataoo
Sé u ki vòyé zèklè	It is you who throw it
Tònè, grôdé	The thunder grumbles
Sé u ki vòyé tònè	It is you who send the thunder
Badagri-o, jénéral sâglâ	Badagri oh! Ferocious general.

The spirit of vegetation is Loco. He is mainly associated with
trees of which he is in fact the personification. It is he who gives
healing power and ritualistic properties to leaves. Hence Loco

is the god of healing and patron of the herb-doctors who always invoke him before undertaking a treatment. He is also the guardian of sanctuaries, and that is why he is compared to an invisible *hungan* with authority over all the sanctuaries of Haiti. In one of the hymns addressed to him, there are these words: 'The key of the *humfo* is in thy hand.'

The worship of Loco overlaps with the worship of trees—in particular of the *Ceiba*, the Antillean silk-cotton tree and the tallest species in Haiti. Offerings for a sacred tree are placed in straw bags which are then hung in its branches.

The attributes and character of nature-spirits are not always revealed by their outward appearance, that is to say, by the get-up or bearing of the people they possess. Hence, although Loco is a personification of plants, he is only recognizable by the pipe smoked by his servant and the stick which he carries in his hand.

Crops and agricultural labour are the province of the *loa* Zaka—the 'minister of agriculture' of the world of spirits. First and foremost a peasant god, he is to be found wherever there is country. People treat him with familiarity, calling him 'cousin'. When Zaka possesses devotees, they appear in peasant dress: straw hat, dark blue denim shirt, matchet slung and short clay pipe in the mouth. Their manner of speech is rustic. By nature the Zaka take after the peasants of the region: they are suspicious, out for profit, fond of quibbling, and they fear and hate town-folk. In the following song Zaka is shown up:

Kuzê Zaka u ârajé	Cousin Zaka, you're in a rage
O diab-o	O devil-o
Kuzê u ârajé	You're in a rage
O diab-la	O devil la
U vlé kité fâm dé byê	You want to leave a good woman
Pu alé viv-ak vagabô	And go and live with vagabonds
Kuzê Zaka u ârajé	Cousin Zaka, you're in a rage
O diab-la	O devil.

Local political life has inspired other songs in honour of Zaka. These revolve round election-talk, the chamber of deputies and the Senate; in them the divine right-honourable 'Minister' witnesses electoral triumph. The favourite offerings of the Zaka are the dishes which peasants feast on—boiled maize, bread soaked in oil, *afibas*,* *rapadous*,† all washed down with a glass of *trempé*.‡

Gods associated with a profession or a function are not tied down to strictly prescribed tasks. They are invoked whenever an affair seems to come within their province, but no one hesitates to seek their support for undertakings which logically should not concern them. Voodooists seem to attach more importance to the character and personal tastes of a *loa* than to the specific functions attributed to him by mythology. Let us take Ogu as an example. In Dahomey, Gu is the blacksmith of the mythical world. Ironwork having lost most of its importance in Haiti, he has become mainly a warrior *loa*, symbolized in *humfo* by a sabre stuck in the earth in front of the altar. A few vestiges of his former rôle are nevertheless still preserved in the homage paid to him and in the accepted idea of his taste and character. 'Ogu's forge' is the name given to the iron rod (*pince*) stuck in a brazier which represents him. Because of Ogu's passion for fire, people possessed by him wash their hands in flaming rum. The most worked-up among them think nothing of handling red-hot spirits. For this reason they are never offered a libation, as are other *loa*. The water-pot is tilted three times in their direction without a drop being spilt. Ogu-balindjo, on the other hand, lives right in water and must be constantly sprinkled with water whenever he leaves his element.

Ogu is seen in the guise of an old veteran of the 'time of bayonets' (the civil wars). People possessed by him dress themselves in red dolman and French képi, the better to incarnate him. Those who do not possess such cast-off military clothing wrap a red cloth round their heads and tie other scarves of the same colour round their arms. The 'Ogu' always wave a sabre or matchet. They affect the brusque and lively language of a soldier and season it with coarse oaths. They chew a cigar and demand rum in the time-honoured phrase: '*Grèn mwê frèt*' (my

---

* Slices of the small intestine with fatty membrane, fried in the bottom of a pan.

† Unrefined sugar.

‡ *Clairin* (white rum) with an infusion of aromatic herbs.

testicles are cold). The members of this celestial family are great drinkers. Alcohol has no effect on them. We learn as much from a song in their honour, which goes thus: '*Mèt Ogu bwé, li bwé jâmè su*' (Master Ogu drinks, he drinks but he is never drunk).

Ogu would not be a genuine soldier if he had not got a weakness for 'a bit of skirt'. He ruins himself for pretty women:

Ogu travay o li pa mâjé	Ogu works, he doesn't eat
Li séré l'ajâ	He puts money on one side
Pu l'al dòmi kay bèl fâm	In order to sleep with a pretty girl
Yè o swa Féray dòmi sâ supé	Yesterday evening Ferraille went to bed without supper
Ogu travay-o	Ogu works o
Ogu pa mâjé	Ogu doesn't eat
Li achété bèl rob bay fâmli	He has bought a dress to give to his girl
Yè o swa Ogu dòmi sâ supé	Yesterday evening Ogu went to bed without supper.

Ezili-Freda-Dahomey is usually compared to Aphrodite. The two goddesses resemble each other in so far as a pretty Antillean half-caste is capable of evoking an Homeric divinity. Like Aphrodite, Ezili belongs to the family of sea spirits but she has become so completely divorced from her origins as to be now almost exclusively a personification of feminine grace and beauty. She has all the characteristics of a pretty mulatto: she is coquettish, sensual, pleasure-loving and extravagant.

In every sanctuary there is a room, or corner of a room, dedicated to Ezili. Her red and blue dresses and jewels are kept there, and on a table, always ready to hand, lie basin, towel, soap, tooth-brush, comb, lipstick and orange-stick. As soon as Ezili possesses a devotee, man or woman, the chosen person is led into this room to be dressed and titivated. While this is going on the choir sings the following song:

A ñù bèl fâm	Ah, the lovely woman
Sé Ezili! (bis)	Who is Ezili!
Ezili m'a' fè nu kado	Oh, I will give you a present
Avâ u alé, Abobo	Before you go away, Abobo.

At last, in the full glory of her seductiveness, with hair un-
bound to make her look like a long-haired half-caste, Ezili makes
her entrance to the peristyle. She walks slowly, swinging her
hips, throwing saucy, ogling looks at the men or pausing for a
kiss or a caress. She likes to get presents and she gives them. Her

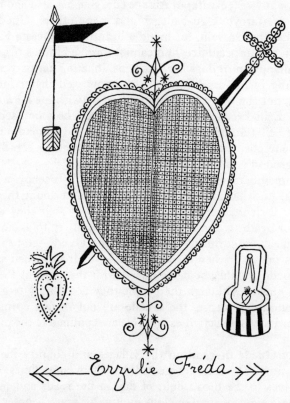

FIG. 4. The symbol (*vèvè*) of the goddess Ezili-Freda-Dahomey,
drawn by the *hungan* Abraham

caprices are sometimes expensive: has she not been known to
moisten the dried mud floor of the peristyle with scent? She is so
fond of men that she instinctively mistrusts women as rivals; she
treats them haughtily and greets them by hooking her little

finger in theirs. Ezili is 'a woman of etiquette' and when she pretends to speak French, she purposely talks in a high-pitched voice. When she goes back to her boudoir men flock to escort her.

The life of Ezili is a succession of scandals: she has been the 'kept woman' of Damballah-wèdo and this automatically makes her the *matelote* (co-wife) of Aida-wèdo. She has also had liaisons with Agwé-taroyo, Ogu-badagri, and many others. Guédé-nibo courts her, but in vain, for being a beautiful half-caste Ezili has a certain colour prejudice, and cannot forgive him his black skin. The unhappy spirit dogs her footsteps, inhaling her perfume and mumbling in his nasal voice: 'You know well that I love that woman, but she won't have anything to do with me because I'm black.' Ezili-Freda-Dahomey should not be confused with Grande Ezili (Grandmother Ezili) who is an old woman, crippled with rheumatism and only able to walk by dragging herself along on the ground with a stick.

The members of the main Guédé family occupy a rather marginal position in relation to other *loa*. No doubt the ambiguity of their status proceeds from the fact that they are the spirits of death. Other spirits fear them and try to avoid them, which means that during ceremonies the Guédé tend to arrive towards the end, when the other *loa* have already been saluted. The Guédé should not be confused with the souls of the dead, or with ghosts. Although the people they possess try to give the impression of a corpse, the Guédé are not in fact corpses but *loa*—spirits, whose activities and rôle are confined to the province of death.

Many Guédé descend on the villages and countryside at All Saints time. Devotees possessed by them sometimes exhibit themselves in the broad light of day in the roads and markets. The mere sight of the Guédé is enough to scare people, simply because of their funereal associations. The fear and ill-defined anxiety they provoke is, however, tempered by their cynicism, joviality and broad jokes. Their entry on to the peristyle stage is always greeted with joy by all present. Everyone knows they can be relied on to introduce a vein of frank gaiety into the most serious ceremonies. Their habit of talking through their noses is by itself comic enough—even though meant to be like the speech of Death. Their language, too, is full of the unexpected. They distort the commonest word or substitute others with filthy connotations. *Lunettes* (spectacles), in their mouth becomes *doubles languettes* (double clitoris), rum becomes *pissetigue* and *clairin* becomes *claleko*. They have a fine repertoire of obscene songs which they sing with a stupid look, raising one finger and prolonging certain notes indefinitely. Their favourite dance is the well-known *banda*—remarkable for its violent agitation of the hips and lascivious positions. In some *humfo* a huge wooden phallus is kept on the altar in case such an attribute is suddenly required by the god. The possessed masquerade with it, dance obscene dances or abandon themselves to prurient fooling. Tradition requires them to carry out certain tricks and they usually manage to do so. One is to drink a beverage made from twenty-one different kinds of pimento, or to wash their faces with it. Only a person possessed by a Guédé, seemingly, can touch this infernal liquid. The Guédés usually pour rum into their ears and they complete the joy of the crowd when they start pinching things out of spectators' hands or seizing the food they were about to put in their mouths. The Guédé are also bare-faced liars; their shamelessness earns them the title 'vagabonds'. They are also accused of being stingy, for they love burying their surplus food and coming back a few days later to eat it rotten.

The trappings of the Guédé are in keeping with the ambi-valence of their nature. From some angles they look terrifying, from others merely ridiculous. They wear top-hats, bowlers or straw hats decorated with crêpe, ancient frock-coats or thread-bare dress-coats. This is done in order to look like undertakers' mutes or officials in grand mourning. Sometimes they round matters off with a collar and starched cuffs. The Guédé also wear mourning dresses and black or mauve veils. Spectacles, pre-ferably black, are an indispensable part of their equipment. If people possessed by the Guédé are not provided with spectacles, they steal them from the noses of spectators. Such is their passion for spectacles that some Guédé wear several pairs. They also dress up as corpses. Cotton is put in their mouths and nostrils and a strip of linen round their chins. Thus apparelled they dance, emitting, from time to time, a death rattle.

Baron-Samedi, Baron-la-Croix, Baron-Cimetière, Guédé-nibo and Madame Brigitte are the best known representatives of this terrible family. The 'barons' form a sort of triad, so closely united it is difficult to say whether they are three distinct spirits or three aspects of the same spirit. Baron's emblem is a black cross surmounting a false tomb covered with a top-hat and a black coat. The tools of a grave digger (spade, pick and hoe) are all properties of Baron-Samedi and that is why he also goes under the names Three-spades, Three-picks and Three-hoes. The receptacles in which the offerings for this god are placed are black, decorated with skulls and crossbones.

Baron's wife, Big Brigitte, Maman or Mademoiselle Brigitte, also has authority over cemeteries, particularly those in which the first person buried was a woman. From her union with Baron she had issue: General Jean-Baptiste-Tracé (General Jean-Baptiste the Outliner) who 'outlines' the periphery of graves, General Fouillé (General Dig), who digs them, Ramasseur-de-Croix (Collector of Crosses), and finally at least another thirty Guédé whom we shall speak about later.

It was à propos Guédé-nibo that I came across one of the rare vestiges of African myth still extant in Haiti. Loco, walking near Miragoane, stumbled on a package. He picked it up, opened it and found in it a stone. This he took to his humfo where it turned into a child. Loco, greatly perturbed, consulted his neighbour, Ogu, who advised him to baptize the little boy. He called him Guédé-nibo. Ogu became his godfather and later adopted him in order to educate him. Nibo even wishes to pass himself off as the brother of Ogu-badagri, who despises him and will have nothing to do with him. If, during a ceremony, Ogu-badagri meets Nibo he chases him or makes him kneel and beg forgiveness. In point of fact the functions of Guédé-nibo do get mixed up with those of the chief of the Guédé family. He takes care of tombs and if magicians wish to use some dead person, for ritual oath-taking—then it is to him they must address their prayers.

I will add some impressions of other members of this interesting family. They are based on the behaviour of people when possessed by them. Guédé-brave, in spite of his name, has always appeared to me as a thieving impudent swashbuckler. He is celebrated in a song which is not without a certain lyrical power:

Mwê di brav-o	I say brave-o
Rélé brav-o, gasô témérè	Call him brave!—he's a bold fellow
But' bânân li, témerè	His banana end is bold
Mòso pul li témérè	His bit of chicken is bold
Gnu ku klérè li témérè	His bowl of clairin is bold
Mòso patat-li témérè	His bit of sweet potato is bold
M'apé rélé brav Gédé	I call Brave-Guédé
V'ni sové z-âfâ la-o	Come and save the children
Brav-o rélé brav	Brave-o he's called brave!
Gasô témérè	He's a bold fellow.

For me, Captain Zombi, or Captain Guédé, is always linked with memories of *hungan* Baskia who was possessed by him in the middle of a dance. With trousers rolled up above the knees, a fat cigar in his mouth, Captain Zombi came round offering his friends bumpers of rum. Guédé-double, so called because he is a *loa* who can endow people with second sight, incarnated himself in a beautiful *hunsi* of Abraham's *humfo*. Abraham was himself possessed at the time by Guédé-souffrant (Suffering Guédé). When this *loa* entered him Abraham put on a black dress, a bowler hat and held in his hand a crystal ball in which he read what the future held for his guests. It was in this same sanctuary I became acquainted with Guédé-z-araignée who used to oblige his 'horse' to imitate the movements of a spider. Guédé-ti-pe'té always entered an unfortunate girl, a victim of yaws, who had lost her nose. She wore a sou'wester for the occasion and danced in the gayest manner imaginable, kicking her legs as high as possible. Guédé-fatras always possessed the *hungan* Tullius who thereupon carried out his famous *danse de Fatras*. A song in honour of Fatras includes, in the form of question and answer, an encomium of Guédé's powers: 'If you need *wanga*, where do you go? To the house of Guédé. If you want advice where do you go? To the house of Guédé. If you need treatment where do you go? To the house of Guédé.'

Linto is a child spirit of the Guédé family. He induces puerile behaviour in those he 'rides'. They walk clumsily, with a certain stiffness, like a baby who scarcely knows how to use his limbs. They babble and weep for food. The company treats Linto like a little child and teases him good-humouredly. Guédé-fait-que-paraître (Guédé who just appeared), who appeared only once when I was present, behaves like an ordinary Guédé and has no distinguishing trait. He speaks through his nose, utters obscenities and sings dirty songs. One day when through the mediation of Lorgina I had offered a feast to the Guédé, the whole lot of them came rushing in a crowd and danced with joyous abandon till dawn. Among my guests the following were pointed out to me: Guédé-caca, Guédé-antre-toutes (Guédé among all), Pignatou-Guédé and Madame Kikit. Achille-piquant (The sharp Achilles) is a relation of the Guédé and takes after them in his nasal way of speaking and the curious habit of tipping rum into his ear.

Never having had an opportunity of observing people possessed by the other Guédé, I will content myself with listing them and remarking upon a few of their peculiarities. Guédé-vi bears the name given in Dahomey to the former inhabitants of the Abomey plateau, who regarded themselves as descendants of Gédé (*vi* means 'children'). Guédé-usu is well-known in Haiti, but still more so in Dahomey. Guédé-loraye (Guédé the storm) is a woman of small stature who reveals herself during storms. Guédé-ti-wawé is only known to me by a song in which he complains of the injustices he suffers and of the bad food served to him. Guédé-masaka is a female spirit who 'goes about with an umbilical cord and poisoned leaves in a bag'.

In this brief outline of a mythology room must be made for a number of *loa* of the *petro nanchon*, who, through their cruelty and their liking for evil have earned the title of 'devils'. In this category there are several Ezili. Ezili-jé-rouge, whose wicked nature I have already mentioned, is said to be the wife of Simbi-yandézo. The latter would seem to be more violent than his wife, so much so that whenever he is drunk she has to leave him. The other Ezili of the *petro* group are Ezili-mapyang, Ezili-coeur-noir (Ezili of the black heart), Ezili-bumba and

Ezili-kokobe (Ezili the shrivelled). In the following song Ezili-kanlikan is accused of eating 'two-footed goats', that is to say human flesh:

Ezili kâlikâ elu	Ezili kanlikan elu,
A la loa ki rèd (bis)	Ah, what a hard *loa* (bis)
Ezili u mâdé kochô	Ezili you ask for a pig
M'apé ba u li	I will give you one
Ezili mâdé kabrit dé pyé	Ezili, you ask for a goat with two feet
Kòté pul'prân pu ba-li	Where could I get it, to give it to you.

Marinette-bwa-chèch (Marinette of the dry arms), one of the most dreaded *loa* of the *petro* class, is particularly well-known to us thanks to the excellent monograph on her by Mme Odette Mennesson-Rigaud and M. Lorimer Denis.[3] She is a she-devil, the sworn servant of evil and agent for the underhand dealings of Kita who is, herself, an outstanding *loa* sorceress. The screech-owl is the emblem animal of Marinette—or it could be said Marinette *is* the screech-owl, since those who are possessed by her do 'beak to earth' (lower their heads), let their arms hang by their sides like wings and crook their fingers like claws. Marinette is particularly respected by werewolves who hold propitiatory 'services' for her whenever they need her help. She wanders through the woods and it is there, in secret places, that her servants come to leave their offerings. Being a stingy divinity, she goes there at night so that she need not share her food with any other *loa*.

Worship of Marinette-bwa-chèch has not spread all over Haiti. At the time of my stay there, it was growing in the southern departments. Ceremonies in her honour are celebrated in open country under a tent. A huge fire is lit and petrol and salt are thrown into it. The *hungan* induces possession among the company by striking people with a red cloth. From the mouth of those she possesses Marinette confesses her crimes and boasts of the number of people she has 'eaten'. *Hungan* and possessed alike finally throw themselves into the flames and stamp about till they have put them out. For sacrifice she gets chickens—which must be plucked alive—goats and black sows. These offerings have to be buried and no one may touch them. Marinette-bwa-chèch is the mistress of Petro-é-rouge, but also wife to Ti-Jean-pied-sec, known also as Ti-Jean-pied-fin, Prince Zandor, and Ti-Jean-Zandor; he is a little man dressed in red, who jumps about on one leg and perches at will on the tops of palm trees whence he keeps an eye on the roads and jumps on passers-by to kill them for food. To appreciate the violent and passionate nature of Jean Zandor I had only to study the expression and gestures of a woman possessed by him. With fixed and dilated eyes she walked slowly backwards, hands behind her back. When the drums were silent she sank to her knees beside the ditch, in which lay remains of a sacrifice, and began to fling her arms furiously from side to side as though she were prey to immeasurable grief. Then, crossing her arms on her breast, she bit them deeply. When small charges were detonated round her, she stretched her arms towards the smoke and plunging her head into the ditch, shook it with demented energy.

Bakulu-baka, who drags chains behind him, is such a terrible spirit that no one dares to invoke him. And he himself possesses no one. His habitat is the woods. Offerings are taken to him there.

The Mondong-mussai *loa* also form part of one of the many Congo groups; they are very well known, even outside Voodoo circles, on account of an unusual custom in their cult; live dogs are offered to them so that they may bite the ends of their ears. Since they are evil spirits it is dangerous not to give them enough. At Marbial a family was cruelly punished for taking lightly a request from these Mondong, a child died and during the funeral a Mondong *loa* 'came down' into one of the relations and said that if he had only been offered some dog to eat the child would still be alive.

This brief outline of Voodoo mythology would be incomplete if it did not include some mention of the Creole *loa*—products of the fanciful imagination of the people in Haiti. First we have Taureau-trois-graines (Bull with three testicles), 'great *loa*' of the Jacmel region. His appearances are terrible. People possessed by him are seized with destructive rage and create havoc all round unless appeased by the offer of a handful of grass. This they munch at once. During trance they bellow ceaselessly. The Taureau is greeted with the following songs:

M'tòro m'béglé (bis)	I'm a bull, I bellow
Nâ savân mwê	In my pastures
Sa m'wè la? Mwê sa	What do I see? I see that
Mwê béglé	I bellow
Tòro mwê tòro	Bull, I'm a bull
Sa ki mâdé pu mwê	Whoever asks for me
U a di o	You must tell him
Mwê mèm kriminèl	I'm a criminal
Tut fâmi mwê kiriminèl	My whole family are criminal
A ro â ro â ro	High up high up high up
Di yo mwê kriminèl	Tell them I'm a criminal.

The *loa-taureaux* are a family which includes Taureau-belecou and Ezili-taureau—both mooing and brutal spirits.

The world of *loa* also has its divisions of nationality. Melle Chalotte and Dinclinsin are French 'mysteries'. People possessed by them talk excellent French although in normal life they may not speak a word of it. Milo Rigaud,[4] who drew our attention to these seldom-seen *loa*, told us that Chalotte is 'particular', that she 'insists on the most refined form of ritualistic protocol'. When she speaks *langage* she expresses herself clumsily which at once gives away her non-African origin. As for Dinclinsin, he murders Creole like a typical foreigner. He may be recognized by his habit of putting any *tafia* offered to him straight into his pocket. And that is the last you see of it.

The Krabinay *loa*, of the *petro* family, behave in a truly devilish way. Possessions induced by them are so violent that *hunsi* advise spectators to keep their distance. They are dressed in red and execute impressive leaps. They are tough and take pleasure in cynicism. However, they assist *hungan* in their hardest work and undertake treatment of desperate cases. As devils they avoid mentioning the name of God and declare they have no connection with Him. They admit they were created by Him, but say it was a favour they never required of Him. They take care not to go near images of St Michael, the bane of demons.

IV. POSSESSION

RELATIONSHIPS BETWEEN SPIRITS AND MEN

Intercourse between the visible and the invisible world is easy and constant. The *loa* communicate with the faithful either by incarnating themselves in one of them, who then becomes his mouthpiece, or by appearing to them in dreams, or in human form. Also priests and priestesses have the power of calling gods down into jars whence the gods converse with those who wish to question them.

We shall deal first with the phenomenon of possession, or trance, which has a fundamental rôle in the framework of Voodoo.[5]

The explanation of mystic trance given by disciples of Voodoo is simple: a *loa* moves into the head of an individual having first driven out 'the good big angel' (*gros bon ange*)—one of the two souls that everyone carries in himself. This eviction of the soul is responsible for the tremblings and convulsions which characterize the opening stages of trance. Once the good angel has gone the person possessed experiences a feeling of total emptiness as though he were fainting. His head whirls, the calves of his legs tremble; he now becomes not only the vessel but also the instrument of the god. From now on it is the god's personality and not his own which is expressed in his bearing and words. The play of his features, his gestures and even the tone of his voice all reflect the temperament and character of the god who has descended upon him. The relationship between the *loa* and the man seized is compared to that which joins a rider to his horse. That is why a *loa* is spoken of as 'mounting' or 'saddling' his *chual* (horse). Possession being closely linked with dancing, it is also thought of in terms of a spirit 'dancing in the head of his horse'. It is also an invasion of the body by a supernatural spirit; hence the often-used expression: 'the *loa* is seizing his horse'.

The symptoms of the opening phase of trance are clearly psychopathological. They conform exactly, in their main features, to the stock clinical conception of hysteria. People possessed start by giving an impression of having lost control of their motor system. Shaken by spasmodic convulsions, they pitch forward, as though projected by a spring, turn frantically round and round, stiffen and stay still with body bent forward, sway, stagger, save themselves, again lose balance, only to fall finally in a state of semi-consciousness. Sometimes such attacks are sudden, sometimes they are heralded by preliminary signs: a vacant or anguished expression, mild tremblings, panting breath or drops of sweat on the brow; the face becomes tense or suffering.

In certain cases trance is preceded by a sleepy condition. The possessed cannot keep his eyes open and seems overcome with a vague languor. This does not last long: it suddenly gives place to a rough awakening accompanied by convulsive movements.

This preliminary phase can soon end. People who are used to possession pass quickly through the whole range of nervous symptoms. They quake, stagger, make a few mechanical movements, and then, suddenly—there they are: in full trance. Even as much preamble as this may be dispensed with when a ceremony is in full swing and demands instantaneous entries on the part of the gods.

The intensity of this crisis varies according to the character of the spirit who is seeking incarnation. The great and terrible *loa* rush into their fleshly envelope with the violence of a hurricane. Those of a gentler nature spare their mount. The nervous attack also varies with the ritualistic status of the possessed: the less experienced he is, the more he will throw himself about. As long as his head has not been washed,* that is to say as long as his *loa*

---

* The 'head-washing' (*laver-tête*) is a ceremony which varies in importance according to regions and sanctuaries. Its purpose is to baptize the *bosal loa*. Bread soaked in wine, *acassan*, maize, grilled peanuts and other eatables are made into a sort of paste which is wrapped in *mombin* leaves. It is then fixed to the head of the *loa*'s elect by means of a cloth. He must keep it there till the following day and must wait several days before washing his head. Herskovits was present at a head-washing in the Mirebalais region. The novice was shut up in a room for three days while his friends and relations sang hymns in a neighbouring room. A *hungan* in a state of trance washed the head of the elect with a concoction of aromatic herbs and wine. The *loa* then came down on to his 'horse'. The family offered him a sacrifice and the possessed novice drank the blood.

has not been formally installed in his head, he behaves wildly. His chaotic leaps and gestures are like the bucking of a wild horse, who feels the weight of a rider on his back. Is not initiation the breaking-in which prepares the faithful as mounts for the deities? The horse which at first rears becomes accustomed to its master and at last scarcely moves when ridden and guided by an invisible hand. Such metaphors are not out of place in a system which continually makes use of equestrian terminology.

The possessed are protected from the possible effects of their own frenzy by the crowd which surrounds them. They are prevented from struggling too furiously and if they fall, arms are ready to catch them. Even their modesty is shielded: a woman rolling on the ground, convulsed, is followed by other women, who see to the disorders of her dress. This sympathetic concern on the part of the crowd for the gambols of the possessed certainly provides an atmosphere of moral and physical security which is conducive to total abandon in the state of trance.

Sometimes—though not often, it is true—the person possessed seems unable to come out of his stupor. I remember one woman, seized by the *loa* Agassu, who remained a long time on her back with eyes closed, her arms flung out like a cross. She might have been thought to have fainted, had she not thrown her head from side to side and had her body not been subject to mild spasms, gradually reaching her shoulders which she shook rhythmically. With great difficulty she managed to kneel. She then opened her eyes: they were fixed and estranged. She kissed the earth and got up with the heavy movements of a person weighed down by pain. Like a sleepwalker she went and kissed the *poteau-mitan*. Tears rolled down her cheeks. Losing balance she fell to the ground, where she resumed her previous position. The *hungan*, rushing up to her, alternately cajoled and entreated her gently. She wiped her tears, got up and went and sat on a seat where she remained motionless, her face fixed in a sad, farouche stare.

A person emerging from trance remembers nothing of what he did or said while possessed. Even if the trance seemed obviously 'put on', he will deny it categorically. No possessed person is supposed to know that he has been the receptacle for a spirit, unless he has learnt as much from someone else. Many, when informed, seem to disbelieve the account of their words and actions. A woman whose dress had been torn while she was in trance, came and asked me the reason for the damage by which she was much vexed. Her pained surprise radiated good faith.

Such amnesia, or more exactly reserve, does not embrace the initial stages of trance. Some informants say that before darkness engulfs their brain, they feel pins and needles in their legs or a strange heaviness which glues their feet to the earth. Some compare the first inrush of the spirit to a blow on the nape of the neck. Then all sense of time vanishes.

Possession may last any time; and sometimes, when the subject is what is known as 'saoulé', that is to say slightly dazed, it only lasts a few seconds. This state of drunkenness results from any contact with a spirit or a sacred object. Thus, a possessed person may cause mild intoxication in others if he spins them around as a gesture of courtesy. The priest who carries the necklaces of the *hunsi* staggers as if overcome by the sacred energy contained in these ornaments. It is then said that they have been brushed by the *loa* whom for a moment they approached.

With some people trance lasts several hours or even whole days. I was told of a woman who was ridden by Ezili for fifteen days in succession. Throughout this time she wore the clothes of the goddess and remained powdered and made-up. From time to time the goddess gave up her seat on her *chual* to her friend the Siren. A person visited by a *loa* for as long as this usually experiences difficulty in sustaining the condition of trance. Oversights and omissions betray his weariness and obscure the personality of the god incarnate in him. Unless warned, a visitor may fail to realize the situation and so address the possessed as though he were in his normal condition. The unrecognized *loa* then takes offence and scolds. To avoid such confusion *loa* usually have the good grace to withdraw their essence if their minions forget to establish their identity for them. Mistakes of this kind are more excusable when a god deserts his 'horse' in mid-conversation. A visitor imagines he is talking to a god . . . and finds himself face to face with a man or woman, who listens gaping with astonishment.

Such mix-ups are rare. Usually signs of fatigue in the subject give clear indication that trance is ending. He loses momentum and if he does not collapse in a corner, he falls semi-conscious on the knees of spectators. Motionless and dazed for a few minutes, he at last opens his eyes and looks round him with the astonished air of a person waking in unfamiliar surroundings. Often out of respect for the departing god, the face of his 'horse', during this phase, is covered with a cloth.

Once the acute stage of the crisis has passed, the footwear, necklaces, rings, hairpins—in short any form of dress or adorn-ment that could get broken or lost, or might put the *loa* off and so 'stop' him—are removed. When a subject has difficulty in mastering his convulsions a priest goes up to him and soothes him by shaking his rattle softly, close to his ear. Sometimes, too, if the subject is rolling on the ground the officiating priest will keep him still by straddling and gripping him.

The frenzy of the *criseur* wears off gradually. Suddenly a new person takes shape: it is the god. At once his attributes are brought to him: hat, sword, stick, bottle, cigars—or if he has to be dressed up he is escorted to one of the sanctuary rooms used as a dressing-room. The spirits, whatever their sex, incarnate themselves in men or women as they please. Subjects must in-dicate by dress, or simply manner, whatever change of sex may have taken place in them. In the chapter devoted to mythology we tried to characterize the principal *loa* by the dress or behaviour of their 'horses'. We must here take the liberty of referring the reader to those descriptions. But let it not be forgotten that such impersonation is achieved with degrees of success which vary according to the imagination or resources of the *hungan* or the *mambo* concerned.

The appearance of a *grand loa* is greeted by a special rhythm called *aux champs* (flourish): singers, men and women alike, burst out with redoubled enthusiasm. The god is fanned and his face is wiped free of sweat. If he is one of the accredited, guardian spirits of the sanctuary he is given an escort with banners in front. Such adulation does not exempt him from observing strict Voodoo procedure. Admittedly the 'ground is kissed' in front of him—but he, in his turn, prostrates himself before the resident priest or priestess, before the drums and before the *poteau-*

mitan. Usually he dispenses small favours among the onlookers
—clasping both hands of some rather roughly, anointing the
faces of others with his sweat, or shaking their clothes to bring
them luck. He lifts in his arms those whom he wishes to favour,
or he wriggles between their open legs. He is expected to effect
cures, so he must touch the sick and improvise treatment. This
can miscarry—as when a man possessed by Agwé tried to cure
Lorgina of rheumatism . . . and bit her cruelly in the leg.

The possessed—or to be more precise, the gods—prophesy,
threaten sinners and gladly give advice. What is more they give
advice to themselves, for often a *loa* will ask the spectators to tell
his 'horse' to behave differently or follow his advice. These
messages are faithfully transmitted to the person concerned as
soon as he is in a fit state to receive them.

A description of one of the many possessions which I witnessed
will give a clearer picture of this essential aspect of Voodoo than
any amount of general observations. The following passage is
from notes taken on the spot: 'The *hunsi*, with red cloths round
their heads and coloured dresses, dance in honour of Ogu. At the
very first dance *mambo* Lorgina is possessed by this god. In spite
of her age, her infirmities and her weight, she dances nimbly in
front of the drums, hands on hips, shaking her shoulders in time
to the music. She then fetches a sabre and jams the hilt of it
against the *poteau-mitan* and the point against her stomach. Now,
by pushing with all her strength, she bends the blade. She repeats
this dangerous practice, this time basing the hilt on the post's
concrete plinth. A *hungan* sprays rum from his mouth on to her
stomach and rubs her legs. Lorgina in a sudden frenzy fences
with the *la-place*; he, too, being armed with a sabre. The ceremonial duel degenerates into a real fight, so that spectators, fearing an accident, have to intervene. Lorgina is then seized by
another wave of bellicose frenzy. She hacks the *poteau-mitan* with
her sabre and chases the *hunsi* who flee in terror. She is on the
point of catching them when prevented by the shafts of the sacred
flags which two women cross in her path. At once she becomes
calm—and thus will it always be whenever Lorgina-Ogu gives
way to an attack of rage. A priest comes up to talk to her, keeping
prudently in the safety-zone of the banners. The *mambo* winds

up by going back to the *hunsi* whom she beats violently with the flat of her sabre; and this outlet has a soothing effect upon her. Suddenly all smiles, she salutes everyone present and overflows with politeness in every direction. She has a cigar brought to her which she smokes in a nonchalant way. Then she gives orders that the meat-safe hanging on the *poteau-mitan* should be placed before her. She eats heartily and distributes what is left among the *hunsi*. She calls up a trembling and excited little girl whom she has already spanked hard with the flat of her sword: she gives her a long lecture on her future behaviour and foretells a terrible fate for her unless she takes the warning to heart. Having forced the little girl to prostrate herself before her, Lorgina— still in the tones of Ogu—lectures her *hunsi*, giving them detailed advice on dress. Then, speaking of herself in the third person, she boasts of her own labours, and tells how she managed to save up to build the sanctuary. The *hunsi* listen with respect. Shortly afterwards the god leaves the *mambo*, who then returns to herself.

A *hunsi* is possessed. She begins by tottering and then flounders doubled-up, strikes her forehead and twists her arms. Very gradually, almost insensibly, her movements fall into rhythm, become more supple, more harmonious until they can only be distinguished from those of the other dancers by a nervous quickness. She comes out of the trance by imperceptible stages.

Two young girls are possessed by Ogu-balindjo. At the mere sight of this event Lorgina bursts out laughing and with a pretence of impatience chases them from the peristyle. The two women jump into the pool where they romp like children. They come back streaming and the public greets them with gibes and laughter. Proud of their success, they return several times for a bathe. Finally Lorgina orders them back into the sanctuary where they will be given a change of clothes since, says she, 'the horses of Ogu must not catch cold'.

Every possession has a theatrical aspect. This is at once apparent in the general concern for disguise. Sanctuary rooms serve to a certain extent as the wings of a stage where the possessed can find all the accessories they need. Unlike an hysteric who shows his own misery and desires by means of a

symptom—which is an entirely personal form of expression—
the man who is ritually possessed must correspond to the
traditional conception of some mythical personage. The hysterics
of long ago who thought themselves the victims of devils, also
certainly drew the devilish part of their personality from the
folklore in which they lived, but they were subject to influences
not entirely comparable to those felt by the possessed in Haiti.

Adepts of Voodoo make a very clear distinction between possession by *loa*, which is sought after and desired, and possession by
evil spirits which is frightening and morbid. In Voodoo there is
nothing comparable to the dialogues between the two personalities of the demoniac. With the ritually possessed consciousness is
entirely obliterated, at least in appearance, and the individual
obeys the *loa—perinde ac cadaver*. As soon as he has chosen the
personality which the folklore mystique suggests to him or, to
speak in Voodoo terms, as soon as the *loa* has, at his own wish,
or in response to a call, descended into him, the subject fulfils his
rôle by drawing upon the knowledge and memories which have
accumulated in the course of a life frequenting cult congregations.
The amount left to his own whim will be governed by his relations with other people. He can be benevolent if he wishes or,
on the contrary, he can be angry with certain people; but he
cannot alter the characteristics or the appearance of the divine
personage he incarnates. Some, in the eyes of spectators, succeed
better than others in representing such and such a god. That is
why you hear in Voodoo circles statements such as 'You should
see her when she's got Ezili in her head'.

Similarities of this kind, between possession and the theatre,
must not obscure the fact that in the eyes of the public a possessed
person is never really an actor. He does not play a character part,
he *is* the character as long as the trance lasts.

And yet, what else can it be called except 'theatre' when the
possessed turn the simultaneous manifestation of several gods in
different people, into an organized 'impromptu'? These im-
promptus, which vary in style, are much appreciated by the
audience who yell with laughter, join in the dialogue and
noisily show their pleasure or discontent. Take an example:
someone possessed by Zaka appears under the peristyle in the

get-up of a peasant. By canny movements he mimes the anxiety of a countryman come to town, and who fears to be robbed. Now another possessed person joins him, one might almost say 'comes on'. It is Guédé-nibo, of the Guédé family, which watches over the dead. Zaka is clearly terrified by the presence of his gloomy colleague and tries to propitiate him, inviting him to have something to eat and to drink some rum. Guédé who is making a show as a townsman exchanges courtesies with him, trying to tease him. He asks him: 'What have you got in your bag?'; he searches it and examines the contents. Alarmed, Zaka cries 'Stop, stop'. The bag is returned to him only to be surreptitiously lifted off him while he is examining one of the sick. Zaka, in despair, calls for cards and shells in order to discover the thief by means of divination. The audience chants: 'Play, Zaka, play.' Zaka: 'I have come to complain about Agau-wèdo.' 'Play, cousin Zaka, play.' The objects he has called for are brought.

Several people are suddenly possessed by Zaka and provoke what in Haiti is so aptly termed 'a scandal' (*youn escandale*). One of them accuses a woman of having stolen certain objects which had been left in her keeping. Protests from the woman; screams, temper and backbiting. It is Zaka who is at last accused of thieving. He has not got an easy conscience and is on edge whenever anyone goes anywhere near his precious bag.

The following anecdote is also indicative of the theatrical nature of possession. During Voodoo ceremonies each divinity is honoured in turn by three dances accompanied by songs; the order of the dances is laid down and cannot very well be changed. During one of them, consecrated to Ogu, a priest was suddenly seized with a *loa*. At first it was thought to be the expected god. So there was general astonishment when it turned out to be Guédé, making a premature appearance. A priest addressed him and asked him kindly to go away and come when it was his turn. Guédé refused and demanded his paraphernalia. Priests and other dignitaries returned to the attack. From prayers they passed to threats. Guédé laughed at them. Weary of strife they sent for his clothes. He proceeded to dance gaily, took the liberty of a few farcical jokes and then collapsed on a chair. The possession was finished. Returning to his senses the possessed was disconcerted to hear songs and drum-beats which in no way corresponded with the normal order of events. He became angry and sharply reproached the *hunsi* for this breach of discipline. It was in vain they told him the only person to blame for the deviation was Guédé, who had possessed him. He would not hear of it. In fact he had his work cut out insisting, as do all people possessed, that he knew nothing of what had taken place.

Some of the possessed have a considerable repertory of tricks. Their talent is particularly evident when they are possessed several times in succession and have to change their identity without intervening pause. They can, like a *hungan* I saw one evening, become successively Ogu-balindjo, a shrill god who sprinkles his head with well-water, and then on the spur of the moment turn into Guédé-fatras and carry out an acrobatic dance which in its turn gives place to transformation into Petit-Pierre— a gluttonous and quarrelsome spirit who to the joy of the gallery tries to pick a quarrel with the audience. Another time it was a woman who, prey to the goddess Veleketé, racked her body into strange shapes with her tongue hanging out and her neck twisted. She had managed to distort her body in the most terrible manner when suddenly she stopped incarnating the hideous Veleketé and became a blithe and frolicsome divinity.

Whenever a depressing atmosphere develops as a result of the violence of possessions, then Guédé appears, puckish and obscene. He sits on girls' knees and pretends to be about to rape them. The congregation revels in this sort of fun and laughs heartily.

Ritual trances pose a fundamental problem: are they genuine dissociations of the personality, comparable to those found in certain cases of hysteria, or are they entirely simulated—merely part of the traditional cult and obedient to ritualistic imperative? To put it differently, when a man becomes the vehicle of a god, has he lost all sense of reality, or is he simply an actor speaking a part? This question can only be answered by firmly establishing the basic data relevant to the problem. First and foremost it is essential to realize the part played by possession within the

social and religious system which has attached so much importance to it.

Trance usually occurs during religious ceremonies, private as
well as public. Spirits must take part in the homage which is
paid to them and must themselves receive the sacrifices offered.
Their appearance is expected and takes place at the desired
moment. When the feast is being celebrated in a private sanctuary
the spirits only 'enter into' the members of the family. If a
stranger went into a trance it would be thought bad taste and
he would be asked to remove himself. As a general rule it is the
same people who are visited by the same spirits each year.
Possessions are as arranged as the details of family 'services'.

But when a public sanctuary organizes a dance or a grand
ceremony, possessions are not restricted to office-holders of the
cult, *mambo*, *hungan* and *hunsi*. Many spectators, mere visitors,
are abruptly picked upon by a god and for a few moments take
part in the dances and rites.

The confusion caused in the smooth working of a ceremony
by successive possessions is more apparent than real. Only very
seldom is the arrangement of worship disturbed by *epiphanies*.
The main rites are always accompanied by possessions since it is
desirable, and even necessary, that the main *loa* concerned should
take part in them. They usually go into the person officiating and
also into the man or woman who is paying for the ceremony. In
showing themselves they give an earnest of their goodwill and
guarantee the efficacy of the ceremony. If the gods kept away
it would be a sign of their indifference, or worse, hostility. When
a present is brought for the *loa*, the priest, who will be the only
real beneficiary, is careful not to thank the donor. Marks of
divine gratitude will be shown later during a feast when the god
incarnates himself in the priest or some other person.

Collective possessions take place without fail whenever in the
course of a ceremony the crowd get worked up by some spectacular effect such as the leaping flames of alcohol burnt in honour of
Ogu, or when the *zin* (sacred pots), coated with oil, suddenly
catch fire, or when small charges of powder are detonated to
greet a god. Moreover some connection may be noted between
possessions and certain drum-rhythms: the musicians seem to

be capable of inducing trance by redoubling their effort. They themselves, then, seem subject to delirium; though they are seldom genuinely 'mounted'. *Hungan*, too, know how to overcome the resistance which certain people put up against the god. They dance in front of them, staring at them all the time and making certain gestures which seem to have the suggestive power of hypnotic passes. On the other hand people who are subject to 'attacks' of possession but who, for one reason or another, do not wish to give in to them, make use of various magic procedures to 'moor' the god where he is. Sometimes they do their hair in a certain way or sometimes they carry in a corner of their head-cloth some ingredient effective against an attack of *loa*, such as wax. Spirits who have been 'moored' can do no more than make a person 'tipsy'; their passage is quick and has only a moderately inebriating effect. To avoid being mounted a person can also remain seated with arms crossed and wearing a forbidding cast of countenance.

Possessions also occur in ordinary, daily life. In fact it is in lay surroundings that the psychological function of possession becomes clear. Trance sometimes amounts to an escape-mechanism in the face of suffering, or simply fatigue. Dr Louis Mars witnessed an attack of *loa* which took place in someone undergoing an operation; it broke out at the very moment when the pain was at its sharpest. On another occasion he saw two people became possessed just after a motor bus accident in which they had been involved.

People who have to make some exceptional effort sometimes ask a spirit to help them—in other words they hope their task will be made easier if attempted in a state of trance. Stories are told of shipwrecked sailors who were able to reach land thanks to the god Agwé entering into them. In the course of a pilgrimage to the Balan cave, in the neighbourhood of Port-au-Prince, *mambo* Lorgina who was moving over stony ground slowly, because of rheumatism, was suddenly possessed by Legba: instead of limping and pausing every few seconds as she had been till then, she went on her way with a resolute step and without apparent weariness. Apart from this sudden access of energy the possession had no other effect upon her.

It was freely said in Port-au-Prince that the dancers who had taken part in a dance marathon were all 'mounted by a *loa*'. *Hungan* and *mambo* who had 'doped' them as an inoculation against the nostrums of their rivals, took care that their possessed condition was not too apparent. But the malicious and uncontrollable Guédé could not contain themselves. In the very middle of the competition the nasal voice of a Guédé cried out '*Sé mwê Papa Gédé—mwê fò . . .*' (It's me, Papa Guédé, I'm strong.)

The characteristics of a *loa* can be very useful to the person in whom they are temporarily vested. A thief who has Damballah within him can slide through the narrowest openings like a snake. He can also climb with the utmost speed and even if he falls from the top of a telegraph pole he suffers no ill effects, because 'nothing is impossible for a person possessed by a *loa*'.

Trance does indeed make strange exploits possible. Mme Mennesson-Rigaud witnessed the most appalling gluttony on the part of the *loa* Guédé-cinq-jours-malheureux (Guédé Five Days Unhappy), who had revealed himself at the end of a big *manger-loa* (food offering for the spirits). Dragging himself along on his knees and elbows, he moved among the offerings all of which he gobbled, only pausing to distribute occasional handfuls to the children. Having returned to his normal state the possessed complained of hunger and asked for food. He was given a plateful which he cleaned up as though he had an empty stomach.

Trance can provide a person with a means of escape from an unpleasant situation. One of the ordeals of initiation obliges novices to beg in public places. Some are ashamed to do so. They ask the *hungan* to call down a spirit into them. Once possessed they need not feel embarrassed since it is not they but the *loa* who stretches out his palm.

The individual in a state of trance is in no way responsible for his deeds or words. He has ceased to exist as a person. Someone possessed can express with impunity thoughts which he would hesitate to utter aloud in normal circumstances. It is an observed fact that the possessed hold opinions or give free rein to aggression which can only be explained by repressed grudges. Their indiscretion is sometimes shocking and throws the whole crowd into a flutter. People show their disapproval and implore the god to shut up. Possession in this respect has much in common with drunkenness in America, which often excuses outbursts of frankness in the same way.

The state of possession gives weight to advice which a priest, or anyone else, wishes to give the congregation. How often have I seen *mambo* Lorgina transformed into one of the mighty *loa*, scolding her *hunsi* or exhorting them to be obedient and grateful to the good Lorgina.

Certain *hungan* hide behind their *loa*, protesting to their clientèle that it is not they who care for and counsel them, but the spirits of which they are merely the servants. Lorgina attributed the success of her medical treatments to Brisé, the 'master of her *humfo*'. Possession allows a spirit to take the place of his 'horse' and assume his functions. Some *loa* have a liking for the profession of *hungan* and incarnate themselves in those who are officiating in order to control the ceremony in their place. This was done, it seems, by Guédé-Achille-piquant who finished up by being regarded as the true master of the *humfo* of a certain Dieudonné, who, not being a *hungan*, always performed the offices with this *loa* in his head.

Possessions sometimes occur in the middle of the market at Port-au-Prince. A prospective buyer may suddenly perceive that the woman behind her stall is saying the most preposterous things to him in a nasal tone. He need not be surprised. It is Guédé who is 'riding' her and indulging in a bout of frankness, just to cheer everyone up.

Some possessions satisfy obscure cravings which have a masochistic tendency. The possessed, in fact, sometimes hurls himself to the ground as though flung there by some power greater than himself, or bangs his head against a wall. In certain exceptional cases, rare it is true, women have ripped up or burnt expensive clothes. These acts are interpreted as punishments for some ritual fault which the 'horse' has committed. The vengeance of a *loa* can also take other forms, scarcely less cruel. He will come down into his 'horse' in the middle of church, at the Elevation of the Host, and so cause a distressing scandal.

Loa who wish to humiliate their 'horses' put them in a dangerous or ridiculous position or abandon them suddenly, to such effect that the person possessed, becoming aware of and pained at his plight, suffers for it. M. Marcelin told me that during one ceremony a woman was possessed by Damballah and climbed up a tree where she prepared to hang by the legs from a bough which might have broken beneath her weight. The congregation became frightened and did not know what to do. An old woman traced out a *vévé* in the middle of which she put some sweetened water and an egg. She then sang: 'Damballah-wèdo everyone is perfectly happy. It's you who are in a bad temper. If you see Damballah, give him a caress from me.' When she saw the offering the possessed woman came down from the tree, drank the water, swallowed the egg and immediately returned to her normal state.

Last, but not least of the functions of possession, is the pleasure which it gives to poor souls ground down by life. They are able, by virtue of such a mechanism, to become the centre of attention and play the part of a supernatural being, feared and respected. Histrionics and exhibitionism undoubtedly do play a large part in the phenomenon of possession, just as they do in the case of genuine hysterics.

Voodoo adepts say that spirits prefer to come down into people who resemble them. In other words there would seem to be a correlation between the character of the god and that of the devotee who represents him. Gentle people are inhabited by calm and friendly gods, while the violent harbour fiery and brutal spirits. It is true that the practice of Haiti, unlike that of Dahomey and Brazil, allows one person to be 'ridden' by several different divinities. The analogy of a *loa* and his 'horse' should only be applied therefore to the *loa-tête*, that is to say to the spirit who first possessed the subject and became his official protector. Not uncommonly, however, devotees are possessed by *loa* whose character is the very opposite of their own. Trance, then, acts as a form of compensation.

This last aspect of trance suggested a Freudian interpretation to Professor R. Bastide.[6] In his view, possession allowed the repressed personality to come to the surface in a symbolic form 'in a jovial, festive atmosphere without any of the sinister colouring which Freud gives it'. It was 'a confessional which was played not spoken, a physically active cure—based on the muscular exaltation of dance instead of on a horizontal, disguised couch, in clinical half-darkness'. The comparison is slightly forced and attributes too much to individual pressures, when very often trance is a ritualistic reflex. We are also entitled to ask just what are the repressed drives which a person 'exteriorizes' through the medium of trance. Apart from the cases mentioned above, a subject's behaviour is rigorously laid down by tradition, and far from expressing *himself* the possessed tries to personify some mythological being whose character on the whole is foreign to him. Most of the possessed apparently get nothing more out of their condition than does an actor who lives his part and gains applause. And the approval of the congregation is measured merely by the amount of attention it devotes to his words and actions.

Too often people imagine that a crowd exalted by mystic enthusiasm is the usual setting for Voodoo possessions. In fact those who attend ceremonies as spectators only cast an occasional absentminded glance at the goings-on. They gossip on the edges of the peristyle, smoke cigarettes, or nibble at *tablettes* (pralines). At no time is the crowd subject to collective delirium, or even to a degree of excitement propitious to ecstasy. The traditional dances of Voodoo—*yanvalou, doba, Dahomey, petro*— all carried out with great seriousness, a subtle sense of rhythm and admirable suppleness—are far from being dionysian. Only at certain ceremonial moments does the degree of excitement reach enthusiasm.

Ritual possessions are often attributed to nervous disorders of a hysterical nature. Twenty-odd years ago Herskovits had already refuted that explanation by drawing attention to the stylized and controlled nature of the phenomenon and its frequency in a society in which it was the normal means of communicating with supernatural powers. The number of people subject to possession is too large for all of them to be labelled hysterics, unless the whole population of Haiti is to be regarded as prone to mental disorders.

If trance is suited to an innate disposition in Haitians, then we may well wonder what mutation can account for the fact that the same faculty has disappeared from regions with the same ethnical composition, but where African religious tradition has either disappeared or been preserved less faithfully.

Possession could hardly be explained entirely in terms of psychopathology. Such an explanation is probably only valid for a limited number of people who are unquestionably true neurotics, people subject to what has been called dissociation of the personality. Is hysterical anaesthesia to account for the impressive performance of those men and women who while inhabited by a god, handle red-hot bars of iron, without apparent discomfort? In ceremonies which I attended the possessed brandished plenty of *pinces* (bars of iron) reddened in fire, but they contrived to hold them by the very end. The *hunsi* who danced in the fire jumped prudently on logs which the flames had spared. All the same I have no reason to doubt the word of those who have seen the possessed grasp red-hot bars with wide-open hands. It is difficult for me to give an opinion of feats such as may be found in other religious manifestations, and among sects which practise an extreme form of asceticism. As for those Haitians who while in trance munch glass—their performance is of the same order as that of our own travelling showmen. According to Voodoo logic the 'horse' should not suffer for actions initiated by the god on his back.

Apart from chaotic preliminaries there is in most cases of possession a theatrical element which unavoidably suggests a certain amount of simulation or at least of intentional delusion. We are entitled to doubt the authenticity of possessions which come, so to speak, on request, the moment ritual requires. The loss of consciousness, without which, from an absolute stand-point, there can be no possession, is at most partial with many subjects, if not actually non-existent. Take the woman who when wearing a new dress is possessed by Damballah. She avoids throwing herself on the ground in case she spoils it, although the serpent-god normally requires his 'horse' to wriggle along the ground. Take the person who refers to events or matters which she could only know about if she has remained in full possession of her memory. Take another, finally, who too obviously uses his divine immunity to give vent to his spite or his greed. How often,

when talking to someone possessed, I have learnt that the god I
was hoping to meet is none other than himself! More than one
person possessed has been guilty of such give-aways and lapses.
Here are a few examples: one day Lorgina, who was supposed to
be possessed by Brisé, nevertheless begged for help from this
very *loa* and praised him just as if she were merely his 'servant'
and not Brise himself. Her attitude would have made sense if the
god had in fact left her, without warning, and without anyone
noticing; but Lorgina then sprinkled her speech with oaths—of
which Brise is prodigal—and this showed that she had forgotten
her rôle and, becoming aware of it, was trying to recoup.

Organizing the details of a fête, which I wished to offer
Guédé, I found the *mambo* and her acolytes, who were allegedly
possessed by Guédé, became only too human when the question
of money arose. Once the discussion was over and agreement
reached, they again remembered their rôles and behaved like true
Guédé. I remember one possessed who completely forgot she
had a god inside her the moment I gave her news of a woman
from her own village.

Thanks to imperceptible signs it is sometimes possible to fore-
see when a person intends to fall into a trance. When I was on the
sailing boat which was taking me back from the Islets where we
had been sacrificing to Agwé-taroyo, a *hunsi* asked me to jump
into the water. Feeling that she was going to be possessed I
replied that I thought it wiser to stay with her and prevent her
from jumping into the sea should a marine god suddenly visit
her. I had scarcely finished speaking when she closed her eyes
and began breathing heavily. Two men seized her but she
managed to break free and threw herself writhing into the lowest
part of the boat. There it was possible to overpower her. She
grew calm and of her own accord went and lay down on a mat.
She had been possessed by Agau who is a 'diving' god, which
explains the efforts made to keep her from the side. The in-
sistence with which this woman pressed me to jump into the
sea suggests that even then she was intending to identify herself
with Agau.

The obviously stylized behaviour of people possessed does not
in itself allow one to be sure whether the origin of possession is

voluntary or not. Only very rarely do you see a subject genuinely fight against trance and be overcome in spite of himself. I remember seeing a well-dressed woman in a crowd which was admiring the dances of people possessed by Simbi. She was certainly a member of the Port-au-Prince petite bourgeoisie. She seemed ill at ease and was looking at the dancers with an abstracted expression. Suddenly she shut her eyes, and her face contracted as though she were in pain. She began to sweat profusely, her shoulders and arms became stiff. In a few moments she was shaking all over and then was violently convulsed. The *hungan* came to where she was swaying, quicker and quicker, from side to side on her chair. From his closed fist he stuck out a thumb and pressed it into her forehead as though he were driving in a peg. With face still convulsed she closed her eyes as tight as she could, but in less than a minute her tremblings came to an end. She looked round about her and her sweating eased off. She seemed relaxed and remained seated as though nothing had happened.

Song, or more often drumming, has an undeniable effect on certain subjects. The *hungan* Tullius, during an audition in Paris, was listening to the tape recording of a ceremony which he had himself conducted when he was suddenly seized with dizziness at the exact moment when he had been possessed during the 'live' recording. There and then, dancing on a Parisian stage, he was properly 'ridden' by the god Damballah, much to the annoyance of his colleagues.

That possessions can occur during ceremonies which formally rule them out affords another proof of the suggestive nature of the phenomenon. One evening, during the rites which celebrate the seclusion of initiates—rites from which gods are carefully kept away—three people showed signs of possession. Two calmed down of their own accord but the third had to have his forehead pressed by the *mambo* before he returned to his senses.

The preliminary crisis has a contagious effect, particularly upon people who are nervous and unstable. That is why the sight of a possession often has the effect of provoking others, not only among the *hunsi* who are ready to be ridden by the gods but also among the spectators who have come as visitors or out of curiosity. In Voodoo circles, among the masses, a nervous crisis is not regarded as cause for shame or even anxiety. There is nothing mysterious or abnormal about it; on the contrary—it is a mark of divine favour. It would seem that those who have once been affected by and given in to suggestion become gradually more and more likely to succumb to trance. Their crisis, which is at first incoherent, ends by attaining the stylized behaviour which I have tried to describe.

Among the apparently stylized possessions which are presumably spontaneous, it is impossible to distinguish between those initiated by psychic infection and those which reflect a private impulse on the part of the subject. We may well wonder whether the convulsive and trembling phase may not be for many—I was on the point of saying for most—devotees of Voodoo, a sort of physical technique* which induces the 'delusion' of divine possession. This of course is merely hypothetical yet is it not possible that such a simulation of a nervous attack might actually assist the evacuation of the real personality in favour of a borrowed personality? Might not the exaltation and dizziness consequent upon such frenzied agitation, create a mental climate propitious to a certain amount of auto-suggestion? If this were so, then possession would engulf the senses in the wake of the heralding symptoms.

When watching some of the possessed it is tempting to compare them to a child who is pretending to be, perhaps, an Indian or an animal, and who helps the flight of his fantasy by means of a garment or an object.

Adults are the accomplices of this waking dream by supplying helpful disguise. The possessed then move in an atmosphere which is even more propitious than that of the child: the public does not *pretend* to believe in the reality of their play, it does

---

* I remember seeing some young *hunsi* at the beginning of a ceremony, dancing without any sort of conviction even though the rhythm of the orchestra was perfect. Like schoolgirls, turning the inattention of the master to good account, they took every opportunity of riotous giggling and of playing with the young men. The latter kept on teasing them; finally chased them and brought them back into their midst where they lurched on to them as though suddenly possessed and about to lose their balance. Their behaviour showed clearly that the preliminary crisis is merely a technique—of which they had perfect mastery.

believe in it sincerely. Among the poorer people and even in certain circles of the Haiti bourgeoisie, the existence of *loa* and their incarnations are articles of faith. Anyone possessed shares this conviction. Having undergone or simulated a nervous crisis his state of tension is such that it is not so easy for him to distinguish between his own self and the person he has been representing. He plays his part in good faith, attributing it to the will of a spirit who got inside him in some mysterious fashion. In short it would seem that merely for a person to believe himself possessed is enough to induce in him the behaviour of a person possessed—and that without any intention of trickery. Filliozat[7] compares possession to a 'suggested state' and explains it as 'a momentary forgetting either of intentions based on normal activities, or of any real sensation of one's actual condition', all of which results in a person 'acting against his normal will or believing himself to be in some other state than the actual one'.

The 'forgetting' of the possessed is not always a piece of crude mystification. For a person to admit that he remembers what he has said or done as a god, is to admit that he was not genuinely possessed—it being impossible to be oneself and a *loa* at the same time. Better convince himself that he has forgotten everything than admit that he pulled the wool over the eyes of everyone present, and of the divinity too. Whoever puts himself into a trance must keep up the pretence right through to the end. To simulate possession does not necessarily imply a sceptical attitude. The *hungan* Tullius whose possessions were often 'done' to oblige, was haunted by fear of the *loa* and took very seriously— even tragically—the threats and warnings which he received from the mouths of other people possessed.

The state of possession can be explained, therefore, by the extremely religious climate which obtains in Voodoo circles. The ubiquity of the *loa* and their incarnations are the object of beliefs so profound and so unquestioned that possessions are received with less fuss than the arrival of a friend. If a woman rolls on the ground or writhes, the spectators merely say 'she has a *loa*'. This faith is contagious: it is shared by part of the Haitian clergy who naturally see in this phenomenon the work of the devil. A

few cultured Whites accept possession as a supernatural manifestation and take an interest in Voodoo which borders on faith.
The frequenting of sanctuaries demands from the detached and
polite observer the use of expressions which in fact amount to
an acceptance, by him, of the authenticity of possession. Indeed
it is impossible to mention the behaviour of someone possessed
without attributing it to the god who has gone into him. It would
be improper to make the 'horse' responsible for the actions or
utterances of his invisible rider.

The following story gives an idea of the conviction to be found
among the possessed themselves. A young woman 'ridden' by
the goddess Ezili had danced during a ceremony with a young
man to whom she afterwards accorded her favours. While still
in a state of trance she gave the young man a hundred dollars—
all her savings. In this she conformed to the generous nature of
the goddess. Next day, no doubt regretting her gesture, she pretended she had been robbed and would not accept the explanation of her friends—who said simply that she had no memory at
all of what really happened. She brought an action against the
young man. When the judge was informed of the circumstances
he ordered the young man to give the money back; but the girl
was at once seized with fear and refused to accept it. She was
rightly afraid of going back on the divinity who had guided her
while she was supposed to be unconscious.

V. EPIPHANY OF THE GODS

Spirits when they wish can take on material shape and reveal
themselves to men without making use of the body of someone
possessed. Several peasants assured me they had seen Ezili in
the flesh during the terrible flood which ravaged the Marbial
valley in 1935. Just when the people who lived along the river
Gosseline were fleeing in panic toward the high ground, they
saw a boat lighted by candles coming down the river. In it was a
splendid Negress surrounded by women who were chattering,
laughing and singing the following song:

Ezili, Ezili o fâm kay mwê ralé kò (bis)
Si u mâdé-m pu m'a ba u-li
Si u mâdé-m kòchô, ma ba u-li
Ezili, o, si u mâdé krétyê vivâ m'a ralé kò mwê
Ezili, Ezili, o women of my house go away
If you ask for a chicken, I will give it to you
If you ask for a pig I will give it to you
Ezili, o, if you ask for a live Christian I shall steal away.

Hungan and *mambo* have more opportunity than ordinary devotees of meeting the *loa* in broad daylight. Lorgina prided herself on a conversation which she had in the sea with Agwé-taroyo. She described what happened with a wealth of detail. She had to go to Miragoane. Remembering a previous awkward crossing, she had this time decided to go by land. On the eve of her departure Agwé-taroyo appeared to her husband in a dream and told him to go by sea without fear. As a token of good faith she gave him a snuff-box and told him to make use of it. During his voyage his boat was hailed by another boat whose captain was a handsome Mulatto with green eyes and a luxuriant beard. The sight of him filled everyone with fear, but Lorgina had an intuition that she was face to face with Papa Agwé. The Mulatto turned to her and said in good French 'Lorgina, how are you?' He then inquired politely about the purpose of her journey and assured her all would go well; and with these words he vanished. The journey went well and it was from then on that Lorgina continually took snuff.

Of all Voodoo divinities it is Zaka the peasant god who most often reveals himself in concrete form. He appears abruptly in the guise of a rather rough peasant, clad in a deep blue shirt, trousers rolled up to his knees, a big straw hat and carrying the *alfo* (basketwork bag) which is an indispensable item of the countryman's equipment. Often he limps, for he suffers like many a peasant from a *crabe* (a yaws lesion) on the sole of his foot. With the awkwardness and tone of voice which is attributed to people of the hills he begs a glass of rum or a bit of cassava. Woe to those that refuse him. Zaka disappears without more ado and whoever spurned him for his shabby, boorish appearance will soon feel the edge of his anger. He does not forgive easily and his victim must humble himself for a long time at his feet before obtaining a pardon. It is certainly no mere chance that stories concerning Zaka nearly all centre on the theme of his being despised for his lumpish and ragged appearance. Such tales unquestionably reflect the feeling of the peasants who, when they come to a town, are exposed to the rebuffs and disdain of its citizens, without ever daring to show temper or even drop the subservient tone they affect.

VI. DREAMS

Spirits are apt to communicate with the faithful by means of dreams.[8] It would be hard to find a Voodooist who has not at some time or other been visited at night by a *loa*. In this respect priests and priestesses are particularly favoured. Spirits constantly come and give them advice and medical prescriptions, or talk over with them some new rite which they hope to see introduced. That is why people are always reluctant to waken a *hungan* or *mambo*.

Supernatural beings seen in dreams usually have a human form. They readily assume the appearance of a friend or relation —a guise which serves them as well as does a person possessed. The dreamer is not deceived: one detail of dress, a symbolic object or simply his own inner certainty reveals to him the identity of his nocturnal visitor. One young woman of Marbial, lying ill, was visited by Ogu who appeared to her in a dream in the form of her brother. At no time did she think it was the latter since the apparition was in uniform and her brother was not a soldier. She decided therefore that it must be some warrior *loa*, a member of the Ogu family. He led her out of the house by the hand and showed her plants which she must use in the preparation of a magic bath. When she woke up she faithfully followed the god's prescriptions and never had cause to regret it. A female *loa* can appear as a man in a dream just as in ordinary possessions. Often when telling of a dream, people omit to mention the form taken by the god, just as when awake they speak of encountering a *loa* without paying any attention to his 'horse'. It is possible to be possessed by a *loa* during sleep. Whoever has had this experience remembers it well, unlike the person who, possessed when awake, remembers nothing of what he did or said.

It sometimes happens that while sleeping a person takes part in dramatic events which ai ? no mere simple fantasies of the imagination but genuine visions which reveal to the sleeper that his life is in danger and the spirits disputing it among themselves.

Marie-Noël who was 'queen-chorister' for a grand *hungan* of Port-au-Prince told me of an extraordinary dream[9] in which she learnt that if she were persecuted by wicked people who wanted to kill her by sending dead souls against her, she could none the less rely upon the protection of powerful divinities. In the dream a policeman in khaki uniform had come to ask lodging for the night. He warned her he would have to leave early and that he had no money with which to pay. Marie-Noël replied, 'That doesn't matter, stay and sleep here and tomorrow morning I'll call you punctually at four o'clock.' The policeman went to bed and slept. Meanwhile some malicious people slandered Marie-Noël. One of them said, 'I'm going to have Marie-Noël arrested; I'm going to send a he-dog to open her door.' And indeed a male dog did jump against the door and pulled it, whereupon she opened it. Behind it Marie-Noël saw three policemen all in white. Her guest who had been asleep protested: 'This is all wrong: you have no right to behave like this! Only if someone steals are policemen called in to arrest him.' Marie-Noël began to weep but her defender said to her, 'Don't cry. Dress. Wherever you go I will be beside you.' And in fact when Marie-Noël went out he placed himself at her left hand while the three policemen took up positions behind her.

Marie-Noël was taken by the policemen to the station which lay near the cemetery. There were many people there, each with a candle in his hand. They were dead. A big sergeant sat behind a desk with a corporal beside him. They had black stripes on their sleeves. They alone carried no candle. The corporal told Marie-Noël to light a candle. Marie-Noël refused and a lively argument broke out between her and the corporal. The sergeant called her before his desk and said to her, 'You will light one here.' Marie-Noël refused with heat and said, 'Even if you put a pistol to my head I'll never light a candle.' She then asked to be taken to the central police station to be judged, whereupon the sergeant asked her: 'What is your name?'

'Marie-Noël Auguste.'

'Auguste who?'

'Auguste Gustave.'

He went on like this till he had reached back to the fifth generation. Then in an outburst of rage he shouted, 'Good heavens—whenever this woman comes into my office I never manage to get her name. You can go.' Marie-Noël went out of the police station with the khaki policeman who all along had kept beside her without opening his mouth. They parted at a crossroads and she woke up. A few days later when she was asleep the god Ogu, sword in hand, appeared before her and said, 'Do you recognize me? It is me Ogu-badagri, the *nago royo* Negro, who came as a policeman in khaki uniform . . . The other policemen who came to fetch you were dead men. The man you were hauled in front of was Baron-Samedi [the god of the dead]. If you had lighted a candle you would have been lost.'

Loa appear to their servants in dreams to warn them of sorceries by which they are threatened. A woman of the Saline quarter, in Port-au-Prince, told me she had escaped being poisoned thanks to the intervention of Damballah-wèdo. She had dreamed a Mulatto advised her not to touch a dish which someone was going to offer her. And indeed on the following day she was visited by a neighbour who brought her a fine plateful of white rice. She immediately threw it out, well clear of the house. The dish was poisoned for out of it there crawled a huge, hairy, green worm.

The *loa* also appear to their servants in sleep to tell them that some favour which they asked for has been granted. I knew one devotee, the mother of a very fair-skinned baby, who said this child had 'been given her by Damballah'. Before it was born she had dreamed of a very tall, thin white man (the snake Damballa is a white god) who was holding a white baby in his arms. She said her child moved in a supple and undulating way, which proved that it was the serpent god who had sent him.

VII. THE CULT OF TWINS

Twins (*marassa*), living and dead, are endowed with supernatural power which makes them exceptional beings.[10] In the Voodoo pantheon they hold a privileged position beside the *grands mystères*. Some people would even claim that they are more powerful than the *loa*. They are invoked and saluted at the beginning of a ceremony immediately after Legba; in some regions, notably Léogane, they even come before him.

Any family which includes twins, either among its living members or in one of its ancestral lines must, under pain of 'chastisement', serve them with offerings and sacrifice. Sometimes a family reeling under a series of misfortunes learns from a *hungan* that it has been neglecting twins far back in its ancestry 'at the time of Guinea'. A child counts as a twin when it is born with webbed feet, for this is a sign that it has 'eaten' its brother in the womb.

Dead twins are deified and their spirits are as formidable as they are made out to be—quite the equal of living twins—choleric, violent and extremely touchy. There is a link between *marassa* and rain. They can foretell it and even bring it on if sufficiently wooed with offerings. The twins are represented by images of Cosmas and Damian, the martyr twins. Saint Nicholas (who brought back to life the three children which the wicked butcher put in the salting-tub) passes as their father; Saint Claire as their mother. To obtain a favour of the *marassa* it is customary to appeal to Saint Nicholas, with face turned toward the east.

Like *loa*, the *marassa* belong to different *nanchon* (nations). Hence there are 'Guinin' *marassa*—and also Dahomey, Nago, Ibo, Congo and Anmine *marassa* etc. Those born in Haiti are called 'Creole *marassa*'. Among the different categories of *marassa* some enjoy a special prestige by virtue of their close association with the *petro* spirits who confer on them a certain power for ill: these are the *marassa-bois*. Their cult differs from that of other *marassa*: food set aside for them is taken into the woods and placed in the branches of a tree. To this already extended list we must add, according to Odette Mennesson-Rigaud, the White *marassa* and the *marassa giro* who are dead twins, unbaptized.

Possessions attributed to *marassa* are rare. Those whom they do seize become like little children, 'tyrannical and capricious'. They roll on the ground, get up, walk uncertainly and ask for food. A manuscript note which M. Milo Marcelin was kind enough to give me describes a *mambo* possessed by the *marassa*:

'She had gone back to being a child. She asked for sweets in childish tones and for a bit of stuff to make a dress for her doll. To tease her, people refused what she asked; so she began to cry. She was comforted and offered a large basin full of sugar: "There—help yourself. You can eat as much as you like." She put her head on one side and rocking gently from side to side said, "No. If I eat any I'll be smacked." She was reassured; and ran to the basin, jumping with joy, and took a little cake. Someone interrupted her sharply: "Who said you could take the cake?" Terrified she put it back and falling to her knees implored: "Don't beat me. It's not my fault. I was told I could take as much as I like. Please don't beat me." Tears ran down the cheek of the possessed. Once again she was comforted and invited to stuff herself with sweets. Then she asked for a lesson book to show how advanced she was, and she began to read— humming and hawing like a very young scholar.'

The child who follows twins immediately in order of birth (the *dosu* if it is a boy, *dosa* if it is a girl) unites in its person the power of both twins and therefore can dispose of greater powers than they. 'The *dosu* is stronger than the *marassa* and stronger than the *loa*.' Hence he is treated with the greatest respect and in the event of offerings being made, he has precedence over the twins. On the other hand, the child born before twins—the *chuket* or *dosu avant*—has no great standing, though it is said of him that he 'dragged the twins after him'.

The presence of twins in a family involves its members in constant attentions and a thousand precautions. It takes very little to make a twin turn against his parents and, as is his wont, 'grip' them in the stomach—that is to say inflict serious trouble upon their intestines. It is true that twins are prepared to be punished for some fault which they have really committed, but they take cruel revenge if they think they have been unjustly treated.

The *mambo* Florémize, one of my informants, fell foul of her daughter Ti-so (little-sister) aged twelve, who was both *marassa* and *dosa* and by virtue of this combination possessed quite

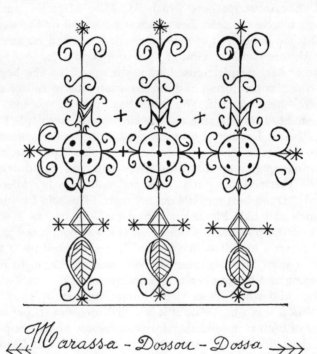

FIG. 5. The symbol (*vèvè*) of Twins (*marassa*)

exceptional powers. Her mother had punished her for some peccadillo and the child was outraged. Florémize saw that she was almost asphyxiated with rage, such was her wounded pride. Two or three days later the mother fell seriously ill. Her husband was the first to suspect the cause of her condition. The same night Florémize heard in a dream a voice saying to her: 'This illness is the result of what the *dosa* holds against you. Tomorrow morning ask Ti-so to make you an infusion and promise her a pretty dress and a cake. You'll get better straight away.' Florémize told her dream to her husband who called Ti-so and said: 'My child, is it you who are doing this to your mother?' Florémize chimed in, imploring: 'Ti-so, fetch me an infusion. Let me off, Ti-so. I'll go to Léogane and bring you back a lovely dress.' The father began to sob: 'Ti-so, you can't "hold" your mother, it's she who gave you life. Let her go for my sake, I beg you, Ti-so.' The child smiled and said: 'I'm going to prepare an infusion. If mother Mimize doesn't get up when she has drunk it then there's nothing that can make her get up.' She went off and did in fact boil some leaves and draw off a tisane which she gave her mother to drink. During the afternoon Florémize felt better but next day she was not absolutely herself. Ti-so said to her: 'What's the matter? It's time mother Mimize was able to give us something to eat.' The following day Florémize was quite better and resumed her household duties.

A worker employed at Marbial told us that he and his twin sister almost killed their mother for refusing them a dish of crabs and gomboes which their father, out of concern for their health, had advised her not to give them. The boy placed a stick in the moist earth beside a tree and each day he went and pushed it in a little further. His mother fell dangerously ill and would have died if the twins, as the result of family entreaties, had not acknowledged the wrong they were doing. They were offered a feast and a pig was killed. The two children did themselves proud—and then consented to break the spell.

On another occasion our informant made use of the same magical method, this time without his sister, against a woman who had jilted him. He only alleviated the sufferings of his victim when she offered him a kid, some syrup and bread.

More energetic action is taken against *marassa* who merely make their parents ill out of jealousy. Two twins who had cast a spell on their mother for having given a coconut to the *dosu* and none to them, were beaten with a strap until their bodies were 'pink and blue'. It was only then they owned up to their wicked intention and agreed to remove the charm.

It is normal for twins to hate each other: '*Marassa yo raisab*' (twins don't get on) is a proverbial saying. At Marbial I knew a boy Andreno and a little girl Andreni, who were twins in a large and poor family. Each of them grew with difficulty for want of adequate food; but the little girl was bigger and stronger than her brother. The parents said she was 'eating' her brother and explained that the two children had dedicated themselves to mutual hatred before they even saw the light of day. The moment she was born Andreni had tried to strangle Andreno by looping the umbilical cord round his neck—to such good effect that as he came into the world Andreno found himself 'hanged like a young goat'. Usually when twins are of different sex it is the boy who prospers, at the expense of the girl.

Twins can hardly be too carefully supervised if they are to be prevented from harming each other. As soon as one of them shows signs of failing, the other is implored to give up his criminal intention. At meals, when they are not looking, parents seize the opportunity of switching round their plates so that each eats the food of the other—which has the effect of restoring a good relationship. They also get given a dose which has the power of changing the hatred they feel for each other into affection. Such is the power of twins that no one will take any steps against one twin who causes the death of the other; indeed, people will even take care not to show him the slightest resentment.

Twins must be treated exactly alike if jealousy is to be avoided. Their clothes must be identical, their share of food equal and any praise exactly divided between them. As to twin sisters, they must be married as far as possible at the same time. If a woman with a twin brother marries, she and her husband will load him with presents to obliterate any possible resentment he may secretly feel. Even death does not break the ties which link twins together. The survivor puts to one side, for the deceased, a symbolic portion of whatever he eats or receives by way of presents. Herskovits[11] traced these practices to that belief, so widespread in West Africa, which attributes but one, shared soul to twins.

The power of *marassa* is not entirely negative. Certainly their ill-will is all the more to be dreaded for being sometimes in-

voluntary. But provided they are happy and satisfied, they turn
the strength which is in them to good account. Their intervention
is often sought on behalf of the sick; in serious cases recourse
may be had to ancestral *marassa* who, either by dream or by
medium, will prescribe appropriate remedies.

Once a year, on the day of Kings, on the Saturday before
Easter or on Christmas Day, whoever is connected with *marassa*,
living or dead, must offer them under pain of 'chastisement' a

FIG. 6. Dish and pitchers consecrated to *marassa*

manger-marassa. This sacrifice is the usual kind so we will only
touch on its main peculiarities. When a *humfo* of some importance
pays homage to all the twins worshipped in it, there may well be
as many as fifty *marassa* dishes, grouped by *nanchon*, beneath
the peristyle. Eatables and the blood of the sacrificial victims are
laid out. A usual sacrifice for the *marassa* is a brown-skinned kid
and a speckled hen. The task of distributing offerings is entrusted
to a *mambo* and must be done with great fairness so there may be
no jealousy. Taboos peculiar to each category of twins are

scrupulously observed. These are of many kinds: some will not eat such-and-such a dish, others require their food to be put on a banana leaf, others on a mat. They cannot stand the sight of knives, forks or spoons. Any mistake runs the risk of offending them and in their childish susceptibility they take cruel and sometimes quite disproportionate vengeance. Vegetables are forbidden them, it seems, in case they 'dissipate their powers'. Food offerings are buried in three holes dug near the sanctuary or family house, if that is where the fête has been celebrated.

The meal of twins ends with the same rite which sometimes terminates fêtes for the dead. The remnants of the offerings are mixed in a huge calabash or wooden basin. With this on her head a *hunsi* does the round of the peristyle three times, then, having shown it three times to the children present and asked if they are pleased with it, she abandons it to their greed. The children hurl themselves on it like so many seagulls and fight for the contents. They are warned however not to break any bones with their teeth.

If the meal prepared is for living twins, then naturally the latter are the first to eat and it is only when they are satisfied that they offer the remainder to the guests; they are saluted and people continually inquire if they have had enough. This concern for the feeling of twins is apparent in a song which is sung on such occasions:

Marassa m' apé mâde m' apé mâdé	Twins, I ask you
Sa u wé la si u kôta	Look around and say: are you satisfied
Agoé	Agoé.

Among the songs you hear in the course of this ceremony there is one which seems to reach from across the centuries like an echo of the slave lamenting his African homeland.

Marassa élo, m'pa gêñê mâmâ isit	Marassa élo, I have no mother
pu palé pu mwê	here who can speak for me
Marassa élo	Marassa élo

Mwê kité mâmâ mwê lâ péi Géléfré	I have left my mother in Africa
Marassa élo	Marassa élo
Mwê kitê fâmi lâ péi Géléfré	I have left my family in Africa
M'pa gêñê fâmi pu palé pu mwê	I have no family to speak for
Marassa élo	me
Mwê pa gêñê parâ sak palé pu mwê	I have no relations to speak for me
Marassa élo	Marassa élo.

VIII. ANIMIST BELIEFS

A number of rather vague animist beliefs are to be found floating, so to speak, in the margin of Voodoo. They seem adapted to small, very primitive tribes and do not fit into the main pattern of the Voodoo religious system. In fact they are of minor importance and give rise only to very rough and elementary rituals. The idea of a 'soul' existing in any object that moves or has life, seems an over-simple and too convenient explanation of the interplay of supernatural forces.

However, care must be taken not to confuse the word *nanm* with *âme*. The meaning which the former word has taken in Creole is much vaguer than that of the latter; *nanm* corresponds with the idea of 'spiritual essence' or 'power', or simply of 'what is sacred'. Any object that has been ritualistically consecrated possesses a *nanm*.

A soul is attributed to the sun, to the earth and to plants because they all influence man and nature. It is the *nanm* in food-stuffs which makes children grow, and *nanm*, too, which gives plants their medicinal powers. The *nanm* of plants is understood in a more personal sense than the *nanm* of other things. When the herb-doctors go to gather them, they choose a time when they think of them as being overwhelmed with sleep, and then go up to them gently so as not to aggravate the *nanm*. As they pull them up they murmur 'Get up, get up, go and cure someone who is sick. I know you're asleep but I need you.' They are careful to put a few pennies beside the main stem—to pay the soul for the effort which will be required of it. In placing this pittance the picker must say: 'I take you so you may cure so-and-so. Go and cure him immediately, for you have been paid.' When a plant dies, its soul leaves it in search of residence in something else that grows.

A woodcutter about to chop down a tree will give the trunk a few taps with the reverse of his axe, so as to warn the resident soul and give it time to get out. To be on the safe side he will even recite a prayer and invoke the Holy Ghost.

The souls of the big *mapous* (*Ceiba pentendra L.*) wander along roads at night, and their monstrous forms strike terror into the hearts of travellers. On certain nights of the year, the souls of the 'wicked plants' gather at the foot of a giant tree and hold a sort of sabbath there and discuss the crimes which they propose to commit.

In addition to the 'great soul of the earth' every field has its own spirit which assures it fertility, through action on all that grows there. The soul of the earth is not un-material. A worker in the fields, under the midday sun, can feel its presence in the form of a breeze stroking his face, and can see its shadow outlined behind it. Anyone who owns a piece of land expects its soul to increase the crop; expects also, and above all, that it should know how to resist anyone who wants to acquire it. In fact there are magic procedures which enable the envious to steal the soul of a person's garden, either for their own use or simply to cause the ruin of someone they hate. People protect themselves against these underhand dealings by digging four empty dibble-holes at each corner of a field when sowing is finished: thus any soul upon whom pressure is brought to bear, has a ready excuse, for, says he to his would-be seducers, 'How could I follow you? You can see perfectly well that sowing is not over: some dibble-holes are still empty.' Sometimes small fish are buried in a field. To the thief who tantalizes the soul with the hope of a good meal, it replies: 'I have already eaten, my father has come.'

It is the soul of rain which strengthens the soul of the soil; and this, in turn, works upon the soul of the crops. Rivers, lagoons and springs all have souls which seem to be clearly anthropo-morphic: these are 'the mistresses of the water' who are represented as beautiful, clear-skinned women with long hair.

The *nanm* of a star can be so worked upon as to make it go into a plate, but it must be replaced in the sky or your life may be forfeit. This sort of activity is 'big magic' and lies within the scope of only a few *hungan*.

The auspicious and inauspicious nature of certain days and months was explained to me as the manifestation of the soul, good or bad, inherent in the nature of any division of time. There would seem to be a difference in sex in souls connected with days: the auspicious days (Monday, Tuesday and Thursday) being feminine, the inauspicious (Wednesday, Friday, Saturday) masculine. Sunday, devoted to rest, is the only day without a soul. Friday is the day chosen by sorcerers to bring their evil designs to fruition and the day preferred by evil spirits for their sabbath.

January, March, May, July, August and October each have a 'good soul', which is not the case with the other months. December is regarded as particularly dangerous because the 'evil soul' associated with it has power of rendering amulets less efficacious. Many sorcerers pick on this period for their spells, knowing these will be more effective through having less resistance to contend with. Hence December is looked upon as the month with the highest rate of deaths due to magic causes.

From the examples cited it can be seen that the soul may either be conceived of as a spirit scarcely different in kind from a *loa*, or as an impersonal power, an active essence which belongs to the domain of magic. What the peasants understand by *nanm* is something very vague and ill-defined. We are entitled to wonder whether the word may not have been adopted by my informants as a subterfuge which always enabled them to give an answer to my questions about the causes of natural phenomena. I do not think so. Once the animist explanation is admitted in certain cases, it subsequently suggests itself whenever a need is felt to understand the properties, not only of natural objects, but also of abstract concepts such as the division of time.

No connection is made between the soul of things and the spiritual essence which every human being carries within himself. The latter is conceived of in the form of two spirits usually designated under the name of Big Good Angel (*gros-bon-ange*)—

and Little Good Angel (*ti-bon-ange*). They are visible in the shadow cast by the body which in certain lights is edged with a lighter margin. A guardian rôle is attributed by some to '*ti-bon-ange*', by others to '*gros-bon-ange*'. The latter is sometimes identified with the main dark shadow, sometimes with the paler marginal shadow which surrounds it. This double shadow is not to be confused with an ordinary shadow which is called 'corpse shadow'. A person's general condition reflects that of his *ti-bon-ange*. Even the sleepiness which comes over you on a hot afternoon reveals that your *ti-bon-ange* is in need of a siesta. Serious illnesses only take hold when your 'protector' has been overwhelmed by spirits stronger than himself or when, through weariness or any other reason, he finds himself unable to cope with an evil spell.

He is not allowed to lie. It is even very unwise to doubt his word. If having said the same thing three times he then says solemnly: 'Verily three times I've said this is true,' anyone who still remains incredulous can count on not having very long to live. Knowing the sincerity of *ti-bon-ange* some *hungan* invoke him just to find out whether the person he is protecting is telling the truth, or not. A woman who refused to give her lover any money, under the pretext that she had none, was obliged to admit that she had lied when a *hungan* summoned her *ti-bon-ange*. The latter announced straight-away that she was hiding the true state of her finances.

The *gros-bon-ange* occupies a position subordinate to that of the guardian soul. Nevertheless it is he who is responsible for the faculties of thought and feeling: for our whole affective and intellectual life, in short. He is closely connected with the body and leaves it only to wander far afield during the night. What he sees and experiences in these nocturnal excursions forms the matter of our dreams. When a *gros-bon-ange* fails to rejoin his carnal abode in the morning the person concerned sinks into a profound lethargy. The spirits sold by some sorcerers to clients are *gros-bon-anges* which they have managed to capture. They are called *zombi* but they must not be confused with the flesh-and-blood individuals—the mindless slaves of sorcerers who have stolen their souls.

IV
Ritual

I. RITUAL

It is too often assumed that Voodoo ceremonies are mysteries from which the profane are excluded. This is not the case. True, certain rites, that of initiation for instance, are veiled from the sight of the uninitiated, but services—unless tainted with black magic—take place in public. The head of a sanctuary will debar only people liable to create a disturbance or people whom he regards as enemies. Any white visitor is usually well received and has only to put up with the importunities of beggars—and sometimes of the *hunsi*. Provided he is prepared to pay a few gourdes* for the privilege of seeing an impressive spectacle, then he will be treated as a guest of honour and the *loa* will not fail to do him a few small favours.

There has for long been much amused or indignant commentary on the number of Catholic practices which are mixed in, during ceremonies, with African ritual. We shall go into them in detail in Chapter VI. On the other hand, it would seem insufficient emphasis has been placed on the influences which have affected Voodoo ritual to a lesser extent; for instance the army. The parading of flags, the play made with swords, the *aux champs* (flourish) of the orchestra were all borrowed from military life and bear witness to the chauvinistic spirit of the Haitian nation. Has Freemasonry also contributed its quota to Voodoo ceremonial? People say so. They even insist that some *hungan* are affiliated to lodges. Certain it is that in some symbolic devices of the gods masonic signs may be recognized. There are even *loa* masons, such as Agassu, Agau and Linglessu. For all this, masonic influence on Voodoo has been weak and is limited to a few superficial touches.

The originality of Voodoo lies as much in the multiplicity of

* A gourde is worth $0.20.

its social uses as in the disparity of the many different elements which it has managed to absorb smoothly. To grasp its true nature, we should remember that each ceremony is also an opportunity or pretext for profane rejoicing. Certain Voodoo society leaders, anxious to revivify the lustre of the rites they were celebrating, have striven to introduce a vein that was spectacular, almost theatrical. Evincing a genuine talent for showmanship they turned to good account the darkness, lights, fires, processions and dresses, in fact anything which would help to inspire the hearts of the poor, who frequented their *humfo*, with an illusion of magnificence and mystery.

At first sight the richness of the ritual and the respect for the traditions of 'Guinea Africa', which the priests use as their authority, might suggest that Voodoo was tainted with rigid formalism. In fact it is nothing of the kind. Considerable freedom is left to the imagination of an officiating priest and he can always set off his ceremonies with new and piquant details provided he respects the basic general scheme. Every sanctuary has its own individual style which often reflects the personality of the *hungan* or *mambo* in charge. The same ceremony can show many variants according to the region in which it takes place. In describing a Voodoo ceremony allowance should always be made for this personal factor—otherwise too general a value will be attributed to every detail, and significance seen where perhaps it does not exist.

All the various activities treated as sacred in Voodoo, form a large—perhaps too large—part of ritual. To spare the reader minute descriptions I have thought it best to separate from the mass of our observations the basic elements which together constitute what the Haitians call 'a service'. Connoisseurs of Voodoo will no doubt reproach me with many omissions, but these seemed necessary if analysis were to be kept lucid.[1]

II. THE RITUAL SALUTATIONS

The purpose of ceremonies is often obscured by the innumerable casual practices which complicate ritual. This is the case with the salutations—gestures or attitudes of the officiants which are marks of respect for each other, and for the spirits and sacred objects. Here, on the divine level, we find the same etiquette which in West Africa governs relations between social inferiors and superiors. The subtleties of this interplay are taught at initiation.

The code of manners has its nuances and these are reflected in the various gestures and positions. How, for instance does a *hunsi* greet a *mambo*? Facing her squarely, she will turn first to the right, then to the left and then again to the right. After each turn she will drop a deferential curtsey (a *cassé*) bending her knees and leaning slightly backwards. Then she will prostrate herself before the *mambo* and kiss the ground three times. The *mambo* replies to this homage by taking the *hunsi*'s hand at the moment when she gets up from the ground, and making her pirouette three times. These 'twirls' (*virés*), which have no equivalent in Africa, suggest the figures of the minuet. Since the ground is only kissed before a superior, good form demands that a person so saluted by someone only slightly his junior, should hasten to refuse such an obeisance and seize the hand of the man or woman on the point of self-prostration. Persons of equal rank go into a 'twirl' at the same moment; taking each other's hands, they turn together in such a way as to bring their foreheads and the backs of their heads alternately into contact. Another form of greeting between *hunsi* is to grip both of each other's hands, with arms crossed, and flex knees together.

If in the course of ceremonies pirouettes and prostrations become monotonous then it must be remembered that such marks of respect are not only for the dignitaries present but also for the spirits who are coming to incarnate themselves in their 'horses'. It is only right people should accord them equal courtesies so that in return they may be 'twirled' by them.

The greetings which priests exchange among themselves are of a quite indescribable complexity and loaded, in every detail, with symbolic meaning. These ritual courtesies or *gangance* are always carried out 'four-sided' (*en carré*), that is to say they must be repeated towards all four cardinal points. The *hungan* turn right round three times before facing each other. Extending their rattles they shake them for a few moments, stoop and rap them on the ground, then, walking towards each other, they take each other by the arm and turn together. When the greeting is between *hungan* and *mambo* they strike their rattles against the palm of their left hands or rub each other's hands with an undulating movement of the wrist. All movement is done in a dance-step and is followed by a triple kiss on the mouth or by a simultaneous prostration—*un baiser terre.*

Every rite has its own peculiar salutations. When two people of rank meet each other in the course of a *petro* ceremony they alternately raise their hands to the height of their eyes, then with bent arms bring their left elbows into contact, and then their right elbows. They hook the little fingers of each hand together and end with a sort of accolade in three-part-time, shoulder against shoulder.

The 'ground kiss' is carried out, not only before human beings and gods, but also before sacred objects—the threshold of the sanctuary, *poteau-mitan*, drums, *vèvè*, etc. Whenever the name of one of the *humfo*'s protecting *loa* is mentioned in prayer the *hunsi* prostrate themselves for a triple 'ground kiss', or, touching the ground with their fingers, they then raise the fingers to their lips. The same thing happens when during a prayer mention is made of *hungan*, *mambo* or the *hunsi-kanzo*. The dignitaries of the society limit themselves to a mild striking of the ground with their rattles.

Any distinguished visitor is greeted by drums rolling out the *aux champs*, a courtesy to which you are expected to reply by offering a few gourdes. These you clamp against the perspiring foreheads of the musicians or put in their mouths.

III. THE FLAG PARADE

Each sanctuary possesses at least two flags which symbolize the society attached to it. They are expensive objects, made of silk or velvet fringed with gilt and covered with glittering spangles. The embroidery is purely decorative but often includes inscriptions or the outline, in silhouette, of sacred emblems or of a

saint identified with some *loa*. The association between flags and
the army must surely be the reason why most of the flags bear an
armed and helmeted figure on a rearing horse—none other than
Ogu-ferraille under the guise of Saint James the Elder. Their
colour is red—the red of this warrior god. Their hardwood
shafts are surmounted with an ornamental, slanting S.

The flags are kept in the sanctuary, along with other objects
used in worship. They are brought out at the beginning of a
ceremony or when a 'great *loa*' possesses one of the faithful.
Also, important visitors are entitled to the honour of walking
beneath two crossed flags. When the moment comes to fetch these
flags, the flag party, which consists of two *hunsi*, goes into the
sanctuary escorted by the *la-place* waving his sword. They come
out backwards and then literally charge into the peristyle behind
their guide who is now twirling his weapon. The choir of *hunsi*
intones a hymn to Sogbo, protector of flags. The trio manoeuvres
and from the four cardinal points salutes the *poteau-mitan*, the
drums, the dignitaries of the society and finally any distinguished
guests, each according to his rank. The *la-place* and the standard-
bearers prostrate themselves in turn before them. These show
their respect by kissing the guard of the sabre, the staff of the
flag, and make the *la-place* and the standard-bearers pirouette.
The return of the standards is accomplished in a remarkable
rite: the two *hunsi*, still preceded by the *la-place* pointing his
sabre before him, run round the *poteau-mitan*, often making
quick changes of direction. This musical-ride goes on till the
la-place leads them off towards the sanctuary door through
which, having first recoiled from it three times, they pass at the
double.

IV. INVOCATION FORMULAE

For every great *loa* there exist invocation formulae and these
constitute the most singular examples of oral ritual. They are
catalogues of saints' names, surnames and odds and ends of
Creole or *langage* phrases. The use of these formulae is in line
with an African tradition: the gods of the Dahomey pantheon

are likewise greeted with stereotyped phrases the meaning of which is obscure. There is magic in these formulae and they help to make the *loa* come down. Here are two samples: '*Au nom Monsieur Damballah-wèdo-tôka-mirwazè, dâ, sa lavatyo pasa wilinò wilimê odâ kòsikòs odâ kòsikòsa odâ ayika siuka, odâ owèdo nêmê odâ misu wèdo, diêké, Damballah-wèdo têgi nêg ak-â-syel.*' Invocation to Brisé: '*Par pouvoir Brisé montagne, nèg krasé lez o, nèg krasé le mâmb, nèg kasa mâblabila kôgo, bila lûvemba,*' etc.

Probably the *langage* texts are more or less distorted phrases from Fon liturgy. Mme Comhaire-Sylvain quoted an invocation of Guédé, '*Zo wan-wé sobadi sobo kalisso*', which in Fon is the same formula as: '*zo wenne sobadi sogbo kolissou. . .*' This seems to be an appeal to the god of tombs and death for his co-operation in a criminal design. The language employed appears to be not ordinary Fon but some secret language understood by a few initiates.

V. THE LIBATIONS

In the eyes of voodooists, libations of water performed in front of the sacred objects amount to 'salutations'. At the beginning of, and several times during ceremonies, the *hungan* or *mambo*, equipped with a pitcher called the 'cooling pitcher', carries out three libations in front of the *poteau-mitan*—or four if it is done facing the four cardinal points. He then kisses the central-post three times and moves towards the drums which he greets by striking the ground with his rattle and by 'throwing' water three times. These greetings are then repeated by all the dignitaries present. The priest who has poured a libation to Legba at the entrance to the peristyle, takes care when he comes back to sprinkle a trail behind him right up to the *poteau-mitan*, so as to lure the spirits to come in and appear.

VI. ORIENTATION RITES

The different forms of salutations are not the only ritual actions to be repeated continually during ceremonies. If you watch the movements of an officiant you will see that he never picks up an object associated with the cult—be it plateful of flour, sacrificial knife, pitcher of water, chairs for dignitaries to sit on during 'Guinea prayers', kindling wood for the *boulé-zin* etc.—without quickly presenting it to the four points of the compass. This concern with orientation extends to offerings and, as we shall see, to the victims of the blood sacrifices. *Loa*—that is to say people possessed—raise the hands of those upon whom they wish to confer 'luck' four times in succession towards the sky. When a man 'orientates' an object he says 'God the Father, God the Son and God the Holy Ghost,' or '*Apo Lisa, gbadia tamènâ dabò*'. In this formula, probably Fon, the name of Lisa occurs—Lisa being the sun-god of Dahomey. No doubt some link exists between this rite of orientation and that which consists of rocking extremely heavy objects, such as the cisterns containing the water for the 'Christmas bath', three times.

VII. MATERIAL REPRESENTATIONS OF DIVINITY

Spirits revealing themselves in people to whom they lend their own customary features and mannerisms, have no need of statues or images in order to be conceived as anthropomorphous. Sanctuaries are decorated with images of saints identified with *loa*, but as I have already shown, this assimilation is entirely superficial and has scarcely affected the way in which spirits are represented to the faithful.

In Haiti it is the symbolic drawings, called *vèvè*, which fulfil the functions elsewhere devolving upon statues and images. These are traced out, according to the *nanchon* of the *loa* whose emblem the officiant wishes to represent, in flour made from corn or maize, brick-dust or powdered bark, ashes or even coffee-grounds. The procedure is as follows: the officiant takes from a plate a pinch of powder or flour which he lets slip from between his index-finger and thumb in such a way as to leave a thin regular line. Thus he traces out geometrical motifs, objects or

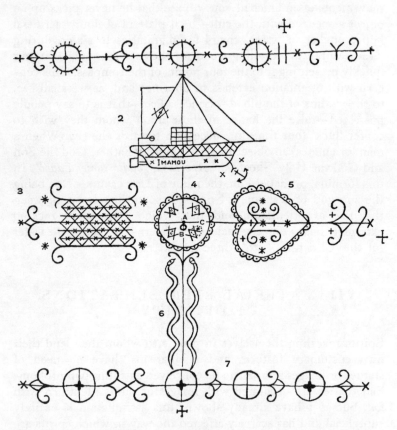

FIG. 7. The symbols of various *loa* traced on the ground during a ceremony at Croix-des-Bouquets. This combination of *vèvès* covered an area more than six yards by six yards. 1. The emblems of the drums. 2. Agwé-taroyo's *vèvè*. 3. Ogu-badagri's *vèvè*. 4. Ornaments drawn round the central post of the peristyle. 5. Ezili's *vèvè*. 6. Damballah-wèdo's *vèvè*. 7. The emblems of the drums.

A. The central post (*poteau-mitan*). B. Stone at the foot of the *poteau-mitan*. C. Dish containing flour and an egg.

animals which may cover fairly large areas. Some *vèvè*, comprising the symbols of several gods, stretch from one end of the peristyle to the other. Usually they are arranged symmetrically round the *poteau-mitan*. While they are being traced out the *hunsi* choir sings:

Vèvè-lò sé hûnsi ki fè hûngâ	Vèvè-lo it is the *hunsi* who makes the *hungan*
Hûnsi tôbé hûngâ lévé atò	Hunsi falls down, the *hungan* then gets up
Vèvè-lò sé hûnsi ki fè hûngâ	Vèvè-lo it is the *hunsi* who makes the *hungan*.

Each *vèvè* is consecrated by putting on it little piles of grilled maize and other dried foodstuffs which are sprinkled with *acassan*,* kola, rum or any other drink. Each libation is made three times over. The *hungan* shakes his rattle over the drawings, mumbling ritual formulae in *langage*. Finally a lighted candle is placed on the *vèvè*. The *hungan* and the other dignitaries of the *humfo* come in turn and 'throw' water on the outline as a form of 'salutation'.

These *vèvè* reveal the presence of the god in a tangible form. On them are laid the offerings for the *loa* and the bodies of sacrificed victims. When chalked on cult accessories, *vèvè* constitute the 'mark' of the god and are intended to establish a close link between the object and the divinity. In the *boulé-zin* ceremony each pot is placed on the symbol of whatever *loa* will be invoked during the climax of the fire ritual.

These emblematic drawings have a magical nature. Merely by tracing them out a priest puts pressure on the *loa* and compels them to appear. Their function is to summon *loa*. In order to oblige a person possessed by Damballah-wèdo to come down from the tree in which he or she has perched you have merely to trace out snakes in white flour on the ground. These are the *loa*'s symbols and if you add to them an egg dimpled into a little pile of flour, the *loa* will be irresistibly attracted by the magic of the *vèvè* and then of the offering.

---

* Soft drink prepared with maize starch and flour.

Though the *vévé* are Dahomean in origin their actual style is clearly European, as may be seen from an examination of figure 7. The scrolls and traceries recall the iron-work and embroidery motifs of the eighteenth century. French inspiration is as evident in them as it is in some of the folklore music and dances. In spite of the stylization, characteristic attributes of *loa* may be easily recognized: the sabre of Ogu, the boat of Agwé, the serpent of Damballah, the heart of Ezili, the dishes of the twins etc. The stars which may be seen round the main motif are called 'stopping points' (*points d'arrestation*) or simply 'decoration marks' (*points d'embellissement*).

Not all *mambo* or *hungan* are equally gifted in tracing *vévé*. Some show a sureness of touch and speed of execution which is absolutely prodigious. In less than half an hour they cover a space several metres square with perfectly symmetrical drawings —and this without the slightest rubbing-out.

Other objects too can symbolize *loa* and partake of their sacred nature. The mere attributes—sabre of Ogu, crutch of Legba, wrought-iron snake of Damballah, cross of Baron-Samedi—are enough to convey identity and witness a presence as clearly as any statue, though such emblems are not surrounded with the reverence which would be the due of idols. Many libations are poured out at the foot of Legba's crutches, but the latter are merely a simple accessory for the use of people possessed by that god. An iron bar can symbolize more than one god—Criminel, Lemba, Zau, Adum in particular. The big cemetery crosses or those which crop up round *humfo*, consecrated to Guédé, are probably the things which come nearest in Voodoo to tangible representation of a divinity.

The worship of 'thunder-stones' centres in Haiti—as in Africa —round old neolithic axe-heads, still plentiful in the areas once occupied by Arawak Indians, the island's first inhabitants. Failing these axes, stones of a particular shape are used. The supernatural properties attributed to these stones derive from their association with the *loa* whose power they symbolize. Hence they are called 'Stone of Ogu' or 'Stone of Brisé', whichever the case may be. On some a mirror is stuck to increase their magic powers. They must be kept in oil, otherwise they lose their powers. Their association with the *loa* gives them all kinds of abilities. They sweat when touched, or they whistle or talk. One of their special characteristics is the ability to go long journeys by themselves. It is not unusual for one of them to leave the altar where it lives and slip beneath the pillow or into the pocket of a 'servant'. One Voodooist told Lorimer Denis[2] how he found a crystalline stone on his bed and at first paid no attention to it. In fact he threw it out. But the stone came back into his room. Suddenly it turned into a snake. The man chased the animal and killed it. A few days later he fell ill and so learnt that the stone and snake were none other than Damballah.

Finally the numerous pitchers (*gòvi*) ranged on altar tables should also be regarded as so many material symbols of *loa*; these receptacles are all consecrated in a special manner and after the baptism which procures them a place among the ritual objects, they are 'dressed' in colours which symbolize the god whom they are supposed to house. In spite of the anthropomorphic appearance which this clothing gives them, they can scarcely be likened to idols. Rather should they be classed with the jars which house the dead and with the *pots de tête* which hold the hairs and nail-parings of the *hunsi*.

Among objects which derive a sacred nature from their association with *loa*, mention must be made of the *hunsi* necklaces. These are made up of china beads of various colours, alternating in groups of seven. Each *loa* has its representative colour—red for the Ogu, white for Damballah, blue for Ezili etc.—so that a mystic connection is to be presumed between the necklaces and the various gods. This, however, was vigorously denied by a *hungan*. Thinking he saw doubt and astonishment in my face, he took out his own necklace and, pointing out each colour, insisted they corresponded with *loa* who had no particular connection with him and that therefore aesthetic considerations alone had dictated the choice and disposition of the beads.

In Dahomey the necklaces are important cult accessories and are supposed to contain a spirit. Some vestige of this belief still lingers in Haiti: when a dignitary of the society fetches the *hunsi* necklaces from the sanctuary in order to serve them out, he is usually in a state of near-trance; in other words he 'has been made tipsy by the *loa*'. Spectators seeing the *hungan* select, un-hesitatingly, for each *hunsi* the necklace which belongs to her, conclude that his hand is guided by the gods themselves. This is not the case. Each necklace is specially marked in such a way as to prompt the memory of the priest or priestess.

VIII. THE SACRIFICE

All faithful worshippers must help to provide the *loa* with food—that is why Voodoo ceremonies are often called *mangers-loa*. From the attitude of Voodooists and from their opinions it may be deduced that, as in Dahomey, offerings and sacrifices 'give strength to the gods' and the more numerous and magnificent the sacrifices, the more powerful the gods will become.

The blood sacrifice is the climax of the series of Catholic or pagan rites which make up what is called a 'service'. Seldom are the gods approached without being offered at least a chicken. In the course of *mangers-loa* it is not only chickens which are immolated in great numbers but also goats and bulls and in the case of *loa* of the *petro* family, pigs. Beneath a complex exterior the Voodoo sacrifice follows the classical pattern of immolation rites. The latter tend to concentrate in an animal sacred powers which are liberated by its being put to death.

Is the person who performs the sacrifice bound to go through preliminary rites of purification, and practise certain abstentions? On this point I possess no other information than that which was supplied to Jacques Roumain[3] by the *hungan* Abraham in con-nection with the 'sacrifice of the *assoto* drum'. On the eve of the ceremony the officiating priest, he tells us, must 'take a special bath to which are added pure milk, cinnamon, star-anise, *fleurs pectorales* roses, jasmine and anis flowers called *trois paroles*. Then he must sprinkle himself with holy water and carry out a fumigation with incense and benzoin laurel. He dries himself in the open air since he must not touch himself with a towel. In addition *hungan* and *hunsi* are bound to practise strict sexual abstinence before the ceremony.' All this preparation before sacrifice does not seem to be a general rule and, like many other details furnished by Abraham, could represent merely an ideal of conduct, seldom practised.

The choice of victim depends on precise conditions familiarity with which is part of priestly science. The animal is only acceptable to the god if it suits his tastes and if it embodies some of his own qualities. It would be tedious to list all the various preferences attributed to each spirit or group of spirits. Let us mention just a few examples: black pigs are set aside for the *petro loa*, guinea fowl for the Ibo, turkeys for the Kaplau-ganga, dogs for the Mondongue. As far as possible the dress or the plumage of the victim should be the *loa*'s own symbolical colour. Thus white animals are offered to water spirits (Damballah-wèdo, Agwé, Simbi, Clermerzine, etc.), black to the Guédé, spirits of the dead, russet or red to the Ogu. Speckled hens are kept for Brisé and some of the other *petro loa*.

Nothing that is concerned with sacrifice, either closely or remotely, is exempt from ritual. Indeed the very type of wood for the stake to which the victim is attached and the details of the ceremony for consecrating this stake, are all prescribed by ritual.

The consecration of the victim is carried out by degrees and continues right up to the moment of death. These steps towards sanctification we shall now describe. First comes the victim's ceremonial bath: head, neck and feet (sometimes only the latter) are washed with a scented infusion of *mombin* leaves. The beast is then dried with a spotless towel, liberally perfumed and sometimes even powdered.

Bulls and goats are 'dressed' in a pall of silk or velvet, the colour being suitable to the *loa* to whom they are destined, and as a 'head-dress' wear a cloth tied to the base of the horns. Those who persist in regarding Voodoo as a form of sorcery read a satanic meaning in the lighted candles which are normally fixed on to the horns of goats; in fact these candles merely affirm the semi-divine nature of the victim. It is customary in Voodoo to light some kind of candle whenever you get in touch with the *loa*. The animal thus accoutred is *croix-signé* (cross-signed), that is to say marked on the back with trails of dried food (grilled maize, bits of cassava etc.) and various liquids (water, syrup, rum or coffee) spread out into crosses.

The act of killing is always preceded by a rite which is akin both to Communion and divination. The victim can only be put to death if it has first eaten some food and drunk some liquid of a sacred nature. If it refuses this, then it will be understood to have refused its death and thus, being unacceptable to the divinity, should be replaced by another victim. Chickens which undergo this test are stationed near little piles of food which have been placed on the *vèvè* representing the god. Their greed is further tempted by bits of maize or cassava floating in a glass of water ('Guinea water'). When the victim is a goat or a bull, his muzzle is teased with a tuft of Guinea grass, or branch of *mombin*, a plant possessed of purifying powers and supposed to have come from Africa. Sometimes an attempt is also made to make the beast drink some 'Guinea water'.

As soon as the animal has eaten or drunk, it becomes the property of the *loa* and partakes of his divine nature. Usually, exactly at this moment, the person who is to perform the sacrifice and often several spectators as well, become possessed by the *loa* to whom the animal is to be sacrificed. By appearing thus the god intimates his readiness to accept the offered victim.

The people offering the sacrifice, having established as close a link with the god as possible, are anxious to absorb the beneficent effluvia, with which the animal is now impregnated, by establishing as close a link with it as possible. If it is a goat, they carry it in turn on their backs and dance with it. Sometimes members of the *humfo* society kneel, in order of rank, in front of the victim and taking it by the horns rub their foreheads against its own forehead, three times over, and then kiss the ground in front of it three times as a sign of respect. This participation in the sacred nature of the victim can be taken as a total identification of the people performing the sacrifice with the creature sacrificed. Thanks to the kindness of M. Kurt Fischer, I acquired a copy of an anonymous document which describes the sacrifice of a goat in the north of Haiti. The details are all the more interesting because they explain the bewildering scene described by W. H. Seabrook in his *Magic Island*. Seabrook says he witnessed a sacrifice in which a woman and a goat changed rôles, that is to say at the moment when it was being immolated the animal groaned like a human being and the woman bleated like an animal. There we have a highly romanticized version of a rite whereby the person making the sacrifice is symbolically assimilated to the victim. In the case which concerns us the sacrifice is supposed to be offered by a woman. She is led to the foot of an altar where she is greeted by an officiant who embraces her tenderly and weeps just as though she must soon die. He gives her rum to drink and the woman in sudden despair revolts against her fate. Nevertheless she kneels before the altar and her head is done up in a sort of turban just as is the goat's. In plaintive tones she sings, '*Kabrit marô chaché. Chimê kayli. Mwê mâdé li, sa li gêgnê. Na Giné tut mun malad. Mwê pa malad m'pralé muri.*' (The wild goat which escaped is trying to find the way home. I wonder what's the matter. In Guinea everyone is ill. I am not ill. I am going to die.)

The goat and the woman making the sacrifice are placed in front of each other and look into each other's eyes. The man who is to perform the sacrifice puts a leafy branch between the animal's muzzle and the woman's mouth which are so close together that their breath intermingles. The woman pulls the leaves away from the animal who is about to munch them; she says 'God be praised'.

The woman kneels again in front of the altar. The priest puts his hand on her head and recites the formula: '*In nomine Patris et Filii et Spiritus Sancti.*' Then he pours wine, oil and water on her hair and whitens her eyelids with flour. The woman then eats the food and drink on the altar. The goat has its throat cut and with its blood a cross is traced on the forehead of the woman and she is given three mouthfuls of it to drink.

Another means of entering into contact with the sacrificial victim is to ride it. Here is a description of what I saw last year at a *petro* service which took place at a settlement on the road to Kenskoff. 'A woman staggers, hangs on to the *poteau-mitan*, then collapses. She lets herself fall, with arms dangling, on to the neck of a little black bull tied to the *poteau-mitan*. Other people possessed come up to the bull and stroke it in a loving manner. The *hungan* says a few Catholic prayers and goes round the victim shaking his rattle. Water from a pitcher is poured over the

bull's back and the *hunsi* catch it in their hands and rub it on
their faces. A big girl jumps on to the back of the little bull with
all the appearance of ecstasy; she rides it and shakes her shoulders
in time to the rhythm of the drums. Another girl follows her and
both remain, jigging up and down, on their mount. A man
possessed by the *loa* Bakulu sits on the withers of the bull and
lying along its neck, grasps its muzzle which he then sucks for
some time. Then he slides along the animal and embraces it
again, hanging on to its head. Next he stretches out on its back
and presses his lips to its rump. Thus he remains for a few minutes,
his whole body shaken by tremblings. Another person possessed
lifts the bull's tail and embraces its buttocks or anus—I don't
know which. An old peasant, likewise possessed by Bakulu,
unravels the hairs on the bull's tail and uses it on his face like a
shaving brush. The *hungan* launches the song "*Béñê béñê
susu . . .*" (Wash, wash, susu). Men and women crowd round
the bull and rub it with their hands as though soaping it. They
lead it several times round the peristyle singing at the top of their
voices "*Béñê susu*" and rubbing its back for all they are worth.'

This same rite when done with chickens is called *passer poule*
(it must not be confused with *ventaillage* which merely consists
of waving the birds in the air or crossing them in front of the
body with one large, generous, sweeping movement). Contact
between the victims-to-be and devotees is effected by the
sacrificer, who, holding one bird by the legs in each hand, walks
them in turn or at the same time, along the head, the back, the
flanks and the chest of the person bowed before him.

The *passer poule* brings luck, but is also part of the scapegoat
rite. If the officiant knows that among the faithful before him
there are some who are ill, he will touch with the chickens whatever parts of their bodies are afflicted. This action suggests he
intends to permeate the patient with the effluvia which earlier
ceremonies have accumulated in the sacrificial victims: but
since, when the operation is finished, the officiant shakes out his
chickens like dusty feather-dusters, we may equally suppose he
has accomplished a rite of expulsion.

This last interpretation agrees with another, which was given
me by a *hungan*. 'The *passer-poule*,' he said, 'takes away bad luck.'

The victim is then 'orientated', in other words presented to the supernatural powers of the four 'sides' (*façades*) of the universe. The sacrificer raises the fowl with a swift and sometimes even a merely sketchy movement, four times. When the animal is a goat the rite is not so simple: having stripped it of its 'robe' and head-dress the two assistants take it by the horns and feet and 'swing' it three times towards each cardinal point. After each orientation they touch the ground three times with its back, then carry it round the *poteau-mitan* at the double, first in one direction then in the other. Finally they run out of the peristyle and, stopping before the doors of the different 'chapels' they raise the victim as though to present it to the gods. Then, zigzagging across the *humfo* court they come quickly back under the peristyle.

Before immolating chickens it is customary first to break their wings and legs. Death is usually inflicted by pulling their heads off with a quick, twisting movement. Some sacrificers whirl the body of the bird until the head comes off in their hands. For *petro loa* the throat must be cut with a knife. At the moment of sacrifice the tongue or even the windpipe is often torn out with the teeth and these parts are then offered up separately. In order to realize full union between the victim and the supernatural powers, its limbs are sometimes broken against the *poteau-mitan*. Often, too, the officiant sucks the bird's bleeding neck. After the sacrifice a few breast feathers are plucked and stuck on to the *poteau-mitan* with blood, or on to the edge of the altar or on to the rim of the sacred jars.

Just as chickens are mutilated before being put to death, so goats have their beards and testicles cut off a few moments before having their throats cut. Hair and organs are placed on the altar or on the *vèvè* after the priest and *hunsi* have sucked the testicles. The sacrificer 'orientates' the knife before using it and if he is painstaking he will make three feints before piercing the throat. Sometimes, too, he traces a cross with the point of his knife on the victim's back. Very often the sacrificer is possessed by the *loa* to whom the animal is dedicated at the moment of immolation; in this way it is the *loa* himself who cuts the throat of his own victim.

Michel Leiris[4] was present at the sacrifice of a bull by a *hungan* in the Plaine du Cul-de-Sac. His description is so precise and detailed that I shall give an extract here:

'The bull is brought close (till now it has been kept a few yards from the peristyle, to the right and rather to the rear); it is reddish brown, its back is covered with a pink or crimson pall and a cloth of the same colour is wrapped round its horns. It is tied to the *poteau-mitan* and a very old woman . . . comes out and dances in the centre of the peristyle. Before long she is staggering, "tipsified" and gives vent to a few brief shrieks; she has been seized by Ogu-badagri. She goes on to perform libations with rum and syrup and spreads out bits of food on the bull's back. She pours "Three-star Barbancourt" over his head and raising his jaws by sheer force puts the bottle into his mouth and so makes him drink: the rum trickles down the bull's fetlock. Then the old woman, bottle in hand, puts her back against the bull's right flank and leans backwards against him, in an attitude of triumph. She remains like this for a moment and then returns to the space between the *poteau-mitan* and the *hunsi* and has a good long drink herself from the mouth of the bottle.

'Kissing of the earth by all *hunsi* positioned in a half-circle round the bull.

'During the consecration of the bull, standard-bearers and *la-place* race from the peristyle to the "barrier" and return running to the peristyle.

'The bull is freed from his finery; he is set loose and a halter is put round his neck. The low wall has two openings, one near the entrance, the other on the far side of the orchestra; it is by this latter that the bull, like the goat, was brought in, and now by the former (when it has been cleared of people) that he is quickly led out, drawn by the halter and followed by a procession including the *la-place*, the two *hunsi* standard-bearers and a number of the congregation, of which I was one.

'The bull, which is made to run, is escorted by several men. The procession disperses over the courts in a wild rush with much fooling, laughter and general din. After a few minutes of complete confusion the bull may be seen still running, pulled along, and being taken clear of the houses; the whole procession, *la-place* and standard-bearers in the van, run along behind him. In this way a field of sugar-cane is passed and an uncultivated area reached. On one side is a big tree, on the other a building. Having looked for and found the right spot in the bull's neck a man drives in the blade of his matchet, almost vertically, behind the horns, slightly behind where matadors place the thrust called the *descabello*. The bull falls, as though struck by lightning. The base of his throat is then deeply cut into with a knife. The blood flows over the ground.'

The blood of victims is collected in a calabash containing salt, ashes, syrup or rum. Care is taken to prevent coagulation by stirring it with a stick. The officiant and sometimes all the *hunsi* in turn drink a spoonful of warm blood. I remember often seeing Lorgina dip her fingers in the blood, taste it and then dab it on the lips of her *hunsi*. Sometime she traced a bloody cross on their foreheads or mouths. The blood of sacrificed animals, with cinnamon, star-anise, nutmeg and other spices added, is made into a strange beverage called *migan*. A spoonful of this is given to each member of the family celebrating the service. The rest is kept for ceremonies of a magical nature.

The body of the victim is put on the *loa*'s *vèvè* where it is again 'cross-signed'. All present come up and throw money into a plate. This is either distributed among the cooks or buried along with other offerings in a ditch. The sum given to the cooks is not strictly speaking a payment for their services. It is intended to make it possible for them to make offerings or libations to their own *loa* who would otherwise resent their having neglected them in favour of rival deities.

The cutting up of victims is a rather dangerous operation. It releases dangerous powers against which it is as well to protect yourself in advance. When the victims have been cooked, the pieces for the *loa* are put out on the altar and then buried in a ditch or thrown to the four cardinal points. The bones of the victims are sometimes buried separately or hung in the branches of the *arbres-reposoirs*.

A *loa*'s portion of the sacrifice is determined by rules which are not fully known. One example will be sufficient: when a goat is sacrificed the *loa* Linglessu is entitled to the ends of the tongue and the ears as well as to the front feet and the extremity of the tail. Any meat set apart for him must not be cooked with salt.

IX. OFFERINGS

A 'servant' seldom communicates with *loa* without first inviting them to eat something which he knows they like. Ritual meals are made up in accordance with traditional Haitian recipes, but the kind of dishes, the way of preparing and serving them, must follow exact rules which it would be dangerous to ignore; in culinary affairs the *loa* are hard to please. The choice of foods, and the method of preparing them, are often determined by the symbolic attributes and the character of a *loa* or by the group to which he belongs.

All these ritual minutiae would provide enough matter for a treatise on ritual cookery, but we shall limit ourselves to mentioning a few recipes.

Foods—meat, tubers, vegetables—prepared for Legba, must always be *boucanés*, that is to say grilled on a fire. A cock sacrificed to him is cut in four quarters and prepared without removing the crest or feet of which only the nails and spurs are pared off. It is regarded as important not to break any bones. These dishes sprinkled with oil are served up in a red calabash.

Foods prepared for the white *loa*—Damballah, Ezili, Agwé, Grande-Bossine etc.—must be as far as possible of that colour. An example of this may be seen in the following menu of a *manger* offered to mistress Ezili: rice cooked in milk, greengage jam, cinnamon milk, fried egg, bananas fried in sugar, maize biscuit, mangoes and a glass of water.

Each *loa* has his favourite drinks. We have already mentioned the very pronounced taste of members of the Ogu family and of the Nago *loa* for rum and *clairin* (white rum). Ezili being a white *loa* and 'a woman of the world' has a fondness for pale and sugary drinks. Nearly all *loa* like to quench their thirst with coca-cola or any of those sugary kola drinks of which the Haitians consume such a lot.

The way in which offerings are presented to the divinity is

similarly prescribed by ritual. Each of the main *loa* worshipped in a sanctuary owns a large calabash (*assiette de Guinée*), painted in his own colour and decorated with his emblems and in this he is served with the foods donated to him. The Ibo *loa*, for instance, get their *manger* in an oblong dish called *ékuey ibo* (*écuelle des Ibo* —Ibo basin) and they are summoned by a special rhythm which is beaten out with a rod on the edge of this receptacle. According to the *loa*'s group and the circumstances, offerings not eaten by the faithful are either buried, thrown away at random or left at a crossroads.

When a person possessed eats food prepared for the god who is lodged in him, then it is the god, and not he, who is supposed to get the benefit.

While the food for the great *loa* is being arranged on a table or at the feet of the guests, the *hungan* goes round the house, scattering far and wide grilled maize, peanuts and bits of cassava for the little *loa* and the dead, wandering on the outskirts. Like the other *loa* they have been drawn by the songs and drumming, but being poor and often sickly they do not dare come in under the peristyle. They too are hungry. Were they forgotten they might take revenge. For even a weak and humble *loa* becomes dangerous when irritated.

Among the offerings are to be found foods and drinks not specifically for the consumption of the gods and spirits but possessing intrinsic virtues of a kind that justifies their inclusion in rites of consecration. Among the sacred foods in this category there is one—a mixture of grilled maize, peanuts, bits of cassava and bread—which is arranged in little piles on the *vèvè* and spread over sacrificial victims. The *manger-dyò* or *manger sec* which is served in calabashes alongside other foods consists of yams, sweet potatoes, pumpkins and other tubers raw and cut-up.

X. MUSIC AND DANCE

The drum[5] on which the rhythms are beaten out for the dances symbolizes Voodoo. 'Beating the drum' in popular speech has come to mean 'celebrating the cult of the *loa*'. Whenever the

State has tried to suppress paganism it has begun by forbidding the use of the drum. That the drummer himself may be only a professional musician, not even initiated, is neither here nor there: he remains the linch-pin of every Voodoo ceremony. The fervour and concentration of the dancers and a general nervous tension conducive to trance depend upon his mastery of rhythm and upon the vitality of his touch. A musician who has not got all the rhythmic formulae at his finger tips will certainly throw dances into confusion and directly hamper the epiphanies of the *loa*. On the other hand a talented drummer can induce or terminate possessions at will.

The *tambouriers* (drummers) are endowed not only with a delicate sense of rhythm and a vast musical memory but also with exceptional nervous stamina. For nights on end they make their instruments speak with a passionate violence which at times attains frenzy. To see them with their eyeballs turned back, their faces taut, to hear the rattling gasps in their throats you might easily suppose them to be possessed. But their delirium is not the work of a god. In fact only very seldom are drummers possessed by *loa*.

Their talent is all the more admirable when you consider that Voodoo orchestras are polyrhythmic and each musician is striking an instrument of a different pitch from that of his neighbour and developing his own theme which must nevertheless fit in such a way as to give an impression of over-all unity. In addition to a knowledge of rhythmic formulae he must also have an enormous repertoire of Voodoo songs and be capable—as soon as the choir leader intones the first bar of a song—of following on at once with the rhythm which belongs to it.

Such virtuosity is not merely the expression of innate gifts but also the fruit of a long apprenticeship. During ceremony intervals it is not unusual to see a little boy go up to a drum with a look of grave concentration and start beating it after a fashion. Sometimes a drummer comes and guides his inexpert fingers and teaches him a simple rhythm which the child repeats under the approving eyes of the congregation. Thanks to small encouragements like this, children gradually develop their talent until the day they feel ready to take their place in an orchestra. An opportunity for young people of showing their skill in public occurs at the end of ceremonies when the exhausted professional drummers go to bed. The apprentice musicians then take over the instruments and play for the last dancers till dawn. To be a good *tambourier* is a lucrative profession but above all it is a means to fame and honour. Some members of this profession have acquired an international reputation.

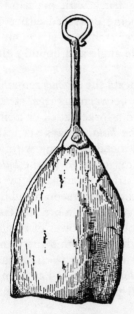

FIG. 8. *Ogan*, or iron bell, with its clapper on the outside (Musée de l'homme, No. 50.29.1).

As we have already shown, the difference between the main rituals is reflected in the diversity of the rhythms and in the form, or even the kind, of instruments which belong to them. We shall first examine the latter. The drums assigned to the cult of *rada loa* take after the typical drums of Dahomey; their shell, carved from the trunk of a tree, is in the shape of a truncated cone; the head—bullock or goat skin—is stretched by means of pegs braced with cords. They are usually painted in bright colours that symbolize the patron god of the sanctuary.

Rada drums are never played by themselves but always in groups of three. Identical in shape, they differ in size—the biggest, the *adjunto* or *manman*, being more than a yard long; the second (*ségond*) occupies a middle position between the big óne and the *bula*, the height of which varies from forty to fifty centimetres. Each of these drums is beaten in a different way; the *manman* is struck with the hand and a small wooden hammer, the blow being delivered either on the rim or on the drumhead. The player stands or sits behind the drum which is kept at a considerable angle and bound either to his body or his chair with a rope.

The person who beats the *ségond* remains seated with the instrument held firmly between his legs, striking it either with his left or right hand and a forked stick or a small bow (*agida*) held in the free hand. The *bula*, always vertical, is struck with two sticks. The *ogan* is a metal bell rung with an iron rod: this it is which sets the rhythm, followed by the *bula*, the *ségond* and the *manman*. The orchestra is dominated by the *manman*. In the rhythm of the latter there is a freedom and intensity which stands out clearly from the sonorous, more regular, background and to its voice people attribute the power of bringing down the *loa*. In fact the musician who plays this instrument can, by sudden changes of beat and ingenious *feints*, induce trance in dancers who are avoiding a *loa*'s hold. It has been said of the *manman* that, within the total percussion, it is 'what song is to accompaniment'.

Drums used in the ritual of the *petro loa* go in pairs; they differ from the ones just mentioned in size (they are smaller) and particularly in the Y-shaped attachment of the cords. The bigger of the two is called *manman* or *gros baka*, the other *pititt* or *ti-baka*. The latter has the more important rôle. It is struck with the flat of the hand. The grave tone of the *manman* is called *ralé*; the slighter sound of the *pititt*, *taille*.

The Congo orchestra consists of three drums of different sizes called *manman*, *timebal* and *ti-congo*. In their cylindrical shape, double heads and method of head-attachment they are remarkably like European drums of which they may be merely copies. The head tension is obtained by two wooden rings. Unlike the other drums which are positioned vertically or sloped, the *timebal* is kept horizontal on a chair or some other support. It is played with sticks. A small board is often fixed to its casing and this serves as a percussion instrument. It is the *timebal*, people say, which gives the true Congo music, the other drums being merely there to back it up with *crié* and *ralé*.

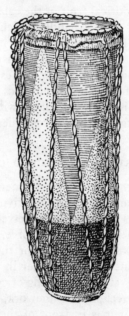

FIG. 9. *Petro* drum

The *djuba* or martinique drum only appears in a religious ceremony when the peasant god Zaka demands, via the mouth of someone possessed, that the dance which goes by the same name, *djuba*, be danced for him. The *djuba* is a small cask; it has only one head which is attached as on the *petro* drums. Two musicians can play it at the same time, one striking the skin with his hands the other striking the casing with sticks.

The cylindrical Ibo drums are related to the *petro* but their heads are attached in a different way since they have to be made of sheepskin. This is pierced with a series of holes through which strings are passed and laced through other holes arranged along the base of the instrument.

Sometimes in the north of Haiti large calabashes take the place of the drums and these are struck with thimbled fingers.

Dance rhythms, notably those of the *petro* rites, are beaten out with a rattle, the *chacha* which unlike the *asson* of the *hungan* is made from the cylindrical fruit of the calabash tree (*Crescentia cuyete*) and furnished with a handle which crosses it from one side to the other. The beads with which it is filled make a metallic sound when it is shaken. It is usually decorated with engraved or painted pictures and sometimes covered with a piece of stuff. It is used for both sacred and profane music. The marine conch (*lambi*) is rarely associated with worship. None the less it is sounded during certain ceremonies and at wakes.

THE DRUM AS A SACRED OBJECT

The drum is not only a musical instrument, it is also a sacred object and even the tangible form of a divinity. The mysterious power with which it is endowed is conceived of either as a *nanm* (soul), a sort of vaguely defined life-force, or as a spirit called *huntò*, a Dahomean word used also for the big *manman* drum and the man who beats it. If the order in which the *sacra* of a sanctuary are 'saluted' at the beginning of ceremony is any guide to their position in the religious framework, the highest rank then goes to the drums, for it is in front of them that people pause first and only afterwards in front of the *poteau-mitan* even though this is the very symbol of the peristyle and the pathway of the *loa*. Time and again in the course of ceremonies, *hungan* and *mambo* will kiss the ground in front of the drums and pour out libations to them. Like all divinities the drums need men to renew their energy and strength. Sacrifices and offerings to the drums are part of the ritual obligations of Voodoo societies and constitute a ceremony known as 'putting the drum to bed' (*coucher tambour*), or *bay manger tambour* (feeding the drums). The instruments are placed on banana leaves near the *vèvè* which represent them symbolically. They receive offerings of food and libations; chickens are sacrificed to them. *A propos* this ceremony, M. Rigaud[6] makes a very interesting observation (though it needs checking): 'The drums are put to bed to the sound of *bohun*—that is to say funeral songs. The congregation affects great sadness, for this music is announcing the departure of the drums across the sea—to Africa where they will renew their powers and then return.'

The making of a drum is accompanied by rites and precautions which foretell its sacred nature and which, at the same time, help to augment its supernatural quality. In fact the early ceremony endows it with a *nanm*. Even before the axe has cut down the tree from which the drum is to be shaped, the *hungan* celebrates a 'ceremony of adoration' to the *loa* who will answer its call when the instrument is finished. In the hollowed-out trunk rum is burnt.

Particular reverence is shown for the first hole made—for the peg called *manman* which occupies a privileged position. The fastening-on of the drumhead is accompanied by pious formulae and ritual movements. Before drums are absorbed into the business of worship they are consecrated with special baptism. For this occasion they are arrayed in 'robes' the colours of the *loa* and then a *père-savane* gives them a name in the presence of godfathers and godmothers. These Catholic rites are followed by a second ceremony, according to the traditions of 'Guinea',[7] conducted by a *hungan*.

No drum is so sacred as the huge *assoto*, a veritable monster more than six foot high, which is only beaten on solemn occasions. Most of the *assoto* disappeared during the anti-superstition campaign. I have only seen one—in a *humfo* where it had a special room to itself. It was 'dressed'—that is to say covered with a white robe which gave it a vaguely human appearance. The Bureau of Ethnology of Port-au-Prince has an *assoto* which is certainly very old. It has been described by Jacques Roumain in the excellent monograph which he devoted to its ritual consecration. The drawing shown in figure 10 was taken from a photograph in that work.

Jacques Roumain's monograph, so rich in details of Voodoo

ritual, is unfortunately not based on personal observations but upon the description of a ceremony which the *hungan* Abraham would have celebrated had he been able to.

The sacrifice of the *assoto* drum comprises a whole assortment of ceremonies in honour of various *loa*, the general pattern of which is standard so I need not describe them. Instead I will

FIG. 10. *Assoto* drum, from Cabaret, to the north-west of Port-au-Prince (Museum of the Bureau of Ethnology, Haiti, SEM 100).

merely cull from Jacques Roumain's work the parts which concern the worship of the *assoto* drum.

So sacred an essence is attributed to this drum that it could almost be called an idol or a fetish. It must be hewed from kinds of wood laid down by tradition, particularly from *mahaudème*

(*Ochroma pyramidalis* cav.) 'wood which has much blood'. It must be cut in the full moon and the membrane which covers it must be laid as midday is striking. The first ceremony which the *assoto* undergoes is the baptism which must 'install the soul'. Seven, or three times seven, godfathers and godmothers are selected for this ceremony. Here is the song sung on this occasion:

Asòtò micho	Assoto micho
N'a po rélé ja	We call Jean
Jâ asòtò n'a po rélé	Jean Assoto we call you
Pu nu batisé tabu asoto	So we may baptize the assoto
D'yé li Pè, Dyê li Fi,	God the Father, God the Son,
Dyé li Sê Espri	God the Holy Ghost
Aprè Bô Dyé m'ap batisé	After the good God I baptize you
U sòti nâ Giné	You left Guinea
U vini wè kéol-la yo	To come and see the Creoles
Nu kôtâ wè, Asòtò micho	We are glad to see you, Assoto Micho
M'ap batisé Asòtò	I baptize you Assoto.

After ceremonies in honour of different *loa*—Legba, Ayizan, Loco, Ogu—a black or a white goat or more often still a russet coloured ox (*boeuf rada*) is sacrificed to the drum. The animal is put to death according to a subtle ritual, and with its blood the *hungan* traces a cross on the *assoto* which is then beaten alternately by seven *hunsi* dancing round it. If any of them misses her turn to beat a member of her family will die.

The ceremony ends with the 'sending back of the spirit' of the *assoto*. As we have so far had no opportunity of describing the rites by which a spirit is at one and the same time appeased and driven out, we shall follow Jacques Roumain's text[8] as closely as possible. 'The *hungan* mixes some cooked and some raw food in a basket; adds victuals, needles, cotton, linen, pipe, tobacco, matches, plates, spoons, knives, forks, small change, all sorts of blood known as *tchiman-assoto*. All members of the family sign a paper witnessing that they have offered something to the *assoto* to eat and have sent him away until the next ceremony, owing him nothing more. This document is put in the basket.

'At midnight a good strong man is chosen to accomplish the

actual send-off. The *hungan* rubs his limbs with a magic oint-
ment and puts a special powder in his nose to protect him from
the 'evil spirit' of the *assoto*. His clothes are turned inside out.
Three times the basket is alternately put down and raised.
Finally it is balanced on the head of the strong man and all the
congregation sing.

'The drums beat mournfully. The sacred rattles are sounded
with intensity. It is the *rumblé*. The *hunsi* weep with lowered
heads. There is great sadness, for it is a god.

'A whip is cracked three times behind the strong man. Thus
is he sent off. He goes and throws his sacred burden into the sea
or into the depths of a wood. A certain sum of money has been
paid him because he is thought to run a serious risk. The send-off
rite is finished.

'The ceremony continues with songs and dances. Many are
possessed by *rada loa*. The *assoto* is beaten alternately by seven
hunsi until—with a special stick with a nail in the end—its
diaphragm is burst.'

SONGS

All dances and even the main ritual acts are accompanied by
songs. These are short musical compositions sometimes with a
melody that is European though sung rather stridently. They
are 'launched' by the *hungenikon* who, rattle in hand, fulfils the
function of choirmaster and intones the first strophes which the
hunsi choir takes up in unison.

The many quotations from song texts which sprinkle this work
will suffice to give an idea of their style and content. They are
often short invocations to supernatural beings or brief descriptions of what the officiant is doing, added to a nominal roll of the
loa for whom the ceremony is being held. Here for instance, is a
song which is intoned at the moment when food offerings are
being prepared:

> I am making ready a meal for the Twins of Guinea
> O—may they come!
> I am making ready a meal, it is for the dead, agoé
> I am making ready a meal, it is for the Saints.

Come eat this food
Rada, Mondongue, Don Petro, Mussondi, Ammine
Come, come and eat this food,
Motokolo, the earth is shaking, where are you?

Judging by their wide diffusion most of the songs heard during
ceremonies belong to a repertoire of long ago; though a contemporary incident, connected with the intervention of a spirit,
can also give birth to a new song full of allusions to the circumstances which inspired it. At Marbial I had an opportunity of
attending the improvisation of a religious song; a woman possessed by Zaka, who was on her way to Marbial market, came and
asked alms of me. Dancing all the time, she made up a song for
the occasion and kept repeating it: it told of her 'nudity', of a
curé who was hostile to us, and of the power of the *loa Zaka*. The
theme of her nakedness and of our quarrel with this clergyman
got so mixed up that the text of this song would have been quite
incomprehensible to anyone not acquainted with the niceties of
the whole situation. There is no doubt that in this way were born
many of the Voodoo songs which, through obscurity or insigni-
ficance, put us on false scents. The unknown artist who made
them up managed to impose them on the *hunsi* of his sanctuary;
their subsequent diffusion was due either to the prestige of a
particular sanctuary, or to their intrinsic musical merit, which the
profane cannot easily assess.

Interpretation of these songs is often complicated by the
difficulty of knowing whether they express the sentiments of the
faithful or if they are supposed to be the words of the god. Within
the same melody the utterances of the *loa* and of the human
heart can alternate without any clue being given as to when a
change of subject took place. Little attention is paid to what the
words mean. Many are incomprehensible, particularly when the
song contains passages in '*langage*'. *Hungan* and *mambo* make no
attempt to hide their embarrassment when asked to interpret
them. They get out of it by making things up. What is most
important in ceremonies is the celebration of *loa* by song and
dance and not by phrases, often meaningless, foolish or absurd,
which merely serve as vehicle for the vocal music. Nevertheless

some of these songs are far from being insignificant; some of them have a certain lyric power which they owe to unexpected imagery or even to the simplicity with which they proclaim the attributes of the *loa* whom they celebrate. In its very bareness the account of some state or action of a god takes on a certain religious majesty.

In spite of their impoverished content some songs formulate a moral judgement in an elliptical way as might a proverb. They are even used in quarrels and arguments; a *hunsi* or a *mambo* will begin chanting the song which has a bearing on a situation emphasizing the verses which express her thought. Thus at the time of a quarrel between the *hungan* Tullius and his rival Joseph, the former only agreed to make it up after the *hunsi* had intervened, all singing to him in turn a hymn about harmony and the forgiveness of injuries.

Many of the liturgical songs originate from a *chant point*, that is to say a satirical song improvised during some ceremony by someone possessed. These songs are taken up by the choir who memorize them and if they are in some way exceptional, either for their malice or their knack of sententiousness, they will be adopted and sung again in honour of the same *loa*. The following song was quoted to me as an example of a *chant point* composed by a loa:

> *Z-âmi lwê sé ajâ séré*
> *Z-âmi pré sé kuto dé bò*
> (Friends far away are like money laid on one side, friends near are knives which cut both ways, they can help you and harm you too.)

These songs are no different from those improvised during communal work by the *samba* or *simido*. Repeated in chorus by the workers, they, too, are inspired by small incidents of country life and are usually meaningless for those not 'in the know'.

DANCES

Dance is so closely linked with the worship of *loa* that Voodoo can be regarded as one of the 'danced religions'. Dancing is a

ritual act from which emanates a power that affects the supernatural world. Drum rhythms and dances attract the spirits.
That is why they are assigned a predominating rôle in nearly all
ceremonies. If the music and dancing pleases the spirits to such
an extent that they are affected, even against their will, then it is
because they themselves are dancers who allow themselves to be
carried away by the supernatural power of rhythm. They prefer
to make their appearance when dances are done specially in their
honour and they generally use incarnation as an opportunity to
make their 'horse' dance. Spurred on by the god within him, the
devotee who a few moments earlier was dancing without gusto,
throws himself into a series of brilliant improvisations and shows
a suppleness, a grace and imagination which often did not seem
possible. The audience is not taken in: it is to the *loa* and not to
the *loa*'s servant that their admiration goes out.

Each *loa nanchon* (nation) has its own batteries of drums and
dances. That is why you hear of Dahomey, Congo, Petro and
Ibo dances though this classification by race includes, in each
case, different kinds of dances. Thus under the heading Dahomey
or Voodoo are bracketed the *yanvalu*, the *Dahomey-z'epaules*,
the *mahi* etc. The Petro dances comprise the *petro* proper, the
kita, the *bumba* etc.

The classical distinction between dances sacred and profane is
not always very clear. Some, which are merely entertainments,
can work their way into a ceremony simply because they are
regarded as pleasing to the god or because the god particularly
asked for them through the mouth of his 'horse'. Similarly
at certain public jollifications dances are done which differ little
or not at all from ritual dances. This is particularly the case
with the Congo dances. Finally there are some dances such
as the *gabienne* and the *mascort* which are not addressed to
the spirits but merely fitted into services to fill in blank periods
and provide a certain relief.

In trying to portray, as many authors have, the principal
Voodoo dances I have resigned myself to giving only a very brief
outline of them. A more complete description would have been
wearisome and would only have made for confusion. I would
have tried to list and classify them if that task had not been made

superfluous by the excellent monograph of Courlander, *Haiti Singing*.

Dancers revolve in no particular formation anti-clockwise round the *poteau-mitan*. Each of them dances as the whim takes him without regard for his neighbours, except when, as quite frequently happens, two or more dancers face each other and compete in agility and improvisation. The whole art of the dance is expressed less in the play of the feet than in the shoulders and hips. It is above all in *feints* that a dancer's virtuosity is revealed. Such is the term given to the improvisations which are permitted whenever the *manman*, beaten with redoubled energy, introduces a 'break'—off-beat—into the orchestra rhythm. These *cassés* which interrupt the flow of the dance throw people into a state of paroxysm propitious to 'attacks' of *loa*. In the short confusion which follows the dancers try to adapt their movements to the new beat by doing pirouettes or sudden strides. Often while dancing, women grasp the hem of their dress with both hands and raise and lower it gently in strict time to the music; the men let their arms hang slightly bent as though to maintain their balance. Some of them, with their heads hanging, pull the two ends of a cloth thrown round their necks.

Among those who dance in honour of Agwé, god of the sea, movements may be observed which suggest the undulation of waves or the motions of a swimmer. In the same way to please Zaka, the god of the soil, *hunsi* take on the heavy gait of the peasant and try to evoke the labour of the fields by their positions.

The *yanvalu* is danced with the body leaning forward, knees bent, and with undulations which seem to spread from the shoulders all down the back. Movement is effected by sliding the feet sideways with a pause on the fourth beat. The undulations of the *yanvalu* are much more pronounced in the *yanvalu-dos-bas*; to such an extent, indeed, that it is taken for an imitation of waves or a serpent. Thus it is often danced in honour of Agwé or Damballah-wèdo. In this dance the body is considerably bent and the dancer goes gradually lower until he is virtually squatting with hands on knees.

Another version of the *yanvalu* is the *yanvalu-debout* or *Dahomey-z'epaules* which, as its name indicates, is a dance characterized by the play of the shoulders. The dancer, body upright, rolls his shoulders ever more rapidly following the beat of the drums.

The *nago-chaud* is particularly for warrior-spirits. It is akin to the *yanvalu* but distinguished by its rapidity and violence. The steps are short and hurried, the pirouettes numerous, the shoulders seeming to be shaken by a continuous trembling accompanied by a certain swinging of the hips requiring an unbelievable muscular suppleness.

Maya Deren[9] describes the *nago-grand-coup* as a sort of salutation to Ogu, characterized by rotating the shoulders alternately. Nothing is more lively than the gay *mahi* with its crossings and twirlings.

The *petro* rhythm—rest-two-three—has such a special quality that even an untrained ear can pick it out. Beaten on two drums, it is regarded as particularly exciting. In it the play of the feet is more important than other movements of the body. In one of the typical *petro* attitudes, found also in the Congo dances, the dancer stretches one hand in front of him while the other rests on his hip.

The Congo dances are perhaps the hardest of all to describe, if not to carry out. The dancer moves his feet imperceptibly and gives small shakes to his shoulders while gently undulating his loins. From this controlled pulsation he suddenly changes to the more violent movements during which he turns round and round.

The only dances which are frankly obscene are those carried out in honour of the Guédé or by devotees possessed by them. The rhythm is brisk and gay and the dancers sway their hips as much as they please. The dance of the Guédé-fatras was the speciality of the *hungan* Tullius. Wearing a police hat and leaning on a *coco-macaque* (walking stick), bent double, he rolled his buttocks in time to the drum-rhythm. Then he raised and lowered his head mechanically with an idiotic smile. Sucking in his cheeks to give his face an even sillier aspect he threw the upper part of his body backwards and danced rapidly throwing up his legs as high as possible. He was accompanied by the *hunsi* who weaved their bottoms in and out and sang an improper parody of a Catholic psalm. When they came to the refrain they stretched out one arm with the index finger raised and prolonged the last note as long as possible.

The *banda* too is a Guédé dance and marvellously indecent. Nevertheless it also has a sacred aspect for it is danced at funerals to dismiss a dead person's spirit to the other world, and it occurs in ceremonies to provide relief in the wake of dire and awful *loa*.

The *mazone*, the *crabigné* and the *gragement* have the power of making *loa* go away either when they have not been invited or when they are outstaying their welcome. They provide a tactful means of hinting to a *loa* that he is *de trop*. With their gay and lively rhythm they break the tension which possesses dancers or spectators after a terrifying *loa* has spread fear all round.

XI. INITIATION RITES IN HAITIAN VOODOO

The Significance of the Initiation Rites

Initiation into Voodoo (*kanzo*)[10] demands much from those who undergo it: financial sacrifice (often considerable), absence for quite a long time from usual occupations, great efforts of memory, patient acceptance of a severe discipline and strict observance of moral obligations. Those who do not recoil from such a mystical adventure are motivated by considerations which, in varying degrees, combine genuine religious aspiration and practical concern for the main chance. *Kanzo* makes for a more direct contact with the divinity and puts the initiate under the immediate care of a *loa*. It also acts as a guarantee against the tricks of fate, bad luck and above all, illness. An initiate leaves the *kanzo* both purified and fortified. Thanks to these rites initiates not only ensure for themselves a supernatural ally, but also steep themselves in beneficent effluvia. *Kanzo* 'gives you a *nanm*' (soul). Some of the rites have an entirely magical nature and even though superficially they may appear to be tests of endurance and courage, in fact their real function is to increase the luck and health of the novice. Initiation ceremonies are therefore 'myste-

PLATE I. Lorgina Delorge, *mambo* of Port-au-Prince

PLATE II. *La-place* (master of ceremonies), carrying a matchet and leading a procession of *hunsi*

PLATE III. *Left:* a death spirit, painted on the door of a sanctuary consecrated to *loa* of the Guédé family. *Right:* Baron Samedi, spirit of death

PLATE IV. Chango, one of the Nago *loa*, painted on the wall of a sanctuary in Port-au-Prince

PLATE V. *Left*: a small sanctuary consecrated to divinities of the Guédé family whose funereal attributes are depicted on the building's walls. *Right*: the *pè* (altar) of a Voodoo sanctuary. The bottles contain drinks favoured by *loa*. The white pots are the *hunsi*'s 'head-pots'. The symbols on the walls are those of Ezili and of Damballah-wèdo

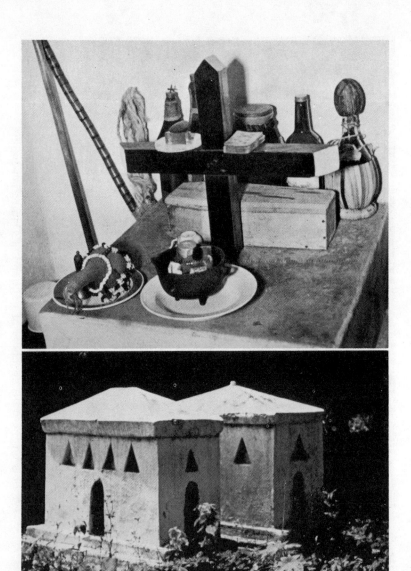

PLATE VI. *Top:* Altar consecrated to divinities of the Guédé family. Cards for divination lie on the arm of the cross. In the background, the bottle surmounted by a small cross contains *kimanga. Below:* Stone tombs in the Marbial Valley

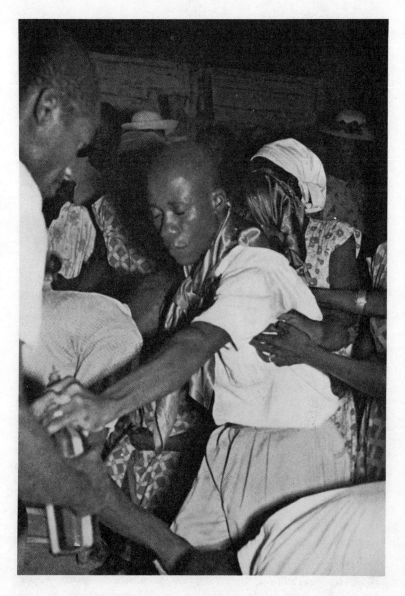

PLATE VII. The first stages of possession. *Hunsi* restrain the possessed man while his footwear is removed

PLATE VIII. A *hungan*, possessed by a *loa*, dances round the
central post of his peristyle

PLATE IX. Ritual salutations. Two dignitaries of a Voodoo Society are 'twirling' each other

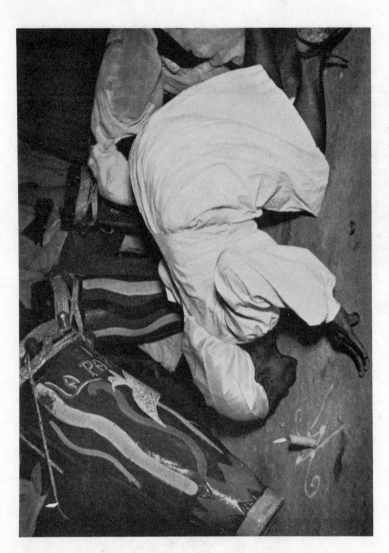

PLATE x. A *hunsi* kissing the ground before the *rada* drums

PLATE XI. A *mambo* 'twirling' the *hunsi* standard-bearer, while another *hunsi* goes into a trance

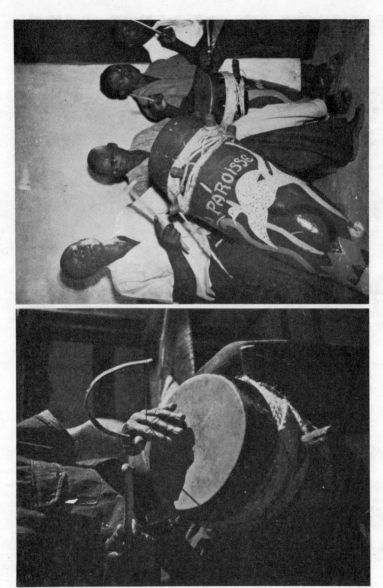

PLATE XII. *Left*: The *segond* or *hunto* drum of the *rada* orchestra. *Right*: Drums of the *rada* orchestra

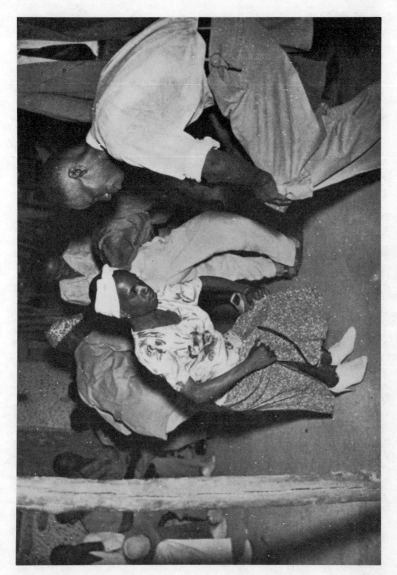

PLATE XIII. Dancing the *yanvalou*

PLATE XIV. 'Passport' issued by a society of sorcerers

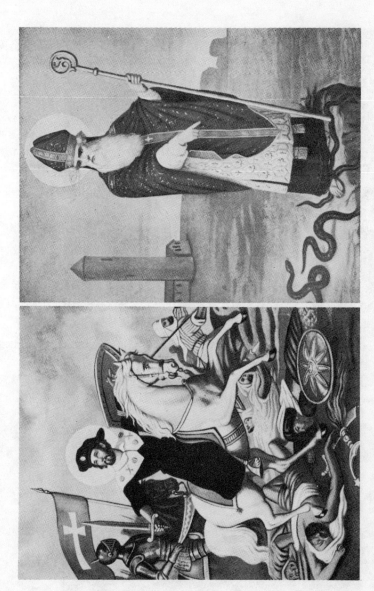

PLATE xv. Prints of Saint James the Elder and Saint Patrick. In Voodoo sanctuaries the first represents the warrior spirit, Ogu; the second, Damballah-wèdo, the serpent spirit

PLATE XVI. *Left*: Pilgrims at Saut-d'eau, burning candles before a sacred tree. *Right*: a crowd of pilgrims following the Virgin of Saut-d'eau

ries', but their salutary effects primarily concern life on this earth—an aspect of *kanzo* so important that for some ill people it becomes their one supreme hope, makes them expect a cure or have faith that the illness from which they are suffering will not strike them down again. This conception of the *kanzo* makes sense when we consider how many illnesses are attributed to supernatural causes. A priest prescribes initiation for his patient to appease the *loa*, whom the patient may have offended, or to obtain a protector to save him from the persecutions of other *loa* or of sorcerers. Initiation is, let us bear in mind, at the same time both death and resurrection. It gives those who undergo it the chance of rising from the profane state to a new life in which they will be dependent upon—but also in the good graces of—the *loa*.

In many cases it is the *loa* himself who insists that his servant should be initiated. He will appear to him in a dream, or make known his wishes to him in the course of some ceremony, through the intermediary of someone possessed. Woe to him who then turns a deaf ear. A series of disasters will bring home to him that the *loa* do not speak lightly and that if he wishes to escape worse misfortunes still, he had better make up his mind quickly.

Whatever may be the mystical reasons given by initiates to explain their candidature, the hope of practical advantage is certainly not far from their minds. In the address given by one *mambo* whom I knew to the *hunsi-kanzo* at the end of their novitiate, exhortations to piety and good behaviour were mixed with descriptions of the immediate profit they would derive from their new condition. 'The *kanzo* is a ceremony which brings luck' she declared and gave examples of women who had lived in poverty up to their initiation, but were afterwards loaded with good fortune. Very different was the case of a woman who owned land and houses but was ruined—because she neglected the *loa* and had not answered their call. The *mambo* reminded the new *hunsi* that the *humfo* was now their home, they were the children of it—the *pititt-caye*—and that if ever they needed money they could always come there for help and would be given 'anything from two to fifty gourdes (*sic*)' (i.e. from $0.40 to $10). This address of which we have here given merely the main points, shows the emphasis on one important consequence of initiation: a *hunsi-kanzo* is no longer alone, she has a spiritual mother and father—the *hungan* and *mambo*, from whom she can ask help and advice. The *humfo* is a refuge for people who are weighed down by poverty and have nowhere to lay their head. The priest who made them *kanzo* has a moral obligation to help them and welcome them in. Think, for a minute, of the isolation and destitution of the proletarianized peasants in a town like Port-au-Prince—then the attraction which the *kanzo* holds for these up-rooted country people becomes easily understandable. There, in the shade of the sacred trees, and in the 'house of the mysteries', they find family and home.

There is another consideration: the title *hunsi* flatters a person's vanity. And we know how much store the ordinary people of Haiti set by social distinctions and prestige. Initiates at once acquire rank which separates them from the mass: they are in possession of secrets which they cannot share with just anybody and whenever there is a dance or ceremony in the *humfo* they appear before the spectators in the coveted rôle of sacred actors.

With the exception of those who get themselves initiated as a means of completing a medical treatment, novices are recruited from people living in the neighbourhood of a *humfo* and who have already taken part in ceremonies and dances over a long period of time. That is why most of them know the dance steps, the drum rhythms and the ceremony details long before being taught them during their *kanzo*. Having watched many possessions, *hunsi*-to-be are familiar with the customary bearing of each deity and can recognize the gods on sight, by their tone of voice or mannerisms. Many novices out of friendship for—or to secure the favour of—a *hungan* or *mambo*, take an active part in the preparation of ceremonies. In this way they acquire a fairly intimate knowledge of the details of the cult.

It often takes many years of hard work before a candidate can put by enough to get himself initiated: apart from the fees of the priest, which can be substantial, he must also buy clothing and many ritual accessories. The *mambo* Lorgina told her novices of one *hunsi* who had come to her to discuss details of her initiation with nothing more than a straw-mat to bargain with. To cope

with the costs of initiation she had started a small business and
saved up penny by penny. Priests sometimes make allowances
and scale down their fees if, in return for training, the *hunsi* will
stay with him and serve him faithfully.

The difficulties which many find in getting the necessary
money, and the multiplicity of circumstances which can lead a
person to get himself initiated, explain why novices vary so much
in age. Some very young children undergo initiation if the
parents think it will do them good and if they can afford the cost.
I know of a little girl of five who was made *kanzo* by a *mambo* as a
mark of affection and to help her future. A pregnant woman who
becomes a *kanzo* shares the benefits derived therefrom with the
child she is carrying.

Once their decision is made, candidates for initiation usually
have whole weeks in which to prepare themselves. It is in a
priest's interest to get together as many novices as possible.
These assiduously frequent the *humfo* and seize every opportunity of picking up ritual routine and the dances which every
hunsi must be able to do.

About a week before the date fixed for the *kanzo*—a date
which the priest often keeps secret for fear of sorcerers—the
novices gather in the sanctuary equipped with their white
clothes and all the things they will need. This preliminary period
is devoted to the carrying out of pious practices in the local
churches and to frequent ablutions, particularly on the last three
days before the retreat starts. They 'freshen' their bodies with
'baths' that is to say with water into which leaves with medical or
magical properties have been infused. At the same time they
abstain from foods likely either to blunt or excite their nerves.
The morning of the 'putting-to-bed' ceremony (*le coucher*), they
merely take some soup and something light to go with it, and
instead of coffee they get a decoction of *pois piante* (*Cassia
occidentalis L.*) or an infusion of *corossol* (*Annona muricata*)
which is held to be a most effective sedative. .

THE 'PUTTING-TO-BED' OF THE 'HUÑO'

The *coucher* of the novices—to whom I will sometimes refer

by the Haitian name (of African origin) *huño*—is the ceremony
which marks the beginning of the initiation and precedes the
period of withdrawal which initiates must complete within the
sanctuary. It usually takes place on a Sunday evening and is
marked by mutual salutations, libations, offerings and possessions,
but includes also ritual acts which give it a character of its own.
These last are: 1) the *chiré aizan*, 2) the public lessons which the
novices receive, 3) the consecration before retreat.

The *chiré aizan* is the ritualistic fraying of palm leaves into
strips from which are made fringes which the neophytes wear
over their shoulders or in front of their faces. In Dahomey these
fringes are used as talismans against evil spirits. After a few preliminary songs and dances, a newly-cut palm branch is placed
on a chair covered with white stuff, having first been formally
raised, three times, and then 'orientated'. The chair is put on
the *vèvè* of the *loa* Aizan which has been duly consecrated by
libations and offerings of ritual food.

The *hunsi* place themselves in a row, facing the palm, and sing
and dance where they are; they then start tearing the leaves into
strips with their nails or with pins. Here are the songs in honour
of the god Aizan:

1.	*Aizâ sé loa*	Aizan is a spirit
	Legba e!	Legba e!
	Chiré Aizâ	Tear the Aizan
	Aizâ tâdé!	Aizan listen!
2.	*Aizâ vélékété*	Aizan vélékété
	Imamu tôkâ	Imamu tokan
	Lésé bo loa-a	Let me kiss the god!
	Aizâ e, nu tut alé	Aizan e, we are all going.
3.	*Aizâ e, Aizâ e!*	Aizan e, Aizan e!
	Nu rêmê vivâ	You love the living
	Nu arivé	You arrive
	Aizâ dèr Ibo	Aizan after Ibo
	Aya Aizâ!	Aya Aizan!

4. *Aizâ pûngwé Aizâ*   Aizan pungwé Aizan
   Aizâ géléfré   Aizan of Africa
   Aizâ, go, o   Aizan, go, o
   Aizâ, go, o   Aizan, go, o.

5. *Aizâ e (bis)*   Aizan e (bis)
   M'pralé   I will go
   M'pralé Géléfré   I will go to Africa
   P'pr'alé   I will go
   Se u ki maré mwê   It's you who tie me up.

6. *Aizâ Aizâ e*   Aizan, Aizan, e
   Nèg-sòt maré chwal li   The stupid man ties his horse up
   Nèg l'espri di l'a lagé The intelligent says he will let him go
   Aizâ nu tut parèy   Aizan we are all the same.

Throughout the operation the strips of leaf which fall to the ground are carefully picked up by the *hunsi* who plait them into a whip—used, eventually, to punish the initiates. Another palm leaf, but this time a dried one, is brought and taken to pieces in the same way. The stems are split and cut into lengths and these strictly speaking are the *aizans*. They are once again placed on the chair and a *père-savane* blesses and baptizes them.

The *hungenikon*, holding the fringes at arms' length, twirls on his toes, dances round the *poteau-mitan*, and running with quick little rhythmic steps, salutes the doors of the *hᵘmfo*, the drums, the sacred trees—particularly that of Legba—the 'side-chapels', and returning to the peristyle holds out the fringes first to the *mambo*, then to the *hunsi*, finally to important people among the spectators. Everyone kisses the *aizan* with the utmost respect and then the *hungenikon* hastens to put them away in the initiation room. Several times over in the course of the ceremony the *hunsi* make the novices repeat the salutations and dance steps which they have taught them. These are the last lessons to be received in public. The pupils perform all together, facing the *hunsi*, who only take them on one side if they need advice. The *mambo* does not hesitate to scold the ones who make mistakes and even knock them about a bit—as well as showing them where they went wrong. These repetitions are known as *balancer* (swinging). They also include the hand-clap rhythms—which are the salutations proper to initiates.

When the *mambo* thinks the repetitions have gone on long enough she orders the novices to lie down, full length, round the *poteau-mitan* with their heads resting against the pediment. First she pours water on their mouths and feet and then traces a cross with some green powder on their faces, their palms and chests. Then she whips them on the legs. In our opinion this chastisement is not entirely symbolic for it varies from person to person and is followed by reproaches and admonitions. The novices are no doubt paying for ritual faults they have committed in the privacy of the sanctuary. Before they may get up the *mambo* goes up to each and taps forehead, mouth and cheek with her rattle.

The priest now places a large stone on the head of each neophyte. Holding it with one hand they go dancing, in procession, to salute the sacred trees and the *poteau-mitan*. It was only many years after I saw this rite that the *hungan* who presided explained to me its significance. The dance, apparently, was to imbue the novices with a spirit of solidarity and obedience. To show what he meant, he described circumstances in which the *hunsi* had been made to 'jump to it' at the mere reminder of this rite. It can happen, he told me, that a *hungan* visiting a *humfo* with his *hunsi* may be dissatisfied with his reception. He has only to put his hands to his head and mime a dance step for the *hunsi* to remove themselves—and promptly. They withdraw, singing the refrain of the song which accompanies the dance with stones.

Now there are yet more salutations to dignitaries and to the *hunsi*. The 'putting-to-bed' (*coucher*) of the *huño* is at hand. The *mambo* who has never stopped 'launching' songs, breaks off in order to give them a short talk. She outlines the beneficial effects of the rites which have been performed for them, exhorts them always to behave irreproachably and to be loyal to the *humfo* which made them *kanzo*.

In obedience to signs from the *confiance* and the *hungenikon*, the novices, two by two, approach the *mambo* to kiss the ground at her feet and get themselves 'twirled' by her. They are then ordered to take off their shoes which are put in a pile. They line up once more facing the *mambo*. The latter kisses each of them on the mouth, her face distorted with emotion. All the *huño* begin to weep silently. Becoming more and more emotional the *mambo*, singing and walking with rattle in hand in front of them, gradually gives up all attempt at holding back her tears which end by drowning her voice. The *hunsi* and the spectators crowd round to embrace the departing initiates and press their hands as though they were going away for ever. It is in these farewells that the deeper meaning of the *kanzo* shows up most clearly. The initiates will soon return—everyone knows that. But the point is, they will not be the same. They will have become different people and it is for their symbolical 'death' that spectators are now mourning, no less symbolically.

The *hunsi* remain stationed behind those candidates for whom they have acted as personal teachers and when the moment of departure comes they wrap a cloth round their protégés' eyes. Then, rather roughly, they push them into the room—the *djèvo*—where they are to remain shut up for a week.

THE RETREAT

What goes on behind the locked doors of the *djèvo* is a secret which initiates may not reveal. However, they are not all so discreet. Piecing together scraps of information and using some of the written sources, I believe I have succeeded in reconstructing the main outline of the series of rites which lasts the whole week—from the *coucher* to the *bulé-zin* on the Saturday night. Some facts cannot be reconciled with each other and a few inexactitudes may have managed to creep in, but on the whole I am convinced that the picture here presented is correct.

Once they are in the *djèvo* the novices put on a tunic of plain white cloth which is the initiate's normal dress. With their backs to the door, legs stretched out, they sit on a heap of *mombin* leaves. The priest cuts a lock of hair from the tops of their heads, removes the hair from their arm-pits and pubes, and takes nail-parings from their left hands and feet. These bits of the body, which represent the 'good angel' (*le bon-ange*) or the soul, are wrapped in a banana-leaf with grilled maize, sweets, *acassan* and the blood and feathers of sacrificed chickens. The whole is placed in a pot of white china—the head-pot (*pot-tête* or *pot-kanzo*) which stays with the novice throughout the retreat. Later this is placed on the sanctuary altar where it remains as a token of the good behaviour and obedience of the initiates-to-be. In this way the *hungan*, the custodian of the pot, gains complete control of his *hunsis'* souls and either with threats or by witchcraft, can bring to heel any who behave rebelliously or badly. Those who don't wish to remain attached to a sanctuary take their head-pots away and hide them carefully in some nook of their houses.

The novices now undergo a second head-washing (*laver-tête*), and a much more important one than that which takes place automatically whenever a person is first seized by a *loa*. On the novice's head, carefully washed with an infusion of medicinal herbs, the officiant clamps a poultice of bread soaked in wine, vermicelli, grilled maize, *acassan*, rice cooked in milk etc—the whole sprinkled with syrup and blood. These ingredients, wrapped in *mombin* leaves, are held together in the folds of a white cloth which envelops the head and covers the eyes. They are removed seven days later but the initiate's hair, fouled by the decomposition of so much organic matter, may only be washed when initiation has been completed—just before the new *kanzo* goes home. The infusion of *mombin* leaves which is used for this final washing, is carefully saved and put in a bottle for the initiate to use whenever he feels heavy or 'hot' in the head. If need be, the whole of this ceremony can always be repeated.

The main effect of the *laver-tête* is to establish a permanent link between the neophyte and a *loa*. In ritual language this ceremony corresponds with the placing of the *loa maît'-tête* (the *loa* master of the head). From then on the novice is consecrated to one particular spirit who will be his protector and will 'dance in his head' more often than other *loa*. Whereas in Dahomey and Nigeria a person is visited solely by the spirit to whom he has been pledged, in Haiti no *loa* claims a monopoly. Despite the rights a *maît'-tête* holds over his servant he does not take offence when another *loa* uses his 'horse'.

How is a *maît'-tête* chosen? Theoretically Loco, the sanctuary guardian, is invoked by the priest and then tells him the *maît'-tête* of each initiate. In fact most neophytes have been possessed long before their initiation. They therefore take as their protector whichever *loa* first descended upon them or visits them most often. If troubled by doubt they put themselves in the hands of a priest who is experienced in such questions and knows how to recognize signs which clearly reveal the identity of the *loa* looking for a new servant.

In some sanctuaries the priest or the priestess, flanked by acolytes, calls upon the *loa*, beginning, as is proper, with Legba. As soon as a neophyte, by trembling or any other symptom, shows that the *loa* is wandering round him, he is made to sit down and is asked if it is really this spirit which he wants as guardian. If he says yes his mat is carried to the far end of the room. A novice who has never yet fallen into a trance should experience a mild *frisson* during the invocation of the spirits, otherwise initiation is not complete.

The placing of the *loa maît'-tête* does not always pass off without incident: other *loa* sometimes try and turn him out and take his servant for themselves. Then the officiant must induce the possession desired by calling the *maît'-tête* with appropriate songs and by tracing his emblem on the ground.

In honour of the *loa* the sanctuary flags and other sacralia are put round the walls of the retreat-room. The very ground is covered with every kind of receptacle all full of the *maît'-tête loa*'s favourite dishes. The mats on which the initiates are to lie are placed on the *vèvè* of their respective *loa* protectors. For pillows they are issued with large stones which have been taken into the *humfo* at night in great secrecy. Small coins, worth about 77 centimes, are put under the stones or knotted into a corner of the cloth of each novice. Before lying down on the mat the *huño* kiss the ground three times, then they lie on their left side, covered with a sheet. During the seven days retreat they may neither move, laugh nor speak without permission. They are put under the supervision of an experienced woman, the *manman-huño* who sees to their needs and prepares their food. A bell or rattle is placed in their reach so they may call her if they need to. A whip hanging on the wall is the sign of the discipline which must obtain in the *djèvo*. The *hungan* uses it liberally at the first glimpse of disorder. All the novices are punished for the fault of one.

They are kept to a rather strict diet which could not exactly be called a fast. Nonetheless they must eat nothing salted. They get nothing but *afibas* (dried tripe) and chicken in the way of meat. Offal (head, feet, gizzards etc) is particularly reserved for them. The bulk of their diet consists of *gumboes*, *acassan* and maize soup without fats. They only drink water or infusions of *piante* (*Cassia occidentalis*), *corossol* (*Annona muricata*), *bois-dine* (*Eugenia fragans*) or cinnamon.

Every morning the novices wash in hot water. Twice a day their bodies are rubbed with oil. At these moments they are allowed to turn over on their mat or sit up for about ten minutes.

Only people who have themselves passed through the *kanzo* rites may enter the room where the *huño* are lying. A visitor greets them by clapping his hands in a conventional rhythm and the novices reply with a beat which varies according to the visitor's rank. A parent or uninitiated friend may come to the door, but not past it. When his presence is announced, he too is saluted with hand-clapping. Such are the limits of communication with the outside world. According to one *hungan*, who had initiated a great many *kanzo*, novices are not allowed to leave the *djèvo* to satisfy their natural needs. Other informants told me they may leave before dawn, muffled up with a sheet.

Every attempt is made to withdraw novices from outside influence simply because during their retreat they are particularly vulnerable. They are in a state of diminished resistance and their weakened organisms lie open to the wiles of sorcerers. All precautions taken are therefore merely dictated by elementary prudence.

OFFERINGS TO THE 'MAÎT'-TÊTE'

The eve of the day upon which the novices have to make their solemn exit, a ceremony is celebrated in honour of all their *loa maît'-tête*. During the preparation of each *loa*'s favourite dish (soups, sugary things, *acassan*, chocolate, coffee, sweets, syrup, cakes, cassava and fruit) the *hungan* draws on the ground, in flour, the emblems of the spirits to be invoked. These drawings are covered with mats on which the offerings are then laid out.

The novices sit down with legs apart. The officiant sanctifies their heads by letting fall handfuls of food upon them and sprinkling them with water, kola and liqueurs. A choir sings three songs in honour of each *maît'-tête*. The priest goes up to the novices with the chicken each has given him and makes it peck at their head and hands. If the auguries are favourable he walks the bird on the postulant's head and gives it to him or her to hold in such a way that within his crossed arms it is held against his breast. The *hungan* takes back the bird, breaks its wings and legs, tears its tongue out with his teeth and allows three drops of blood to fall on the initiate's head. He finishes the bird off by wringing its neck; then he tears out a few tufts of down which he sticks, with blood, to the rim of the 'head-pot', and to the novice's head. He also traces out crosses, in blood, on the nape of his neck, forehead, palm of the left hand and on the left foot. Pigeons are sometimes sacrificed under a cloak. Their bodies, duly 'cross-signed' and sprinkled with maize and various drinks, are heaped up in a pile between the novices' legs. Any initiate not possessed when the name of his *loa* was called out, usually makes up for it at this juncture.

The *hungan*, using his fingers, puts bread soaked in wine and other foods in each *huño*'s mouth and between the big and second toe of his left foot. In fact it is the god who eats this offering since the person receiving it is possessed. The song which is now sung explains the meaning of the rite: 'The saints [that is to say the *loa*] want something to eat. Kneel down. A *loa* in a pot is incapable of eating; you must eat instead of him.'

THE CEREMONY OF THE 'BURNING-POTS'

The *bulé-zin* ceremony which takes place on the Saturday evening, closes the retreat and precedes the grand ceremonial exit on the morning of Sunday. I shall base my description of this on what I saw at Lorgina's in 1949.

The *bulé-zin* begins—as custom demands—by invocations of Legba, 'opener of the barrier', and by libations in front of the drums and the *poteau-mitan*, these rites being first carried out by Lorgina and then by all the dignitaries present. Then comes the long series of salutations between priests, *hunsi* and *mambo*, and finally between *hunsi* and *hunsi* who, equal facing equal, 'twirl' each other simultaneously. Then comes the parade of standard-bearers, with the *la-place* in front. One by one, with great cere-mony, they salute their flags and present them to be kissed by members of the *humfo* society.

Suddenly a man bursts into the peristyle. He is loaded with necklaces which he wears round his neck and arms. It is the *confiance* or the *hungenikon* who has been to fetch the necklaces of the *hunsi-kanzo* and who, from contact with the sacred orna-ments, has been made drunk (*saoulé*) by the power emanating from them. He staggers, totters and regains his balance, like a ballet dancer imitating a drunk. The *mambo* shakes her rattle and the orchestra of three *rada* drums adds a ceaseless rolling to the clear sound of the *ogan*. The carrier of necklaces falls to his knees and the *mambo* relieves him of his burden.

Each *hunsi* comes and kneels before the *mambo* to receive her necklace. The *mambo* picks out the right one from the pile with-out hesitation and puts it on her, crossing it over each shoulder. She also adjusts her *awèssan* (silk band).

The *mambo* is brought a plate of flour and a lighted candle and after a few ritual movements, she traces out, all round the *poteau-mitan*, the *vèvè* of the various *loa* honoured in her *humfo*. Circles, near the symbols of each *loa*, show the positions of the *zin*.

A song calls the *hunsi* who go into the sanctuary in a group to fetch the things they will need for the 'service' from the foot of the altar. There, on a mat covered with white stuff, everything necessary for a meal has been arranged—pots, plates, dishes, large wrought-iron nails, calabashes, small pinewood sticks, wreaths of *mombin* and *lalo* (*Corchorus olitorius* leaves), chickens with tied feet, maize meal, grilled peanuts, *acassan*, oil, wine, liqueurs. Of course, it is really a magico-religious meal since the pots, nails and sticks are all decorated with small crosses and symbolic designs done in chalk. They have already been 'cross-signed', at a consecration ceremony during which the protecting spirits of the sanctuary were called. The number of *zin*—globular clay pots—may vary but the cookery section of a *bulé-zin* must include a small cast iron pot consecrated to the *loa* of the Nago nation, and to its most celebrated representative Ogu-fer or *Ferraille*.

The earthenware pots are regarded as living pots with the exception of two consecrated to the dead. Each object is orientated towards the cardinal points before being given to a *hunsi* who receives it on her knees and who prostrates herself—'kisses earth'—as a sign of respect.

Carrying their burdens either on their heads or in a fold of their skirts, they form a long procession which advances towards the peristyle under the guidance of the *confiance* or the *hungenikon*. The latter holds two chickens which he waves above his head and whirls rather as a drum major whirls his staff. The movements of his outstretched arms by which he raises and lowers the birds, while giving small flicks to his wrists, is known in the language of the liturgy as *ventaillé* and has a ritual meaning. The person at the head of the file leads it swiftly, keeping in time to the ever increasing tempo of the drums. This progress is almost a farandole, particularly when the *confiance*, juggling with his chickens, does an about-turn and, three times over, by means of sudden feints compels the *hunsi* to retreat or change direction thus throwing their ranks into disorder. These gallopings-about often result in outbreaks of near-trance which never quite mature into fully fledged possession. Many *hunsi* are seized with giddiness though none of them actually succumb to convulsions.

At a signal given by the drums the *hunsi*, jumping and bounding as though at the sound of wonderful news, and crying '*abobo*', kneel, facing the *vèvè*, and lay down their burdens. Carefully they place each pot in its allotted circle, facing the emblem of the god to which it has been pledged. They prostrate themselves and kiss the ground before the *mambo*. The latter is seated on a little chair and raises each for three little pirouettes.

The dignitaries present come and sit on chairs placed near the *vèvè*. The *mambo*, with one hand over her eyes to help her collect her thoughts, and the other clasping her rattle, begins to recite the 'prayer of Africa' (*priyè Ginè*). This begins with three Paters, three Aves and three C redos; then come Catholic psalms followed by a long enumeration of widely assorted saints, whose names finally flow into, and get muddled up with the *loa*, now finally invoked. The name of each divinity is framed by words in *langage*: *Heyá . . . sindyóe* and the litany is punctuated by other words in this mysterious language—the sound of *lisadolé zo, zo, zo* recurring most frequently. (Here let us remember that *zo* in Fon means 'fire' and Lisa is one of the great divinities of the Dahomey pantheon.)

The *hunsi* who have taken their places on mats or chairs remain motionless with eyes closed and only bestir themselves to say over and over again '*é zo, é zo, é zo*' and to prostrate themselves whenever there is mention of a *loa* venerated in the *humfo*. When the *mambo* recites prayers in *langage*, adding many incomprehensible syllables which are bits and pieces of Fon and other African languages, the *hunsi* provide responses.

A few terse blows on the drums herald the end of the African prayer. The *hunsi*, after new prostrations, come and get themselves 'twirled' by the *mambo* and the dignitaries present. Then, to cries of '*abobo*', they resume their dancing round the *poteau-mitan*.

The dignitaries who have come to help the *mambo* and who are to become 'the servants of the *zin*' take off their shoes. The *hunsi* who are to help them do the same. First a glass is taken and filled with a mixture which includes water, wine, syrup, grains of maize, peanuts and bits of biscuit. Then to the rhythm of drums and of the song:

E o plâté pòto, Papa Legba, o	*Hé*, knock in the nails, Papa Legba o.
Plâté pòto e, Papa Legba, e.	Knock in the nails, Papa Legba, o,

they take three pegs and having orientated them, drive them into the ground in a triangle: these nails are to be the tripod-base for the pots. On each side of the triangle a handful of ritual food is

placed and over it three libations are made with the mixture
described above and a lighted candle is placed in its middle. The
servants sit on their chairs and using their bare feet raise the
bulé-zin, placing each on its respective support. The sticks,
having been presented to the four points of the compass, are
lighted and put beneath the *zin*. In some *humfo* they are given to
the *hunsi* who dance for a few minutes by torchlight. Water is
poured into the *zin* as well as a little mixture from the glass. The
so-called 'living' pots get a few grains of salt.

The 'servants of the *zin*' take the two chickens, 'orientate'
them, 'cross-sign' them with flour, then, having broken their
wings and legs, pull their heads off with one quick twist. In the
twinkling of an eye the chickens are plucked, singed, 'drawn' and
cut up. The pieces are washed, rubbed with sour oranges and
given to the 'servants of the *zin*' who, having passed them three
times over the pots, plunge them into the boiling water. When
the meat is cooked the *hunsi* in charge of the kitchen, soak their
hands in a mixture of oil and wine and take out the bit which they
put on the *mombin* leaves, repeating the whole manoeuvre three
times. Maize meal is added to the soup. The iron pot, *zin nago*,
only gets *akra* (maize balls).

Meanwhile the novices are waiting. Since dawn they have been
ready for the evening ceremony. They have washed themselves
as usual in hot water and have drunk sedative infusions. Repeating in a low hum the songs which the *hunsi* are intoning under
the peristyle, they wait for the moment when they will be fetched.
Their entry is very impressive: entirely covered with a white
sheet which makes them look like ghosts or huge cocoons, they
walk leaning on the dignitaries of the *humfo* who with bent backs
advance slowly, dancing. The *hunsi* take care during this progress
to see the sheets don't get lifted and so reveal to the public the
identity of the novice beneath.

The rites to which the initiates are subjected during the *bulé-
zin* are carried out in the middle of the peristyle, but are hidden
from the eyes of the curious by sheets and coverings which the
hunsi stretch over the *mambo* and her assistants seated in front
of the pots. One by one the novices are put into this improvised
tent.

Having soaked their left hand in a mixture of oil and wine and *amasi* (a *mombin* infusion) and placed it three times flat down on the ground, they now close it three times in succession round a handful of hot maize-flour. Since the oil constitutes a thick layer of insulation the risk of being burnt is slight. The same is not true however of the fritters drawn from the boiling oil in the *nago* pot. These would cause grievous burns were they not lolloped up and down until cooled off. Finally each initiate has to pass his left hand and foot through the flame which rises from the *zin*.

These rites, which are compulsory for initiates, are not regarded by Voodooists as tests of courage; in their eyes they are magical procedures which endow novices with a supernatural power (*nanm*), health and good luck. Once the initiates are back in the sanctuary the *hunsi* and spectators who have passed through the *kanzo* are invited to come and take their turn at handling the little balls of hot maize and so benefit from the powers of the flames. Those who are willing to do this, have their eyes bandaged but are not hidden under a sheet.

The last episode of the ceremony is the *bulé-zin* proper. The 'servants' having retired, still with bare feet, remove the pots from the fire and clean them with *mombin* leaves and using a brush made from feathers of the sacrificed chickens, smear the insides with a thick coat of oil. The pots are put back on their stands and a little oil is poured into each. As many sticks as possible are placed beneath them so as to get up a good blaze. The *mambo* and her colleagues recite prayers and incantations and sound their rattles. The *hunsi* sing and run round the peristyle: here is the text of a song sung on this occasion:

Atchasu bâ mwê zê	Atchasu give me the pot
Pòté li tu maré (*bis*)	Bring it all wrapped up
Atchasu bâ mwê zê	Atchasu bring me the pot
Zê-lâ tu fèlé (*bis*)	That pot is all cracked
Atchasu bâ mwê zê-là	Atchasu give me that pot
Zê-là tu maré	That pot is all wrapped up.

When the flames leap up high and vivid, excitement does the same. The *hunsi* prostrate themselves, 'kissing earth', and resume

their wild circling of the *zin*. Possessions break out among them
at this moment but they are only partial as before. The priests
take care the women are no more than 'tipsified' by the god. The
hunsi, standards in the lead, go into the sanctuary to fetch the
head-pots, the *govi*, the necklaces and the *paquett*. These objects
are passed rapidly through the flames and then taken back to the
altars.

The peristyle is lighted entirely by the flames leaping up from
the *zin*. Dancing wildly, the white-clad *hunsi* disappear in the
murk only to reappear for a few moments in the field of light.
They stagger and everything suggests that many of them are
tipsified by the *loa*. When the moment comes for the *nago zin* to
burn, and the rum, tipped into the fire, throws out its bluish
flames, excitement increases and a number of *hunsi* totter or roll
on the ground in a state of trance. But those possessed return to
the dance after a few convulsions.

Once the fires have died down the *hunsi*, with their bare feet,
remove the pots, some of which have split under the stress of the
heat. A *vèvè* is traced out with a circle in the middle: this circle
is the circumference of what is soon a hole. The inside of it is
'cross-signed' and consecrated with libations of water and
liqueur. The sacred food wrapped in a white cloth is laid out on
mombin leaves. The *zin* and the pegs are broken up and the
fragments thrown into the hole. The *hunsi*, grouped round, fill
it in by hand and then tread it level in time to the music; Guédé
is called in a song:

> *Dya rélé, dy dya kékékéké dya dya rele dya*
> *Gédé-nibo, dya ké ké ké ké dya*
> *Barô-Samdi, dya ké ké ké ké dya.*

The ceremony ends on a gay note. The *hunsi* possessed by the
Guédé carry out the *loa*'s favourite dances: the *banda* and the
crabinié. Suiting their movements to the character of the gods
whom they incarnate, the *hunsi* swing their hips and amuse the
audience with their licentious gestures and obscene attitudes.
When the *loa* have left their 'horses' the *hunsi* kneel and their
necklaces are removed. After a few salutations and a quick turn
round the *poteau-mitan*, the standard-bearers and the *la-place* go

back into the sanctuary. But in the peristyle dancing goes on till dawn.

The exit of the initiates takes place on the Sunday morning, a few hours after the end of the *bulé-zin*. In the interval they have made a big effort with their appearance and are wearing clothes of spotless white. Over the kerchiefs which cover their heads, they wear broad-brimmed straw hats. The fringes of the *aizan* disguise their faces. They hold in their hands bunches of flowers or platefuls of offerings.

During their time in the initiation room the *mambo* has grouped them into pairs. Two people thus associated regard themselves as bound by particularly close bonds and so come out side by side. The procession of neophytes, headed by the *la-place* and the standard-bearers, threads its way under a sheet which the *hunsi* hold up with outstretched arms as a sort of panoply. The initiates move towards the sacred trees, beginning with that of Legba. Having paid homage to the *loa* of the sanctuary they return to the peristyle where the *mambo* once again lists the advantages of their new condition and reminds them that the sanctuary is from now on their second home. She warns them finally of the serious consequences of any failure in their duties towards the 'mysteries'.

In the afternoon, dressed in their finest clothes, the neophytes make another exit not less solemn than the first. Escorted by the *mambo*, the *la-place* and the standard-bearers they prostrate themselves before the gates of the sanctuary, the *poteau-mitan*, the drums and the *humfo* dignitaries. Candle in hand they are led before an altar which has been put up in the peristyle and decorated on either side with curtains. A *père-savane*, called in for the occasion, reads a few Latin and French prayers. Then each initiate, escorted by his godmother or godfather, is baptized by the *père-savane* and sprinkled with a leafy branch soaked in a glass of water. It is then the *hunsi* get the title of *kanzo*. The godfathers and godmothers can from now on call themselves *compère* and *commère*.

After the baptism dancing goes on till the middle of the night. The *mambo* calls upon the *loa maît'-tête* of the new *hunsi* and the latter are thereupon possessed by them. The congregation breaks up but the novices, exhausted by their long day, rest for a few hours in the peristyle. At dawn they once more put on their white clothes and each goes off on his own account to perform devotions in neighbouring churches and at the foot of the various calvaries. They return to the *humfo* in the evening but leave again next morning to make pilgrimages in different directions. Until the Friday evening they are allowed to do nothing. But on the Friday a *loa* comes down into the *mambo* or some other member of the *humfo* society and gives them permission to go home. They go in small groups and as self-effacingly as possible.

THE DESCENT OF THE NECKLACES

For forty-one days after their coming-out—that is to say until the ceremony of the 'descent of the necklaces'—the initiates remain in a weakened condition which lays them open to various dangers of a supernatural kind. They protect themselves by carefully obeying the prohibitions and by disciplining themselves to a pure and calm life. They do no work and do not leave their houses. They avoid the sun and the evening dew. They keep off pig meat, cold foods and iced drinks.

On the eighteenth day of this semi-retreat, they go to the market, equipped with a basket, to beg. With the alms which they receive, either money or produce, they buy a meal which they offer to the poor. This ends with an issue of old clothing, tobacco and soap. The beneficiaries of these gifts pray for the initiates.

The ceremony of the descent of the necklaces brings initiation to an end. The novices clothed in white, wearing large hats and carrying their *kanzo* necklaces under their shirts, go to the sanctuary where the priest has traced out on the ground the *vèvè* of their *maît'-têtes*. Under the guidance of experienced *hunsi*, they repeat for the last time dance-steps and salutations. Then, facing the symbols of their *loa*, they prostrate themselves, at the first rolling of the drums, three times over. In turn, they go and kneel in front of the *mambo* who removes their hats, their *awessan*, their *aizan* and their necklaces which she puts on the *vèvè* of their *maît'-tête*. She shakes her rattle quite close to their faces and raising them to their feet 'twirls' them three times over. Then there is an interminable interlude of salutations between *hunsi*.

The initiates return to the sanctuary where they wash themselves with hot water and rub their bodies with a *manger guinin* (African food offering). They put on new clothes and take the things they have worn during initiation to the *mambo* who is supposed to own them. Those who wish to keep them may buy them back for a sum which, though symbolic, still gives rise to bargaining and hard words. The *mambo*, or more precisely the *loa* inside her, does not always conceal his impatience for the *hunsi*'s haggling. The small coins kept under the ears or stowed away in the folds of a kerchief are also collected. Some of the total is given to the drummers, some put aside to pay for a Mass.

The *hungenikon* gathers up all the necklaces and tottering and staggering carries them into the sanctuary. The ceremony ends with dances during which many *loa maît'-tête* make a point of coming down into the initiates. With heads now strengthened, their possessions are free from the brutal and chaotic. The *loa* is now 'in the saddle'—for good and all—and his 'horse' need never again be afraid of 'losing its footing'.

XII. MYSTICAL MARRIAGE IN VOODOO

A Voodooist seeking the co-operation of a god in order to achieve some ambition, or simply wishing to put himself under the god's special protection, can make the god a formal proposal of marriage; and the same course can be taken by a god who wishes to bind himself more closely to a devotee. Does not the marriage sacrament provide the most permanent and unbreakable legal bond which can unite two beings?[11]

When a god and his mortal partner have pronounced the ritual phrases and exchanged rings, as a sign of plighted troth, they know that henceforward they will have a common destiny and will be able to depend upon each other. Marriage entails obligations and responsibilities; if the *loa*'s duty is to watch over his spouse, then in return he must be given presents. One night a week must be reserved for the *loa*; the night of the day consecrated to him. To give this night to a mortal would amount to adultery which might be seriously punished. Some human spouses make up a bed for the *loa* and sleep in it the allotted night.

Many Voodoo adepts think twice before uniting themselves to a god on account of the expense: for it is the mortal who provides the trousseau; and if the divine half is a coquette like Ezili, the cost of this can be considerable. There will have to be a silk dress, head-scarves, scent, jewels and much else. What is more, the divine spouse will take umbrage if cakes and wine are not available at the wedding reception; the price of these, added to the fees of officiating priests, can swallow up the savings of several months or even years. That is why many are afraid to obey when gods ask for their hand in marriage.

Ezili, patron goddess of lovers, has strong matrimonial tendencies. She usually ends by offering her hand to any man who serves her with zeal, particularly if he is himself about to take a wife. Then she insists on marrying him first, fearing she may be supplanted. Usually the two marriages are celebrated within a few days of each other. If the human fiancé hesitates or procrastinates too much, then supernatural warnings become ever more numerous and insistent. Should he persist in turning a deaf ear, minor disappointments, setbacks and finally serious accidents remind him that Ezili is not to be trifled with. If he marries a mortal without first marrying the goddess, then his human wife will not live long. More patience is shown by the gods to a devotee who has no intention of marrying. He can then fob them off with assurances of respect and vague promises. A person who wishes to marry a god or goddess in the hope of securing protection has therefore everything to gain by remaining celibate for the time being: he will thereby save himself a great deal of bother.

The first marriage I ever witnessed between a *loa* and a human being took place at Jacmel on the day of the Kings. Some friends had taken me just outside the town to a little sanctuary where I found myself in a considerable throng of people, many of whom belonged to the local petit bourgeoisie. At one end

of the peristyle, beneath a red satin canopy, a table had been set
up complete with candles, holy water, prayer book and a variety
of things to eat. This altar was surmounted by coloured posters
representing the saints. Two *vèvè* drawn on the ground showed
a heart (Ezili), and a snake (Damballah).

The ceremony began with the 'baptism' of the wedding dress
and of two silk handkerchiefs. Having sung a few liturgical songs
in a beautiful bass, the *père-savane* signed to the 'godparents' to
come forward, each couple carrying a different object. Opening
a prayer book he intoned a few prayers and then asked them in
an almost threatening manner whether they were good Christians
and if they really intended to baptize the head cloths and dress
which they carried. He inquired the first name of each article
carried. The godmothers, perceptibly frightened, answered un-
easily in whispers. The *père-savane* trumpeted out the names as
soon as they were given and sprinkled holy water on each piece
of clothing.

After an interval devoted to dancing, the woman who was due
to marry Damballah appeared in the peristyle. Serious and
anxious, as though overawed with the solemnity of the moment,
she took up a position seated on a chair near the *poteau-mitan*.
The *père-savane* sat beside her on a stool and chanted more
prayers; then, without change of tone and to the noise of his
sacred rattle, he proceeded to invoke the gods of Africa. The
fiancée, who till now had remained impassive, began to show signs
of nervousness. Her features contracted and her body became
agitated by an ever more pronounced trembling. She seemed prey
to violent emotion which she mastered with difficulty; clearly it
remained liable to burst out. Suddenly her mouth opened and
from it came ceaseless rapid staccato sounds. From then on all
doubt was at an end: the woman was possessed by Damballah.
No one seemed at all surprised by this metamorphosis. The
père-savane continued to roll out his litanies, pausing only to tell
the possessed to go and get ready. She complied and went off to
one of the sanctuary rooms. When she came back she was dressed
in white from head to foot; she was wearing a silk turban and
held in her hand one of the handkerchiefs which had just been
blessed. Supported by two women she made a tour of the hall,

walking face to face with the *hungan* who walked backwards in front of her shaking his rattle as though luring her with it. The women stopped and finally with flexed knees they did three pirouettes to 'salute' their guide. The *fiancée* moved toward the altar, flanked on one side by her 'godmother'—a pretty girl dressed in town clothes—and on the other by her 'godfather'—a prosperous-looking person with a distinguished bearing. Since Damballah is in fact a mute *loa* it was necessarily the 'godfather' who was asked by the *père-savane* if he would take the lady to be his wife. He asked the *fiancée* the reciprocal question and slipped two rings over her finger: her husband's and her own. He then read out the marriage certificate which ran as follows:

LIBERTÉ, ÉGALITÉ, FRATERNITÉ

Republic of Haiti, 5.847.—The year 1949 and sixth day of the month of January at 3 o'clock in the afternoon. We, Jean Jumeau, Registrar of Port-au-Prince, certifies (*sic*) that citizens Damballah Toquan Miroissé and Madame Andrémise Cétoute appeared before us to be united by the indissoluble bond of the marriage sacrament. Inasmuch as Madame Cétoute must consecrate Tuesday and Thursday to her husband Damballah without ever a blemish on herself, it being understood Monsieur Damballah's duty is to load his wife with good luck so that Madame Cétoute will never know a day's poverty: the husband Monsieur Damballah is accountable to his wife and owes her all necessary protection as set down in the contract. It is with work that spiritual and material property is amassed. In execution of artile 15.1 of the Haitian Code. They hereto agreed in the affirmative before qualified witnesses whose names are given. [Signatures.]

Assuming that the witnesses take on the heavy responsibility and answer in the affirmative.

This deed to abrogate all laws and legal statements which are contrary to it.

Asked whether they agreed to accept each other as husband and wife they replied separately in the affirmative in front of qualified witnesses hereinafter named; and they signed the register . . .

By virtue of which we certify the act of marriage stated here-under has been registered as required by the law.

Certified true copy.

The witnesses were asked to put their signatures at the bottom of the deed. The bride made signs which suggested she wanted something to eat and was led to a small pile of flour in which had been embedded an egg. She knelt and was immediately covered with a sheet. When she had gulped down the egg, some rice pudding and other dishes, all white, were passed in under the sheet. As soon as she had tasted a dish it was taken away and put on the altar. Once the meal was over the bride—still possessed by Damballah—made three libations of water before the drums and then clasped both hands of each guest in turn. While doing this she seemed to have forgotten her divine rôle for she no longer flickered out her tongue or hissed. Suddenly, without any sort of warning, she was abandoned by her invisible husband and possessed by Ezili. As 'horse' of this new divinity she proceeded to simper for all she was worth, rub herself shamelessly against the young men and give them long kisses. Possession by Ezili finished as abruptly as it began; the bride regained her calm and serious manner and went off to don her town clothes again. The fête ended with the usual set of traditional dances in honour of the main 'Guinea' divinities.

The second marriage to which I was bidden was that of Mlle L. C. who was to become one of the most popular folk singers of Port-au-Prince. When I met her she was still a *hunsi* in one of the town sanctuaries. To ensure success for her artistic career, then at its outset, she had thought it would be a good idea to unite herself in matrimony with Ogu-balindjo, one of the pro-tectors of the sanctuary to which she was attached.

I went with her, as godfather, to the altar where the *père-savane* pronounced the ritual formulae. During the ceremony L. C. bore herself quietly and gently, even timidly. But at the very moment when I slipped the two wedding-rings over her fingers she let out a vigorous 'Thunder and F——', followed by other oaths equally violent. Her features had hardened and she stamped her foot in rage. She was no longer a young bride but the soldier-god, Ogu. Quickly her shoes and jewels were removed, as always happens when someone is on the point of going into a trance. In haste the drums beat an *aux champs*, the roll of drums to salute an important person or a god, as a sign of homage to the *loa*, and the flag-bearers rushed up to provide an escort for him. Indifferent to these marks of respect, the possessed danced a joyous *mahi*, during which, proud and smiling, she lost no opportunity of showing off her rings. The god within her, a real tippler deep in his cups, demanded a bottle of rum of which he proceeded to drink a brimming cup while the choir sang 'He drinks, he is never drunk. Ogu drinks, he is never drunk.' The bride was soon deserted by her husband who vanished as quickly as he had come; she continued to dance, but was soon 'seized' by Ti-Jean-Dantor, whose incarnation was rather brief. Scarcely had he, in his turn, vanished when the face of L. C. which had in turn mirrored the rough and ferocious features of the soldier-god and the rather depraved jollity of Ti-Jean-Dantor, became positively hideous. She lay doubled up on the ground with head twisted so that her face was pressed against one shoulder, eyes turned up till the whites showed, an inordinately long purplish tongue stuck out of grimacing mouth, and arms thrown back with hands tensed like claws. This living gargoyle was laid out on a mat and the crowd came pressing round it. Each spectator in turn stepped over the possessed and hooked a little finger in hers. There was a large crowd so the procession lasted a good hour. L. C. remained fixed throughout in the same grimacing, uncomfortable position. When Vélékété—for such was the name of the visiting divinity—had disappeared, L. C. got to her feet in one leap and resumed her normal expression as though she had torn off a mask. Mingling with her companions she did some more dances until for the fourth time she fell into a trance. The god who 'rode' her now was undoubtedly her husband, for occasionally she let out an oath or an obscenity and demanded rum. This she shared generously with the other dancers who had no sooner taken a mouthful than they too were possessed by Ogu.

A few days later, meeting the bride in town, I made a discreet reference to her transformations. She had no recollection of them

and listened to my account with amusement and scepticism. Such
a reaction was normal since it is generally understood that a
'horse' knows nothing of what he does or says while ridden by a
supernatural being.

If the consort is rich enough the mystic marriage ceremony is
just as brilliant as a bourgeois wedding. An example of this was
the union celebrated by M. Baskia, one of the Voodoo priests of
Port-au-Prince, a man who had enough money to do things on a
certain scale. He had invited almost every *hungan* and *mambo* of
the region and they had all spent a lot on their appearance. Many
of the women were in long silk or satin dresses and the men wore
coloured shirts and newly pressed trousers. Some of the Voodoo
clergy were escorted by junior officials attached to their *humfo*.
As they arrived the guests were placed round the peristyle in
order of importance. Mme Baskia, a large and robust negress,
wore an embroidered white dress and sandals of the same colour.
She bustled about like a good hostess receiving important people,
always ready to put them at their ease, and keeping a weather eye
open for the smallest hitch. Her husband, in khaki shirt and
trousers, was as zealous and genial as she. For two hours priests
and priestesses exchanged greetings according to Voodoo
etiquette.

The wedding took place in one of the little chapels adjoining
the peristyle. The groom wore a white starched suit and a pink
and blue tie in honour of his divine bride, and polished shoes.
The proxy for the bride was a dumpy, ugly little *mambo*; in her
the goddess of love became flesh. Mme Baskia, who was to be
the sponsor of the wedding, went and changed into a pale blue
dress. During the ceremony four young women sang some
beautiful songs which were taken up and repeated outside by a
women's choir. After the blessing the doors of the chapel were
closed with the couple left alone, inside. When they came out
the woman, possessed by Ezili, was entirely dressed in pink and
her husband, still in white, was carrying a bouquet of white
flowers and a bottle of scent.

The standard-bearers of the sanctuary stationed themselves
behind the newly-wed and crossed the shafts of their red flags
above their heads: the *hunsi* fell in behind and the procession

went dancing round the *poteau-mitan*. Ezili, true to her nature, had to flirt with the young men and pay them indecent attentions. The couple then went up to a table, under a canopy, spread with the most sumptuous meal: decorated dishes, cakes, biscuits, bottles of champagne and rum and a great variety of liqueurs. The goddess herself cut the wedding cake and slices were served round with champagne to the important guests. The small fry had to be content with beer and biscuits. While the couple ate in a seated position, the flags were waved over their heads. Ezili and her husband received the congratulations and good wishes of all the guests. The goddess rose to embrace the women present and in her customary manner hooked her little finger into theirs. She then danced with her husband upon whom she lavished marks of affection, then she sprinkled scent on the other dancers. The couple sponged each other's faces with a silk cloth and the husband fanned his wife to cool her: an attention for which the gods have a weakness. When they had thus paraded their harmonious relationship the couple withdrew, escorted by the standard-bearers and the *hunsi*. A few minutes later the woman who had personified Ezili came modestly back and took her place among the spectators. Her husband on the other hand, who had already changed into a pink shirt and striped trousers, stayed in the place of honour. The remainder of the cakes were taken up to the altars or distributed among the guests.

It would be wrong to interpret such marriages as just so much rather ridiculous play-acting. The union of a god and a human being, as carried out in a modern bourgeois setting, can be traced back to an ancient African custom. Among the Ashanti, a spirit who wishes to favour a certain person throws himself upon him and puts him into a state of trance. The victim of such sudden and apparently involuntary possessions is regarded as the object of the spirit's matrimonial desires.

XIII. THE CONJURING UP OF *LOA*

Loa, having higher knowledge and being very well informed about what is going on both above and below, are in a position to warn their servants of what lies in store for them. But they are capricious and it would be unwise to count entirely on their goodwill. When a situation requires an urgent solution it is better to question them through the intermediary of a *hungan* or a *mambo* who 'calls them into a pitcher' (*rélé loa nâ gòvi*). Such consultations are a common occurrence in a *humfo*; often the priest himself will resort to such a method to learn the success of one of his undertakings or to set the date for a ceremony. He will use the same procedure to consult the *loa* whenever a sick person comes to him for a cure. It is the spirits who will have to indicate both cause and adequate remedy.

With Lorgina I was often present at these séances which could almost be described as shamanistic. The *mambo*, equipped with her rattle, shut herself up in the sanctuary, and by dint of prayers and invocation brought down the spirits and souls she wished to question into the pitcher. The profane who remain outside the closed room can hear noises and voices. Each spirit speaks in a different manner but nearly all affect a cavernous tone. The sceptics attribute such changes of voice to ventriloquism but the simplest explanation, suggested by the very name of the operation, is that the pitcher acts as an amplifier and distorts the voice of the *mambo*. Dialogues between the spirits, the priestess and the public are both naïve and racy. They show up the nature of Voodoo much better than any amount of speculation based on ritual or mythology. That is why it has seemed worth while putting down in full notes taken during a consultation which a certain Choisi had requested of Lorgina. Choisi, having heard that her younger sister had been seduced and abandoned, was anxious to get in touch with and consult her mother who had died a few years earlier. Throughout the séance I sat beside Choisi in a room next door to the sanctuary in which Lorgina had shut herself up. Tullius, sitting beside me, whispered in my ear the names of the *loa* as they appeared and explained allusions which escaped me. Here is the account of that séance.

For quite a long time there is no sound but the regular and monotonous clicking of Lorgina's rattle. Then she repeats a few Catholic prayers only to switch abruptly to a Voodoo invocation, mostly in *langage*, of the *loa*. '*Yâvalu gitô ladé môsago bôjago*

Yâvalu wèto, nu tayòvi, gwèru, gwèru ladè . . .' But suddenly her
voice changes; it becomes deep and muffled as though it were
resounding in some empty tank. Someone whispers to me that
it is Ogu. All the people present intoned: 'Good morning Papa
Ogu'. The god addresses Tullius with a breezy: *'Yâvalu* Tullius'
and adds: 'Don't be afraid of what you've got in your head'—an
obvious allusion to Tullius's fear that he was under a spell, and
to his endless complaints during the last few days. Papa Ogu who
is one of Lorgina's *humfo* 'masters', gives a violent dressing down
to the *hunsi*, reproaching them for their ingratitude and idleness
and several times refers to them as 'sluts'. After delivering this
reprimand Ogu, saluted by the congregation, takes his leave.

Lorgina resumes her invocations and in turn I hear her call
upon Maître-Carrefour, Baron-Samedi and the Guédé (gods of
death). She has to get their permission for Choisi's mother to
appear in the sanctuary. The noise from the next room is now a
sort of whistling which is seemingly produced by blowing over
the mouth of a bottle. It soon becomes a mournful moan: it is
the dead mother who has just arrived. Lorgina puts the utterances of this ghost into human language: the deceased recom-
mends resignation: there is no help, she says, for this embarrassing affair and above all the poor girl must not be beaten.
Lorgina, still interpreting for the ghost, says to Choisi: 'Your
mother is cold, she is in the water; you must sing a Libera to
release her good angel. You have also four brothers whose soul is
in the water.' She interrupts herself to ask Choisi if her father
is still alive. Choisi says that he died a long time ago. Lorgina
replies that his soul also is in water. The ghost once more asks for
the girl to be forgiven, pointing out that if she has done wrong
she is nevertheless not entirely to blame having been brought up
so extremely badly. The father of the child should be sent for as
soon as possible and seriously spoken to. A noise is heard in the
pitcher—the ghost has departed.

Lorgina begins to shake her rattle and recite prayers. A new
loa enters the sanctuary. First comes a grunting which turns into
a sad quavering voice. The congregation whispers that the new
inhabitant of the *govi* is Maîtresse-Mambo, protector of Tullius.
She calls Tullius who replies, 'I am in thy hand.' Everyone

present repeats the same respectful formula. The *loa* has a grudge against a certain Valérius. He reproaches him for getting into bad ways and abandoning himself to shameful practices. The accused defends himself with vigour and makes a show of laughing at some of the charges. He asks the *loa* to show him just what

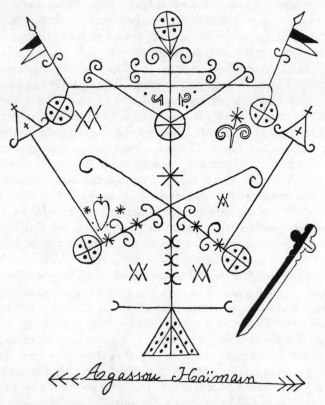

FIG. 11. The symbol (*vèvè*) of the *loa* Agassu-hayman

ways he ought to follow. Maîtresse-Mambo exhorts him to stop wasting his money and change his way of life which is not good. Immediately after this the spirit departs amid the sound of plates clashed together.

After a few minutes she is followed by another *loa* who talks in hiccups from the back of the throat, like an old man. The congregation greets him with 'Good morning, brother Linglessu' and Tullius adds 'We are in thy hand, you are our patron and protector' . . . Linglessu speaks, but his voice is so distorted I cannot understand him; then he gives place to Ogu-balindjo. Tullius is much gratified by the arrival of his patron *loa* and greets him in a confident and affectionate voice, 'I am in thy hand, Ogu Saint-Jacques, my father and protector . . .' Ogu-balindjo replies in the same spirit and passes some remarks which make Tullius laugh. He promises to become 'Linglessu's servant'. Balindjo then speaks to the congregation and inveighs against a certain *hunsi* whom he dubs 'a bad lot'—a judgement which he pronounces with disdain. He advises the *confiance* to be careful because 'bones wear the dog out'. Tullius whispers in my ear that this proverb means it is wrong to make trouble between people. It was directed against a certain Joe who seemingly was addicted to making mischief.

Suddenly a horrible lowing accompanied by the noise of clashing plates comes out of the sanctuary. It is Agirualinsu who has burst in without being called. He is amusing himself by terrifying Ogu-balindjo with fearsome cries. Agirualinsu can be heard saying, 'You have stayed long enough with me, now it's my turn.'

However he does not stay long and Lorgina explains to everyone present that he went off in a huff because they forgot to greet him. The *hunsi* protest, saying it is for the *mambo* to greet him first.

Lorgina recites various formulae in *langage* and each time she stops a cavernous voice is raised in reply. No one can identify the visitor who, as I learnt later, is none other than Agau-léfant. He has a grudge against Joe who answers him vehemently and cries out in despair: 'Don't say that.' Tullius intervenes and implores: 'But she's only a child: she doesn't know what she's doing.' The *hunsi*, stricken, cry out 'Have pity, have mercy, don't kill her, forgive, forgive! She is a little angel!' Joe begins sobbing and begs the *loa*: 'Comfort her, don't eat her! Have mercy—pity.'

Agau-léfant then tells Vertilis of traps which have been set for him at a crossroads but assures him he has nothing to fear, that he will protect him in spite of having good grounds for complaint against him—Vertilis having neglected him and favoured another *loa*.

My notes end thus: I find Joe leaning weakly against the door of the sanctuary, his face tense, frowning and anxious. I ask him what it all means. He snubs me, saying 'I can't give my mind to anything after what I've just heard . . .' Lorgina who seems well pleased with the séance explains to me the incident which created such a stir. Joe's niece had been entrusted to the *mambo* to be trained for and passed through her initiation rites, but her family had withdrawn her before she was 'brought to bed',* thus depriving Lorgina of her fees, upon which she had counted, and offending the *loa*, in particular Agau-léfant who had no doubt been selected as *maît'-tête*-to-be. This spirit had intimated to Joe his intention of killing the girl! Moreover the latter had just had a dream in which she had seen her dead mother bringing her money. With this she was to buy provisions for a journey. The dream had been interpreted as a premonition of death, since the voyage in question could only be beyond the grave.

Some *mambo* work more simply. They put themselves in a state of trance and become possessed of a god whose speciality is divination. Certain Guédé like to foretell the future; the seer's crystal ball is one of their attributes. With one of the grand *hungan* I got to know a young *hunsi* who was often 'ridden' by Guédé-double. She assumed the attributes of this spirit and then revealed the future by looking into a glass of water beside which she lit a candle.

XIV. THE FEAST OF YAMS

Although Voodoo is practised mainly by peasants it is not strictly speaking an agrarian religion. Magic rites are the commonest means by which a peasant tries to increase or maintain the yield of his acres, and it is this which gives the relationship between agriculture and religion an individual rather than a collective stamp. The only public ceremony directly related to harvests is

* This expression refers to the seclusion period of initiation.

the one known as the *manger-yam*: this corresponds with the sacrifice of the first-fruits which, among the Fon of Dahomey and Togo, is practised in exactly the same way.

The *manger-yam* is celebrated in all Voodoo sanctuaries shortly after the yam harvest. Its purpose is to allow the peasants to eat the tubercles they have gathered from the soil with perfect safety. Here are the exact words in which a Voodooist explained the object of this fête: 'When the yams of Guinea appear they cannot be eaten under the peristyle until a *manger-yam* has been held for the mysteries of Guinea. The fête does not take place at a fixed date but must follow the first harvest as closely as possible: in the south of Haiti this falls about the middle of October.'

The *manger-yam* comprises the usual elements of any Voodoo grand 'service'—African prayers, libations, consecrations, dances, sacrifices, parades. These rites substantially agree with those which we have described elsewhere; only the general outline of the ceremony and the actual treatment of the yams need concern us.

The ceremony goes on for two days. The rites of the first evening are in essence designed to confer a sacred character on the yams, on the bananas and on the dried fish collected round the *poteau-mitan*. All these are cross-signed with flour, sprinkled with libations and finally carried into the *bagi* by a procession of *hunsi*. There they are laid down on the *vèvè* and thus come in contact with the *loa*; then they are covered with *mombin* leaves, whose supernatural powers we have often remarked upon, and with an *aizan* made beneath the peristyle, as in the rite described above (see page 196). This first part of the ceremony is the 'putting-to-bed of the *yams*' (*coucher des ignames*).

The following morning the rites called the 'rising of the yams' (*lever des ignames*) are carried out and go on all day. In particular they include the sacrifice of chickens and goats. When the bodies of the victims have been put down on the *vèvè*, the *mambo* installs herself in the *bagi*. There she lines up the yams which have 'slept' under the eye of the gods and spirits and cross-signs them again with maize-flour mixed with ashes. Everyone present is invited one after the other, according to his rank in the society, to cut a tubercle into several pieces. When the yam has been divided with the matchet it must then be 'orientated'; the ground is kissed both before and after the cutting-up. This ceremony is repeated in the different *caye-mystères* (houses of gods) of the sanctuary.

In the evening the yams are boiled up with fish and everyone feasts himself. The *loa*'s share is buried in a hole dug in front of the altar.

XV. VOODOO CHRISTMAS IN HAITI

THE QUEST FOR THE MAGIC WATER

The voices of Haitian church bells and sanctuary drums mingle on Christmas night, but they summon people to very different kinds of ceremony.[12] On the one hand the birth of Christ is celebrated, on the other, beneath the watchful eye of African divinities, magic powders are prepared to afford immunity from the machinations of sorcerers, from the evil deeds of werewolves and from misfortune of all kinds. The coincidence of dates is certainly no mere chance for 'Christmas' has come to indicate rites which formerly fell about the winter solstice, or which heralded the new year. A similar phenomenon is known to have occurred in Europe at the dawn of Christianity. Voodoo, standing closer to its origins, has not bothered to establish a link between the two festivals. Extensive rites of preparation for Christmas are begun a long time ahead and are themselves occasions for complex ceremonies. Voodoo Christmas is the culminating phase of a veritable cycle of rites. The picture of them which we shall give here is incomplete; much is missing, in particular the practices observed during the picking of the magic plants. On the other hand I had the opportunity of accompanying the whole staff of a *humfo* in their search for the water used in the preparation of the 'baths'. At Port-au-Prince these ablutions are made with the sulphurous water of the Source Balan, situated at the foot of one of the mountain chains which border the Cul-de-Sac plain on the north side. The subterranean cavern from which it emerges is said to be the dwelling place of numerous *loa*: Damballah-wèdo, Agwé, Maîtresse-la-Sirène and Grande-Bossine.

The quest for this sulphurous water is carried out with great pomp and all members of sanctuaries—priests, acolytes and servants of the spirits—take part, treating it as a pilgrimage. In 1947 I was invited by Lorgina to join one such pious expedition. On the day agreed for the start, the *mambo* made a sacrifice to the water *loa* in her *humfo* room. 'I ask you,' she said firmly, 'to open the way for us tomorrow to go to the Balan spring. Give me your help throughout the journey. Grande-Bossine, I've promised you a present, I've given you a chicken; the other chicken was for all the *mystères*. I killed the chicken this evening so that I might give it to you tomorrow at the Balan spring. It is tomorrow that you'll get it. All mysteries, help me, watch over me, let me make profits. Let those to whom I have done good be grateful to me. The mysteries know very well that I am good. Take away the bad luck which has been afflicting me and which is preventing people from being grateful to me. Let people come and succour me when I am ill and let them remember the good I do instead of abusing me. Give me your help so I may have the means of sleeping, eating and living, and so that peace may be in my house.'

When she had finished this speech, with all its implied reproach of the *hunsi* of her society, she threw whole handfuls of food in the pool of Damballah-wèdo and made libations. With this gesture, the first ceremony of the Christmas cycle came to an end.

The next day, turning up early at the *humfo*, I found *mambo* and *hunsi* in the process of loading packages wrapped in white cloth into a motor-coach. Before its departure Lorgina shut herself in one of the sanctuary rooms in order to consult two of her favourite *loa*—Ogu and Linglessu. Those who like myself kept near the door heard monotonous incantations punctuated rhythmically and ceaselessly by the clinking of the rattle, then the noise of plates being clashed together, finally a hoarse voice—which meant Ogu had come down into the *govi*. I did not understand much of the dialogue between the *mambo* and the two *loa* but the consultation must have been satisfying for she left the *humfo* in a cheerful mood. We piled into the coach as best we could and set off at a good speed. The *hunsi*, like a band of schoolgirls on holiday, sang hymns loud enough to split your ears and waved the 'Society's' banners out of the windows.

When we had gone about twenty miles towards the mountains the vehicle left the main road and began to plough through a forest of acacias whose thorny branches whipped our hands and faces. Despite the efforts of our chauffeur who hoped to save Lorgina and her rheumatism a long march, we were compelled to stop in the middle of the bush. We unloaded the bus and the *mambo*, followed by her *hunsi*, boldly set out along a narrow path towards the chain of hills in which lay the Balan spring. Arriving at a crossroads we halted so that we could pay homage to the patron spirit of crossroads—Legba. The god's emblem was quickly traced out in flour in the middle of a clearing, a small fire was lit and into it each in turn made libations and offerings. The *hunsi* sang hymns to Legba, and the standard-bearers, having done the rounds of the fire, kissed the earth. Legba chose this moment to possess a girl who was still almost a child. She fell to the ground convulsed and struggled as though trying to escape from the clutches of the invisible being who was trying to take root in her. She finally gave in and her abandon made it possible to lift her to her feet. She then fell to her knees and stayed thus, her arms hanging slackly, her head loosely slumped on her chest, amid the *hunsi* who, with their songs, saluted the presence of the god. The possessed girl at last came out of her torpor and went back to her place in the procession as though nothing had happened. Legba having departed, we moved on again—everyone having made four libations and four offerings of dried food, as before.

A nauseating stench of sulphur showed we were approaching the Balan spring. Now we found it, in a hole about a yard wide, lying at the foot of a mass of rock. The water which keeps it filled escapes into the forest in a thin stream. An arch rose up near the source; some *vèvè*, partially rubbed out, bore witness to the recent passage of other 'Societies' come here to get water for the Christmas ablutions. Without losing a minute, the *hunsi* opened their parcels of provisions and put out a great variety of foods in the dishes and calabashes which they laid out on the ground. These were offerings for the guardian spirits of this place. Tullius, who

was very active, dug near this picnic-place a shallow ditch, doubtless to inform the 'mysteries' that when the time came they would
get their share of the feast. After a few Catholic prayers recited
by Lorgina, Tullius 'launched' a song, probably composed specially for the occasion.

Marie, vini Jésus moi	Mary come Jesus to me
Grâce ô grâce	Mercy, o mercy
Deshabillé deshabillé	Undress, undress
Grâce, Marie, grâce	Mercy, Mary, mercy.

At this the *hunsi* began to undress in readiness to enter the
cavern from which came the waters of the Balan spring. This subterranean pilgrimage is quite an adventure. Indeed the only
means of access to the cave is the spring itself and you have to
slip through it, into a narrow enclosed channel which leads to
the bottom of a tiny lake. Tullius and another young man acted
as guides. They set off ahead, as path-finders, their cheeks
stuffed out with candle-ends and a box of matches to light the
cave.

After a quarter of an hour the head and the hands of Tullius
could be seen at the bottom of the spring. He had come to let us
know that all was ready: the *hunsi* could come to him; and he disappeared again. First to go down into the hole were the men.
When my turn came I slid as best I could into the narrow opening having first taken a deep breath to last out my period of sub-
mersion. This was short, for I was no sooner under than I felt
myself seized by energetic hands. When they let me go I was able
to reach the surface with a few strokes—and found myself in a
darkish pool. By the feeble light of the candles I could make out
a low vault of basaltic rock and at one end a sort of beach lighted
by daylight which filtered down through a narrow crack in the
wall. Those who had gone on before me had gathered there and
were rubbing their bodies with bunches of herbs which they
subsequently laid on a ledge of rock where other such bunches
were in the process of decomposition. Everyone was silent as
though afraid of disturbing that abode of *loa*. Noise, however,
there suddenly was—and violent too—yappings and gurglings
such as might have been made by someone drowning. A young

woman who had just emerged, possessed by Damballah, was giving in to a crisis. She struggled violently, fell into the water, came up and tried to hiss like a snake, but failing, broke into a sort of barking which may have been shouts of terror. Since she seemed unable to keep herself afloat Tullius and his acolyte went to her assistance and pulled her up on to the beach where she might stay till her trance was over. Another possession gave us even more anxiety: the man concerned had fallen into a state of torpor which verged on catalepsy. When an attempt was made to bring him into the open air, it proved exceedingly difficult to get him through the neck which he blocked with his inert body. It took the combined efforts of all the *hunsi* to get him out of the hole. They lifted him on to the edge of the spring where he remained stretched out as though dead. Lorgina seemed unmoved by the incident. She came and shook her rattle over him, recited a few prayers in a low voice and finally 'rode' him—stood astride him—as is customary when a *loa* prostrates itself in front of a priest. Clearly the *mambo* was trying to make the spirit leave the man whom it had so seriously endangered. Her treatment proved effective for gradually he came to his senses. When he was quite himself he seemed to have no recollection of his misadventure.

Inside the cavern there were more and more possessions and soon everyone there, with a few exceptions, succumbed to Damballah or Grande-Bossine. This cavern, this dismal pool, these people possessed, convulsed on the surface with their eyes turned up, their mouths agape, their tongues lapping the air, put one in mind of the damned teeming on the banks of the Styx. But the attacks did not last long. Whether it was the god that quitted them or whether they found calm in giving in to him, they managed to get to the beach where they rubbed their bodies with handfuls of vegetation. The heat, the lack of air and the darkness began to trouble me. This feeling of oppression was shared by people near me who also seemed anxious to get out. After some lively discussion it was decided that the women, who seemed the most frightened, should be evacuated first although several men insisted on going out before them. Those who could dive were guided by the ferrymen towards the neck which was not easy to

find among the rocks. The others were carried on the backs of
guides to the opening where they had to start climbing. The two
ferrymen who were continually diving to show the pilgrims the
way out, only paused long enough to get their breath. When
everyone was out Lorgina and the other women who had been
kept from entering by their *embonpoint*, soaked themselves in the
waters of the spring.

Having given the bathers time to dry themselves and dress,
Lorgina led them to a small pond situated not far from the Balan
spring. We had hardly arrived there before the other *mambos*
went down into it and rubbed themselves vigorously with
medicinal plants. While they were going through with this ritual
toilet Tullius did a fine *vèvè* on the bank representing Damballah
the snake. As before he lit candles which this time he stuck in the
hollow of a tree. Lorgina came out of the pond and went and sat
on a palm trunk by the water's edge. She stayed there motionless,
her eyes half-closed, when suddenly she was shaken by tremblings
that became more and more violent. It was Damballah possessing her. People busied themselves round about her and gently
and respectfully she was helped back into the water. She remained near the edge, up to her waist, and the expression of pain
remained on her face. Then darting out her tongue she made the
staccato sounds which pass for the language of the snake Damballah. With index and small finger raised she pointed out the
hunsi on the bank and splashed them gaily until they came up to
her as required. Two *hunsi* entered the water and unfurling the
flags of the society took up position behind Damballah as his
guard of honour. Tullius came and offered him an egg nestling
in a pile of flour. Lorgina having taken it was immediately hidden
from view by a sheet which was stretched over her. Other *hunsi*
poured almost the whole contents of a bottle of scent over her but
she, tearing it out of their hands, motioned the other two *mambo*
to come near. As a token of goodwill the 'god' poured scent over
their heads in the outline of a cross. The *hunsi*, fully dressed,
joined them in the pond where they sprinkled each other. This
game, which must have been basically ceremonial, was followed
by many crises which may either have been provoked by the
sprinkling or simply due to the fact that the moment had come

for the *hunsi* to receive the master of the pond, the god Damballah, into their bodies. Soon they stopped hissing and darting their tongues, and climbed out again on to the bank along with Lorgina. Then came the turn of the men to go down into the water. They too sprinkled each other and were 'mounted' by the spirit of the pond.

We all went back to the Balan spring where we had to take in a supply of water and offer the spirits the food which had been prepared for them. When the *loa* had been saluted with songs and prayers the share of food allocated to them was thrown into the hole prepared in the morning. Then, quickly, the hole was filled in and a *vévé* traced on the loose earth. The remainder of the food was divided out and the ceremony ended with an open-air luncheon which was both sumptuous and gay. The journey back was full of incidents. These were due to the enervated condition of the *hunsi* for whom the sudden pleasures of a brief holiday had alternated with strong mystical emotion. When we got back to the *humfo* the *hunsi* formed up in procession behind Lorgina who made a tour of the sanctuary, stopping at the four points of the compass to salute the spirits. She also came and shook her rattle and prayed before the house of the Guédé and the entrance to her peristyle. Finally she scattered four libations of water and rum in front of the *poteau-mitan*. The *mambo* saluted each other according to *rada* etiquette and the *hunsi* came and pirouetted and prostrated themselves before Lorgina. Just when we were about to disband a woman who, on the way back, had already shown signs of excitement and who had quarrelled with her companions, became subject to a strong 'attack of *loa*'. She rolled on the ground, violently convulsed. It was Damballah again. His appearance at such a late hour was certainly regarded as ill-timed, for the *mambo* and her acolyte at once set to work to get rid of him.

Between this water quest and Christmas there was, to my knowledge, no other ceremony. But in the course of my sojourns in Haiti I twice was present at the actual ceremonies of Christmas, once with Lorgina at Port-au-Prince and the second time in the Léogane neighbourhood with a rural *hungan*. The contrast afforded by the two interpretations of an identical ritualistic theme is worth showing in some detail as it throws into relief the extent to which Voodoo varies from one milieu to another.

CHRISTMAS EVE AT PORT-AU-PRINCE

The ceremony which I am about to describe was conducted according to the *petro* rite. The orchestra was made up of two drums beaten in a rapid and staccato rhythm accompanied by blasts on a whistle out of the depths of the night. From the first dances onwards the *hungan* and his acolytes carried out sprinkling of *kiman*. They filled their mouths with this liquid and sprayed it over one shoulder whilst throwing one forearm on to the opposite shoulder in a gesture which was full of arrogance.

A strong spicy smell engulfed the peristyle. The *hunsi*, dressed in red and blue, went in procession to the house of the Guédé where they received packets of leaves. They put them on their heads and in Indian file came back dancing under the peristyle. As they entered they were sprinkled with *kiman*. They went through a few dance movements and then knelt before a large tank decorated with *vèvè* traced out in chalk. They put down the leaves and before rising piously kissed the earth. The leaves must first be crumpled and stripped of their stalks so as to liberate their salubrious powers. This operation, like all the other preparations for the fête, takes on a ritual character.

A dozen *hunsi* gathered round the receptacle and set to work amid dancing and singing. Lorgina, standing in the middle of the peristyle, gave out a series of veritable croaks and showed signs of dizziness: a *petro* spirit whom I was unable to identify had come into her. Her arms were rubbed with scent and a green cloth tied round her loins. The *hunsi* came to salute the divinity who, in reply, 'twirled' them. Lorgina, or rather the god within her, did not always seem entirely well-disposed towards her servants for occasionally she 'twirled' them with such sudden violence that they lost their balance. It is true though that movements which appear brutal may, when they come from a 'god', be no more than the expression of a desire to induce possessions.

Towards ten o'clock in the evening a mortar was brought in decorated within and without with *vèvè*. It was in this implement

that the dried plants used for magic powders were ground down
as prescribed by ritual. The following plants were listed to me
as ingredients: *trois-parôles* (*Allophyllus occidentalis*), *bois-dine*
(*Eugenia fragrans*), *grand-bois* (?), *zos-douvant* (*Eugenia crenu-
lata*); but the strong and piquant smell which emanated from
the powder and which made those who took it sneeze, was due to
the presence of bloodwort and *ogan*. Two men with silk cloths
round their necks approached the mortar. Each took from the
hungan a pestle which had first been presented to the four
cardinal points and which, like the mortar, was inscribed with
symbols in chalk. They saluted each other, crossing their pestles,
and then brought them down alternately in the mortar, keeping
exactly in time to the drums. The *hungan* came back with ashes
to trace out symbolic figures all round the mortar. Lorgina, once
again possessed by a spirit, smoked a big cigar in a corner. From
time to time one of her acolytes came and emptied the mortar
and filled it again with dry leaves. He passed the results of the
milling through a sieve before tipping it into a calabash. So strong
is the magic power of this mixture that, while dealing with it, he
sometimes reeled as though a spirit were trying to enter into him.
The powder is not fully effective unless the blood and flesh of a
chicken are contained in it, so one was now brought by the
hungan who, having brought it into contact with the *poteau-
mitan* and 'signalled' it to the four cardinal points, placed it on
the edge of the mortar where Lorgina, still entranced, executed
it with one blow from a sabre. The priest then sucked the blood
which pumped out of the palpitating body and cut the bird up
into several slices which he threw into the mortar. Now the
heavy pestles resumed their battering and in a few seconds the
chicken was nothing but a pulp of blood and feathers. The same
hungan sprinkled this with *clairin* and set fire to it. The uprush of
flames induced a number of possessions. Jean-Dantor—that is to
say a woman possessed by the spirit of that name—took a little
boy, three or four years old, by one leg and dangled him for a few
seconds over the flames. The child screamed with terror but
suffered no harm. The remains of the chicken scorched by the
fire were added to the powder. Thus ended the rite called 'grind-
ing-leaves' (*piler-feuilles*).

Those who take part in the preparation of the 'bath' hope
their health will be the better for it and their luck improved. That
is why women freely offer their services for the stripping and
crumpling of the leaves, and why men volunteer to grind them.
With such a crowd of willing helpers the work is soon finished.
The sulphurous water of the Balan spring, mixed with *clairin*, is
poured into the mortar along with various ingredients, intended
to increase its efficacy, such as pepper and pimento and a
chopped-up bullock's heart. Then small charges of powder are
detonated on the edge of the tank and this results in yet more
possessions.

A large *boucan* fire was burning in the court. Out of it reared
up an iron bar, the *pince* of the *loa* Criminel. The *hungan* went and
took out a brand which he threw in the 'bath'. This then burst
into flames while the *hungan* stirred it like a cook with a bit of
wood. He then returned to the pyre and brought out the reddened
pince (he wisely gripped it by the very tip) and threw it into the
tank. As the sizzling marriage of fire and water was consum-
mated, the *loa* Brisé possessed Lorgina and her face immediately
changed: now a hard and furious god, whip in hand, she threw
herself on the *hunsi* lashing them cruelly—doubtless to make them
dance with more ardour. The drum-beat became more urgent,
the dance faster, more hectic and 'hotter'. Clearly the *hunsi* were
giving in to a growing exaltation. Several among them even
became all but entranced. They tottered and staggered or, seized
with giddiness, remained struck still where they stood. None,
however, were ridden by a *loa*. They were merely 'tipsified' by
spirits who had settled on them briefly.

The whole ceremony coming under the sign of the *petro* and
magic, it followed that it should be used as an opportunity for
undertaking spectacular treatments. A sick man advanced on the
hungan with arms outstretched. The *hungan* poured on to his
palms a charge of powder which immediately exploded, throwing
out an enormous flame. Burning spirit was spread over the hands
of a *hunsi* who rubbed them as though she were soaping heself.
Spectators and *hunsi* alike gave themselves willingly to these
spectacular but not very dangerous ordeals. The *hungan* then
went the rounds of the gathering with a calabash full of magic

powder of which he gave everyone a pinch to snuff. This substance is said to cure physical disorders and also to remove bad
luck. The magic bath was first taken by a little girl of about five.
She was put in the tank and was rubbed from head to foot with
the leaves. The receptacle was then taken into the house of the
Guédé where all the *hunsi* shut themselves in to be washed by the
hungan and his acolyte. The bath ceremony lasted all night but
naturally the highly developed sense of modesty of the Haitian
made it impossible for me to attend.

Here is the description of the same ceremony carried out in a
country setting. An arbour, specially built for the occasion,
served as a peristyle. The fête began with the consecration of a
vast pyre which was to burn all night. The site for it had been
marked out with a *vèvè*: the drawing of a circle sliced with eight
radii, these being produced beyond the circumference. Branches
were laid along these radii, leading out from the centre where pine
sticks and glowing embers had been heaped up. The *hungan*
sprayed *kiman* with his mouth, proceeding as follows: three times
over his shoulder with the arm folded back, four times on the
fire, three times in the air and again three times on the fire. A
large mortar was brought in under the arbour and placed on a
mat. The *hungan* sanctified it, tracing *vèvè* inside and out, then
'dressed' it with white cloth as is sometimes done with certain
drums. Two large pestles, also covered with symbolic designs,
were leant against the mortar. Shortly afterwards everyone
assembled for the 'thanksgiving' (*l'action de grâces*). The *hungan*,
sitting on a little chair in front of the drums, chanted a series of
Paters, Aves, Credos and Confiteors which were punctuated by
the responses of the congregation. Passing without transition
from God and Saints to *loa*, he recited a long prayer in which
Creole words alternated with passages in *langage*.

Three verses of this interminable invocation are engraved on
my memory. The first evoking cockcrow and waking up in an
African village is moving in its simplicity.

> *Nâ Guinê ju l'uvri, kok l'ap châté kokoliko*
> *Twa Pater, twa Ave Maria*
> *Wâgolo, ki menê l'Afrikê sòti nâ Guinê*

Day is dawning in Africa and the cock crowing cocoriko
Three Paters, three Ave Marias
Wangolo, who is leading the African who has left Africa.

This invocation was accompanied by piercig blasts on a
whistle and the sharp, dry sounds of the *petro* whip which was
cracked near the tank.

The prayer lasted nearly an hour and a half. As soon as it was
over, there came the sound of the quick, staccato rhythm of the
petro drums. Two men with the lower half of their faces covered,
one by a white cloth, one by a red, advanced on the mortar and
seized the pestles. After being sprinkled on their arms and hands
they began to pound the leaves (*piler feuilles*) while the congregation celebrated the divine twins (*marassa*—in this region they are
invoked and saluted before Legba). The choir then went on to
hymns in praise of the *petro loa*. Spirits seldom fail to come
quickly when they are sung or danced for. A sudden scuffling in
the congregation made me think a riot had broken out; in fact it
meant merely that a number of spirits had arrived and were
struggling with their 'horses' in order to 'mount' them. The latter
rolled on the ground at the mercy of crises which threw them
from side to side in a sort of sacred frenzy. The tumult only
ceased when the *loa* finally got the better of their 'mounts'. The
spirits who revealed themselves were Simbi, Simba, Malalu,
Kita and Grand-Bois. Two women were even possessed at the
same moment by Grand-Bois!—one of them was Docelia, the
daughter of the master of the house. She was a Negress of about
twenty, well filled-out and built and muscled like a fair-ground
wrestler. In order to look more like Grand-Bois she had put on
a ferocious mask. Her heavy chin sticking out in front, and her
dilated nostrils gave her the muzzle of a beast. Her loins were at
once encompassed with a cloth and her sandals removed. With a
sort of wild barking, she jumped on to the mortar where she
remained balanced with legs apart and hands on hips—her head
pushed out she shook her shoulders in time to the drums, jigged
up and down, shouted and sang her head off, only pausing to ex-
hort the men with the pestles to redouble their exertions. Here are
a few couplets of her song, taken down on the spot as they came:

Grâ bwa zilé . . . zilé o (bis)	Grand-Bois zilé . . . zilé
Grâ bwa môté bwa, l' álé	Grand-Bois climbs on the wood, he has gone
Aaa dié	Aaa dié
M'alé lâ Grâ bwa	I am going to Grand-Bois
M'pralé kéyi fèy mwê	I am going to pick my leaves.

The other Grand-Bois climbed the mortar in his turn. At first she was resisted by her companion who as daughter of the house felt the position was hers by rights, the other girl being merely a distant relation. However, soon reconciled, the two danced and sang as one. While the pestles were rising and falling without pause between their separated feet, Docelia, carried away by frenzy, caught on to the roof beams, raised herself and hanging for a moment in mid-air, flourished her legs in time to the music. She let herself slip down back on to the mortar, only to repeat the whole performance a few minutes later. The acrobatics of the two possessed girls would have upset the mortar if some men had not run up and held it firm. The pestles only paused when those wielding them were relieved or when the receptacle was emptied and refilled by the *hungan*. Halts were marked by blasts on a whistle. Bark and roots were pulverized before the leaves. The bunches were 'orientated' to the four cardinal points before being thrown into the tank while the choir sang:

Fèy o vini sòvé mwê	Oh leaves, come and save me
La misè, mwê yé	I am so wretched.

The supply of leaves having been exhausted, the last multure was about to be taken out of the mortar when Docelia jumped down and stretched herself out on the ground on a mat. Several peasants lifted the mortar and set it down on her back. She took the whole weight while people once more set to work with the pestles. Such a feat required a rare degree of strength; consequently the faithful gave the kudos not to Docelia but to Grand-Bois who in her goodness permitted this powder to be pulverized on her back and thus endowed it with new powers. This performance brought the 'grinding of leaves' to an end. The mortar was now emptied and the hollow meticulously combed so that not a grain should be lost. When the interior had been well cleaned the *hungan* poured in some *clairin*. This he ignited with a brand taken from the bonfire in the court. The leaf pounders came and scooped up some of the flaming liquid in their calabashes and raised it to their lips. Then, plunging their hands into the fire they rubbed their hands and faces with it. Sometimes it was the possessed who took this fire-bath and passed their flaming hands over the body and face of the *hungan* or the leaf-pounders. The *hungan* taking a calabash full of powder went round the company giving everyone a pinch. Wherever he went he was followed by a concert of sneezing for no mucuous membrane can stand up to the powder. This distribution brought the first part of the fête to an end.

The second act which was due to take place round the bonfire, at some distance from the make-shift peristyle, opened with hymns in honour of the *loa*, notably of Maître-Cimetière-Bumba. Docelia, still possessed by Grand-Bois but much calmer now that she was no longer presiding over the leaf-pounding, seemed to be nervous and on edge. She finally sank down on to a chair and covered her face with her cloth. When she took it away she had resumed her habitual expression: Grand-Bois had left her. But suddenly she again tottered, completed a few erratic steps and slumped to the ground where she remained stretched out, her eyes fixed, her limbs rigid. This time it was Maître-Cimetière who in descending upon her had changed her into 'a corpse'. Immediately a symbolical funeral toilet was carried out: a strip of cloth was tied round her head, cotton wool put between her teeth and in her nostrils and ears. Other dancers, among whom were many women, collapsed in their turn on the ground. They too 'became corpses' and were therefore ceremonially laid out. Soon their bodies, motionless at first, were overrun with mild tremblings which built up into sudden starts. Some of the 'dead', using their elbows and feet, crawled towards the pyre. Others, sprinkled with *kiman*, got up and walked to the fire helped by the *loa* Malulu. The latter, who had perhaps drunk more than was wise, buzzed and bumped around like blind bees. The spectators, gathered round the brazier, watched the *loa* with curiosity and amusement tinged with alarm. As well as Maître-

Cimetière-Bumba, an essentially terrifying *loa*, there were a few comic Guédé in funny hats and wearing dark-glasses as is their custom. These walked up and down in front of the fire with rigid legs, uttering obscenities in a high-pitched nasal tone. The orchestra had left the peristyle and installed themselves outside near the bonfire. From the first drum-beats the possessed came round the fire dancing, and jumped with great agility into the middle of the flames to 'bathe' there. They did not linger and despite their apparent state of trance, took care to put their feet on parts of the logs not yet alight.

Other less bold members of the Guédé remained at a distance and continued to provide light relief for the whole performance. One Guédé, sinking down in front of the drums, pretended to want to rape a woman seated nearby—a farce which earned him a huge success.

Some *loa*, Malulu in particular, tried to provoke possessions among the spectators by stationing themselves face to face with them and staring straight into their eyes. They even pressed themselves against people and rubbed foreheads, but these efforts were not always crowned with success. Maître-Cimetière-Bumba, despite the chin-support and the wad of cotton-wool stuck in their mouths, felt it incumbent upon them as living corpses to emit lugubrious death-rattles rather as children will when trying to frighten each other. Docelia, who had put on a black dressing-gown and a strange Chinese hat, did her best to live up to her part. Spirit though she now was, she did not forget her responsibilities as daughter of the house and so watched over the smooth-running of the ceremony. Every time the crowd came too near the fire and got in the way of the possessed, she drove them back, threatening them with a flaming torch. The Maître-Cimetière spirits, taking some *hunsi* by the hand, pirouetted them so violently that several, losing their balance, all but fell into the fire. One *loa* seized the hand of a young woman which he held in the flames a few moments without her wincing. At that moment one of the spectators cried out, 'I would never submit to anything like that; if I did an ambulance would soon be on its way.'

The preceding year there had been plenty of comedy. Knowing the Guédé's dread of fire, one of the other *loa*, Brisé, had

seized Guédé-nuvavu and tried to drag him into the flames. The
poor Guédé had struggled without managing to get free. When
he felt the heat of the fire on his naked feet he screamed in terror.
Maître-Cimetière-Bumba then 'came to his assistance and pre-
vailed upon Brisé to have pity. The latter let go whereupon the
Guédé fled amid general laughter and jeers.' This impromptu
which the possessed had enacted round the fire had attracted a
lot of people. People crowded round, the better to see, and the
spectators in the front row, finding themselves pushed towards
the fire, reacted vigorously, protested and resisted the crowd
behind. From the direction of the sanctuary came an appeal loud
enough to quell the disturbance. It was the *loa* Loco-atissu who
had come down into Sino, the brother of Calixte, to demand that
everyone present should get back beneath the arbour. The drums
changed rhythm to 'salute' the *loa* and the choir intoned the
song which begins:

Loco-atissu, nu la agoé.   Loco-atissu, we are here, agoé.

A few minutes later, since the crowd was still milling about the
fire, Loco-atissu, clad in a black frock-coat, came in person to
hasten the withdrawal. This god is regarded as a sage whom it is
worth consulting. He did the rounds of the congregation full of
friendliness for one and all. Of some he took the hands and raised
them to the four points of the compass, of others the clothing and
shook it to free them of bad luck, and all the time he was prodigal
both with advice and reproaches.

The last part of the fête was entirely given over to dance. The
Guédé in particular proved gay companions—particularly Guédé-
brave who kept sitting on the knees of the women, lied shamelessly, stole food and suggested to those present that he should
change clothes with them. All this with furtive gestures, timid
evasions and rodomontades.

Docelia, who as we have said had been mounted by Grand-
Bois and then by Maître-Cimetière-Bumba, finally fell prey to
Damballah-wèdo. Instead of the god's usual 't-t-t-t', she yapped
or more precisely barked like a cur. She disappeared in the
direction of the *humfo* and came back clad in red, her *hunsi*
necklace worn crosswise. She resumed her barking louder than

ever and danced with her arm stretched out, the fingers of her right hand forming horns. She was given an egg nested in flour which she took and threw away. After this she demanded a bath in the *humfo* pool. The *hungan* addressing himself to the *loa* who was lodged in her head, begged him to spare his 'horse' a bathe which might be harmful to her so soon after exposure to the flames of the bonfire. Damballah vanished as though by magic— to give place to the marine god Agwé whom everyone hastened to revive with towels and sponges as though he were a wilting boxer—for Agwé suffers from the heat whenever he leaves water. At more or less the same moment a woman rolled on the ground, seized with violent convulsions. She knelt, tore the top of her dress and flung herself into a dishevelled dance, the upper part of her body quite naked. She resisted all attempts to calm her and went on with her frenzied prancing. When finally she was soothed she burst into tears. Recovering quickly she danced until she was finally overcome by an excess of weariness. A child *loa* came on and began to cry, begging for something to eat. Among the supernatural personages who mingled with the dancers there was a certain Pierre-Boucassin, one of whose peculiarities is a weakness for salted coffee.

At dawn when the drums were silent the last exhausted dancers went and flung themselves down on mats. The 'horses' of the gods were there before them, sleeping deeply.

The following day some of them woke up already possessed by their *loa* and continued to adhere to their various divine personalities. But on the whole their hearts were not in it. Worn out by the agitation of the previous day the *loa* dawdled and made insignificant remarks.

The cycle of ceremonies, beginning with the quest for the sulphurous water and ending so brilliantly with Christmas night, is mainly designed to bring good luck to the devotees by means of the 'baths' and to give priests an opportunity of preparing, with all due pomp and circumstance, the magic powders which they use in their 'treatments'. The fête which we refer to as 'Christmas', on account of the coincidence of dates, is at root only a magic ceremony designed to ensure the capture of that vague power called 'luck' and to confer immunity against sorcerers.

However, other stray rites seem to have got grafted on to the magic ritual. These are doubtless vestiges of other ceremonies which had to do with the winter solstice and the visiting of the earth by the dead. Of this the part played by fire, as well as the presence of the funeral deities, are signs which cannot be altogether dismissed.

XVI. THE CULT OF THE DEAD

The dead, after the *loa* and the Twins, are the third category of supernatural beings to be worshipped. But before a deceased person is promoted to the rank of tutelary spirit, and becomes in his turn a *loa*, his family must first complete various ceremonies which are usually spread out over several years. The funeral customs of the Haitian peasantry are extremely complex. Alongside rites borrowed from Catholic liturgy—and scrupulously observed—there exist many practices which are dictated by fear of ghosts and the simple desire to put death at a distance as soon as possible. Strictly speaking such precautions are no part of Voodoo, in so far as 'Voodoo' is taken to mean a religious system. They are magic precautions whose exact origin is hard to establish; and they are common to the folklore of both Europe and Africa. These funeral rites are much more elaborate and much stricter when the deceased has been an initiate holding some rank in a Voodoo cult-group.[13]

It would be somewhat arbitrary merely to describe Voodoo funeral ceremonies without giving some attention to rites which, although apparently not linked with the cult of *loa*, nevertheless are always observed over every dead body no matter whether it is that of a Catholic, a fervent Voodooist or an uncompromising Protestant. Christian churches tolerate many pagan customs either because they are ignorant of their origin or because they do not dare to condemn traditions whose roots lie deep in the life of the people.

Fear of the dead is such that their close relations would never dare, under any pretext whatever, to avoid those duties which custom exacts. Even the most destitute family does not hesitate to sacrifice its last pennies to ensure a proper funeral for one of its members. In such spending—which may seem unreasonable to us—there may be an element of vanity and concern for 'what the neighbours might say', yet this ostentation has a deeper cause. That the style of funeral actually determines the fate of the soul in eternity may not really be believed or given clear expression, but it does somehow influence the reaction of peasants when confronted by death. The anguish which gnaws at the heart of some, when they imagine they will have no funeral vigil and perhaps only a coffin of rude planks, cannot be explained away merely in terms of peasant pride. Any man who respects himself takes forethought for his funeral. If his cattle are insufficient to defray the costs he designates plots of land to be sold as soon as he enters his last agony or after his death. The needs of heirs are pitilessly sacrificed to their duties towards the deceased. I was told of peasants who, having no direct heirs, actually adopted a child to make sure they would get a proper burial. Others fearing their children may prove stingy when it comes to the quality of the coffin, make one for themselves and keep it carefully in their homes. In a report which reached Unesco, someone speaking for the Marbial community thanked the International Organization for having provided them with a carpentering shop and so paved the way to coffins on account. Let us forbear to smile: the dead are demanding and these poor country folk were truly glad that their burden had been lessened.

Initiation serves to create a mystic bond between *loa* and devotee, making the spirit into a *maît'-tête* for the human being. Later, other spirits may possess the initiate but the one who first made him his 'horse' remains his particular patron and protector. This link must, however, be broken after death or else the *loa* will rain vengeance on the heads of neglectful relations. The ceremony by which this separation is effected, between the deceased and his *loa*, is called the *déssunin* (from the French *déssonner*), or *dégradation*. It takes place immediately after death but can equally be celebrated at the cemetery some days or even weeks later if, for some reason or other, it was impossible to celebrate it at the desired moment.

The *déssunin* ceremony begins with appeals to the *loa* and ends with a scene which people have always described to me with terror—provoked by the mere mention of it. The *hungan*, having motioned the spectators to stand at a distance, advances towards the death-bed, gets under the sheet which covers the corpse and crouches over it. Shaking his rattle he beseeches and invokes the *loa*. Then, having murmured some mysterious formulae three times over in the corpse's ear, he calls the deceased loudly by name. Now, apparently something horrible and strange happens: a shudder runs through the corpse and slowly it raises its head, or shoulders, as though trying to sit up—then it slumps back—an inert mass. This is not a spark of life, struck into being by the *hungan*'s art, but merely a muscular contraction—the effect of the *loa* leaving the mortal remains of his servant. It is not unusual for the released *loa* to go, there and then, and take up residence in some person who, appointed by him, will immediately become, so to speak, the spiritual heir of the deceased and will take over the obligations which the latter may have contracted *vis-à-vis* the god.

This description of the most dramatic moment of the *déssunin* is based upon eyewitness accounts, honest—certainly—but carried away by faith so that every detail was seen in terms of marvel. To separate truth from fantasy is not always easy. A Haitian teacher who had witnessed a *déssunin*, told me that the *hungan* straddling the corpse had pulled it up by the arms. No doubt it is this striking scene which for believers becomes a miracle.

I have left out of this chapter many details, which were generously contributed by various informants, simply because they are to be found in the majority of Voodoo ceremonies. One episode, however, which I got from an excellent source, I will mention. It takes place shortly before the departure of the *loa*. The *hungan* marks a cross on the head of the corpse with flour, then places a tuft of its hair in a little white pot, some of its body hair, and parings of nails from the left hand and foot. To these are added feathers plucked from a chicken which the *hungan* has first passed to and fro several times over the head of the corpse. The meaning of this rite seems clear to me: it is the soul of the 'good angel' of the departed which is put in the white pot and

not the *loa*, as some Voodooists make out. The soul of the dead
person, since it is destined to become a *loa*, is often referred to
as such—which makes for confusion. As we have seen in another
chapter, *hungan* transfer the soul of initiates into a *pot-tête* by an
identical procedure, and magicians gather, similarly, into a bottle
the souls of those who wish to protect themselves from evil spells.
Hair, body hair and nail-parings thus become the vehicles and
symbolic matter of the soul. Whoever possesses them has power
over the person from whom they have been taken.

The pot containing the soul of the deceased is carefully sealed
and placed in a safe place—often in the boughs of a tree—until
the day when it is opened and exposed to the sacred flames of
the *bulé-zin*.

In the Plaisance region the *déssunin* rite is observed not only for
the adepts of Voodoo but also for anyone who excels in his
profession. Thus musicians, photographers and experienced
sailors are all 'dismissed'. The talent, or simply the ability which
such people have shown during their lifetime, is taken to be
supernatural, therefore the work of a *loa*, who must of course be
withdrawn from the body.

THE LAYING-OUT OF THE DEAD

This takes place after the *déssunin*. The body is washed with an
infusion of aromatic herbs of more or less magical powers, the
nostrils and the ears plugged with cotton-wool, the mouth closed
by means of a sling knotted on top of the head and the big toes
tied together. In the course of these last attentions the deceased is
treated as though he were still conscious. Rubbing him with
leaves of the custard-apple the 'washer' explains to him that he is
only washing him to make him more beautiful and to ensure that
even in his condition he shall not lose one jot of dignity. If, in the
course of dressing him, he experiences any difficulty in putting
on his shirt or trousers he politely asks for a little co-operation.
It is reported that the limbs of the deceased then become flexible
as though the request had been heeded. Friends and relations
come up to the body and entrust it with messages for the other
world. It is assumed, too, that the deceased can take illnesses with

him. A woman of Marbial who was suffering from yaws told me in confidence that she had bribed a 'washer' to use water in which she had soaked her wounds for the last washing of a corpse. Convinced that the deceased would thus relieve her of her complaint, she had rewarded him with an offering of a few *sous*.

The pockets of the deceased are either torn or turned inside out, to make sure that he does not retain on his person any article which would give him power over members of his family. Care is also taken that he shall not go shod, in case the noise of his footsteps disturbs the living. The custom of burying people with the tools of their trade is still observed in certain regions but is far from being a general practice.

THE WAKE

The *rèl*—the piercing cry which proclaims to neighbours that someone has given up the ghost—is no sooner heard than the news is passed from hut to hut and within a few hours the whole region has been informed. Friends and relations hasten to the side of the deceased to help him pass a happy last night on earth.

A death watch is enjoyed, sincerely, like any other party, and young people, starved of distraction, welcome with joy the news that one is to be held.

To attend a death watch is, furthermore, a mark of respect to the bereaved family which takes pride in the number of people who turn up to share its mourning. The home is invaded by the 'watchers' who first repair to a room in which the menfolk of the family are gathered. They commiserate with them; the relations return thanks for the time-honoured phrases, and seize the opportunity of mentioning the virtues of the deceased, of repeating his last words or recounting his last actions. The consolations offered to the family are the kind that counsel resignation and obedience to divine will. Since the reputation of the household depends on the welcome given to the watchers the women of the family, hard-pressed with their hospitable tasks, can only lend a distracted ear to the sympathy addressed to them. They busy themselves round the huge cauldrons, boiling water for coffee and ginger tea, and go from kitchens to arbour serving each according to his rank. From time to time the closest relations of the deceased—husband, wife, mother, sister or daughter—who a moment earlier had seemed unaffected by grief, break off whatever they may be doing and pour out a sudden heartrending lamentation. This, preceded by a pathetic *'way way'*, takes the form of short sentences in which terms of endearment are mixed with reproaches or with allusions to some affecting memory. They end with the announcement of the dead person's name followed by a prolonged 'O'. For instance a woman bewailing her child will cry out *'A la trâché ki rèd mézâmi'* (Ah, what agony in my entrails, my friends), comparing her present suffering to that of the child's birth. Another, pretending to be angry or desperate, will say to the body of her husband: 'Why did you desert us? Why did you go and do that? Just look at the state you left us in . . .'

Such an outburst—the *vocero*—only lasts a few minutes and then comes suddenly to an end. The wailers wipe their eyes, return to whatever they were doing or to their interrupted conversations as though nothing had happened. But if some circumstance—the arrival of the coffin or of the corpse-washer or the appearance of some friend of the deceased—revives their sense of loss then once again, and with the same suddenness, they give tongue. When exhaustion or domestic chores oblige them to stop, then friends and relations take over from them, or 'support' them as the local expression has it. Formerly professional mourners came and helped out the female members of the family. If during a death-watch lamentations are thought to be lacking either in loudness or frequency, then it is held against the family and the deceased is pitied for having been so little loved and respected by his own kin. You hear for instance: 'So and so? Oh, he had no family worthy of the name. If he had he would have been better mourned at his burial.'

People who were deeply disliked by the deceased take care not to attend his funeral for fear of putting him into a rage which might be vented in the most terrible way. One woman who had suffered much at her husband's hands forbade him, when she was dying, to come anywhere near her corpse. The man thinking propriety demanded his presence at the vigil paid no attention to her prohibition. Not only did he come but he brought with him a bottle of paraffin to feed one of the lamps which, on these occasions, burn all night. No one turned him away even though the stomach of the deceased began to inflate as soon as he came in.

In the course of the evening one of the lamps was replenished —but it still refused to burn. Seven boxes of matches were expended on it—in vain. Only then was it noticed that the new paraffin had come out of the bottle brought by the husband. Quickly it was replaced by paraffin from someone else's bottle: the lamp then lit without difficulty and burnt all night with extraordinary brightness for, I was told, the deceased herself had 'looked after her light'. As to the intruder, confronted by general reprehension—he fled.

Among the distractions which help to pass a peasant's evening of mourning the most extraordinary is the sung reading of the *Marseilles*, a collection of poems the full title of which is as follows: *Canticles of the Religious Soul, Said to Originate from Marseilles, Adapted to Common Tunes.* Alongside verses which are as stupid as they are flat, it contains endless descriptions of Church mysteries, of the lives of the Saints and paraphrases of the Gospel. These insipid compositions are sung by professionals of the *Marseilles* who mouth them by feeble candlelight without understanding a word of what they read. Sometimes two singers intone alternately a few verses of a poem up to the moment when one of them 'launches' a refrain which is then taken up by everyone present.

The tunes which form the basis of the *Marseilles* are of European origin and derive from Church music and the Cantilena, but rhythm and register are certainly in the African tradition. Voices are true and the whole effect would be tolerable if only the singers would not disdain unison and seek, each on his own, to obtain special vocal effects, thus achieving a veritable braying which, coupled with lamentations, noises of conversation and clapping of hands, results in a deafening din—and the more deafening, the better the funeral. Most adults play dominoes and a card-game called 'three-seven' or 'wood on the nose' on account of the penalty which the loser must pay: wear a piece of slit bamboo over his nose. Those who prefer the pleasures of conversation to playing games make high-spirited remarks, not even sparing the deceased. Witness a certain observation I heard: 'Have you noticed how many women there are at this vigil? It's because they found the dead man a good lover!'

The young people organize all sorts of games on their own, called *plézi* (pleasure), which take on a ritualistic flavour by virtue of their being associated with the deceased. But if the dead person is very old and highly respected then the vigil does not include entertainment of any kind.

THE BURIAL

The deceased must leave his house before dawn—or else he will shortly be followed where he has gone by another member of his family. On crossing the threshold of the dead person's house those who are carrying the coffin pause as though in doubt, then advance. They recoil like this three times. They stop long enough for the *père-savane* to bless the deceased, sing some hymns and mumble some prayers. Then they take the road to the cemetery deviously and at a run—trying all the time to disorientate the dead man by swift and subtle detours and changes of direction so that he may not find his way back to his house. The lowering of the body into the grave, presided over by the *père-savane*, is carried out according to Catholic ritual except that before the coffin is allowed to come to rest it is turned round one last time, as a final precaution. Anyone who has touched the coffin should wash his hands before going home with a brew made from *médicinier* leaves which are believed to have purifying properties.

For a few days after the burial the family of the deceased lives under the perpetual threat of the dead man's return. In spite of all the precautions taken he may yet haunt the living. He is regarded as being consumed with dread of his new loneliness and obsessed by a desire to come and fetch someone he was fond of. In this respect there is nothing more dangerous for children than the love of parents who cannot bear to leave them behind. That is why surviving children are protected by the marking on their forehead of an indigo cross, or by being given some garment of the deceased to wear round their necks—though this last is dangerous as it may attract, instead of repel, the dead person. Little bags of garlic are said to have prophylactic powers against the return of the dead. A child who has lost its mother must kiss the corpse on the forehead and step over it. A lamp lit on the grave of a child prevents it from coming out to look for its brothers and sisters. A few days after a death, the Novena starts. It is called 'last prayers' and friends and relations are expected to attend. Every evening they gather in the house of the deceased where an altar is set up in a corner of a room. This altar is just an ordinary table covered with embroidered cloth and overhung by a canopy. On it are placed coloured pictures, crucifixes and flowers. Calabashes and plates of food for the deceased are laid out on the ground. These, on the ninth day, are thrown away close to the hut. Such offerings strike the only note of paganism in the ceremony which otherwise falls entirely within the competence of the *père-savane*. The latter says French and Latin prayers, following them with hymns which are taken up in chorus by all present. On the last evening the prayers become more solemn. They are interrupted by deafening manifestations of grief, cries of '*way way*' from near relations, and by exhibitions of despair which verge on hysteria. The *père-savane* sings a Libera in the cemetery and a permanent cross is set up at the head of the grave.

CEREMONIES CELEBRATED IN SANCTUARIES ON THE DEATH OF A CULT-GROUP MEMBER

Just as a family must organize a vigil and observe a Novena on the death of one of its members, so a Voodoo 'society'—which is the equivalent, within the Voodoo order, of a family—must carry out, on the death of one of its members or initiates, certain rites which correspond to the vigil, and celebrate the ceremony of 'last prayers'.

The only Voodoo death-watch at which I ever assisted took place at Lorgina's when one of her *hunsi* died. The women of the cult-group, clothed in white, and wearing on their heads both headkerchief and straw hat, were seated round the peristyle facing Lorgina whose hair was bound up in a black turban. Her

assistant, the *hungan* Tullius, clothed entirely in white, acted as
choir-master. During a long opening spell the women directed
by Tullius clapped their hands in a slow and simple rhythm
without moving from their chairs or uttering a sound. Then in a
sad monotone they sang refrains to the funeral songs which
Tullius chanted. The sanctuary lights were all put out; only one
lonely candle burned on the *poteau-mitan*. The sadness of the
hymns, the darkness, the rapt silence of the congregation invested
this display of mourning with a profound dignity which gave no
inkling of the outbursts to come. One of the *hunsi* who had till
then remained calm, suddenly leapt to her feet as though thrust
up by a spring, and with mouth half open and rigid limbs, then
collapsed on the ground in front of her companions. Hastily she
was helped up—but a few seconds later another *hunsi* began to
emit piercing cries, throwing her arms above her head. This was
the release-signal for a scene of collective despair. The screams,
the tears, the wild gesticulations reached their height when the
choir-master 'launched' a song about the death of a *hunsi-kanzo*.
The women tried to sing through their sobbing, but tears stifled
their voices. Only the men, despite the emotion which engulfed
them, were able to continue. Little by little, calm was restored.
The *hunsi* dried their tears and began singing again and clapping
their hands as though nothing had happened. The ceremony
finished as it began by handclapping which lasted for half an hour.
For the rest of the night everyone stayed on in the sanctuary
drinking coffee and talking cheerfully.

The public death-watch may be a little different from the
domestic variety but this is not the case with the 'last prayers'
which are said every night.

An altar is put up in exactly the same way as described above
and a *père-savane*, paid by the *mambo*, officiates beside it for nine
days.

THE 'CASSER-CANARI' RITE

The *canari* is a large earthenware jar which in the north of Haiti
is formally broken at the end of funerals. This rite is unknown
in the south. It was nonetheless included in the *bulé-zin* which
the *hungan* Abraham celebrated in 1947 in honour of his *reine-*

chanterelle Marie-Noël. The latter was a native of Gonaïves where *casser-canari* is practised. Abraham had decided that she should be honoured after the fashion of her own people. It is quite likely the rite may have been interpreted fairly freely by this *hungan* and that it did not correspond exactly to the traditional form, but an account of it here will serve to give an approximate idea.

The ceremony began with the consecration of the jar. After a thorough washing with decoctions of medicinal plants this was filled with sacred food (bits of cassava, grilled maize and biscuit), cocks' feathers and tobacco leaves. Its outer casing was sprinkled with rum and kola, while the *hungan* slowly shook his rattle over its mouth. It was then carried in procession and offered at the altars and at the sacred trees. From then on it became invested with a *nanm*—a mystical spirit or power. Maize was scattered on the stuff with which it was coated, and the whole was then given over to the greed of two cocks.

Now the jar, placed near the altar, had been covered with a large upturned calabash. The *hungan* came and shook his rattle over it and struck the calabash with a stick. This was the signal for a group of *hunsi*, who had been issued with sticks, to use them on the calabash, beating it as though it were a drum. The choir sang:

Kasé Kanari a (*bis*)	Break the jar (bis)
Papa Pyé Dâbala	Papa Pierre Damballah
Kasé Kanari a	Break the jar
Kasé Kanari mwê	Break my jar
Ibo-lèlè	Ibo-lele (bis)
Nâchô Ibo	Ibo nation
Kasé Kanari mwê	Break my jar.

The jar splits and then breaks completely. When it is reduced to a pile of fragments, a halt is called to allow the *hungan* time to make a libation of rum and kola over the débris. Then the hammering of the sherds begins again, harder than ever:

Hunsi kâso yo	Hunsi kanzo
Gadé n' alé	See we are going

Nu kité regrét	Leaving behind regrets
Kòté nu kité kay-la	Where are you leaving this house
Nâ mê lèsé yo fé	In the hands of just anybody
Mari-Noël u alé	Marie-Noël you have gone
Mari-Noël kòté u kité loa-yo	Marie-Noël where have you left your *loa*
Sé nâ Giné u alé	It is to Guinea you are going.

When the *canari* was reduced to a pile of dust, the *hungan* drew some crosses on it with ash and surrounded it with a circle of flour.

When flames came out of the pots of the *bulé-zin* the *hungan*, taking up the remnants of the jar in a piece of white stuff, approached a ditch dug under the peristyle, and having cradled the parcel in his arms for a moment threw it into the bottom of the hole, where it was soon followed by all the food offerings and accessories used in the service. The *hunsi* sang in French:

> Have pity on his soul
> Pray for all the *mambos*
> Pray for all *hunsi déssunin*
> Mary, holy mother, merciful mother
> Pray for all *hunsi*
> Grant, Saint Philomène, Virgin and martyr
> Grant us mercy
> Her good angel
> Send to heaven
> Mary—have mercy.

Three charges of powder were exploded on the edge of the ditch and a man armed with an iron bar came and smashed up all the pots which had been thrown in. At this the rhythm of the drums became quicker and more violent. The *hunsi*, seized with frenzy, quickly picked up all the bits and pieces which covered the ground as well as the cinders from the hearth and threw all into the ditch. Then singing and dancing in a veritable human chain, they pushed in the earth round the edge of the ditch with their feet, filling it in within a few minutes. A *vèvè* (symbol of the gods) was traced out on the site and the tail feathers of the sacrificed chickens were planted in the newly turned earth.

In these rites can be recognized a corrupted form of the *sihum* —the ceremony which in Dahomey follows all funerals and which is characterized by special rhythms beaten out on calabashes. The tradition of the African *sihum* is preserved in certain sanctuaries but the ritual is only practised for a cult-group's high dignitaries.

THE FUNERAL 'BULÉ-ZIN'

A few days after last prayers the ceremony called 'the burning of the pots' (*bulé-zin*) has to be celebrated. It is, as we have seen, a complex ritual not specifically associated with death—in fact it can be adapted to any occasion and is much in use notably at the end of initiation. Fire occupies an important place in it; indeed, it could be regarded as providing the climax to the ceremony, the moment to which all the other rites tend—the movement when the pots, whose insides have been smeared with oil, all begin to blaze. The purifying powers attributed to flames would suffice to explain their ritualistic purpose in *bulé-zin*. This, nevertheless, is not their main function. They confer strength on whoever exposes himself to them and they invest the objects 'fired' with an increase of sacred energy.

The word *nanm*, 'soul', is best translated as 'energy' or 'effluvium'. One of my informants, wishing to describe to me the object of the ceremony, told me that a *nanm* was what the pots derived from the allegedly miraculous flames which sprang from them. According to others it was the *loa* themselves who got pleasure from being caressed by flames leaping out of the *zin* and who, in return, would give their servants new strength. The ceremony of *bulé-zin* is celebrated when sacrifice is made to the guardian spirits of a sanctuary, when a new sanctuary is inaugurated, at separation from the soul of one of the *loa*'s servants, when the dead are taken out of the water to convert them into protecting spirits and finally at memorial services.

The number of funeral *bulé-zin* held varies according to the rank of the dead person. A *hunsi* is entitled to one *bulé-zin*, a *hungan* to three, the last being celebrated one year and one day after his death. The number of pots burned for an ordinary servant is seven, for a *hungan* or *mambo* twenty-one.

MOURNING

The wearing of mourning is, like burial, a duty to the deceased from which no one is exempt, not even very young children. But the dead are not narrow-minded: they are prepared to wait several years for a hard-up family to buy black clothes; though as soon as they suspect evasion, then—in a dream—they warn the direct heir of their displeasure. It would be as dangerous to disregard such a prompting as it would be to snap your fingers in the face of a *loa*. The dead, too, have the power of bringing down a 'punishment' on the head of a guilty relative. This can take the form of illness or persistent bad luck. Where someone finds it impossible to wear mourning for his parents, then his children must do so for him so they may not become the butt of the offended dead. Inherited mourning takes precedence over personal mourning. Although delay in discharging duties as a mourner may indicate secret antipathies and old grudges, mourning is not a matter of sentiment. Its real nature was well described to me by a peasant woman: 'It is by wearing mourning,' she told me, 'that we rid ourselves of the souls of the deceased; if we didn't mourn the dead would "seize" us and try everything to work us harm. Whoever neglects his father or mother in this respect is taking a big risk.' As for the *loa* they expect nothing from people burdened with mourning—for which tact they are sometimes thanked with offerings and sacrifice.

Parents do not wear mourning for their children: custom requires that black should only be worn for people older than oneself. Black clothes are blessed by a *père-savane* and should not be washed but brushed, for they are on the same footing as the 'devotional clothing' which is worn to expiate a sin.

CEMETERIES AND TOMBS

Each *la-cour* (complex of huts occupied by an extended family) has its own cemetery in which are buried all members of that kinship group—this word being used in the widest sense—to include relations by marriage, concubines, and even sometimes close friends. These cemeteries are dominated by enormous crosses which, in the eyes of Voodooists, represent Baron-Samedi.

The peasants set great store by being put to rest beside the members of their own family and this is the reason why they make great personal sacrifices to bring back to their own cemetery the bodies of kinsmen who die far away. Ground occupied by a family cemetery is jointly owned and cannot be transferred. When a family is obliged to sell its land, the deed of sale will often stipulate that the cemetery must remain in the family's possession, likewise the right to use it for the burial of their dead.

To build a fine vault for a relation is a compelling duty which can be disregarded only at risk of incurring supernatural punishment. Peasants take pride in erecting for their dead monuments which are as sumptuous as their purse permits, and many will deprive themselves of basic necessities over a period of years to realize this ambition.

To whitewash tombs when weather has made them look faded, and also now and again to weed them, is a mark of affectionate devotion to the dead and a way to their goodwill. Such duties are incumbent on all relatives though each branch of a family has a particular responsibility to its own dead. Heads of family have the additional responsibility of caring for the tombs of the distant ancestors.

THE FATE OF THE SOUL AFTER DEATH

No coherence is to be found in the vague and contradictory notions of life after death which at present hold sway. Although everyone carries within him two souls, the *gros-* and the *ti-bon-ange*, each of which has a different fate, in practice the distinction is often forgotten. A dead person is spoken of as though he had survived himself in the form of a disembodied soul.

From discussions which I had with peasants of Marbial—about life beyond the grave—it transpired that the *ti-bon-ange* does not leave the earth until the ninth day after death—that is to say after 'last prayers'. He it is who presents himself before God and accounts for the sins committed by the person who was in his charge. As to the 'big good angel' (*gros-bon-ange*), he appears to be the same thing as a ghost. Only very reluctantly will he leave the places he frequented and he lingers in the house where he died.

A dead person will only harass the living if they neglect him, if they omit to wear mourning, if they fail to withdraw the *loa* from his head and finally if they show themselves dilatory in giving him a worthy burial-place. He shows himself in dreams and explains his disappointment; on those who pay no attention he calls down a 'chastisement'. Whoever dies as a result of a spirit's vengeance comes back to tell his relations the cause of his death and to warn them to discharge their obligations lest they too be harried by the divine wrath of the spirit. Near cemeteries and in lonely places there is risk of meeting *zombi* (which must not be confused with flesh-and-blood *zombi*): these are the wandering souls of people who perished as a result of an accident and who are condemned to haunt the earth for as long as God had meant them to live. The same fate is reserved for nubile women who died as virgins. This belief is apparently related to a custom which I heard people talk about in a rather vague way: it would seem that in certain regions—from fear of the terrible ordeal which await virgins in the after life—the woman who washes a virgin's corpse is asked to deflower the body before burying it. This is the price which must be paid if she is to escape being raped by such unsavoury *loa* as Baron-Samedi or other members of the Guédé family.

Catholic beliefs about the after-life are of little concern to Voodooists, even to those who profess to be practising Catholics. Voodoo adepts are, on the other hand, most careful about the period spent by the dead man (some say—by his 'good angel') at the bottom of a river or lake. For it is the fate of all who have practised Voodoo to spend at least a year and a day in a stream of water. At the end of a few years they experience a desire to get out. They warn their relations that the moment has come to take them out of the water: they are getting cold, they say, and long for the warmth of the sun and of the flames of the *bulé-zin*.

This nostalgia for the earth is such that if the relative to whom they appeal turns a deaf ear to their entreaty, then he is quickly plagued with an illness from which he can only recover by celebrating the required ceremony. The *weté mò nâ dlo* (extraction of the dead who are in water) is a long, costly, ritualistic operation and therefore several families come to an understanding with a *hungan* or a *mambo* who will then organize a collective ceremony on behalf of a whole list of dead. For it is not merely a question of catching the souls floating in the water, but also of transferring them to a sanctuary where they turn into guardian *loa*.

The ceremony of the *weté mò nâ dlo* which I shall now describe took place in 1948 at Lorgina's. It was watched by Mlle Yvonne Oddon and Madame Odette Mennesson-Rigaud who were kind enough to let me have their notes.

For some time Lorgina had been receiving messages from beyond the grave sent to her by members of her family and by former members of her *humfo* society. From month to month she had put off the fulfilment of her duties—either for lack of money or simply out of laziness. She might even have delayed longer had she not suddenly begun to feel ill. She grew weaker daily and wasted away under people's very eyes. She was too experienced a *mambo* not to know the reason: the dead, growing impatient, had 'seized' her. One night after a ceremony in honour of her guardian spirit, Agirualinsu, she felt a violent pain. She knew then that her vacillation must end and accordingly made up her mind to celebrate the *weté mò nâ dlo* without delay.

She obtained sixteen pitchers (*govi*) and the same number of 'cooling-pitchers' which are shaped slightly differently (and have no other use than to refresh spirits newly risen from water). Along with her assistants she passed a whole day 'cross-signing' these vessels—that is to say marking them all with sacred signs. This done, the pitchers were dressed in white cloth. Branches of *mombin* were attached to them in such a way as to overhang the openings. Shoots of *aizan* were added to this decoration. Throughout these preparations the *hunsi*, clothed in white, sang and danced in the peristyle.

A tent (*bila*), made of white sheets, was put up under a tree outside the sanctuary. It was carefully shut but it was neverthe-

less possible to make out, inside it, a large cylindrical receptacle.*
This, we later found out, was a metal cistern across which a
plank had been put, to support a 'perpetual lamp', that is to say
a wick floating in a pool of oil.

The ceremony began towards nine o'clock in the evening.
Many *loa* had in turn been greeted with song and dance when
Lorgina made her appearance dressed as befitted the solemnity
of the occasion.

The *hunsi* laid out mats on the ground and covered them with
sheets. Pillows were then added and under them *vèvè* were traced
out by an assistant. The *hunsi*, singing and dancing, disappeared
into the sanctuary. A few minutes later a noise was heard in the
humfo. Commotion in the crowd indicated the arrival of a
procession.

First came the standard-bearers grouped round a personage
who was leading a lamb. The lamb's back was covered with white
linen and round its head was a handkerchief. Next came one of
the *mambo*'s acolytes, waving a white pigeon. Some *hunsi* were
carrying an armchair decorated with shawls and curtains on
which had been placed pitchers for the souls of grand *hungan*;
others followed on, dancing, with pitchers on their heads. These
turned, retraced their steps, staggered, 'tipsified' by the *loa*. As
they arrived at the tent they were sent off to lie down side by
side on the mats, having first placed their pitchers beside the
pillows. They were then covered with sheets so completely that
the outline of their bodies could be distinguished only vaguely.

They would not stop chattering underneath the sheets so the
mambo gave them a good scolding. Meanwhile in the peristyle
several groups continued singing and dancing. The *mambo*'s
acolyte, Tullius, came and crouched down beside the *hunsi*, in
front of the armchair. He was wearing a pink scarf and a blue
and white headkerchief. The *mambo* was seated right up against
the tent with her back to the congregation and her head resting
on the canvas. Tullius recited an 'Our Father' and held his
pigeon for a moment underneath the sheet. He then said some
more Catholic prayers including an Ave Maria, a Credo and a

* The receptacle had been 'cross-signed' and consecrated with dry food
offerings.

series of litanies in honour of a number of saints. True to custom, the audience took up the refrain. Finally Lorgina shook her little bell and had the electric light put out. Another *mambo* took her rattle and kept it going for the rest of the ceremony. Finally Lorgina, putting her head through the tent opening, invoked the *loa*, '*maît'-tête des morts*', asking them to help her in her enterprise. Soon a deep, hoarse voice could be clearly heard: it was Papa Loco, come to assure her of his co-operation and to ask for news. Then Lorgina went into the tent. One of the assistants intoned a psalm in which were listed the names of the dead who were to be taken out of the water:

Hé, âhé, hé âhé, hé hé hé!	Hé, âhé, hé âhé, hé hé hé
Ti-mun-lâ yo, m'pralé wété	These children I'm going to take out
Ti mun là-yo là dlo	These children out of the water.

A mild gurgling was heard and then wretched lamentations. The accompanying words were hard to make out, though the voice of Lorgina asking questions could be heard above all else.

Then there were fresh groans and complaints. Lorgina ordered one of the pitchers to be opened. The first dead person to reply was a *hungan* called Romain who had died some years ago. His voice was very hoarse; it was a kind of mumble accompanied by a scraping noise in his windpipe—unintelligible except to Lorgina who interpreted it. She announced that his soul would be placed in a pitcher, whereupon there came the noises which characterize this stage of the proceedings.

Lorgina went on to do the same for other dead people whose utterances were equally obscure. One of the women in the congregation recognized the voice of her mother, burst into tears and began crying out '*Aie Maman*' and, in answer to a certain question 'Yes Mother, he is there.'

As the dead 'appeared' under the tent they sought information about their relatives. The latter hastened to satisfy their curiosity: 'Yes,' they cried, 'so and so is here,' or 'No, he has moved to another district.' A godfather reproached his godson for failing in charity towards him: 'You said you loved me—but that didn't prevent you leaving me to die in hospital alone.' 'Let us forget about it,' replied the god-child. 'What is past is past.'

Among the dead who hurried into the water cistern was an old woman, mother of twins who were in the congregation. When Lorgina told them their mother was present they began to sob so hard they could scarcely answer the questions put to them. Suddenly an agonized voice was heard asking 'Maman—you don't call me—you've forgotten me.' This was a sister of the twins. Probably Lorgina had forgotten she existed; she made the dead person say: 'No my child I have not forgotten you.' Then she added: 'Look—you—sister Ramirène, your mother wants you to bring Dédé to Lorgina who will treat her. Do you hear, child; you're in Lorgina's hands.' The latter then asked what song she should 'send' her, in other words what was the *maît'-tête* of the deceased.

Another dead person appeared but although Lorgina announced him under various nick-names he was not recognized until she described him as a homosexual (*masisi*). He spoke to a *hungan* who had once been his friend and who answered him straight away. The next dead person on the list had also been a notorious pederast. He even reproached a *hungan* about a certain incident which took place 'behind the airfield'. The laughter which exploded from all sides showed clearly that the public needed no introduction to this affair. The *hungan* took it all very seriously and his voice sounded tearful as he sobbed and mumbled in concert with the deceased.

Next came the turn of an old grandmother who chattered away without pause. Having inquired after her family she asked in a rather aggrieved tone what had been done with her cooking-pot and the clothes she had left. People told her, with a touch of impatience, that the clothes had been given away and the cooking-pot, through long use, had finally developed a hole.

When sixteen dead had been taken from the water Lorgina wanted to wind things up for that evening: but the last 'dead' interceded on behalf of a certain 'Mazoutte who,' said he, 'is standing behind me.' Lorgina pointed out that she had no more pitchers available. Among the congregation indignant voices could be heard: the deceased, people cried, 'was a big Negro'—

who couldn't possibly be kept waiting. Since he had turned up, then he must be taken; it was he who had had Guédé Jean-Simon Brutus in his head. Lorgina was accused of injustice. She got very angry and came out of the tent abusing those who were creating the disturbance. A riot almost broke out. But once the lights had been put on calm was quickly restored. Volunteers were called for to carry the armchair up to the pitchers. Others removed the sheets from the *hunsi* and helped them to their feet. They formed up in a row and came forward with the pitchers on their heads, staggering as though affected by vertigo, or hopping on one foot. Having done a dance round the *poteau-mitan* they flooded into the sanctuary to put the pitchers on the altars to the various gods.

The burning of the pots (*zin*) ceremony was celebrated a few days later. The pitchers were solemnly carried under the peristyle and passed across the flames which rose from the inside of the *zin*. With the same pomp as before the *hunsi*, in procession, returned them to their places on the altars. The forty-first day after their withdrawal from the water the dead contained in the pitchers receive food offerings which they share out among the faithful. From then on they are treated as tutelary spirits, a kind of minor *loa*, who look after their relations and who, in return for the sacrifices offered them, attend to the prayers of their kith and kin and respond to their appeals for advice or protection.

OFFERINGS TO THE DEAD

The religious ceremonies called *manger-morts* include offerings to the dead of food cooked without salt and prepared entirely by men. Cooks who help the dead of another family run the risk of offending their own dead; hence they insist on a wage sufficient to pay for their appeasement by sacrifice. The Guinea dead— that is to say African ancestors—get a special stew containing beef, pigs' trotters, maize and scarlet beans.

When a meal is served to the dead, a table covered with food is put in a room which is then shut off for a few hours to give them time to feast themselves at leisure. After prayers and appeals addressed to the ancestors and the unknown dead who have died by steel, fire or water, the *père-savane* or the head of the family knocks three times on the door and goes in. He brings out a calabash full of various foodstuffs which he distributes among the children of the household, having first offered it to the four points of the compass, just as in the *marassa* ceremony. The children hurl themselves on to the swill and fight for it noisily. Another calabash is placed at a crossroads for Legba. The dead having received their share, the living sit down to table and enjoy a banquet. The *manger-mort* ends with dances, particularly the *banda*, done in honour of the Guédé and mentioned in a previous chapter.

In the north of Haiti the fête of the dead forms part of the big services which families celebrate in honour of their gods. The ritual followed in such cases is known to us through the pages which R. P. Peters[14] devoted to the subject and which I will here briefly summarize.

When people wish to honour a dead person in some other house than that in which he died, his soul must first be fetched. A 'reader' (*lecteur*), that is to say a *père-savane*, is entrusted with this task. He goes to the room where the deceased died and puts in it a receptacle containing the favourite dishes of the deceased and beside it a bowl covered with a white cloth. Then he waits. Finally the deceased comes in the form of an insect, a leaf or a little bit of straw which falls on the cloth. The *père-savane* quickly picks it up and takes it to wherever the ceremony is due to take place. Four go to meet him with a sheet which they make into a canopy for his head. Walking backwards the *père-savane* goes to the altar and puts the cloth on it.

The *manger-mort* described to us by R. P. Peters includes some rites which are not mentioned by any other writer. For instance he says the *père-savane* summons the dead twice over 'from the four cardinal points'. He reads the list of a family's dead, pausing after every tenth name to pour out a libation of rum and sing psalms. The nomenclature of the deceased ends with the strange formula: 'Toussaint Louverture—with the dead, to invite all the dead.' At dawn a procession wends its way towards a crossroads to the strains of hymns: 'Go my angel' and 'Send my soul'. When it arrives the *père-savane* tells the dead that 'all is over, and they must stay satisfied and never come back to make demands'. A jar (*canari*), wrapped round with a piece of stuff, or with leaves, is broken against a stone placed in the middle of crossroads. The congregation sings in chorus 'Now is broken the jar of the dead'. Everyone comes away— quickly—without looking back 'for fear of drawing upon themselves the vengeance of the dead'. Once more the congregation dances, in the clearing where the fête was held. The dance is the *bambochard*—which is probably the equivalent of the *banda*.

V
Magic and Sorcery

I. MAGIC AND SORCERY

Many Haitians, in their anxiety to clear Voodoo of the charges which have so often been levelled against it, oppose the cult of *loa* and magic with the utmost vigour. To make this distinction (between the worship of the *loa* and magic) is only possible if the word 'magic' is restricted to meaning black magic and sorcery. In other words the Voodooist regards as 'magic' any rite accomplished with evil intent, with or without the co-operation of *loa*. This essentially moral criterion could hardly be adopted in these pages. We must take—and have taken—magic to include any manipulation of occult forces, any use made of the virtues or properties immanent in things and in human beings and any technique through which the supernatural world becomes submissive to domination and exploitation for personal ends.

Taken in this sense magic is inextricably mixed up with what people are pleased to call 'the Voodoo religion'. Public ceremonies of homage to the gods always include elements which really pertain to sympathetic magic and which neither prayers, offerings nor sacrifices are able to disguise. Reciprocally, magic derives part of its ritual from traditional religion and relies on invocation of *loa*. Indeed, of the many *loa* venerated in the sanctuaries, the most 'pure' are those whose function it is to watch over the efficacy of magic rites. The saying '*Petro* is the art of magic' which *hungan* like to repeat in a sententious way, merely means that, as we have said before, the magic arts fall mainly within the province of that class of spirits.[1]

The grand-master of charms and sorceries is Legba-petro, invoked under the name of Maître-Carrefour, or simply Carrefour. Indeed crossroads are favourite sites for the 'works' of magicians; handfuls of earth taken from them are an ingredient of many beneficent or harmful spells. Some *loa*, the Simbi for instance, prefer white magic; others protect and assist sorcerers: Ezili-jé-rouge, Ti-Jean, Kita-demembré are scarcely distinguishable from the familiar spirits of 'the black art'.

Rites of sympathetic magic which by their very nature should work mechanically, are not effective unless terms are first made with the Maître-des-cimetières—Baron-Samedi: even the most powerful sorcerer cannot kill a man if Baron has not first 'marked out his grave'.

Medicine, as practised by the *hungan*, shares this ambiguity. A 'treatment' usually includes interminable prayers, appeals to patron spirits, offerings and sacrifices—all acts of a pre-eminently religious nature, yet the cure proper, with its symbolic ritual, complicated prescriptions, rites of elimination, belongs to the province of magic in its most blatant form. The ceremony of Christmas for example, one of the most brilliant occasions in the cycle of Voodoo feasts, is it not merely a simple exercise in magical prophylaxis, the efficacy of which is guaranteed by the presence of spirits?

Just as no precise frontier can be laid down between the religious and the magic, so the rôle of priest is difficult to distinguish from that of magician, or even sorcerer. The *boko*, or sorcerer, is only a *hungan* who 'serves with both hands' (*sert des deux mains*) a *nègre mazimaza* (double-faced man) who appears to fulfil his priestly functions but does not hesitate to have recourse, when it suits him, to 'bought *loa*' (*loa achetés*). Driven on by a desire for gain, he uses illicit means to foster the cupidity of his clients and even plays the part of a tool in their various vendettas. A *hungan* worthy of the name knows all the techniques of sorcery since he is constantly required to counter them, but in his honesty he will not allow himself to make use of them. He also avoids any dealings with devil-*loa*. *Hungan* only deviate from this line of conduct if it becomes necessary to protect a client threatened by a sorcerer, or to lay low a criminal. The *hungan* who casts a spell on a thief or an assassin does not incur the opprobrium which falls on a *hungan* who, using exactly the same means, eliminates an innocent person. In short it is neither his 'knowledge' (*connaissance*) nor his functions which distinguish a *hungan* from a sorcerer, but the uses to which he puts them. A *hungan* is 'like a shop. He has a lot of merchandise . . .'²

Does Haiti deserve to be called the 'Magic Island'—the name given to it by Seabrook not because of the charms of its tropical climate but because, in his eyes, it was the country of sorcerers and spirits?

The stories of blood and death which this author raked together assort ill with the open gaiety and gentleness of the Haitian peasant, with his acute sense of what is comic and his love of banter. Nevertheless Seabrook did not invent things. The scenes of black magic which he described with such verve, the mysterious deaths and the whole disquieting world of the *boko*, werewolves and *zombi* which he conjures up, are taken from perfectly straightforward accounts which may be heard today in the country and in the popular quarters of Port-au-Prince. He drew amply, with both hands, on a folklore which in this respect is bewilderingly rich. And it must be remembered that beliefs and 'folklore' practices are not always harmless superstitions. For many they are a source of anxiety and a cause of serious expense. They sow discord between relations and neighbours, foster chronic hatreds and sometimes end in murder.

The ordinary man believes implicitly in magic. He is convinced, also, that among the people he knows there are many who lead a double life, one peaceful and normal, the other criminal and demoniac. The Protestants themselves, who often represent the most educated and enlightened element in the peasantry, firmly believe in the maleficent power accorded by Satan to some of their compatriots. That deep insecurity, which is the lot of most peasants and workers, predisposes them to practise magic and to believe themselves the playthings of occult powers. Ever since his earliest days the Haitian has heard talk of werewolves, sorcerers and evil spirits. Even among educated people there lingers a certain uneasiness and a propensity to believe the most extravagant stories; they disclaim total belief but wonder if behind all this diabolism there may not be ancient 'African secrets' which may enable the *hungan* and *boko* to set our poor science at nought. Left to himself, without much chance of teaching himself or enlarging his horizon, the peasant remains shut up in a world in which mystical powers intervene every moment.

It would, of course, be wrong to see every Haitian peasant as a primitive obsessed by magic. Many of them resist all these beliefs if not with positive scepticism then at least with a healthy indifference. Without actually denying the existence of sorcery, they do not pay much attention to it. But unfortunately rural society has plenty of neurotics or simply troubled and downcast spirits who are quick to suggest that an illness is not 'from God', that an accident is surrounded with suspicious circumstances and that a death was not due to natural causes.

Such people it is who are always hinting at 'bad men' and who take advantage of others' anxiety and unhappiness to sow doubt in their minds and arouse the most absurd superstitions. Those who have been struck down by misery listen only too easily to such mutterings. Is not grief less painful when it turns to hatred? In everyday life the threat of charms, sorcery and spells makes but one more care to be listed with drought and the price of coffee and bananas. Magic is at least an evil against which man is not entirely powerless. He can protect himself with amulets, 'drugs', 'degrees' (degrés) and also by confiding in loa. These last watch over the servant who is dutiful and they warn him if someone has done 'an evil thing' (cast a spell) against him.

Magic has spread in Haiti rather as weeds spread in a tropical clearing. 'Black atavism' some would say. Actually the African cultural heritage has come to a propitious social climate—to a setting of extreme poverty and ignorance which has proved a veritable forcing house for the development of every kind of magic. But in talking so much of Africa we incline to forget France—whose contribution to the magic and sorcery of Haiti is far from negligible. A great many beliefs and practices in Haitian magic originate from Normandy, Berry, Picardy or ancient Limousin. The world of European sorcery is hardly any different from that of African sorcery and so it was with the greatest ease that the Blacks borrowed practices and rites from the Whites; all the more willingly since the Whites, being the feared and admired masters, must therefore have more effective magic. Those who doubt this should remind themselves of the vogue

enjoyed in popular circles, if not among the petit bourgeoisie
too, by *Le Grand et Petit Albert* and *La Poule Noir*. It is from these
books, imported from France, that *hungan* drew some part of
their magic skills. The writer Jacques Roumain, detained in
Port-au-Prince prison for political reasons, found that he was
not allowed to read Seabrook's *Magic Island* because the officer
commanding his guards thought he might use it to escape from
his cell.

The small manual of magic which appears as an appendix to
Seabrook's work was found on the body of a rebel *caco* killed by
American marines in 1920. It is a disappointing document. It tells
us nothing about the secret art of the *boko*: it is only a compila-
tion of old wives' recipes partly taken from works of popular
magic and it gives rather a poor idea of the originality of Voodoo
sorcery.

Until the revision of the penal code the practice of magic was
forbidden under Article 405. This read as follows: 'All makers
of *wangas, caprelatas, vaudoux, dompèdre, macandale* and other
sorceries will be punished by three to six months' imprisonment
and a fine of sixty to 150 gourdes, (a) by ordinary police tribunal;
and on the second offence by imprisonment of six months to two
years and a fine of three hundred to a thousand gourdes, (b) by
the *tribunal correctionel*, this without taking into account the
severer penalties which may be incurred for crimes committed in
the preparation or execution of their maleficent practices.

'All dances and other practices, of whatever kind, likely to
nourish in the hearts of the people the spirit of fetishism and
superstition will be regarded as sorcery and punished accordingly.'

The second paragraph of this text, which dates from 1864, has
often been invoked against the practice of Voodoo but it is clear
that in the minds of the men who drew it up, it was aimed at
sorcery. Since the colonial period both the power and the number
of magicians have been exaggerated. Having said this, however,
we must add that there can be no doubt that in Haiti today many
people are still addicted to the black arts and are encouraged in
this by people who are genuine professionals of those same arts.
The sorceries at crossroads, the vestiges of mysterious ceremonies

which one discovers in the cemeteries, the *'passports'* of werewolves, the objects confiscated in the *humfo* at the time of the
anti-superstition campaign, the occasional inexplicable weird
crime—all prove that even though many of the stories of enchantment and poisoning may be the fruit of unseated imaginations,
the practice of black magic none the less exists. To tell the truth,
however worthy of condemnation may be this form of law-
breaking, it is preferable to real murders. Better cast a spell on
someone than stab him. I am disposed to believe that sorcery
explains the low percentage of murders committed in Haiti. A
person who casts a spell on his enemy already satisfies his hatred
—and avoids the kind of action which, if actually executed,
would be much more serious.

I should like here to contribute to the dossier of Haitian
sorcery a document which is completely authentic. It is the
account of a murder attempted, for magical reasons, on a three-
month-old child. The authoress of the text—an anthropologist—
is no one other than the victim herself.

'I often heard my mother and grandmother tell the extraordinary story of my first contact with a werewolf, a story which
nearly had a tragic end.

'I was only three months old at the time. My parents were pre-
occupied with the health of my sister Madeleine, who was suffering from an attack of whooping-cough which dragged on without
deriving any benefit from the careful nursing lavished upon her.
At about four in the morning the young nurse, whose main
responsibility was myself, was dandling me on the back balcony
of the house. Suddenly my parents heard me give out a sharp cry
followed by an altogether untypical series of screams. My
mother, always quickly concerned if it were anything to do with
one of us, asked the nurse what was the matter. She replied there
was nothing the matter—though her efforts to calm me were in
vain. My mother said, "There's some reason for this screaming;
she does not usually cry like this; make sure she hasn't been
pricked—you've been told before never to pick the child up when
you've got a pin in your dress." The nurse continued to insist
that she had no pins on her and that nothing had happened. My
screaming, however, did not abate.

'My mother had me brought along and undressed me, and there on my chest could be seen the head of a needle. My father immediately went to fetch Dr Audain who lived not far away. He, being unable to draw out the pin because it was so deeply embedded, prescribed a strong magnet. I screamed and threw myself about so much that he feared the needle might start "travelling" and so pierce the heart. He had no course but to perform an emergency operation with whatever lay to hand.

'The nurse it seems swore, when questioned, that a *hungan* had told her he must have "an angel" before Christmas. Apparently she first tried to poison my sister Madeleine in which she was prevented by the continual attention with which the ill child was surrounded. Then, feeling time was short, she made a surprise attack on me.

'No legal action was taken after this affair. My mother, in her revulsion for the girl who had wanted to sacrifice her child, told her to leave at once and never trouble her sight again.'

The classic form of sorcery with a doll or some other object symbolizing the victim is well-known in Haiti but sometimes takes an unusual form. The sorcerer, by means of incantation, tries to lure the person he is required to kill into a bucket of water. When he sees the image of his victim reflected in the water, he stabs it. If successful the water immediately reddens. Naturally a person can be killed if certain rites are carried out on objects which have belonged to him. In this connection I was told the following strange story: a *curé* of the Jacmel area had been called urgently to an old peasant who was on the verge of death. This man had been a *boko* whose whole life had been a tissue of crime. Now to the *curé* he confessed, among other misdeeds, that shortly before falling ill he had cast a spell over him by means of his maniple. He described the place where he had hidden it and advised him to go and find it as quickly as possible because, according to his calculations, the spell should work that very day. The *curé* heard him to the end, gave him absolution and went off in haste to find the maniple. He found it—only to die at the very moment when he was trying to undo the spell. By then only a *hungan* could have helped him since even the originator of a charm is often unable to prevent it taking effect.

Suicide is not regarded as a truly voluntary act, but as the consequence of a state of mental alienation brought about by a sorcerer.

No one will ever know how many crimes are intended and attempted, magically. The number may be less than people say. Whoever casts a spell on his enemy knows that he runs the risk of having his secret discovered by a *hungan* who, in response to demands from the victim's family, will not hesitate to pay him back in his own coin. When the parents of someone deceased suspect poisoning they spare neither money nor trouble to discover the culprit and hit back. And finally there is God, the 'Grand Master' who sees all and will not tolerate sorcery. Even if God does not sooner or later bring down a punishment, the guilty party still runs the risk of finding himself on the wrong side of his own family *loa*. As a sign of their displeasure they may withdraw their protection and abandon him, without defence, to the sorceries and charms of his enemies. Also: whoever practises magic has good reason to fear the magic of other people. Such considerations certainly stop a good many people who are in the way of committing crime. Others prefer slower methods than brutal witchcraft—methods equally criminal but less akin to straightforward assassination. Such are they who use poisons to cause long, lingering and finally fatal illnesses. Some suit the nature of the evils they cause to the degree of hatred they feel, and get satisfaction from painful illnesses, accidents or ruin of which they know themselves to be the cause. *Boko* therefore have to be in a position to meet the widest range of demand; their arsenal must include all kinds of weapons.

Sorcerers' 'works' are carried out in the secrecy of the *humfo*, at lonely crossroads, and at the foot of the Baron crosses in cemeteries. They are shrouded in complete mystery. Nevertheless there are plenty of good people who feel well informed on every little detail of the art of casting spells and preparing lethal poisons. For, let us remember, it is not so much the *boko*'s art which is secret as the act of sorcery itself. Many people have great knowledge in magic but this does not mean they practise it.

I need hardly say that I was never invited to the casting of a spell or to any conjuration of bad spirits. The few 'works' which

I witnessed all pertained to white magic. My information on the whole subject comes from very varied informants, some of them peasants, some town-dwellers. Several stories were told me by friends belonging to the Haitian bourgeoisie. I have thought it useless to go into such technical and irksome details as the enumeration of ingredients of a charm. Recipes of that nature can easily be come by, with the smallest research into the subject of magic cookery. Witch's broth is made up in much the same way whether the sorcerer be black or white.

The magicians most feared are those veritable hired assassins who undertake the murder of innocent people. There are a number of ways of committing murder magically.

SENDING OF DEAD ('EXPÉDITIONS')

The most fearful practice in the black arts—the one which the ordinary people are always talking about, is the 'sending of dead' (*l'envoi morts* or *expéditions*). Whoever has become the prey of one or more dead people sent against him begins to grow thin, spit blood and is soon dead. The laying on of this spell is always attended by fatal results unless it is diagnosed in time and a capable *hungan* succeeds in making the dead let go.

The dead are sent under the auspices of Saint Expedit who is invoked after his image has been placed upside down, in the following prayer:

'Almighty God, my Father, come and find so-and-so that he may be "disappeared" (*sic*) before me like the thunder and lightning. Saint Expedit, you who have the power to move the earth, you are a saint and I a sinner. I call on you and take you as my patron from today. I am sending you to find so-and-so: rid me of (*expédiez*) his head, rid me of his memory, rid me of his thought, rid me of his house, rid me of all my enemies, visible and invisible, bring down on them thunder and lightning. In thine honour Saint Expedit, three Paters.'[3]

The success of this curse still depends on the goodwill of Baron-Samedi, the all-powerful master of the dead. The *boko* strikes his matchet three times against the stone consecrated to this god and at each blow utters the god's name. He is then possessed by Baron-Samedi who, through his mouth, orders the person appealing to him to turn up at midnight at a cemetery and there offer bananas and potatoes, chopped small, in front of the cross which symbolizes him. There too he must take a handful of earth for each of the 'dead' whom he wishes to send and must spread it on some path frequently taken by his victim. Whether the unfortunate man shall step on or step over the earth makes little difference: the dead will enter his body and hold him close for ever. A client may also take as many stones from the tombs as he wishes in the knowledge that each will become 'a dead' ready to do his will, as soon as he has thrown it against his victim's door.

There is another way of rousing the enmity of 'a dead' against someone to whom you wish harm. When a member of the victim's family dies, two nails are surreptitiously driven into a beam of the house in which the decease took place. The dead person then cannot leave the precincts and in revenge begins to persecute his kin, in particular the person against whom the spell was cast. Atenaïze, who complained a great deal about the persecutions she had suffered from her dead husband, had discovered two suspicious nails in a beam of her hut and had had them removed. Unfortunately in the process one of them fell to the ground and was never found. She attributed all her troubles to this lost nail.

The presence of 'a dead' in someone can affect not only his health but also his character. Milo Marcelin[4] tells the pathetic story of a father, good and honest, who overnight became a drunkard and even an assassin because one of his subordinates had dispatched against him a drunken, vagabond 'dead'.

Those who 'send dead' risk the wrath of their messengers if they fail to feed them.

Cattle no less than human beings are vulnerable to *expéditions*. It often happens that out of jealousy or vengeance sorcerers put 'dead' into a cow or a pig which soon seems afflicted with madness. Since an animal possessed is as dangerous as a human being in the same condition, its master is unable to sell it, and so must slaughter it.

TREATMENT FOR 'EXPÉDITIONS'

According to *hungan*, illnesses resulting from *expedition de morts* are not easily cured. The dead embed themselves in the organism into which they are inserted and it is very difficult to make them let go. That this is no exaggeration may be seen from a description of an exorcism of 'dead' which I had the chance of witnessing in all its complexities at Lorgina's sanctuary.[5] The patient who was put through this treatment was a certain Antoine who had been taken into the *mambo*'s *humfo* ill. With earthy complexion and wasted body he lay on a mat motionless as though eking out what little remained to him of life. A few weeks earlier this same man was a sturdy stevedore in the Port-au-Prince docks. His story was simple: he was taken suddenly ill and then went into an alarming decline. His family sent him to a *hungan* at La Salines who diagnosed an *envoi morts*. The magician was confident he could save him. In spite of the high fees he demanded Antoine took him on and endured a cruel and complicated treatment of which burning with seven matches was not the easiest part.

Antoine, seeing the dead would not yield, fell into such a state of prostration that he could no longer swallow. His parents then decided to take him to Lorgina and implored her to do anything she could to save him. She only agreed to take on his treatment after the *loa* Brisé whom she had invoked had promised her full co-operation. She threw shells and learnt that there were three dead in Antoine and there was no time to lose.

Given the nature of the illness the treatment had to be carried out not only under the aegis of the Guédé but even in the house which is reserved for them. There, the Guédé symbols had been traced out in ashes and coffee grounds.

On these *vévé* the patient's mat had been placed in order to establish a more intimate contact between him and the Guédé. Various ceremonial accessories were put on the table, the stone of Brisé (blackish with a mirror inset), five bunches of leaves and three calabashes containing maize and grilled peanuts. In each of these a candle had been planted (one black, one white and one yellow). Two *gamelles* (wooden troughs) under the table contained a brownish liquid. This was the 'bath'—that is to say bits and pieces of plants left to soak in water with bull's bile.

Lorgina ordered her *hunsi* to go and fetch the patient who had been sitting in the peristyle, clad in a nightshirt, with his back against the *poteau-mitan*. He was so weak that it was almost necessary to carry him. From what people said later it seems that on the way the 'dead' inside him continually defied the *mambo* and swore they would not let themselves be driven out. The patient was stripped of his clothes and with nothing on but his pants, was laid out on his mat, his head resting on a stone. Washing and 'tidying up' was now carried out as though the body were already that of a dead man. His jaw was bound up with a piece of stuff, his nostrils blocked with cotton-wool, his arms crossed against his body, palms uppermost, and his big-toes firmly tied together. On forehead, chest, stomach and in the palms of his hands were arranged small piles of maize and peanuts. Lorgina, taking a *zinga* (spotted) hen and a 'curly' cockerel, orientated them and invoked the spirits. She gave the birds to her acolyte who brought them to the patient and made them peck at each pile of food, beginning with the head. The cock's refusal to touch the grain was taken as a bad sign: another cock was fetched. This one attacked the grain with such gusto that the man's eyes had to be shielded from his greed. Now the birds were placed on the body of the invalid, two on the chest and the third between his legs. Meanwhile Lorgina, who had never ceased mumbling Credos, Aves and Paters as well as a long prayer to Saint Expedit, launched into a series of invocations to *loa* and magical formulae which invariably began with 'In the name of God the Father, God the Son, God the Holy Ghost, in the name of Mary, in the name of Jesus and all the Saints and all the dead . . .'

She got up, took the hen and a cock and passed them at length over the body of the patient starting with his head. Into this business she put a certain roughness and repeated several different incantations of which I only picked up one sentence: 'All that is bad is to come out, all that is good is to go in.' The *mambo* and her aide broke off to emit little noises something like the hissings of the snake-god Damballah. The assistant with a bird in each hand went through the whole thing again. He lingered when he came to the chest as though trying to sweep up something tangible. The patient trembled from time to time but the *mambo* cautioned him in commanding tone to keep still. She listed the names of the *loa* of her *humfo* and addressed herself to Brisé, to Agirualinsu and to her other protectors, but she also invoked the ancestors and root-*loa* of her client. She asked them to save him and to give him back his health 'with the help of God'. For one last time the cock and hen were passed over the patient and were then left beside him, so dazed they did not move. It was the spotted hen which had taken *l'expédition*. As to the curly cock, he it was who had taken upon himself the patient's *mauvais-air* (malific emanation). He would be set free. He was supposed to disappear mysteriously a few days later.

Each of the three calabashes with the candles was passed over the patient from head to foot. The same was done with the stone of Brisé. Lorgina continued praying and making the '*tététété*' noise. She dipped her cupped hands into the bath and raising as much of it as she could, threw it brutally into the patient's face. The latter terrified, trembled, shuddered, grunted and tried to get up. He was persuaded to keep still. Lorgina explained that it was not his fault that he moved but merely that the dead were on the move inside him and disturbing him. More of the 'bath' was thrown at him with the same violence as before and now several people took turns at it so the procedure might be continuous. The man was now streaming and covered with leaves and bits and pieces of half decomposed vegetation. This shower-bath was a veritable offensive against the 'dead', an attempt thoroughly to drive them out. Their resistance took the form of incoherent movements which they imparted to the body of the man they possessed. Faced with the spectacle of such brutal treatment, a relation of the patient, who till then had remained quiet, burst into tears, and crying out that she could stand it no longer, tried to escape. She was constrained to sit down. The *mambo* ordered the dead to depart and told them that if they persisted in their obstinacy she would find a sure way of expelling them. Garlic was put in the patient's mouth who, in the violence of his reaction, threw off his chin-bandage and bonds.

Finally he fell back on his mat visibly exhausted. The *mambo*

called him several times by his name: 'Antoine, Antoine, is it you
there? Is it you?' The patient replied faintly 'Yes'; whereupon
the assistant set fire to some *clairin* round the stone of Brisé on a
plate and seizing the flames in his hand, ran them all over the
body of the patient. Lorgina, filling her mouth with *kimanga*,
squirted it roughly into Antoine's face. He tried to shield his eyes
but was prevented. The *confiance* rubbed him vigorously and
struck him with the edge of her hands on the shoulders, the inner
crook of the arm and under his knees.

Baths, rubbings and general massage now brought to an end
this first part of the treatment which had taken place in the 'house
of Guédé'. The second act took place in the court, where a ditch
had been dug. The patient was led there leaning on two *hunsi*,
still walking with difficulty. Seven lamps made from orange peel
were burning round the ditch and with them might be seen the
three calabashes. The patient was helped into the bottom of the
trench and handed a young banana palm which had just been
uprooted. This he held in his arms. The chicken which was used
earlier in the treatment was once again passed over all his body.
Lorgina recited the formula 'By thy will Good Lord, Saints and
Dead, by the power of Papa Brisé, Monsieur Agirualinsu,
Monsieur Guédé-nuvavu, Tou-Guédé, I ask you for the life of
that man there, I *mambo* Yabofai, I ask you for the life of that
man there, I buy him cash, I pay you, I owe you nothing.' Once
the prayer was finished the *mambo* poured the contents of the
calabashes into her hands and with it rubbed the patient's body.
She poured the water from a jug over his head and all over his
body and then broke it against the parapet of the trench. She
anointed his body with oil from the lamps. The speckled hen, all
huddled up, was put at the bottom of the trench against the roots
of the banana palm. It was this hen which, buried alive, must buy
back the patient's life. If Baron-Samedi accepts the deal the
banana palm dies; but if he refuses it the tree prospers and the
man dies.

Quickly the loose earth on the edge of the ditch was pushed in
and the patient helped out. The filling-in of the trench was
completed as quickly as possible. The surface was levelled out
and then crowned with three 'perpetual lamps'.

Now came the most dramatic moment of the treatment, the moment which must bring about the final defeat of the dead. The patient was rubbed vigorously with blazing rum and three small charges were let off between his legs. Lorgina and her assistants squirted *kimanga* over him, blowing some to the four cardinal points—all this done to the cracking of the *petro* whip. A white *maldyoc* shirt with red facings was brought. One of the flap-ends was slightly burnt. With the blackened edge signs were marked on the face and chest of Antoine. The latter put on the shirt and over it the night-shirt which he was wearing at the beginning of the treatment. Lorgina told him to spit as much as possible and go in under the peristyle alone. He did so, stepping almost firmly. There a cloth was bound round his head and his feet were washed with an infusion of medicinal herbs; then he was given tea to drink. He said he was feeling much better.

And indeed the cure was almost miraculous. A few days later Antoine was a changed being. He ate well and having got some of his strength back wanted to get up and move about. Soon he resumed his arduous work as stevedore.

It is not always necessary to endure such a spectacular treatment to get rid of 'dead'. The daughter of a certain Florilon was suffering from a serious illness. Florilon put it down to 'dead' which his own brother had sent against the child to be avenged of the death of his son—an event for which he held Florilon responsible. Florilon first went to herb-doctors, then to the town doctors who all said they could do nothing. He decided—much against his better feelings since he was a fervent Catholic—to consult a *hungan*. The latter diagnosed the illness, prescribed ablutions (*bains*) with herbal infusions and gave the child's father an *arrêtement*, that is to say a talisman to stop the dead. This was a bottle full of magic herbs which he had to bury near his house. The girl was made to wear a *chemisette paman* (chemisette with facings) made of many coloured strips on which had been drawn indigo crosses. The child recovered but ever since then Florilon has felt an implacable hatred of the brother who had thus involved him in heavy expenditure and put him in debt to a *hungan*. At the time when I met him he had not yet finished paying off the fees of the *hungan* who, he feared, would unleash the *morts* which he had succeeded in 'stopping' if faced with further delay.

'ZOMBI'

Zombi are people whose decease has been duly recorded, and whose burial has been witnessed, but who are found a few years later living with a *boko* in a state verging on idiocy. At Port-au-Prince there are few, even among the educated, who do not give some credence to these macabre stories. It is generally believed that *hungan* know the secret of certain drugs which can induce such a profound state of lethargy as to be indistinguishable from death. From time to time a story crops up of a *zombi* being found by the wayside and then taken to the police station. There is still talk of the celebrated case recorded by Zora Houston[6] of a society girl who a few years after her death was found in a house in the town: her family, at a loss what to do with this child returned from the grave, are said to have shut her up in a French convent. Zora Houston also visited and photographed an authentic *zombi* who had been picked up at the hospital of Gonaïves. In spite of the assertions of Zora Houston, who is very superstitious, it really seems that the woman concerned was an imbecile or a moron in whom the peasants had recognized a person who had been dead for twenty years. I myself at Marbial once thought I was to meet a *zombi*. Some distracted peasants came to fetch me to see one in the middle of the night. I found a wretched lunatic with a farouche manner who remained obstinately silent. The people crowding round her stared at her with thinly disguised dread. Only on the following day was the *zombi* identified—as a poor idiot girl who had escaped from the house in which her parents kept her shut up.

Article 246 of the old Penal Code relates to *zombi* as follows:

'Also to be termed intention to kill, by poisoning, is that use of substances whereby a person is not killed but reduced to a state of lethargy, more or less prolonged, and this without regard to the manner in which the substances were used or what were their later results.

'If, following the state of lethargy the person is buried, then the attempt will be termed murder.'

The common people do not trouble themselves with such subtleties. For them the *zombi* are the living dead—corpses which a sorcerer has extracted from their tombs and raised by a process which no one really knows. It is thought the sorcerer passes to and fro beneath the nose of the corpse a bottle containing his soul, obtained with the connivance of the corpse-washer. When there is some reason to fear that a dead person may be transformed into a *zombi*, family feeling calls for measures to prevent such a terrible fate. Normally the dead person is killed a second time by injecting poison into him, strangling or firing a bullet into his temple. My colleague M. Bernot witnessed at Marbial the strangulation of the corpse of a youth. This procedure, it was hoped, would rescue him from the man who was making him into a *zombi*. Whoever has the job of killing the dead man must stand behind him in case he is recognized and reported to the sorcerer who, baulked of his prey, will try and get his revenge. Another way out is to bury the corpse face down, mouth against the earth, with a dagger in his hand so he may stab any sorcerer who troubles his rest. Since a corpse can only be raised if it answers its name, it is important to prevent it from doing so. That is why sometimes the mouths of the dead are sewn up. Attempts are also made to provide a corpse with distractions such as may prevent him from hearing appeals from sorcerers. Just as is done with a *loa* when it is 'limited', an eyeless needle is put beside the dead body so the dead man may spend aeons trying to thread it, or sesame seeds are scattered in his coffin which he will devote himself to counting one by one.

The spark of life which sorcerers wake in a corpse does not wholly give the dead man back his place in the society of men. A *zombi* remains in that misty zone which divides life from death. He moves, eats, hears what is said to him, even speaks, but he has no memory and no knowledge of his condition. The *zombi* is a beast of burden which his master exploits without mercy, making him work in the fields, weighing him down with labour, whipping him freely and feeding him on meagre, tasteless food. A *zombi*'s life is seen in terms which echo the harsh existence of a slave in the old colony of Santo Domingo. A *hungan* is not satisfied with the daily labour of his dead: but uses them

for dishonest purposes such as stealing the harvest of neighbours. There would seem to be a special category of *zombi*
called *zombi-graines* who are trained to steal the flowers of the
coffee bush and graft them on to those of their master.

Zombi are recognized by their absent-minded manner, their
extinguished, almost glassy eyes, and above all by the nasal
twang in their voices—a peculiarity which they share with the
Guédé, spirits of death. Their docility is total provided you never
give them salt. If imprudently they are given a plate containing
even a grain of salt the fog which cloaks their minds instantly
clears away and they become conscious of their terrible servitude.
Realization rouses in them a vast rage and an ungovernable
desire for vengeance. They hurl themselves on their master, kill
him, destroy his property and then go in search of their tombs.
Read in Seabrook[7] the strange story of the *zombi* of *hungan*
Joseph who worked as cane-cutters at la Hasco. The *hungan*'s
wife, to whom these unfortunates had been entrusted, had the
unlucky idea of giving them some *tablettes* (pralines) made with
salted peanuts. The *zombis*, suddenly realizing that they were only
dead men, fled to the valley whence they came. No one dared
stop them because 'they were corpses'. Staring straight ahead,
without paying the slightest attention to their relations who
called to them or tried to stop them, they went to the cemetery.
There each hurled himself on his grave and tore at the stones
with his nails . . . and as their hands touched their tombs they
turned into stinking carcases.

Here is another story which was told me at Port-au-Prince.
The principal protagonists were, it seems, people from the
highest society. A 'Monsieur' who was coming to Jeremie by
road had to stop near a village to repair a puncture. An old man
with a white goatee suddenly appeared beside him and having
said that he would get help from a friend who would soon be
here (a prophecy which was certainly fulfilled) invited him
meanwhile to take a cup of coffee with him. On the way to the
house the little old man, who in fact was a powerful *hungan*, said
—laughing—that it was he who by means of a charm had caused
the puncture, but asked the man not to hold it against him. As
they were taking coffee in the room the *hungan* warned his guest

to be careful of a *wanga* which lay in his car. The visitor, a sceptic, was unable to repress a smile. The *hungan*'s vanity was piqued and he asked if his visitor had known a certain Monsieur Célestin, dead six months earlier. It so happened that this man had been his great friend. 'Would you like to see him?' asked the *hungan* and without waiting for a reply he cracked a whip six times. A door opened and a man appeared on the threshold. He was walking backwards but his silhouette was familiar to Monsieur X. In rough tones the *hungan* ordered the man to turn round. Since he did not obey quickly enough, his master gave him a blow with the handle of the whip. Then it was that Monsieur X recognized his friend Célestin, who now made a move towards the glass which X was holding. Full of pity X wanted to give it to him but the *hungan* stopped him dead with his whip and reminded him nothing could be more dangerous than to give something to a dead person directly, from hand to hand. He told him to leave the glass on the table.

The *zombi* said not a word. He kept his head hanging and his face wore an expression which was both stupid and wretched. The *hungan* revealed to his guest that the issue of blood from which the friend had died was caused by a spell. The sorcerer responsible for this crime had sold him his victim for twelve dollars.

The following story seemed to me interesting in so far as it is typical of this kind of anecdote.

A girl from Marbial, engaged to a young man with whom she was much in love, was unwise enough to reject—rather sharply—the advances of a powerful *hungan*. The latter, wounded, went away muttering threats. A few days later the girl was taken seriously ill and died in the hospital at Jacmel. Her body was taken to her family at Marbial but at the moment when she was being put on the bier, the coffin, which had been got in the town, was seen to be too short. It was necessary to bend the corpse's neck in order to fit it into the space available. During the wake someone dropped a lighted cigarette on to the foot of the deceased causing a slight burn. Two or three months later a rumour spread that the deceased had been seen with the *hungan*. No one believed it. But a few years later, when during the anti-supersition campaign the *hungan* repented and set his *zombis* free, the girl appeared and went back home, where she lived for a long time though without ever recovering her sanity. All those who knew her remember her bent neck and the scar of a burn which she bore on one of her feet.

'WANGA'

Along with sorceries which cause incurable illnesses and destroy crops or cattle there are others, milder, which only inflict transitory trouble and curable illnesses. The magic weapon *par excellence* is the *wanga**—a term which is applied to any object or combination of objects which has received, as a result of magic procedure, a property that is harmful to one or more people. *Wanga* are also called 'poisons'. The word is suitable so long as one remembers that these concoctions are only poisonous on the supernatural plane. The obsession with poison dating back to the colonial era, proceeds from a confusion between matter that is genuinely poisonous and that which is poisonous only in a magic way. The Whites, eternally haunted by their fear of the Blacks, accepted in the most literal sense magic interpretations of every illness or death, provided there was the smallest ground for suspicion. In Haiti the power of a *wanga* is often personified. Its efficacy is then attributed to a spirit which has been vested in the enchanged object.

Many *wanga* are objects which have been 'arranged' (*rangé*) by a sorcerer in such a way that a mere touch from them is enough to produce the desired effect—generally illness. Not least of their marvellous properties is that of being harmful only to the person who has been marked down for the sorcerer's attention. A woman of Marbial had received, in a quarrel, a blow from a stick which had not done her much harm; nevertheless she died shortly afterwards and everyone was convinced that the stick in question had been 'arranged' by its owner.

One of my neighbours died from the effects of a thorn which

---

* In the making of *wanga* great store is set by objects associated with the Catholic religion. The Host is much sought after and goes into the making of the most powerful of *wanga*.

became embedded in his foot. On the evening of the funeral several people came and told me in great confidence that the thorn had been *rangé* and put down by someone whose name they muttered in my ear. On another occasion in the course of a fête, a woman of the dead man's family was possessed by Zaka who told her himself that his servant had been poisoned. The god added that no harm would have befallen him had he only known how to keep on good terms with the *loa* who would have warned him of his danger.

In country districts strange chickens who come wandering unexpectedly into people's back-yards are looked upon with a mistrustful eye. They may well be 'arranged' and therefore the wisest course is to cut off their heads and leave their bodies at a crossroads.

The following story, which I was assured is true, shows the extent magic is feared even in the highest society. Its hero is a historian, whom I knew well, and who at the time was a member of the Conseil d'Etat. On his way to a reunion at the presidential palace, he bought some seed for his pet birds which he put in his dispatch-case. Unluckily for him this had a hole in the bottom and as he went into the assembly hall he left behind him a trail of seed. At the sight of this his colleagues shouted '*Wanga, wanga!*' The following day the councillor was called to the President: who said, 'My dear friend, I am too educated to believe these silly tales of black magic, nevertheless I feel it my duty to ask you to resign.'

Poisoned powders are naturally classed as *wanga*. They are much feared because it needs no more than a pinch of them spread on a garment for the wearer to be struck down with an illness which will resist every kind of treatment. A stronger dose is naturally fatal. A few years ago newspapers of Haiti told of an unfortunate incident which befell a high official in the education department. I had the story from the man himself. In the course of a rather bitter argument which he had had with the Minister, the latter suddenly became anxious and tried to put him out of the room. When unable to do so, he hurried to the office of the President of the Republic before whom he lodged a formal complaint of having been victim of an attempted enchantment. He said he had perceived a suspicious smell and began to feel upset. This was enough for the official to be removed from office—at least this was the reason given in the newspaper for his dismissal. I heard that the Minister in question was obsessed with fear of sorcery. When practising as a solicitor he was visited by a peasant who had come to ask him a favour. His visitor was carrying a stick with which he unconsciously, from time to time, made flourishing gestures. Noticing this the man of law suddenly shouted '*Wanga!*' and the petitioner was arrested and had the greatest difficulty in getting himself set free. The same personage, when sent as government emissary to Saint Marc, suddenly withdrew from that town saying he had seen black hands on the walls of his room and felt himself menaced by werewolves.

MAGIC AND RICHES

The peasants of Haiti never boast of prosperity. Even those who cannot conceal it complain of their lot and belittle their possessions. Indeed, prudence is pushed to extreme lengths: a man congratulated on his healthy, happy looks and plumpness will protest indignantly, 'Me plump? The idea! Alas—it's inflammation—not plumpness.' Dread of provoking fate is even reflected in the small coin of everyday politeness. To someone who asks after your health you must reply: 'No worse.' Such attitudes are very common in rural milieux; the same sort of thing can be found in France and elsewhere. But specifically Haitian is the tendency to attribute the wealth or even simply the well-being of others to shady dealings with evil spirits. The Haitian finds it difficult to admit that anyone might become rich without having made an arrangement with a sorcerer. There are always people ready to pretend they know the exact nature of the contract with a *diab* by which such and such a *grand don* was enabled to complete his fortune: to be rich is to be something of a sorcerer. Naturally all this is the eternal jealousy of the peasant, here taking the form of magical imputations. Nevertheless such goings-on do constitute an important part of the study which we have undertaken.

If we are to believe what we hear in the country districts, the clientèle of the *boko* seems to be made up more of people ambitious or desperate to grow rich at whatever price than people thirsting for vengeance. The 'hot point' (*point chaud*) which is sold to them is usually a spirit who is bound to serve them on certain conditions. It can be represented by a talisman (stone, red herring, etc.) which exercises a direct effect by virtue of an intrinsic property or through the agency of a spirit attached to the object as a 'slave', as was the genie to Aladdin's lamp. The supernatural beings whom sorcerers use as their auxiliaries are 'bought' *loa* or *zombi* souls (*âmes zombi*). The latter are sold to them by corpse-washers who, when members of the family are not looking, seize the opportunity of popping the soul of the deceased into a bottle. The souls most to be feared and also the most magically effective are those of men who were sorcerers in their life-time.

Zombi souls and bought *loa* are often termed *baka*. This word also covers a particular class of evil spirit which wanders in the woods in the form of cats, dogs, pigs, cows or monsters which defy description. *Baka* too are those evil *loa* such as Ti-Jean-pied-chèche, Ezili-jé-rouge, Marinette-bwa-chèche, etc.

Wandering *baka* do not always attack passers-by but sometimes drive them out of their wits by assuming successively, before their very eyes, the weirdest and most varied forms. The following story gives a typical example of their behaviour. A rider travelling by night, far from any dwelling place, saw beside the road a crying child. Moved by pity he took it up behind him to take it to its parents. The child suddenly began to grow bigger and bigger until finally its legs were dragging along the ground; it was a *baka*. It said to him: 'You are innocent, therefore I will not hurt you. But let this be a lesson. In future when you come across a "thing" like me, leave it alone—pass by on the other side.'

These monsters inspire such terror that some people die at sight of them or after they have been 'seized' by them fall seriously ill. There are various forms of protection against *baka* but the best of all is to refuse to give in to the terror which they try to inspire. They must be looked straight in the eyes: then they turn their heads away and vanish.

It is said of someone who has acquired a *point chaud* that he has got a 'commitment' (*engagement*). This agreement—which binds him to evil spirits—usually entails an obligation to feed the *baka* with a human being, preferably some member of his own family: mother, father, husband, child or failing that a neighbour or friend. In point of fact the person who accepts the 'engagement' does not always understand the nature of the deal which is proposed to him. The better to deceive people sorcerers use an ambiguous language in which 'cock and hen' means mother and father; 'a pair of chickens' two children; 'a bottle of water' a pregnant woman. Whoever lets himself be trapped into granting, for instance, the 'chickens' which have been asked of him, unwittingly condemns his children to death. The ambitious man who wants a 'point' should know that he is dealing with pirates of whom he must beware. It is up to him to pick out among the demands of his new partner those which beneath a harmless appearance conceal traps. The life of his family depends on his wisdom; though naturally there are always deprived individuals who for personal ends will not hesitate to sacrifice every member of their family.

The possession of a 'hot point' is only obtained at great risk. Once you are 'committed' to him, a *baka* never lets you go. You think you are its master, only to discover you are its slave. Always thirsting for human blood, a *baka* keeps asking, every time it opens its mouth, for fresh victims. Nothing can bend its will. Sooner or later it ends by killing its partner who, tired of giving it human beings, tries to get out of his commitment. The phrase 'work is getting too much for me' is used to describe the plight of an apprentice sorcerer who has lost control of his 'hot point'.

One story which I heard at Marbial will fully illustrate the fate of those who become 'committed'. An inhabitant of Marbial whom we shall call Novilius, went to ask a *hungan* for a 'point' so that he might become rich. The sorcerer made him bury offerings and food in a coffin. Then he said the following prayer: 'Holy Earth, receive this food-offering and all these medicines. This man is poor: may he within a year ride on a horse and be able to count his money like an important man.'

One year later our friend was prancing about on a horse and

gave the *hungan* 1,000 gourdes. Now extremely rich, he talked gladly of God, whom he thanked for all his good fortune, but he quite forgot about his 'point'. For eight years he gave it nothing to eat. The evil familiar, tired of waiting, 'broke the neck' of one of the man's children. A great deal of money had to be spent on the funeral but the father took no heed of the warning. Then it was the turn of the second child. Then a third fell ill. Finally the fourth committed a crime and his father had to pay a large sum to get him out of prison.

This series of misfortunes made Novilius suspicious. He returned to the *boko* and said: 'What have I done to deserve all these punishments?' The *boko* explained to him that the 'point' must be appeased though this would cost money—a lot of money. Finally Novilius died and the little he left his wife scarcely paid for his burial. The evil spirit, still unsatisfied, turned its wrath on the wife who, soon after, died too. In the absence of heirs the land belonging to Novilius fell to the State. The very first day it was rented the new landlord, who had just settled in, heard mysterious footsteps in the attic. In vain he searched the house from top to bottom: he found nothing suspicious. But every night the same noise deprived him of sleep. Worn out, this man at last fled and since then no one has dared take on the property which could only be lived on again if the evil spirit which haunts it were appeased.

A person can make a deal with an evil spirit by which his life is forfeit after a certain number of years, as stipulated in the contract. There were once two small farmers of Marbial who helped each other. They were very poor. One day one of them said to the other, 'My friend, I'm tired. I work like a beast and it brings in nothing. My life must see a change.' 'What can you do?' said the other. 'Don't you see that this is our fate for life?' 'I don't know what I'm going to do,' replied the first, 'but this is my last year of wretchedness.' And indeed three months later he became the owner of ten acres of fine banana plantation. His friend was surprised. He began to be suspicious when he saw his friend had bought a lorry and then two more acres of land.

But it was much later, after his death, that it transpired how he had managed to make such a quick fortune: he had exchanged

his life for six years' happiness and riches. When the bill fell due
the *diab* of Trou-forban came faithfully to claim his debt.

At Marbial there used to be plenty of gossip about 'commit-
ments' which the rich people had entered into with the devil and
the human victims which they had allegedly sacrificed to him.

Towards the end of my stay at Marbial a luckless fellow called
Jovalis broke his neck falling from the top of a mango-tree up
which he had climbed to shake down fruit. This job had been
given him by a *hungan* who had promised him half the fruit in
return for his trouble. The accident did not strike either the
family of the deceased or the local inhabitants as altogether
straightforward. Everyone agreed in accusing the *hungan* of
having 'given' Jovalis, that is to say sacrificed him to the bad *loa*
he served in return for riches received. It was also said that the
murder was the result of an indiscretion on the part of Jovalis:
rumour said he had been present, by chance, at the sacrifice of a
pig which the *hungan* was offering to his 'point'. Jovalis failed to
keep his mouth shut and his indiscretion was the end of him.
Finally, according to a third version, Jovalis was killed by a
cousin who arranged with the *hungan* that he should be made to
fall from the mango-tree. The peasants based their suspicion on
a curious circumstance: the branch to which Jovalis had been
holding was not broken and someone had heard the *hungan*'s wife
say, 'Why make someone climb a tree which is never climbed by
anyone?' The murderer was held to have finally established his
guilt by paying for part of the funeral costs . . .

Having collected all this evidence I paid a visit on the *hungan*
himself, to hear his version of the affair. Either he had no
knowledge of what people were saying about him or he did not
care—for when I spoke to him about Jovalis's accident he showed
no sign of concern. He assured me the deceased was simply a
stranger whom he had allowed to pick a few mangoes. Nevertheless he regretted the death had occurred so near his house
because it had cost him five gourdes spent on food and drink
when the man's family came to fetch the body.

The following anecdote with its almost Faustian undertones,
was told me as a 'true story': there was at Marbial an important
machinateur (magician) who had for his disciple a young man

called Amantus. The latter was a 'fine lad' who, eaten up with ambition, feared neither sorcerers nor spirits. His master had given him proofs of friendship and had imparted to him some of his 'knowledge'. However, out of prudence he was careful not to reveal to him the nature of his 'point'—the source of all his riches. Amantus did all he could to gain the entire confidence of the *boko* but never succeeded. So he decided to spy on him day and night. His patience was rewarded: he discovered that the power of the *boko* proceeded from a stone which he kept carefully hidden. One day when he was alone in the *humfo* he seized the opportunity of stealing it. The following night he saw in a dream a vast dog with a human head which said to him: 'From tonight on it is you who are my master. Things will go better with you because now you are in with me.' The *boko* having lost his stone found his luck running out. He was defeated in a lawsuit and ruined. His disciple on the other hand grew quickly rich and became one of the notables of the region. But one evening when he was walking in one of his banana plantations he heard a voice saying: 'The time has come to settle our account.' He paid no attention to the mysterious warning. Misfortune overtook him: he contracted such a serious illness that a good half of his fortune went in paying doctors and chemists. He had hoped that once he was cured he would easily be able to recoup his losses, but then epizooty decimated his stock. Weighed down with debt he had to sell his plantations for a poor price and little by little he succumbed to the most abject destitution. His talisman, after being the source of luck, had become the cause of ruin and misery. Not knowing how to pay off the spirit of the stone nor how to appease its ire, he decided to take refuge in the bosom of a Protestant sect. He became a Baptist and from that day forward gave up all dealings with *loa* and magic.

II. THE SOCIETIES OF SORCERERS

Only with the greatest reluctance will the peasants of Haiti go out alone at night. What they fear is not so much an encounter with ghosts or evil spirits but to fall in unexpectedly with a 'column' of criminals of a special kind called, according to region, *zobop, bizango, galipotes,* 'hairless pigs' or 'hairless ones', 'grey pigs', *vlanbindingues, bossu, macandal* or finally *voltigeurs.*

The people designated by these names are sorcerers who have taken a 'hot point', as described in the preceding chapter, and who, in addition, have joined secret societies whose members, united by the crimes they have committed together, give each other help. The *zobop* (the name for them used in Marbial) derive material benefits from membership—wealth and all its trappings—a fine house, luxurious car and a trip to France— though these considerations are secondary to the satisfaction of returning evil for evil, and of 'eating people' during nocturnal expeditions.

Do these secret societies, which are directly descended from the sorcerer-societies of West Africa, really exist or are they merely the fiction of popular imagination worked upon by the perennial fear of magic and magicians?

Countless stories heard about *zobop* really belong to the province of the fairy-tale, but it seems likely that certain people do sometimes band together, in secret, to practise sorcery or to use the popular belief in sorcerer societies to sow terror around them. Proof that the matter is not wholly a question of super- stition is to be found in the passports of *zobop,* confiscated in *humfo* or handed over to *curés* by repentant voodooists.

The most sinister fantasies of a kind sure to capture popular imagination have been centred on the 'red sects'. Hideous or grotesque aspect, weird dress, obscene and bloody ceremonies, gratuitous cruelty—there is no conceivable trait that is not attributed to them provided it is sufficiently repulsive and odious. Here, in Haiti, in mid-twentieth century, we find again every leering apparition of the sabbaths which once crowded the dossiers of ecclesiastical tribunals in the days of witch-hunting. Of the sensational details with which story-tellers season their descriptions of 'grey pigs' and *zobop* there is little point in mentioning here any but those which tally with a tradition which has become more or less established.

The members of the 'red sects' are not recognizable by any distinctive mark or badge. They are often people of quiet and peaceful appearance. You may live cheek by jowl with them for years without ever suspecting their other identity. Some mere chance gives them away—and then the fury of their neighbours can be terrible. I knew a Frenchman in Haiti who had been there for years and made his fortune. One fine day he was suddenly pronounced 'the king devil'. An enraged crowd besieged him in his house. He would have been killed if the police had not fetched him and taken him to the station promising the would-be lynchers to chain him up and punish him.

Zobop commit their crimes at veritable sabbaths. They organize these on certain nights of the week which they say belong to them. Those who attend these reunions must know passwords which sentries will ask for. They are guided to the assembly-place by the sharp rhythm of a small drum. This instrument has the peculiar quality of being audible to sect members at a prodigious distance while remaining inaudible to passers-by even when they are quite close to a band of *zobop* lying in wait. Sorcerers are also convoked by the clashing together of stones—a custom which is not without interest when it is recalled that this same rally-signal is used by the *zangbeto*—a secret society of Dahomey.

The *zobop* wear long red or white garments and are crowned with lighted candles. Sometimes they wear tin horns or a conical straw hat. Holding candles in their hands and cracking a whip they march in column like soldiers; hence the word 'column', used by itself, has come to mean a troop of this sect. Like the *baka* they enjoy the faculty of being able to change their appearance at will: they can elongate their heads, stiffen their features and, whenever they like, turn into giants, dwarfs, cockerels or ferocious dogs. They will go in procession to some crossroad and there celebrate a ceremony in honour of Maître-Carrefour whom they ask to grant success to all they undertake. They meet in cemeteries where they invoke Baron-Samedi and beg him to enable them to kill 'a goat without horns'. They then repair to some highway or bridge where they lie in ambush until their victim comes. Their scouts, armed with cords made from dried entrails, comb the countryside for some traveller imprudent enough to be still journeying after dark. Their tricks are legion:

sometimes they assume the gaiety and general carry-on of a band of young bloods on their way back from a fair: if they know the name of the wayfarer they meet they call out: 'Well! If it isn't old so-and-so . . .' The person accosted, believing himself in the presence of friends, goes confidently up to them—only to find himself surrounded by a band of 'devils'.

The *zobop* do not always kill their captives. If they think they will be good recruits they give them the choice of enlistment or a horrible death. But even when they sign people on they remain as deceitful as ever. Instead of making their offer clear, they ask the prisoner: 'Come in or go out?' If he replies, 'Go out' he is killed on the spot; if on the other hand he says, 'Come in' they spare him on condition he joins the sect. He must drink a glass of reddish liquid—presumably human blood. To prove his devotion and as a joining fee he must, in addition, 'give' someone who is particularly dear to him. In this context I was told the story of a woman who agreed to sacrifice her son—a boy of about fifteen. A sorceress, who was jealous of her, sought out the child and warned him that he would be visited by a woman who would try and lure him away; she advised him to bow very low and say 'Greetings, Queen', but at the same time throw a bucket of water over her. That very evening the young man was in fact called on by an unknown woman accompanied by a group of strange-looking people. He duly emptied the bucket of water over her whereupon the woman fell dead at his feet and her companions fled. When he examined the body he found he had killed his own mother.

A woman of Port-au-Prince whose business was going very badly was one day unwise enough to cry out, 'I would become a *zobop* or *vlanbindingue* if only I could be done with this poverty.' She then perceived that one of her neighbours, who was listening, was looking at her with a strange smile. The following night she was woken by singing and the sound of a small drum which seemed to be coming from a group who had stopped outside her door. She went and looked through the key-hole and saw people dressed in red, wearing three-cornered hats and carrying candles. She was careful not to open the door. The 'column' having sung a song of which the refrain was '*Aye aye zobop, aye ya aye,*

zobop . . .' went on its way. The following day the woman met
her neighbour who said to her reproachfully: 'And me thinking
you wanted to join the society to get your business on its
feet . . .'

The woman, now mistrustful, pretended not to understand.
Whereupon the recruiting-woman's husband, who was a *zobop*,
told his wife to take our woman a glass of wine. She refused to
drink it but seeing her refusal was ill received promised to take
the wine home with her and drink it later. Naturally she did
nothing of the kind but threw the stuff away as soon as possible.
Thus she escaped the trap laid for her. Her neighbour hated her
for it and never stopped trying to get at her in order to be
avenged. But she never succeeded in killing her.

Even among *zobop* the ties of blood and friendship do not lose
their rights; when a member sees that colleagues have seized one
of his relations or friends he has only to say 'no' for the victim to
be released immediately. *Zobop* can be appeased, too, by the
performance of some small service: a man who was going to
Croix-des-bouquets met a person who asked him for a cigarette.
He obliged and was rather surprised to hear the stranger say:
'You don't know what a service you are doing me. I haven't had
a cigarette since early this morning. One day perhaps I will have
an opportunity of repaying you.'

The same day when our friend was going home on foot he met
a man on the road who was quite naked and carrying a rope:
'Stop!' cried this apparition. The man did so. By the light of a
match the *zobop* examined his face and asked him, 'Was it not
you who gave me a cigarette this afternoon?' 'Yes,' said the man.
'You are in luck,' said the *zobop*. 'But you are unwise to walk
about alone at this time of night. It will soon be midnight and
then the column will be out. If you hadn't met me you would
never have been heard of again. Since you did something for me
I am going to do something for you.' From a little bag tied round
his neck he took a scrap of paper on which were drawn cabalistic
signs. He gave him this and told him he could go. 'In a moment,'
he said, 'you will meet the main column. Don't answer the
questions they ask you. Merely show them this bit of paper and
they'll let you pass.' The traveller thanked the *zobop* and every-

thing happened as foretold: he ran into the column, showed his passport—and was able to get home, safe and sound.

According to popular belief *zobop* do their nocturnal raids in motor-cars. A few years ago there was much talk in Port-au-Prince of a 'tiger car' (*auto-tigre*) which took people away by night to 'eat' them. This was no innocent folk tale, as a friend of mine was able to witness. He—Monsieur M. B.—was suspected of being the driver of the phantom car and was almost lynched by a crowd which surged round him, accusing him of having killed a child.

At the same period in Marbial people talked a lot about 'a motor-*zobop*' which drove about at night with bluish beams shining from its headlights. My informants were never tired of telling me about the adventure which befell a certain Divoine Joseph who had been kidnapped by the occupants of this mysterious vehicle. Having heard several versions of the incident I asked the hero of the affair himself to give me an account of what happened. Here, word for word, is what he told me:

'I am a man who at night has no fear because I possess certain mysteries whom I keep well satisfied. They protect me and go with me wherever I go. I am also a herb-doctor and I know from experience that a remedy can never be effective unless it is taken at night. The day I was seized was a Sunday. I had on that day gone to a cock-fight but had no luck. I lost all my bets—a thing which seldom happens to me. I had to go to Nan-Mango to help look after someone who was ill, who was prey to a bad soul. My *placée** wanted to prevent me from going out but I said to her, "Have you ever seen me afraid at night?" Just as I was leaving the back-yard my "bad foot" (left foot) stumbled into a stone. But I paid no attention. Not far from the sick man's house I was seized with sudden fear. My hair stood on end but having seen nothing odd or abnormal, I continued on my way and paid my call as though nothing had happened. When I had finished the treatment I had to go, at about midnight, to a crossroads to throw away the *mauvais nanm* which I had drawn out of the patient's body. Not far from la Gosseline I was blinded by a blue light. This time fear made me lose consciousness. When I came to my

* Common law wife.

senses I was in a car surrounded by hideous masked people. In my horror I cried out *"Tonnerre crasé"*. My captors offered me money if I would keep my mouth shut and never tell what had happened to me. The car stopped and I was made to get out. I woke up in my bed. I asked my *placée* whether she had found any money on me. She said, "You behaved like a raving lunatic. You threatened everyone with a banana-sucker. But you hadn't a penny on you." In the evening I had terrible hallucinations and wandered in my mind. In my delirium I repeated ceaselessly: "They have got me." I was cured thanks to the attentions of a *hungan*.'

Divoine's friends all insist that since that time he has never been quite 'all there'. Indeed he does show signs of extreme nervousness. He never stays still, gesticulates repeatedly, smites his breast, bursts into laughter, frowns for nothing and pours out words. Divoine owes his escape from this terrible adventure to his status as a *kanzo*. The *zobop* had indeed intended to kill him but they changed their minds when they saw they were dealing with a man protected by the *loa*. A *hungan* who had himself been forced to get into a car, driven by *zobop*, also had his life saved by the intervention of one of his supernatural protectors. The *zobop* had already put him in a coffin when the god Brisé 'mounted' him to prevent the evil doers from killing him. Realizing their powerlessness they turned back and dropped him at a cemetery.

The peasants accuse the *zobop* of, among other things, changing their victims into beasts ready for slaughter, for it is a widespread belief in Haiti that among the animals reaching slaughterhouses there are a certain number who are really human beings. How often have I heard the tale of the ox with the gold tooth or the cow with a baby in its womb! People turned into beasts may be recognized by the gentle sadness of their expression. I heard of an ox which, on the point of being slaughtered, threw itself to its knees in front of the butcher and raised its eyes in supplication to his face. It is also said that even after these metamorphoses, human flesh remains always recognizable: rather frothy, and it trembles when spiked by a fork. Many people, even in the towns, believe in these fables and go as far as to say that the

THE SOCIETIES OF SORCERERS

THE SOCIETIES OF SORCERERS 299

injections given by vets are merely a means of making sure an ox
really is an ox, and not a human being. An inhabitant of Morne
Rouge, an enlightened man and a good Catholic, vouched for the
following facts: a merchant of Marbial (who was a *zobop*) reared
on his farm a magnificent pig which was coveted by one of his
friends. The pig's owner, however, was unwilling to sell. Tired
of his friend's importunities he at last advised him to go, at
midnight, to the enclosure where the pig was kept and repeat
three times over: '*So gro, gro cochon*' and then: '*Christien, gro,
gro.*' The man did as he was told and was astounded to see the pig
rear up on its hind legs and turn into a huge Mulatto. He quickly
recited the formula the other way round—and the man returned
to his animal shape.

The 'werewolf point' (*point loup-garou*) confers the power of
being able to turn into an animal. Many sorcerers use it to walk
about at night as black cats, pigs, cows or horses. When they
meet anyone they block their path, follow them persistently and
do all they can to upset them. Some do this merely out of cruelty
to their neighbours, others hoping to induce a 'seizure'. For 'fear
fouls the blood'; and everyone knows that bad blood lies at the
root of many illnesses. There were few people in Marbial who
had not at some time or other in their lives, met one of these
animals. A good friend of mine who had lingered one night near
one of his *placées*, came face to face with a cow who would not let
him pass. He thought he was in the presence of an 'evil spirit'.
Remembering that his whip had been 'mounted' by a *hungan*, he
used it to rain down a storm of blows on the animal and kept on
till he found himself whipping not a cow but the local chief of
police. The official, now full of penitence, implored him to keep
the incident dark, assuring him he had meant no harm but had
merely wished to play a trick on him. The following day it became known the chief of police had taken to his bed. He died a
few days later. People say that his body was covered with weals.

A man who was dogged by persistent bad luck confessed to a
friend that he would do anything under the sun to be rid of his
poverty. His friend then took him to a house where he found
himself among members of the 'red sect'. These people must
have made a pact with him for he managed to become rich. His

wife, whom he had not kept informed of his dealings with the sorcerers, became anxious when night after night she saw him leaving the house and never getting back till the following morning, worn out. More and more anxious, she at last went to consult a priest who told her that her husband at night turned into a horse. Since she refused to believe him the priest gave her a 'mounted' whip and went with her to a crossroads at midnight. They did not have to wait long before they saw a carriage drawn by a horse. The woman, obedient to the instructions she had received, assaulted the animal's head, giving it several good blows with the whip. The animal vanished and she found herself face to face with her husband standing between the shafts, entangled in harness. When he was free he went blind with rage, attacked the coachman (who was none other than his so-called friend) and killed him.

WEREWOLVES

At Port-au-Prince *zobop* are often called werewolves (*loups-garous*), but at Marbial the latter word is reserved exclusively for female vampires who make small children die by sucking their blood. The peasants seemed to me definite on this point: *loups-garous* are always female; the fact deserves a certain emphasis for we find the same belief established in different regions of West Africa. *Loups-garous* are also called 'suckers' (*sucettes*) or *mauvais airs*.

The fear inspired by werewolves is as sharply felt among Protestants and Catholics as it is among Voodooists. At Marbial my friends gave me, in confidence, the names of all the were-wolves in the district. These lists always agreed with each other, which suggests that there is more in this than superstition, a tale with which to frighten children. In 1948 several families lodged complaints with the *Chef de Section* against such and such a neighbour, accusing her of being the werewolf who had come to 'drain' (*sécher*) their sick children. I have also seen an enraged mother who had just lost her baby, insult the woman she suspected of having killed it. Apart from cases where fear or despair drives parents to take violent measures, women regarded as notorious werewolves are left alone. Their neighbours maintain perfectly normal and even cordial relations with them—though these, it may well be true, are no more than a blind. For wisdom counsels a double measure of consideration in dealing with such people, so that their malice may be vented on others.

Only very rarely does a woman become a werewolf of her own accord. She nearly always acts in obedience to an impulse of which, to begin with, she remains unconscious. The occult power which enables her to journey through the air and abandon herself to cannibalism with impunity is often the result of a hereditary taint which has passed from mother to daughter. It can also be a sort of contagious illness which can be transmitted to anyone who, without knowing, wears a garment or jewel which has belonged to a werewolf.

Certain *loa*—Ogu-jé-rouge in particular—can confer this baleful power as a form of punishment upon women who prove neglectful of their duties toward them. When a person has reason to feel threatened by such a curse she had better make the promised offerings and sacrifices quickly and put up an iron cross in front of her house.

The state of werewolf, like that of *zobop*, often proceeds from the penalty-clause in a contract. In other words it is often the 'pay off' for the advantages derived from the acquisition of a 'hot point'. The *boko* who 'commits' a woman to evil spirits gives her a ring or any other object which has first been 'drugged' (*drogué*). This talisman is a pledge of luck, but it also has the power of turning the bearer into a werewolf.

In the early stages of their career werewolves commit their crimes without knowing it. Night excursions, cannibal meals are for beginners no more than nightmares which haunt their sleep. Then, gradually, the terrible truth dawns on them—but by now it is too late to stop: the taste for human flesh which these unfortunates have by then acquired, has become an uncontrollable vice.

Like the *zobop*, werewolves try to get recruits. They lay ambushes for women, surprising them at night in remote spots and obliging them to take part in their sabbath. Whoever has fraternized with werewolves can never again live a normal life. He is bound to them with a complicity which, however involuntary, still alienates him for ever from normal human feelings. Nevertheless a person does not become a werewolf overnight; a novice must learn the secrets of this wretched profession under the guidance of a veteran.

A woman werewolf getting ready for a night outing first raises as many fingers as she expects to be hours absent from her house, or else she lights a candle marked with three notches. Unless she is back before the flame reaches the last notch her excursion may go ill. When she has taken these precautions she frees herself of her skin by rubbing her neck, wrists and ankles with a concoction of magic herbs. She hides her skin in a cool place—in a jar or near a pitcher—so that it will not shrink. Thus, stripped to the quick, the woman werewolf makes movements which have the effect of preparing her for the flight which she will shortly undertake. Flames spurt from her armpits and anus, turkey wings sprout from her back. She takes off through the thatch of her house; sheet-iron constitutes an impassable obstacle to werewolves, not because it is made of metal but because it is fixed to the timbering with nails which have the magic virtue of 'stopping' sorcerers and sorceresses.

Luminous trails—which nearly every peasant says he has seen at night—mark the werewolf's track through the sky. These have some resemblance to comets and are called 'werewolf clusters' (*nids de loups-garous*). The days favoured by werewolves for their night excursions are the 7th, 13th and 17th of each month.

A Marbial peasant, '*fort en Guinée*'—that is to say a practiser of magic—said that he had seen a *loup-garou* at the very moment when it took off from the top of a big *mapou*. The vampire turned towards the four cardinal points and cried out '*Pati fi, yalé pami mové liân*' (Let us be off girls, away among the liana of wickedness). The peasant lost no time in making a *charme loup-garou*, (an anti-werewolf spell) doubtless very powerful, since immediately afterwards one of his neighbours fell seriously ill. No longer afraid, he got together some friends and went to cut the *mapou* down. Just as he was about to deal the first blows the tree suddenly fell of its own accord, and at the same moment there was a loud scream. It was the werewolf woman—dying at the same time as her tree.

A flesh and blood werewolf is much less to be feared than a 'bad soul' (*mauvais nanm*) or a 'bad air' (*mauvais-air*), these being the ghost of a *loup-garou* wandering about at night. Sometimes these spirits take on the forms of glow-worms in order to satisfy their thirst for human blood.

Normally a werewolf never harms children of its own kin. But if no other prey is available, then it knows no scruple. Even less does it hesitate if it cherishes a secret grudge against the child's mother or father. One of the laws of the supernatural world requires that no werewolf may 'eat' a baby unless its mother has expressly 'given' it. Such a gift is obtained by the following trick: having gone up close to the house where the child they want to 'eat' is sleeping they find out their chances of success by shuffling clover-leaves together like playing-cards. Success is certain if all the leaves fall shiny-side down but if only three fall thus it means there will be some snag and the attempt is usually abandoned. When the signs are favourable the werewolf first goes into the kitchen which, in the country, is a small shelter not far from the dwelling-place. From there she calls the child's mother. The latter, half-asleep, hears her name and answers, 'Yes.' The werewolf then asks, 'Will you give me your child?' If then, drowsy and only half-awake, she still replies, 'Yes'—then that's that: the child is lost. Thus it is indeed the mother who 'opens the door to a werewolf'. The sorcerer can also appear in a dream to the mother and promise her a present in the same breath as mentioning the child's name. To accept the gift is tantamount to handing over the child.

The soul which watches over the sleeper—the *petit-bon-ange* according to some, the *gros-bon-ange* according to others—should normally prevent the fatal 'yes' from being uttered, but its vigilance can fail, particularly if the woman it is protecting has omitted to 'give her head something to eat'.

To suck the little victim's blood, a werewolf gets into the house in the form of a cockroach or some other insect, or slides a straw through the wattling so that it rests against the child's cheek. Opinions differ as to how vampires operate. Some say they 'drain' a child gradually, returning each evening to drink its blood, others that they have only to take three drops of blood for the child to die of an illness, caused magically. Therefore, according to the last version, werewolves are not strictly speaking vampires but sorceresses practisirng enchantment. This view is sustained by the popular belief that a werewolf can kill a child by asking it to fetch a spill with which to light its pipe, or by offering it titbits.

That is why children are warned against any woman who asks them for a spill with which to light a pipe or who gives them fruit or a bit of bread. No material link between child and werewolf must be allowed to occur. It is even said that a werewolf can kill a child just by stroking its hair.

Illness caused by werewolves falls within the competence of *hungan*. Some people explain this category of sickness as genuine toxaemia brought about by poisonous substances such as the water with which a corpse has been washed. A small dose of this liquid brings on intestinal swelling or a mass of worms which devour the entrails.

What motives drive *loups-garous* to feed on the blood of children? Peasants say that it starts as a perverted taste and grows into an insatiable yearning. When a werewolf has succeeded in killing a child he goes with his colleagues, digs it out of the cemetery and eats it, having first turned it into 'cod, herring, goat's meat or pork'. There are, however, cases when cannibalism is not the sole motive for these murders. A werewolf may avenge itself on a child for an insult suffered from its parents; others simply kill children out of jealousy.

MAGIC TREATMENT AGAINST WEREWOLVES

The peasants are not entirely helpless in face of their children's danger from werewolves. Since the numerous available talismans are not always effective it is thought wise to immunize new-born babies by 'spoiling their blood'. This is done as soon as possible; during pregnancy, the mother must drink bitter coffee laced with *clairin* and flavoured with three drops of petrol. Then she bathes in water infused with garlic, chives, thyme, nutmeg, *bois-caca* leaves (*Capparis cynophlallophora*), manioc mush, coffee and *clairin*. Some time after its birth the child is plunged into a similar bath. It is also given a tisane made of various herbs. For good measure of precaution *clairin* is burnt in a plate and the child passed through the resulting flames. The exorcizer who is 'drugging' it asks three times: 'Who wants this little one?' The mother replies, 'I do.' In these words she affirms her determination to resist any werewolf who may take advantage of her sleep to come and demand her child. Then the calabash used in the ablutions is buried open-side downwards. If a *loup-garou* turns up near the house and tries by deceitful utterances to obtain the mother's consent to her own loss, the calabash must answer it. In some families the children's blood is made bitter by feeding them with cockroaches—first trimmed of their legs and wings and fried in castor oil, syrup, nutmeg and garlic. Some children have blood that is naturally salty or bitter and these therefore have nothing to fear from werewolves. The werewolf who drinks 'spoilt blood' is seized with violent vomiting. She flees leaving a trail which leads to her house—and to her identification.

III. WHITE MAGIC

A misfortune—unwonted illness, accident, ruin—is either a 'chastisement' sent by the *loa* or the result of an act of sorcery. It is for the *hungan* to decide which. On his diagnosis the remedy will depend. The anger of spirits will yield to *mangers* and 'services', but harm brought about by magic is not so easily put right. The first thing to be done is to determine the nature of the spell and then to undo or impede its effect by appropriate counter-measures. A *hungan*'s greatest triumph is to discover in a patient's house the actual charm which has caused the trouble. Thanks to information provided by their *loa* certain *hungan*—people say— manage to locate the exact place where a sorcerer has hidden his *wanga*. Mean tongues, it is true, allege that it is the *hungan* themselves who 'plant' the objects which they then pretend to discover.

Divination in all its forms makes it possible if not actually to locate, at least to identify the sorcery, and often its author too. Voodoo medicine nearly always comprises preliminary divination as well as 'treatment' proper. Certain cures, stripped of their ritualistic apparatus, appear to us as a judicial combat between the good and the bad *loa* set on by a *machinateur*.

There has grown up within the framework of Voodoo, a complete prophylaxy of which we shall here go into only a few representative aspects.

EXTRACTION OF THE SOUL

A person may obtain a certain immunity from sorcerers, and even from ordinary assassins, by having one of his two souls (the *gros-bon-ange*) withdrawn from his head. The details of this operation which I obtained from a *hungan* show a marked resemblance to those rites by which, during initiation, the soul of a novice is placed in a 'head pot'. The priest puts a lock of hair from the top of his client's head in a bottle along with nail-parings and tufts of hair taken from various parts of the body. Then, as in the ritual of the *manger-tête*, a package containing among other things bread and sweets soaked in white wine, must be clamped to his head. Also a white cockerel is cooked without any flavouring and eaten at a family meal, everyone taking the greatest care not to break any of its bones. These are gathered together after the meal and sewn into the pillow or buried under the bed of the person 'drugged'.

Protection of the soul is such sound policy that a *mambo* of Port-au-Prince had systematically withdrawn the *gros-bon-ange* from all her children. She had shown each of them the bottle containing his soul and said, 'My son, the little fellow in there is your *gros-bon-ange*. I have put it there so that no living creature can harm you.' One of her sons who was divorced lost no time in fetching from his conjugal dwelling the little trunk in which he kept his soul—in case his former wife should get hold of it.

Another more serious danger is that the bottle may fall into the hands of some evil intentioned person. Such an event was the undoing of General Salnave. His rival, Boisrond Canal, who had confided his soul to a *hungan*, a friend of his, learnt as a result of someone's indiscretion that Salnave had 'banked' his soul in the same sanctuary. He kept on at the *hungan* till, at last, the

avaricious and faithless man gave in. Master of his enemy's
gros-bon-ange, Boisrond Canal had no difficulty in defeating him
and then putting him to death.

'RESTRAINING' A BAD 'LOA'

People subject to attacks from a 'wicked *loa*' loosed on them by a
sorcerer, get in touch with a *hungan* who tries to restrain (*marrer*
or *arrêter*) their invisible executioner. A happy chance enabled Dr
Price Mars to be present at the 'stopping' of a *loa*,* a rite which
usually takes place in the greatest secrecy. On this occasion the
offenders were two *loa* of the *petro* family. They were represented
by two bits of wood clumsily carved and enveloped in a piece of
red stuff. The *hungan* recited a *langage* formula, chanted some
liturgy and drove nails into each of the images. He took two strings,
made sure they were strong, had them stretched out in the form
of a cross by his attendants and then wound them round the
images, taking care to tie numerous knots. Every time he pulled
a knot tight, he sang:

Mu pralé maré loa pétro	We are going to tie down the *petro loa*
Hi hi	Hi hi
Jâ-Pétro, chèn ki chèn	Jean-Petro, chain which is a chain
Li kasé li	He has broken it
Ki diré kòd	As if it were a rope.

Finally the *hungan* buried the images at the foot of the altar
along with two crosses of iron and one of wood.

TALISMANS AND AMULETS

Amulets (*gad*) also offer a certain protection against sorcery and

* The operation which prevents a *loa* from doing harm by paralysing it, is
called 'limiting' (*borner*). Bottles containing magic liquid are buried round
sanctuaries or houses and constitute 'limits'; and the crosses which stick up at
the approaches to dwellings are called 'limit crosses' (*croix d'arrestation*). A *loa*
is 'limited' by burying it in a hole with offerings which include eyeless needles
so that he may spend his time trying to thread them. They may also be driven
off into the woods (*renvoi de loa*) or implored to return to Africa (*Guinée*).

in general against all evil influences of a supernatural nature. The objects used to this end are only effective if they are 'mounted' or 'drugged'. Lorimer Denis[8] gives us some information on how to make a 'guard' with an alligator's tooth. The latter should be soaked in a bottle called a 'guard' or *mavangou* bottle which contains gunpowder or Shrove Tuesday ashes, *feuilles trois-paroles* (*Allophyllus occidentalis*), bile of bullock, goat, sow and boar, water from a forge, water from a tannery, red herring, blood of a virgin mouse (*sic*) and alligator flesh. This broth is called *potpouri* or *migan*. The efficacity of the amulet loses its power with time and it is important to feed it every year, that is to say soak it again in the same brew. In 'the time of the bayonets', officers and soldiers alike wore doctored scarves which protected them from sabre blows and bullets. The exploits of certain revolutionary leaders were put down not to their courage but to the efficacy of their *gad* and the blind faith they derived therefrom.

Monseigneur Kersuzan tells how a general who had been doctored by a magician, to make him invulnerable, did not hesitate to have a bullet fired straight into his chest just to prove the dependability of the treatment he had undergone. Naturally he was killed on the spot.

The word 'mounted' is used for any object which has been subjected to any magical process designed to ensure its efficacy or success. An artisan will have his tools mounted to make his work easier. A farmer will do the same for his field. Fighting cocks which have undergone a magic treatment are referred to as *montés*. The verb *monter* is the opposite of *ranger* which designates any magic procedure by which harm is intended to others.

Among the charms favoured by Voodooists are the 'lamps' which are also called 'work lamps' (*lampes de travail*) and 'charm lamps' (*lampes de charme*). These consist of receptacles—an ordinary cup, coconut, calabash, crab-shell—containing oil and a wick floating above two splinters of bone arranged in a cross. These lamps are 'mounted' to bring about the accomplishment of a wish: for successful business, luck or getting a job—and also vengeance on an enemy. A lamp which is burned to harm someone, or even to kill, is called 'black'. The magic efficacy of a lamp depends on the ingredients mixed with the oil burned in it

—on substances which have power or some symbolic analogy with the proposed action. For instance if the object is to build-up a faithful clientèle then glue is included; if to get rid of an enemy, then powdered human bones (*poudre de mort*), powdered lizard and other allegedly noxious ingredients. The lamp is mounted under the auspices of a spirit who to a certain extent becomes the guarantor of the magic operation. This will only succeed if the *conduite*—the maintenance of the lamp—follows certain exact rules: it must be topped-up at certain fixed times (preferably midday), certain prayers must be said each day, etc. Finally the flame must only be put out when the object of the whole operation has been attained.

Any list of charms would be incomplete without some mention of the *oraisons*. These are Catholic prayers addressed to Saint Michael, Saint Claire, Saint Bartholomew, Saint Radegonde. They are carelessly printed on sheets of paper and sold in the market for a few pennies. The *oraison* to Saint Radegonde is not without interest:

> Radegonde Baron-Samedi
> Guardian of the cemetery You
> who have the power
> of going into purgatory
> give my enemies
> something to do
> so they may
> leave me alone.

These prayers are pinned to walls or sewn into pillows. Some people wear them or use them in magical pharmacopoeia.

'BATHS' AND POWDERS

We have seen in previous pages the part played by sprinklings made from infusions of herbs and other things. The liquids with which the sick and unlucky are rubbed all come under the heading of 'baths', although they seldom amount to a proper bath.

Usually baths are given under the auspices of a god and it is often the god himself who, entering the body of the *hungan* or *mambo*, makes the virtue of the 'leaves' available to his servant. These 'leaves'—plants and herbs which grow in the woods—are picked ritualistically under the direction of a spirit. I have spoken earlier of the tribute which on these occasions is paid to their 'soul'.

Baths do not only counteract illness; their virtue extends to a wider field. The 'charm bath' over which Damballah-wèdo presides includes jasmine flowers, orgeat syrup, powdered almonds, scent, holy water and champagne and has the power of 'curing illnesses regarded as incurable, reconciling inveterate enemies, procuring work and securing promotion'.

'Powders' occupy an important position in the pharmacopoeia of magic. They are prepared on Christmas night in the course of solemn ceremonies previously described. The powders are not remedies in our sense of the word. They are antidotes against bad luck and sorcery and ensure certain kinds of advantage— seduction of a woman, securing a job . . .

The spirit of rivalry prevailing among the various *rada* bands of musicians and dancers who perform in the streets of Port-au-Prince during Carnival, prompts their members to take various magic precautions against those who might wish to spoil their success. Before entering town to display their skill, they go to a *humfo* where they are received with whip-crackings and sprinklings of *kimanga*—rites which are observed whenever the *petro loa* are invoked. The *hungan* blows powder over each dancer and gives him a pinch of snuff. Then occur possessions or the preliminaries of possession. Those which I saw were due to the god Simbi who is the patron of magic pharmacy.

Every sanctuary possesses a special kind of talisman called *paquett* (parcels). These are wallets padded with cloth or silk, shaped like an onion or a Chianti bottle. They are provided with handles and other ornaments which give them an obviously anthropomorphic appearance. This resemblance is, moreover, intentional since there are *paquett* men and *paquett* women who are put out together in couples. The 'women' are recognizable by the ear-rings attached to the end of a stem which sticks up from the *paquett*'s rounded body and represents the head. Some *paquetts* are provided with a mirror but most are decorated with a tuft of feathers. Those crowned with a black cross are placed under the sign of Baron-Samedi and the Guédé.

The making of *paquetts* (the ceremony called *marré paquett*) takes place at full moon with invocations of *loa*. The strings with which the *paquetts* are tightly netted must be knotted seven or nine times. As with the Christmas powders the flesh of a 'curly

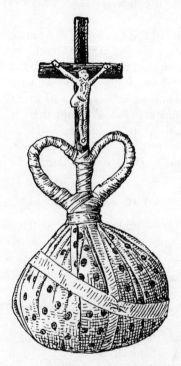

FIG. 12. A *paquett*, or talisman, under the sign of the Guédé, spirits of death

cock' crushed up in a mortar with its feathers is mixed in with vegetable substances. The mat on which rests the powder, contained in a calabash, is placed on *vèvè* of Simbi and other *petro loa*, drawn on the ground with coffee grounds or ginger broken up small. The outstanding rite of this ceremony is the *battre guerre* (*bat gè*). It consists of beating out a particular rhythm with forks on four plates laid on one corner of the mat. The *battre guerre* lasts four days. Major Maximilien[9] has compared it very aptly to the *bohum* which is heard after funerals. The same author says 'the *bat gè* is a call to those spirits which are to be put into someone or into some object. *Hungan bat le gair* (*sic*) for the making of personal talismans, with two sabres and also by beating a sabre against the body of the individual for whom the talisman is being prepared.'

I have never heard the functions of *paquetts* clearly described. I only know they are used in certain 'treatments' and I have been assured that *hungan* pass them over the bodies of people who are ill. One *hungan* whom I questioned at length on this subject explained to me they were 'guards' and that they had the power of exciting and 'heating' *loa*. Without their 'point' *loa* would be weak and unable to 'work' for patients. It is absolutely essential to increase the power of a *paquett* by exposing it during *bulé-zin* ceremonies to the warmth of the flames which rise from the sacred pots.

THE RAIN-MAKERS

In Haiti the power of making rain and fine weather is not the prerogative of *hungan* and *boko*. It belongs to certain individuals who are regarded as possessing in this special department a mysterious gift which they use commercially. When I was in Marbial I visited Examan, the great 'rain merchant' of the region. Before recounting his own explanation of his powers I shall first say what the local people thought of them and thus show, side by side, the public version of the man's function and the man's idea of it himself.

Some people attributed Examan's powers to a white stone which he threw into the fire whenever he wanted to stop rain and make the sun shine. Those who denied the existence of the 'sun-stone' said that he 'limited' the rain by putting a mortar-pestle carefully wrapped in a kind of creeper called *langichatte* (*Eupatorium odoratum L.*) near a fire.

Others insisted that he was the possessor of three bottles containing respectively the wind, the rain and the sun. When he wanted rain he 'signalled' with his bottle towards the La

Selle mountains, made a libation and smoked his pipe with the
bowl downwards. Many peasants told me they had been to
Examan to buy rain. The price of a good soaking for a field in
seed was about a dollar plus a few generous measures of beans or
maize. What was particularly admired in the rain-maker was his
ability to drop a shower plumb on his client's field without the
fields of neighbours getting a drop of benefit.

When my inquiries about Examan were done I went to see the
man himself. He lived in a remote valley and gave me the impression of being rather a down-at-heel fellow. Having boasted
that he was a very skilful healer he confessed without hesitation
that he could 'fix' rain as he chose. He owed this power to the
people of Gonave where every man was a bit of a sailor and could
control the weather. He passionately denied possession of any
'bottles' and said that to bring rain all he had to do was 'say a
prayer in English' (*sic*). 'Rain,' he explained, 'has a soul little
different from our own and can be spoken to.' He addressed
himself to the clouds, asking them to go to the place indicated and
empty themselves.

He complained bitterly that his profession of rain-making
brought him nothing but trouble since people got it into their
heads that he was responsible for droughts and held it against
him. 'And then,' he cried, 'what difference does it make to me
if the sun blazes in the whole valley where there are people unknown to me. I've got enough to do with my own gardens and
those of my neighbours.' He added that he had no intention of
imparting his secret to his children as he wished to spare them
the enmities which he had had to suffer.

MAGIC AND THE SEARCH FOR TREASURE

Popular imagination gives full rein to its fantasy on the theme of
hidden treasure. In the bourgeoisie as among the very poor,
there are people who all their life imagine themselves to be on the
track of a find which will bring them fabulous riches. Some comb
archives, others consult *hungan*, interpret their dreams or give
themselves up to magic practices which will facilitate their
quest. Magic is necessary not only to locate the hoard but also

to appease the spirits watching over it. Treasure myth is always conceived along the following lines: a rich French planter, before fleeing Haiti at the time of the revolution, buried his fortune in a corner of his property. The slaves who carried it there and dug the hiding place were slaughtered on the spot so the secret would be kept and the place guarded by their souls. Special ceremonies must be celebrated to conciliate them. Some treasures lie under the guardianship of a *baka*—the most evil of spirits and very difficult to distract or appease.

Boko naturally possess many magic recipes for the discovery of treasure. These afford excellent opportunities for swindling. The story which you may read in the following pages is the faithful transcription of a law report which appeared in the *Nouvelliste* of November 20, 1944. This amusing but banal story is not without anthropological interest for it gives us an excellent example of the power of popular beliefs, and of the ease with which magicians exploit them.

The Black Hand Again
In the courts

Last Tuesday we reported that a man who had been passing himself off under five different names, as circumstances demanded, appeared in court before Judge Tribié charged with defrauding a Madame Tulia Durand on a colossal scale.

This foxy fellow, assisted in his fraudulent machinations by the no less infamous Robert Jean, a former detective of the Police Bureau, succeeded in milking his victim of 4,000 dollars and valuable jewels as well. Police recovered 3,012 gourdes 50 centimes, partly at the swindler's house, partly at notary Vilmenay's, where it had been paid in for the purchase of a flat.

Here is how the rogue went about it: having well and truly singled out and shadowed his victim, the swindler went alone on a morning in March 1943, called on Madame Tulia Durand and asked her to show him the way to the house of a woman whose name he must certainly have invented—a person who did not exist. Mme Tulia said that being newly arrived in this part of the town she knew no one of that name. Then he said he had come from a long way having been summoned for some 'work'—he did not say what kind—then he said he was very tired by the long walk and asked for a cup of coffee. Madame Tulia gladly gave him a cup of coffee and they got talking.

He said he was the son of a well-known *bokor* of Port-au-faix whose marvellous exploits are remembered by all and who when he was dying passed on to him his secrets. It seems that Madame Tulia, having travelled a lot in the North West, knew of the deceased *bokor*. The swindler asked the woman several questions about dreams which she must have had—dreams about money for example—and finally revealed that a huge treasure lay buried somewhere on her property and to entice her further he said he would only charge twenty-eight gourdes for the few trifles essential to a search ceremony. Madame Tulia Durand hesitated a moment; but the presence and pressure of the swindler soon convinced her.

The twenty-eight gourdes were paid over and a rendezvous arranged for that evening. When the time came, Tulia Durand, who had another woman called Gabrielle Chauvel living with her, received, in the latter's presence, the second visit of Charité Zephirin.

After some smooth talk he announced that the treasure was to be found in the court of the house, but, unable to conduct search in full view of neighbours, he said he must carry out other ceremonies so the treasure might be moved to the inside of a lumber-room situated in this same yard.

To do this he had a huge hole dug in the middle of this room by an odd-job man he brought with him. Dismissing this worthy he said to the women: 'He is now doomed to die this evening.'

Then, after successive ceremonies in which he thoroughly primed Tulia Durand with 'passes' and incantations, he finally conjured up in the bottom of the hole the vision of a human skull and the top of a jar full of gold coins which he said he had brought up from the depths of the earth by the power of his sorcery. He even had the two women touch a genuine gold coin and verify for themselves its great age. This done he now merely had to elicit noises from the bottom of the hole—noises of night-terror; voices of slaves, guardians of treasure. In fact it was Robert

Jean and his accomplices (whom the police have failed to arrest) and who had somehow managed to get into the hole.

Now for the ransom, the sacrifice . . .

Before a finger could be laid on this fabulous treasure the slaves of the Marquis of Caradoux demanded 100 bullocks each (there were five slaves)—at twenty dollars per bullock.

Tulia, horrified by the size of the sum, protested vigorously. The slaves threatened her with death. The treasure having seen daylight, had to be taken. Zephirin the magician told the woman that he would soothe the slaves' anger and obtain for her a reduction of the ransom. He went through a series of fresh cabalistic signs and the woman agreed to give twenty bullocks to each slave—which came to 2,000 dollars. And this money was immediately paid over to Zephirin.

The latter now thought up a ceremony by the sea in which the slaves' payment would be thrown to the waves, as a means of buying back the treasure.

With the money well sealed, the two women, Gabrielle and Tulia, accompanied by the magician, went to the place called Nan Palmiste at Portail Léogane, beside the sea. There Zephirin, shaking his little bell, called upon the mysterious spirits of the Ocean, and threw the precious package into the water. Immediately a thunderous voice (still that of Robert Jean) boomed from the waves telling Tulia and her companion that the slaves could not be liberated because he, the Marquis of Caradoux, was getting nothing out of it. Mme Tulia Durand offered him a Mass for the repose of his soul: Caradoux protested and demanded as much as the slaves.

The two women trembled at such a suggestion. But Tulia was so frightened that she gave in to Zephirin and promised further sacrifices. She was allowed no more than a month to find the money. If she did not pay up by then it would mean death for herself and her family . . .

Madame Tulia Durand, eaten away by fear and anguish, had to mortgage her house with Ernest Caprio (the deeds being held by the notary Maurice Avin) for 1,000 dollars to which she added 500 dollars savings. Two months later Zephirin came back and went with the two women to the same place by night. But

Caradoux refused the 1,500 dollars. He, too, wanted 2,000 dollars, not a centime less.

Tulia had to make another mortgage of 500 dollars, on the same property with the same notary and creditor so as to reach the necessary 2,000 dollars. With the same ceremony as before the money was once again thrown into the sea. Robert Jean, who kept his body hidden under the water so that only his head showed, caught the woman's 'nest-egg' and imitating Caradoux, said he was satisfied.

The phony Caradoux now announced that the slaves were going back to Africa and he himself to Europe and that he intended to send the ladies a letter which must be put under a pillow for twenty-one days and twenty-one nights before being opened, and that in addition it must be Zephirin who should be charged with its execution. At the appointed time Tulia undid it and was seized with terrible fear. The letter did indeed contain the conditions under which she might enjoy the treasure . . . a pact with Lucifer . . . entailing further sacrifice. If she refused . . . it would mean death for herself and everyone in her house. The 4,000 dollars received so far were not enough.

Taken a fourth time to the seashore (we may remember that the first time was to throw in 2,000 dollars, the second time to see the mysterious Caradoux refuse 1,500 dollars, the third time to see this same Caradoux accept the second payment of 2,000 dollars)—taken a fourth time by Zephirin to the seashore Tulia thought she saw a shape in the water and heard a voice demanding 200 dollars for the buying back of human lives. This time the woman was sent to the cemetery and now it was Baron-Samedi who came on to the stage of this tragi-comedy.

The unfortunate Tulia began to find these repeated postponements a little fishy: they always seemed to end in a demand for money. But the fear which had been roused in her by all these comings and goings, these mysterious invocations, with their disturbing surroundings, was stronger than common sense. The devilish Zephirin with his perfidious counsels always swayed her whom he held in his claws: Tulia handed over the 200 dollars for the Master of Cemeteries. They were put down near a hole beside some candles and they vanished at once.

Thanks to the advice of her friend Gabrielle Chauvel, Madame Tulia at last understood that she had been odiously duped and exploited by a gang of scoundrels. She then decided to complain to the police. On May 15, 1943, she got in touch with Lieutenant Jacques Etienne who asked for a written statement which she immediately provided. Subsequently the police put themselves at the disposal of the plaintiff. Traps were laid for the miscreants and Charité Zephirin was arrested by Detective Clement François, on the evening of May 16, 1943, at 8 o'clock, at a rendezvous which he had given his victims—at the 'Palmists', near the water's edge.

Zephirin was found to have in his possession several jewels which he admitted belonged to his victim, 207 dollars and fifty cents in cash, a receipt for 395 dollars from Notary Vilmenay, several cabalistic objects such as playing cards, bells, *chacha* necklace of *mal dioc* and several other receipts for varying amounts, some in the name of Charité Zephirin, some of Charité Toussaint, some of Antoine Zephirin, etc.

He freely admitted that he had received a great deal of money from Tulia to throw into the sea; he put the blame for all his ill deeds on to Robert Jean and said the latter had received on one occasion 300, on another 600 dollars—all swindled out of Tulia. He tried to bribe the detectives, offering them the 200 dollars which he had on him. When they refused to listen to him, he asked them to take him at once to Notary Vilmenay where they would get 400 dollars in addition to the 200 already offered; but there was nothing doing; the bribes were refused and he was taken to Etienne. Once he was in the police station he repeated his admissions made earlier to the policemen. He now added that Robert Jean, during the various ceremonies, had taken the part of Maître Agwé, the Master of the Waters, so as to receive the money and jewels thrown into the sea; and the part of Baron-Samedi, Master of Cemeteries, etc, etc.

Thus ended the sad vicissitudes of Tulia Durand at the hands of the exploiters of superstition.

IV. ORDEALS

All over tribal Africa there exists (as a means of detecting sorcerers) a legal procedure which pertains both to divination and to magic: ordeal. This procedure has disappeared not only in Haiti, but in the majority of black populations in the New World. However, I found in Marbial beliefs and attitudes which show that as far as sorcery is concerned, the custom of ordeal is still very much alive. It was in the course of an argument between two market women that my attention was suddenly attracted by this survival of a purely African tradition. One of the old crones had accused the other of theft, whereupon the accused, choking with rage, rose up in all her outraged dignity, raised her arm and taking the crowd to witness said: 'I have not done that of which I am accused. If I lie—may I be put in the current.' By 'current' she meant an imaginary ordeal which had been suggested to her by local notions of certain police methods. The peasants were convinced that at the police headquarters in Jacmel there was an electric wire which was used to bring criminals to light—particularly werewolves and sorcerers. Thanks to this device a current was passed into the body of the accused: the innocent were not affected but the guilty, especially sorcerers, experienced such a shock 'that they spun on their heels and flames came out of every part of their bodies'. Thus I heard the story of a local woman who, suspected of having murdered her husband, managed to prove her innocence by insisting on being submitted to the 'current'. She survived the ordeal and confounded her accusers. Need it be said that this ordeal of the 'current' is an entirely African interpretation of 'third degree' questioning.

At Marbial children suspected of having committed some crime are sometimes submitted to a not very dangerous ordeal: the trial by *balai*, the name being derived from a plant which is said to have the power of squeezing the neck of a culprit if he does not own up. A theft having been committed in a house at Marbial near which children were playing, the owners decided to have recourse to this ordeal. The principal suspect was an orphan whose unruly behaviour had awakened the deepest mis-givings among the peasants.

A woman who was something of a magician asked for a sheaf of the *balai* (*Corchorus siliquosush*) plant which was duly brought. She sprinkled it with ash, and uttered some spells over it and then squirted water over it from her mouth. She put the children in a long line. Then with a bunch of the *balai* in each hand she went up behind each child in turn, moved the bunches three times round before his eyes, and then put them caressingly against the nape of his neck. When it was the turn of the suspected orphan the two sheaves interlocked round his neck like a garrot.* Terrified, the poor wretch let out piercing screams; but when pressed to admit his guilt, he refused. At this I insisted the ordeal be stopped—much to the disgust of the peasants who reproached me for having let the culprit off too easily. It was later discovered the children were completely innocent and that the money had been taken by a servant. This ordeal is much feared and many young culprits prefer to admit their guilt rather than be unmasked by the plant.

Madame Mennesson-Rigaud told me a variant of this ordeal: Whoever holds the two sheaves of *balai* stands behind a chair and utters the following formula: 'So and so has taken something . . . let the little chair stick fast.' Then the speaker goes through the names of everyone present who is suspect. At the name of the thief, the *balai* branches seize the back of the chair which may then be raised.

V. DIVINATION

In tribal Africa divination is one of the aspects of religion most intimately tied up with daily life. Fate is interrogated before the least venture and invests the smallest incident with omens which inspire fear or doubt. It is the same in Haiti but the methods used

---

* *Balai* stalks bunched into a sheaf have the strange property of interlacing in such a way that it is not easy to undo them. Whoever is conducting the ordeal has only to bring the two sheaves in his hands together for them to interlock and thus form a vice round someone's neck.

to discover the workings of occult powers are much less refined
and complex than they are in Africa.

We have already discovered how *loa* are interrogated. The
hungan and *mambo* bring down a spirit into a pitcher, which then
replies to the questions put to the spirits. This is the more usual
kind of oracle—so much so that it represents an important source
of revenue in a sanctuary's budget.

The questioning of fate with shells is still done in a few
sanctuaries but is tending to give place to more modern techniques. Some *hungan* fall back on it to trace the cause of illnesses
and to help them choose the most suitable treatment. Unfortunately no one either could, or would, explain to me the combinations which provide the desired answer. My account therefore is
limited to the way in which the seer proceeds. The seven shells
which he uses have been 'mounted' in the course of a special
ceremony which includes the sacrifice of a cock. (The skull and
tibias of this bird Lorgina kept in a wallet with the shells.) Having
uttered a few invocations and consecrated the shells with a libation of rum, the *hungan* shakes them in the hollow of his hand and
throws them into a sieve containing a neckl. ce, a magic stone
and a lighted candle. After examining at length the pattern of the
lots he gives his reply.

Divination by *gembo* is also of African origin. The *gembo* is a
sort of shell often decorated with a mirror, stuck on its level side—
the whole threaded, along with china beads or other decorations,
on to a string which finishes at each end with a little buckle. To
consult the *gembo* the *hungan* inserts both his thumbs and holds
the string upright. He begins by calling on Simbi, '*Pa puvwa Mèt
Simbi Yâpaka nèg twa ilè ilè, maza, Simba zâzusi nèg eskalyé
bumba, nèg kêbwa salay, nêg kéké bra . . .*' then he questions the
gembo, phrasing his questions so the answers can only be 'yes' or
'no'. If the shell comes down, the answer is 'yes', if it stays where
it is, 'no'. Sometimes it moves slightly and the string oscillates.
These vague movements are also interpreted by the *hungan*.
This type of divination belongs to the *petro* ritual and the *hungan*
who practise it are usually servants of the *loa* of that family.

All the *mambo* I ever knew were able to tell fortunes by cards.
Thus they ensured themselves a small income. Their clients were

not only women of the people but also well-to-do women of the bourgeoisie. This art, which is doubtless of recent introduction to Haiti, has been incorporated in Voodoo so thoroughly that among the accessories of the priest and priestess kept on sanctuary altars there is nearly always a pack of cards. Many *mambo* tell fortunes while entranced, which naturally gives their predictions a supernatural character.

It would be indiscreet to ask a *mambo* what the cards and their various combinations mean, because this is all part of a science learnt during initiation. However, I can give some account of the rites which accompany any consultation. The cards are laid out in a sieve on the edge of which a candle is stuck. *Loa*-stones which have been put through *clairin* flames are also in the sieve. A *mambo* whom I once consulted out of curiosity told me that white *loa* were favourable to me and I could count on their protection. Then, after a more detailed inspection of the lay-out of the cards she added carelessly that if I wanted to perpetuate their favourable feelings I must offer them a 'smell' (*odeur* i.e.—some scent), rice pudding and some dessert—white in colour. Her attention was further taken by cards which indicated my offerings should be rounded off with the sacrifice of a white chicken and a white pigeon. Remembering my sympathy for the Guédé *loa*, she told me the latter wished me well but desired a sacrifice to themselves, separate from that of the white *loa*. In short, one thing led to another and from my visit transpired the fact that my luck depended on my providing an expensive 'service' for the *loa*—a 'service' moreover which only Mme X was in a position to organize.

Hungan and *mambo* practise many other forms of divination. They watch over the future by examining leaves, coffee grounds, cinders in a glass or the flame of a candle. *L'ange Conducteur*—a pious book published in France—has become an instrument of Satan in the eyes of the clergy on account of the use it is put to for the purposes of divination. *Hungan* use it for 'turn the leaves' (*passer pages*) or 'dot book' (*piquer livre*) which merely consists of turning up at random some passage which then gives the answer to the question asked.

VI
Voodoo and Christianity

VOODOO AND CHRISTIANITY

'To serve the *loa* you have to be a Catholic . . .' These words—of a Marbial peasant—deserve to stand as epigraph to this chapter for they express, very precisely, the paradoxical ties between Voodoo and Christianity. The peasant who sacrifices to the *loa*, who is possessed by them, who every Saturday answers the call of the drums, does not believe (or did not believe fifteen years ago) that he is behaving like a pagan and offending the Church. On the contrary—he likes to think of himself as a good Catholic and contributes to the salary of his *curé* without hesitation. This 'idolater' would be wretched if he were excluded from the Communion or if he were forbidden to marry or baptize his children in church. Not always for truly Catholic reasons does he adhere to such rites, but because he attributes magic virtues to them and fears that if he were deprived of them, he would lose his respectability. Even while scrupulously observing Catholic rites, the Haitian peasant has remained little touched by the spirit and doctrine of Catholicism; chiefly out of ignorance, since such religious instruction as he may have received is rudimentary to say the least. He knows little of the lives of Jesus or the saints. Besides, he feels more at ease with gods and spirits which maintain friendly or hostile relationships with him, in the same way as he does with neighbours. Voodoo is for him a familiar personal religion whereas Catholicism often shares the cold nature of the cement chapels which crown the crests of the hills. Once when I asked a fervent Catholic whether he had finally finished with Voodoo, he replied that he would always be faithful to the Catholic Church but nothing could make him give up the worship of *loa* who had always protected his family. The *hunsi* of Lorgina saw nothing wrong in attending Mass after dancing all night for the *loa*. It takes a white man's mentality to be shocked that a *hungan* or *mambo* can march beside a *curé* at the head of a procession without a trace of shame.

The equivocal reputation which Voodoo has acquired is in fact due to just this very syncretic quality by which it mixes together, in almost equal proportions, African rites and Christian observances. All who have concerned themselves with Voodoo have been pleased to list the many things it has borrowed from Catholicism. The clergy has denounced these same things as so many abominations but no systematic attempt has been made to define, with any precision, the connection between these disparate elements nor the way in which they integrate themselves in the whole system of Voodoo religious values. In other words, no one has raised the question whether the Voodooist ranks the beliefs which he holds from his African ancestors on the same level as those he has derived from the Whites. An example usually cited of the fusion of the two cults is the identification of African gods and spirits with Catholic saints. Authors drawing up lists of *loa* have taken care to mention only the saints which correspond with the most important of the spirits, and have never tried to pin down how this phenomenon works, or establish its real significance. This was a mistake, for in most cases there has been no real assimilation or common identity. The equivalence of gods and saints only exists in so far as the Voodooist has used pictures of saints to represent his own gods.

The walls of *humfo* and sanctuary living-rooms are plastered with posters printed in Germany, Czechoslovakia, Italy or Cuba showing various saints equipped with their attributes or in the act of living some key episode of their legend.[1] Merely by being pinned up in a place sacred to the cult of Voodoo, these personages lose their identity as Catholic saints and become *loa*. But this mutation does not happen in an arbitrary way. It proceeds from some resemblance, in certain particulars, of the picture to the conception which the Voodooists have formed of their *loa* and his attributes.

Often it has needed a mere detail, to our eyes an unimportant one, though important in the context of Voodoo mythology, for a poster to be selected as a representation of this or that African divinity. For instance the snakes chased out of Ireland, which are seen at the feet of St Patrick, have suggested a link between him and Damballah-wèdo, the snake-god. In the same way Our Lady of the Sorrows has come to represent Ezili-Freda-Dahomey because the jewellery with which she is decked and the sword transpiercing her heart evoke the riches and love which are the attributes of the Voodoo goddess. Saint Jacques le Majeur, James the elder, who is shown as a knight encased in steel, has naturally been identified with Ogu-feraille, the blacksmith and warrior god. On the same poster the person armed from head to foot is for some Ogu-badagri, for others one of the Guédé because of his lowered vizor which vaguely recalls the sling put under the chins of corpses.

The cases of common identity which we have just given are, in the apt phrase of Michel Leiris, 'concrete puns'. The same poster can represent different *loa*, according to whatever detail may have struck the attention of the faithful or, reciprocally, the same *loa* can be represented by several different pictures. Thus the name of Legba is applied not only to Saint Lazarus but also to Saint Anthony the Hermit, who in Catholic iconography is traditionally shown as an old man. Agwé, the great sea god, has for long been borrowing the traits of Saint Ulrich because on one poster the latter is shown with a fish in his hand. In the war years, when this picture became rare, it was replaced by that of Saint Amboise. Certain pictures which are completely unreligious in character have been put to the same use. Thus sometimes in a *humfo*, among the sacred pictures you come upon a poster depicting the sad fate of a debauché—a caved-in young man in evening dress. On account of his dark clothes and rather sinister expression he has sometimes been taken for Baron-Samedi or some other member of the Guédé family.

The Catholic clergy seem at first to have had no inkling that the holy pictures and crosses which they were required to bless were to be used as idols. Finally the truth dawned on them. During the anti-superstition campaign, which we will discuss later, the *curés* felt no qualm of conscience when they burnt every picture they could lay their hands on in sanctuary rooms—although these were the same pictures as were being put up in Catholic churches and chapels for the adoration of the devout. In a report written a few years ago Monseigneur X denounced the abuse by Voodooists of sacred pictures: 'They worship the pictures of the saints and one might say no saint in the calendar is excepted from this attention unless it be those whose likenesses have not been imported into the country. In the people's minds the picture they worship does not represent a saint at all—but the pagan divinity which they have substituted for him and which, from then on, constitutes the identity of that particular picture.'

Although we cannot really talk of a true assimilation of *loa* to Catholic saints it remains none the less true that Voodooists have not failed to notice analogies between their respective functions. When they wish to defend, or explain, their beliefs they like to lump *loa* and saints together and say 'all the saints are *loa* which is not to say all *loa* are saints.' In the north of Haiti *loa* are called 'saints' which certainly underlines the homology. All the same, even if the two groups do resemble each other in exercising similar powers, they still stand apart and belong to two entirely different religious systems. Whereas all *loa* reveal themselves in possessions, no one to my knowledge was ever possessed by a saint. In the same way *loa* do not borrow the attributes and characters of the saints to whom they are supposed to correspond. It is, as we have seen, the other way about: the saint, stripped of his own personality, takes on that of the *loa*.

The difference in origin of saints and *loa* is explained in a myth which I picked up in Port-au-Prince: 'When He had created the earth and the animals in it, God sent down twelve apostles. Unfortunately they behaved too stiffly and powerfully. In their pride they ended by rebelling against God. He, as a punishment, sent them to Africa where they multiplied. It is they and their descendants who, as *loa*, help their servants and comfort them when they are unhappy. One of the apostles who refused to leave for Guinea (Africa) gave himself up to sorcery and took the name of Lucifer.

'Later God sent twelve more apostles who this time behaved like dutiful sons and preached the gospel. They and their descendants are what we call the saints of the Church.'

One of those who provided Simpson[2] with information

explained to him that because God is too busy to listen to the prayers of men, *loa* and saints have fallen into the habit of meeting each other half-way between heaven and earth. There the *loa* inform the saints of the wishes of the faithful. The saints then transmit the requests to God who grants them or not, as He chooses.

The assimilation of *loa* and saints is very much more superficial in Voodoo than it is in the Afro-American cults of Brazil. The one and only example of a Catholic saint being substituted for an African god in Voodoo is given us by Herskovits[3] *a propos* St John the Baptist who, in the north of Haiti, has taken the place of Sogbo and Shango in the rôle of storm-god. In this context there is a story which under a Christian exterior still savours of Africa. 'On a given day of the year God permits each saint to have control over the universe. St John the Baptist, however, is so irresponsible, and his rage so violent, that God fears the consequences if he were allowed to exert his power on his day. By plying him with drink the day before, he is therefore made so drunk that when he falls asleep he does not awaken for five days. When he is told his day has already passed, his rage is so terrible that great storms flay the earth, and it is a commonplace in Mirebalais that this day is marked by thunder and lightning storms of almost hurricane proportions. Though he can do some damage, his power is now limited, however, to his own sphere.'

Saint Expedit, once included in the Catholic calendar thanks to a pun, has now in Haiti become a great sorcerer—thanks to another pun.

Then again the title 'saint' is sometimes used to express animist representations which are not out of place in Voodoo. On certain occasions, rare it is true, prayers are addressed to 'Saint Earth', 'Saint Thunder', 'Saint Sun' (identified also as Saint Nicholas), and to 'Saint Moon'.

Voodoo ritual has borrowed heavily from Catholic liturgy: it is customary for most services to *loa* to be preceded by thanksgiving (*action de grâce*). Standing in the middle of their *hunsi* before an altar covered with candles, under a panoply of lace decorated with pictures of saints, priest or priestess recites Paters, Confiteors and Ave Marias followed by hymns to the

Virgin and to the saints. The famous 'African prayer' (*prière Guinin*) which opens the most solemn ceremonies, begins with Catholic prayers and interminable invocations of saints: the *loa* are only summoned afterwards. In giving a Catholic *cachet* to ceremonies which are not Catholic, Voodooists are in no way trying to pull the wool over the eyes of authorities or Church: rather is it that they are in fact convinced of the efficacy of Catholic liturgy and therefore wish their own religion to benefit from it. The singing, prayers and kneelings, which precede a service, are said to 'stir the *loa* up': in other words help to attract their benevolent attentions.

Voodoo has also appropriated the use of holy water with which its devotees are sprinkled from a leafy branch. Father Labat,[4] at the end of the seventeenth century, had already noticed that slave converts used it for magical ends. 'All the Christian Negroes have a great devotion to, and a lively faith in blessed bread and holy water. They always carry blessed bread about with them. They eat it when they are ill or when they fear some danger. As for holy water—whatever quantity may be prepared on Sunday morning for High Mass, seldom a drop is left by the end of the service; they take it away in little calabashes and drink a few drops standing up, thinking they will thus guard themselves against any spell that may be cast upon them. However hard I tried I was unable to discover who had inspired them with this faith: even the elders and most reasonable among them could say no more than that they learnt it from their fathers and handed it down from one to another and found it good.'

The profanation of the Host is one of the most serious charges which the clergy have lodged against the devotees of Voodoo. 'One of the most painful revelations,' wrote Monseigneur X, in the memorandum quoted above, 'was that people were often sent to the Holy Table to steal the Host. To obey a *bokor* people are prepared to submit to any conditions, pay any price, undergo any ordeal: they had to get their Holy Communion. But the catechism which they have been taught has changed nothing in their hearts. It is a formula required of them by the priest and which must therefore be learnt.' The bishop is however wrong not to make clear that it is only the magicians who feel the need to procure the Host—for themselves. No Voodooist, unless he is a sorcerer, would think of committing such a sacrilege.

The symbiosis of Catholicism and Voodoo has resulted in a very close parallelism between their respective calendars. *Loa* feasts often coincide with those of the saints who have been identified with them: the day of Kings is kept for ceremonies in honour of the Congo *loa*: throughout Lent, Voodoo sanctuaries are shut and no service is celebrated in them: sometimes even— in Holy Week—cult accessories such as pitchers containing spirits, *loa* stones, emblems of gods—are covered over with a sheet as are the images in Catholic churches; at All-Hallows the Guédé spirits of the dead overrun the countryside and towns, clad in black and mauve, and people possessed by them may be met not only in the sanctuaries but also in the markets, public places and on the roads: Christmas night, as we have seen, is the moment when Voodoo ritual takes wing, as it were, in its full plumage.

Catholic clergy finally came to realize that some of the patron-saints' days were attended by many more Voodooists than true Catholics. The grand pilgrimage of Saut-d'eau and Ville-Bon-heur, which was started fairly recently, gives us a classic instance of syncretism. The Tombe river, having crossed a green and laughing plain, hurls itself in one leap into the void. All the mysterious charm of tropical forests which have today disappeared survives in that dense grove where the falls gleam like jewels, darkly cased. An iridescent mist crossed by tiny rainbows rises from the foaming water, bedews the ferns and blurs the luxuriant foliage of the giant trees whose roots break the moist ground into humps and valleys. This oasis of coolness is the home of Damballah-wèdo, Grande-Bossine and other aquatic deities. Towards the middle of July it is invaded by thousands of pilgrims from all parts of the Republic. As soon as they reach the foot of the cascade they merge their prayers and hymns with its level roar; and they hasten to expose their bodies to the violence of the healing, saving water. They roll about, frolic and feel at the same time excited, happy and a little afraid to be in the vicinity of spirits. From time to time a bather shaken by tremblings, staggers like a man drunk; his neighbours hold him up so that he shall not sink into the deep pool which the waters have worn away: it is one of the spirits of the falls, usually Damballah-wèdo, who has 'mounted' him. The possessed man reaches the bank, flickering his tongue, eyes upturned and making the characteristic '*tététété*' of the god. The pilgrims crowd round him, speak respectfully to him, squeeze his hand and ask those small favours which the *loa* dispense among those they love.

A huge fig-tree which rears up beside the falls is the resting place of Damballah. Among its roots the pilgrims put little candles and attach their bodies to its branches with strands of wool. Some take pinches of earth from round the tree and store them away in a handkerchief.

The aquatic gods of Saut-d'eau are no longer the only masters of the river. Today they share their domain with Saint John and the Virgin. Notre Dame du Carmel appeared on top of a palm-tree in a little sacred wood, not far from Ville-Bonheur and some few miles from the falls, and from then on the palm also became an object of devotion for the pilgrims and cured the sick who came in their hundreds to petition Notre Dame du Carmel. A zealous *curé*, scenting idolatry, had the miraculous tree cut down. Then, when he found the faithful merely transferred their veneration to the roots, he had these torn out. But the Virgin punished him for his sacrilege for, I was told, he soon lost both his legs in an accident. Faced with the persistence of devotees who, having bathed in the falls, came to pray to the Virgin and Saint John, the clergy made the sacred wood an official place of pilgrimage. On the eve of the Festival of the Virgin of Saut-d'eau, brightly-painted charabancs bring devotees into the centre of Ville-Bonheur. They spend the night in the grove lit by thousands of candles. The bush priests recite prayers, herb-doctors rub the hands of the sick with oil from the lamps which have burnt in front of the sacred trees, and with the water of springs in which medicinal plants have been left to soak.

In the town many peasants make merry, dance to the sound of jazz orchestras and exchange spicy sallies with the prostitutes of whom there is always an influx. Penitents sport their motley costumes, distribute food to the poor, hoping by this act of Christian charity to appease the *loa* whom they have offended.

On the actual day of the fête an enormous crowd crushes round the church built in honour of the Virgin. Those who cannot enter accumulate outside. After the service the statue of the Virgin is tied to the front of a truck and taken round the main square followed by a publicity-car blaring out hymns to the Virgin through a loudspeaker. The crowds of faithful who at dawn bathed in the waterfall of the aquatic spirits, watch her go by with their hands lifted in adoration and their faces transfigured.

The Church must certainly have tolerated many of these 'popular superstitions' in the hope of eliminating them slowly, without violence or outrage. In 1,500 years it has surely acquired some experience in the art of transforming practices and beliefs which could not be supplanted at once. Yet in Voodoo the clergy found themselves faced with a different problem which was formulated very concisely by the bishop just mentioned: 'It is not we who have got hold of people to christianize them, but they who have been making superstitions out of us.' This veritable seizure of Catholicism by Voodoo is nowhere better illustrated than in the sacrilegious use it makes of the Holy Sacraments.

Since the Colonial period the Haitian peasants have attached great importance to baptism. Moreau de Saint-Méry[5] had already pointed this out: 'Since the Creole Negroes who have been baptized pretend, on this account, to a great superiority over those newly arrived from Africa, whom they call *bossals* (a name used throughout Spanish America), then the African Negroes, who are also slightingly referred to as "horses", hasten to get baptized. At certain days such as Holy Saturday and Whit-Saturday, when adults are baptized, the Negroes turn up at the church and too often without any sort of preparation and no concern for anything but the provision of a godmother or godfather who are sometimes allotted to them on the spot, they receive the first Christian sacrament and thus guarantee themselves immunity from the insults addressed to the non-baptized: although in the eyes of the Creole Negroes, they remain always those who were "baptized standing up".'

The haste shown by these slaves in getting baptized cannot be entirely explained by their desire to become assimilated to the Negroes born in Saint-Domingue. Other writers tell us they tried to get themselves baptized several times over. This zeal, whatever people may say, was not based on hope of small presents, but sprang from magico-religious motives. At the first treaty between the runaway slaves of the west, and the French authorities of Saint-Domingue, it was laid down that the rebels who had waged guerrilla warfare for eighty years in the woods should be allowed to go and get baptized at Neybe and that they should retain the liberty they had won with their blood.

Baptism has been adopted by Voodoo as a consecration rite. Not only are men baptized but also *loa* and all objects used in the cult. The ceremony is celebrated with a degree of solemnity which varies according to whether the object baptized is a sanctuary, drums, necklaces, clothing or any other object—but it is always carried out in conformity with Catholic liturgy. The officiant recites prayers, sprinkles the object with holy water and gives it a name chosen by a godmother and godfather who remain beside it and who afterwards call each other jokingly *commère* and *compère*.

Catholic communion is considered by certain Voodoo priests as a sacrament which increases their powers; sometimes they recommend it to their clients. Even further: some *loa* are regarded as Catholics and by virtue of this fact must communicate from time to time. This is notably the case with Damballah-wèdo; when the god feels the need to approach the Holy Table, he tells one of his servants who then prepares himself, as a good Christian, to take the sacrament and when the day comes, putting a stone sacred to Damballah in his pocket, goes and kneels before the altar; at the very moment of taking communion he is possessed by Damballah who communicates in his place. A woman of Jacmel who was more or less a Voodooist told me that one Sunday during Mass she noticed signs of strange excitement in one of her neighbours. She watched her and realized that she had Damballah in her head. This woman went up to communicate and it was only at the moment when she got back to her place that she frankly abandoned herself to trance. While she was being removed from the church the *loa* inside her kept calling out: 'They were saying I couldn't communicate; well I have.'

We have seen how the marriage sacrament serves to unite a

human being with a *loa*, thus assuring the former the protection and favour of the latter. In order to obtain forgiveness from an offended *loa* Voodooists also practise various forms of external, typically mediaeval, Catholic penitence. The penitents, usually women, wear garments made of grey, so-called 'siamese', cloth or a kind of harlequin dress made of bits and pieces which correspond in colour to the various different *loa*; the clothes must be blessed by the bush-priest. Having sung a Mass, burnt some candles and said prayers to the saints, the penitents offer their friends and relations a grand farewell feast. Then they go out, all over the countryside, visiting in turn all the main places of pilgrimage—Saut-d'eau, Vierge du Mont Carmel, Alta Grecia, Saint Dominique—and live on public charity and on the food distributions which certain pious people dole out to acquit themselves of debts to *loa* or saints. They frequent the markets where they are sure to get a few sous and at least some fruit and vegetables. When they think that by their suffering and weariness they have expiated their sin in the eyes of their protecting *loa* they go home and resume their normal life.

At Marbial market I met a penitent who said she had incurred the wrath of the *loa* Champagne-miofré, of the Ogu family. This divinity had inflicted various illnesses upon her but fearing worse, she was trying to placate him with the spectacle of a painful and wandering life. She devoted part of the alms she received to the saying of Masses for the dead.

Some devotees, on orders from a *hungan*, take food to people in prison who in Haiti are usually very poorly fed. Others give food to the poor, not in any spirit of Christian charity, but to obtain the favour of a *loa*.

Voodoo borrows from Catholicism unevenly: whereas the main elements of the liturgy have been indissolubly mixed in with ritual of African origin, the sacraments and funeral rites have not been similarly absorbed. Only partially integrated with Voodoo, and occupying a rather marginal position, they stand outside the competence of *hungan* and *mambo* and fall within the province of the *pères-savane* who have become to a certain extent established as the official representatives of the Catholic Church in the bosom of paganism. They are entrusted with the conduct of all rites—baptisms, communions, marriages with *loa*, funerals —all of which should, if it were possible, be celebrated by a *curé*. These personages are catechists or sacristans on the loose— men who know how to pray and sing in Latin and French with the correct gestures and intonation. They are called in whenever a Voodoo ceremony has to include a Catholic intermediary. Often it is they who carry out the thanksgiving which precedes the invocation of *loa*—the latter being always the responsibility of a Voodoo priest.

All the *pères-savane* I knew seemed to me good-for-nothings who took their functions very lightly. It is hardly surprising. Are they not marginal people who, having learned to despise the beliefs of their brothers, have yet failed to become good Christians? I was somewhat surprised that their off-handedness and buffoonery shocked no one. In actual fact the Catholic sacraments and liturgy incorporated in Voodoo lose part of the religious significance which they have in their rightful context, in a proper church. Voodooists therefore draw a very clear distinction between sacrament administered by a *curé* and the more or less faithful imitation as practised by the *pères-savane*. How can Voodoo communion be taken seriously when you see the absent-minded and amused way in which the servants of the gods kneel down before the bush-priest who crams into their gaping mouths crustless lumps of bread soaked in wine?

In other words we are here faced with a counterfeit which easily explains the indifference and even the irreverence of the participants. Sometimes the bush-priests and the devotees over-do it: then parody turns to farce. Proof of this lies in the 'catechism of the Guédé', which would doubtless be regarded as sacrilege by the Voodooists themselves if they thought it was their own doing; but since it is the Guédé themselves who are fooling, then nobody need be shocked: everyone knows that the spirits of the dead are roguish and rather obscene. I witnessed this game or play—as you please—at the conclusion of a fête which I had offered in honour of the Guédé. A goat had been sacrificed to them with all the usual circumstance and the sacrificial meal had put them in a good mood. Most of the *hunsi*, possessed by various Guédé, were dancing with gusto, rolling their bottoms and behaving like so many clowns. Suddenly the drums stopped and a *hungan*, himself possessed, ordered the Guédé to form up in one rank. He told them he was going to make them undergo an exam. Stationing himself before the leader of the file, he intoned the first question of the catechism: 'Are you a Christian?' The Guédé questioned assumed an idiotic expression, crooked his knees and bleated: 'I am a Christian—yes,' firmly emphasizing the 'yes'. The examiner went on, 'What is a Christian?' to which, still in the same tones, the Guédé gave the first response of the catechism. Questions and answers followed until the moment the possessed man, affecting an ever more stupid manner, finished by singing in an urgent, pressing rhythm a song which described coitus in the crudest terms possible. The *hungan* heard him out with enjoyment, congratulated the candidate and awarded him the rank of 'colonel of the Haitian armed forces' a promotion which was greeted by shouts of joy and capering. The examiner passed to another Guédé who distinguished himself by his understanding of the catechism and the *brio* with which he sang an obscene couplet—a feat which earned him the rank of general. Each Guédé in turn received some prestigious title borrowed from the military, ecclesiastical or political hierarchies. A fat girl with a jolly nature was proclaimed 'pope'. At the announcement of this high distinction the 'popess' let out roars of triumph and despite her size skipped about like a little girl whose success in school has gone to her head.

We would be wrong to look upon this burlesque interlude as a sacrilege. The *hunsi* possessed by the Guédé put no malice into their performance. They amused themselves just as did our ancestors who, however devout, saw no harm in taking off the rites and sacred personages for whom, in another time and place, they showed the greatest respect. The *curés* of those days, more tolerant than the *curés* of Haiti, knew what was not important and cast no anathema on games which, when all is said and done, were quite harmless.

THE ATTITUDE OF THE CATHOLIC CHURCH TO VOODOO

The Church is to a certain extent responsible for the survival of

African cults in Haiti. In the eighteenth century the instruction
of slaves in the religion to which they had been compulsorily
admitted by sprinklings of holy water, was entirely neglected.
Priests who wished to convert the Blacks came up against the
indifference, or more often the hostility, of owners who cared
little if their beasts of burden were, or were not, dignified with
the status of Christians. Then the struggles for independence and
the civil wars which followed each other, practically throughout
the whole of the nineteenth century, were scarcely propitious to
the diffusion of Christianity. The Concordat of 1860, still in
force, provided a formula which was acceptable to national pride
but which was to prove obstructive to the establishment of
Catholicism. What the Haitian country districts needed were not
curés working parishes organized on the pattern of those in
France, but missionaries who would have taught the masses and
fought idolatry. Even today when schools are beginning to
multiply and peasants are no longer cut off in the mountains, I
have heard *curés* say their task should have been approached in
the spirit of mission-work. Most Catholic priests in Haiti come
from Brittany where there is a seminary specially to train them.
When they find themselves confronted, not by good Catholics
who dabble in a few harmless superstitions, but by parishioners
who are visited by—and maintain familiar relationships with—
spirits, they feel bewildered and helpless. Neither the milieu in
which they have lived nor their training fits them to face up to
such a state of affairs. Far from pitying the ignorance and credulity of their flock, most of them, whether they are French or
Haitian, look upon Voodoo as the work of the devil—a demonic
manifestation against which they must fight with every means at
the Church's disposal. In this context one *curé* said to me:
'Judging by what I have seen with my own eyes, I have to admit
that the *loa* are very real beings. Is it not true that there is a
devil? The people of this country are truly possessed by the
Fiend for it is by our prayers that we manage to deliver them.
Before going into a seminary I witnessed many strange happen-
ings. For instance a woman bending a bar of iron made red hot.
Do you suppose such a thing would be possible without supernatural intervention? Was she not possessed by the devil?'

The catechisms used in the country districts give a clear picture of the clergy's attitude to Voodoo:

31. Who is the principal slave of Satan?—the principal slave of Satan is the *hungan*.

32. What are the names given by *hungan* to Satan?—The names given to Satan by *hungan* are *loa*, angels, saints, *morts*, *marassa*.

33. Why do *hungan* give Satan the names of angels, saints, and *morts*?—*Hungan* call Satan after saints, angels and *morts* in order to deceive us more easily.

34. How do men serve Satan?—In sinning, casting spells, practising magic, giving food-offerings, *manger les anges*, *manger marassa* . . .

37. Are we allowed to mingle with the slaves of Satan?—No, because they are evil-doers; like Satan himself they are liars.

Even more precise is this definition, copied into a manuscript catechism which was going about the Marbial Valley: 'A *loa* is a wicked angel who revolted against God and for that reason is in Hell.'

The only divergence of opinion between the pastors and their flock on this point turns on the very different character which they attribute to supernatural beings. To those who tell them the *loa* are so many minor 'satans' they reply that since God created them *loa* can hardly be bad and that anyhow there is no shortage of proof of their goodwill and compassion; it is true certain spirits are prepared to help wicked people and make themselves feared for their violence and cruelty, but they alone deserve the name of *diab*: nice people have nothing to do with them and their victims should try and appease them, without, however, stooping to crime. No more than man does God approve the carry-on of 'bad *loa*' and 'bought *loa*' employed by sorcerers to further their evil designs.

In 1941, given a strong hand by the more or less open support of the government, the clergy determined to intensify its campaign against the outer manifestations of Voodoo and to bring the peasantry as quickly as possible to an undiluted form of Catholicism.

The first official attempt on the part of the Church to combat Voodoo dates back to 1896. The Bishop of Cap Haitien, Monseigneur Kersuzan, launched against 'superstition' a campaign of conferences, gatherings and sermons which resulted in the creation of the 'League against Voodoo', an organization which in the parishes was to work through the *curés*—but the success of this league was apparently moderate. In a synodical address Monseigneur Kersuzan complained of not being supported by the authorities, although the President himself had assured him of his support. He added 'in certain places even intelligent and educated people are siding with fetishism and this is leading the common folk astray'.

In the same breath as he denounced the evils of Voodoo, Monseigneur Kersuzan threatened Voodooists with serious sanctions. Those who took part in a ceremony were deprived of the right to communicate, *hungan* and *mambo* could not become godfathers or godmothers, and for their absolution they had to go to the diocesan bishop. In 1913 the Episcopate returned to the attack. The 'monstrous mixture' became the target of a collective pastoral letter.

These first skirmishes resulted in very little and were quickly forgotten. The real battle between the Church and Voodoo was only joined in 1939, during the presidency of Elie Lescot. Monseigneur X tells us the campaign was set off by 'the discovery, in truly providential circumstances, of the existence of the "mixture" (*le mélange*) and above all by the discovery that this abomination was not only the way of one isolated person but the current practice of the whole body of converts'.

The tardiness of this 'discovery' shows a fine indifference on the part of the Haitian clergy to all that had been written about Voodoo long before it became aware of the existence of this abominable *mélange*. Perhaps they can scarcely be blamed for having ignored the brilliant study which Melville J. Herskovits devoted to the interpenetration of African and Catholic cults in his book *In a Haitian Valley*, but it is impossible not to be amazed by their blindness when one thinks of the daily opportunity of country *curés* to become acquainted with Voodoo belief and practice.

The 'discovery' referred to by Monseigneur X thus hardened the will of the clergy to combat the paganism of their flocks at all costs. The extremely vigorous campaign which it was to undertake to root out Voodoo, had, as its precursor, a man of the people called Ti-Jules (whose real name was St Giles-St Pierre) who lived in the neighbourhood of Trou d'Eau near Hinche. Like all Haitian peasants he was a convinced Voodooist. Three of his children being ill he took them to a *hungan*. At first he strictly adhered to whatever the healer prescribed: his house became full of 'knotted strings', 'indigo crosses' had been painted everywhere, and he gave his children 'ill-smelling baths' (*basins sentis*) to turn away from them the fury of the wicked spirits. However, he was experiencing certain scruples in preferring all this magical cookery to the protection of Almighty God. One morning, rising from prayer, he suddenly began to destroy and throw away not only what the *hungan* had introduced to his house, but all that the *hungan* had ever touched: tables, chairs, plates, cups—all was sacrificed to his virtuous indignation. To his dejected family he explained 'we must rid ourselves of every trace of Satan so that God will take care of us.' The subsequent recovery of his children confirmed him in his rebellion against the *loa*. He became a lay preacher and began exhorting his neighbours to serve God 'without mixture'. A vision soon gave his mission divine sanction: he saw two '*pères*' who came into his hut with radiant faces, made him sit down and told him in the name of God he must 'guide people from magic and put them on the true path'. They explained to him the truths and the prayers he must teach to all who came in search of him, and the means of giving up the *loa*.

News of this miracle spread and a great many people came in search of Ti-Jules to learn how to serve God 'without mixture'. He made them kneel, crossed himself, and having made them say a few prayers such as the Credo and Confiteor, asked them to destroy their sanctuaries and cut down their sacred trees (*arbres reposoirs*). He then made them repeat a text in which as a repentant Voodooist they renounced all service of *loa*. This ended with the phrase: '*Ak pitit ak travo, m'détaché, m'ataché, m'rénôsé*' (with my children with my work, I detach myself, I attach myself, I recant).

Those who declared their intention of renouncing, from then on had to fulfil their religious duties punctiliously, get married if they lived in sin and avoid all contact with Voodoo.

Ti-Jules's success was so great that thousands of peasants of Artibonite and the north went as pilgrims to Trou d'Eau and returned home changed beings. Ti-Jules was soon to know the fate of all prophets. His neighbours, jealous of his ascendancy, and offended in their beliefs and traditions, denounced him to the *curé* as a heretic 'so blinded by his own pretensions as to have invented a new religion'. The *curé*, before whom Ti-Jules was brought, found nothing very reprehensible in his behaviour or in what he said. The *hungan* and *boko* then got at the civil authority and described Ti-Jules as a magician who 'turned people's heads' by means of 'cabalistic words and instruments' and who, at his home, 'organized meetings dangerous to the security of the State.' The reformer was arrested, thrown into prison and although acquitted by the court nevertheless had to pay out a considerable sum of money.

But the persecutions visited upon him merely increased his reputation. The faithful came in ever greater numbers to be freed from the grip of *loa*. On the advice of the archdiocese, Ti-Jules was asked to refer his penitents to the *curés* of their respective parishes. Thus started the movement of those who were called the '*rejetés*'—'rejectors'. Among these a certain Simon who had been seven years under *boko* for treatment, distinguished himself by his zeal. He accompanied the *curés* on their rounds and his words were given greater weight by his habit of accusing himself of those very sins from which he wished to preserve his compatriots.

The Catholic chroniclers of this anti-superstition crusade made no bones about the pain and general disturbance caused by these violent accusings and threats of eternal punishment for all who refused to give up the cult of *loa*. This general *crise de conscience* resulted in a revelation—to the clergy—of the number of 'converts' who had remained faithful to Voodoo. 'All converts or *dévotions*—that is to say all the faithful—were deep in superstition. Even the directors of chapels whose duty it was to catechize others, were no exception. In nearly every dwelling there was to be found a little *loa*-house (*maison-loa*) and all the other objects of superstition. Astonishment gradually turned to stupor but before such an array of facts there could be no more argument: henceforward it was established that nearly all our converts were practising "the mixture".'

The Church then took a step which was to provoke profound indignation even in those quarters from which it might have expected most support. The clergy decided to insist upon an anti-superstitious oath—to be taken by all the faithful. Here is the text of this oath—the oath of the so-called 'rejectors'.

'I before God, stand in the Tabernacle, before the priest who represents Him and renew the promises of my baptism. With hand on the Gospels I swear never to give a food-offering (*manger-loa*) of whatever kind—never to attend a Voodoo ceremony of whatever kind, never to take part in a service to *loa* in any way whatsoever.

'I promise to destroy or have destroyed as soon as possible all fetishes and objects of superstition, if any—on me, in my house, and in my compound.

'In short I swear never to sink to any superstitious practice whatever.

[For married persons] 'I promise moreover to bring up my children without exception in the Catholic and Roman religion, outside all superstition, submitting myself fully to the teaching of this Holy Church.

'And I promise that with God's help I shall abide by my oath until death.'

Members of the 'élite' and even of the middle classes, were outraged they should be required to take an oath which suggested they were suspected of sharing peasant beliefs and practices. Their indignation knew no limits. In vain the *curés* told them that it was precisely because they were good Catholics that they were being asked to make a show of solidarity and separate themselves from those who practised *le mélange*. It was no good: they still saw in this measure nothing but humiliation and persecution. The fact that it was imposed upon them by white priests increased their resentment. It confirmed their suspicions that the foreign priesthood looked upon them as so many savages. Sermons, conferences, reunions, home visits—nothing was neglected in the effort to make them see that the oath was necessary. But in a parish which included some 2,000 regular church-goers no more than a few dozen agreed to take the oath. In the whole of the Gonaïves diocese only 3,000 were sworn in. The bishops attributed this set-back not to hurt vanity but to the attachment of so-called Catholics to Voodoo, and to their refusal to break with 'superstition'. In my opinion priests, thinking thus, had rushed from an excess of optimism to one of pessimism. If indeed it be true that a great many of their parishioners preferred to be deprived of the right to communicate rather than desert their *humfo*, then many others certainly regarded the oath as a shameful admission, incompatible with their personal dignity.

The disillusion, which the clergy confess they felt, was largely compensated by the mass conversions of Voodooists who, seized by a vague collective enthusiasm, 'abjured' in large numbers and came flocking to the priests, asking them to destroy the ritual objects which they possessed and to 'free them from the impossible obligations which had been imposed upon them'. The 'obligations' which Voodoo imposes on its devotees explain in many cases the ease with which many of them abjured and the enthusiasm they showed—probably to cover secret misgivings. Finally, peasant populations are easily carried away—sometimes as briefly as violently. It would be as unjust to deny the spontaneity of some conversions as to pretend there was no coercion. From the Catholic point of view very serious sanctions were taken against all who attended or took part in, actively or passively, any Voodoo ceremony. The mere wearing of an amulet entailed six months' penitence. Fearing they would be deprived of the sacraments, to which they attached the greatest importance, many Voodooists promised to break with the *loa*. Up to this point the Church kept within its rights. Now it changed its tactics and secured the support of the secular arm : on the demand of the clergy, President Lescot ordered the army to co-operate with the *curés* in their hunting-down of all objects to do with the Voodoo cult.

Strengthened by the more or less open support of the government, the *curés* had the *humfo* shut up or destroyed and thousands
of sacred objects were burnt in veritable *auto-da-fés*. I was in
Haiti in 1941 and I remember seeing in the back-yards of presby-
teries vast pyramids of drums, painted bowls, necklaces, talismans—all waiting for the day fixed for the joyous blaze which
was to symbolize the victory of the Church over Satan.

The peasantry whose sanctuaries had been pillaged and who
could no longer *battre tambour* (beat their drums) to summon the
loa of Africa, finally began to express their resentment more or
less openly—in some regions by staging religious strikes. In
addition both Press and public opinion disapproved the often
immoderate zeal of certain priests. The government, aware of
the hostility of the bourgeoisie and people for the clergy, withdrew its support. On February 22, 1942, shots were fired in the
church of Delmas, near Port-au-Prince just when a Haitian
priest was saying a Mass which was to inaugurate a new week of
preaching against superstition. The Catholic newspapers let it be
clearly understood that this affair was an act of government
provocation—alleging that police disguised as peasants had been
sent to Delmas. The fact is the government did immediately
seize on the affair as a pretext for curbing the anti-Voodoo
campaign. Monseigneur X himself relates how, after the earlier
enthusiasm for the *renonce* there was now a massive swing back
to 'superstition'.

With great honesty he admits 'the greater part of that mass
which had rejoiced to be delivered from its slavery, now, once
more, took up their chains'. Voodoo sanctuaries opened again
and, little by little, the faithful gathered again round *hungan* and
mambo. Under the government of President Estimé (1946-52),
Voodoo emerged completely from semi-clandestinity. Many
black intellectuals who supported the new régime professed to
admire Voodoo as an expression of the popular soul. It was
natural for a government which claimed to be sprung from the
masses and to represent the *authentiques*, that is to say Haitians
of pure negro stock, to show itself tolerant of, and even kindly
disposed to, the popular religion. In spite of the economic
distress which afflicted country districts, the presidency of

Estimé was marked by a revival of Voodoo. Many adepts had been nourishing the desire to regain the favour of the *loa* whose worship they had only neglected out of fear of *curés* or police.

The *renonce* has had a very definite effect on the Church's idea of its task in Haiti. The clergy had understood that it was high time the masses received a more solid Christian grounding. An attempt is now made to guarantee clerical influence by means of catechists who are chosen from among the 'rejectors'. These receive training which makes them useful auxiliaries of the country *curés*. On the other hand the war declared on Voodoo by the Church has awakened the peasants to the very real opposition which exists between the cult of *loa* and official Catholicism. The *curés* of today are much more strict on the question of orthodoxy and they are not allowed that lenience which in the past made it possible for the Voodooists to use the Catholic liturgy for pagan ends.

THE ANTI-SUPERSTITION CAMPAIGN
IN THE MARBIAL VALLEY

The Marbial valley is one of those few regions of Haiti where Voodoo has not been able to recover entirely from the blows which were dealt it. There the extirpation of idolatry was conducted with brutal energy by a French *curé* who, by his impetuosity, earned the name of Lavalas (the torrent, the flood) and by a Haitian *curé*—a man who, brought up in a Voodoo-practising milieu, persecuted the religion of his ancestors with tenacious and penetrating hatred.

At the time of my stay in Marbial eight years had passed since the events which I am about to relate. I gleaned them from the accounts of the peasants themselves, and I am aware that they may, by then, already have undergone the distortions to which all oral tradition is prone, and may already have become tainted with supernatural incident; but it is precisely because they tell the facts as the peasants see them that I thought it worth putting them down here. By and large these facts are right, for they were confirmed to me by Father L. C. himself. As to the supernatural incidents, they constitute psychological documents which have their own interest.

The people of Marbial were deeply upset by the anathema hurled down upon their ancestral beliefs from the pulpit. The mystical universe in which they lived was not always so very reassuring, but at least it did not throw up many problems. In it *loa*, saints, the Virgin and Jesus got on with each other pretty well. Masses, sacraments and *mangers-loa* were so many well-tried means of obtaining the favour of the invisible ones and neutralizing their malevolence. Now everything was turned upside down. Imagine the dilemma of a peasant who has spent all his life fulfilling his 'obligations' to his family *loa*, suddenly finding himself branded as an idolater and servant of the devil! What seems to have impressed the inhabitants of the valley most were the expeditions organized by Father Lavalas against the 'houses of the *loa*'. At the head of a band of fanatical converts the Father burst into the farms and demanded that every article connected with the cult of Voodoo be handed over. No violence was committed but by their shouting and general manner the zealots tried to frighten anyone who dared resist them. Even so, the pillage and destruction of the sanctuary living-rooms would have been impossible without the help of the secular arm. At Marbial this was represented by the *Chefs de Section* who fulfil the dual functions of justices of the peace and rural policemen. Many of them must certainly have been Voodoo adepts and therefore surely took part in these raids with considerable reluctance. Such, however, is the sense of subordination among the Haitian peasants that not a single *Chef de Section* seems to have shirked the task assigned to him.

Usually the priests knew very well where to find the objects which people tried to hide. In this respect their perspicacity, attributed to supernatural power, was in fact due to informers— out to gain their favour, or jealous of richer neighbours. Today the *curé* at Marbial is still thought to be the possessor of a magic 'instrument' which enables him to find out the most secret matters and to divine the innermost thoughts of his parishioners.

Many peasants who were either frightened or knew they had been denounced came to the chapel of their own accord and handed in musical instruments, costumes or the attributes of the gods and all the cult accessories which they were keeping at home. Those who pretended to a pure Christianity, without *mélange*, while in fact secretly practising Voodoo, came at night to give up the objects which might have compromised them. Others, fearing a search which might end in a general pillaging of their possessions, took the initiative and themselves asked the *curé* and his acolytes to free them of all 'pagan blot'. Those who on the other hand refused to give up the patron spirits of their family and to destroy sacred objects handed down to them by their parents, or bought at their own expense, could resign themselves to seeing their compounds sooner or later invaded by a band of zealots led by the *curé* or the local police. At first the *curé* tried to convince them that it was in their own interest to forswear their former ways and agree to the destruction of their sanctuary: but if these exhortations had no effect the invaders resorted to force: the priest's escort, headed by the *Chef de Section*, went into the house, took away any suspicious objects, and, according to several of my informants, these self-appointed inquisitors took the opportunity of settling private scores or even of committing small thefts. Then the sacred trees—plentiful round *humfo*—were exorcized and cut down amid hymn-singing and prayer.

All who witnessed these scenes were struck by the behaviour of those who had become the agents or tools of the persecution. They attacked the sacralia of Voodoo as though these were their personal dangerous enemies. While the *curé* was engaged in exorcizing the sacred trees, fanatics threw stones at them, cursed them and blamed them for all the money they had made them throw away on sacrifices and offerings, and of course this rage betrayed their conviction that these trees were in fact duly inhabited by spirits. As to the Voodooists who had to be present during these scenes, which in their eyes were sacrilege, and had to give up with their own hands their talismans—the guarantee of their safety and well-being—they were so dejected, so completely downcast that they burst into tears and showed signs of overwhelming grief. There were, it seems, cases when adepts fainted or were suddenly possessed by the god or spirit whose emblems were being destroyed. These trances gave rise to others. Some of these people were only tipsified (*saoulés*) by the gods and did no more than stagger, but others, on whom the god had truly alighted, shouted their indignation aloud. It was the *loa* themselves crying out against this profanation, repeating again and again: 'I'm not going; I don't want to go.' The *curé* tried to touch the possessed on the forehead with his crucifix but the latter gesticulated and resisted as best they could. Some fled and were brought back by force to the Father, who then exorcized them. When their trance was over these unhappy people wandered about begging for some explanation of what had befallen them.

Sometimes possessions took place in the middle of a church service. The case of Ludalise, which was told me by someone attached to the chapel, is indicative of a certain mental climate and despite its fairy-tale element is grounded none the less on actual fact. The heroine of this affair, Mademoiselle Ludalise, was a young woman who had served the *loa* but who, for reasons unknown to me, had decided to renounce. One Sunday in the middle of Mass, at the elevation of the Host, she was possessed by a *loa*. She was taken to the presbytery where the *curé* followed her in order to drive off this unclean spirit. The *loa* defended itself like a very devil against the exorcisms and kept crying out, 'I shan't go, no—I'm not going.' The mother of the demented woman was quickly fetched and asked if by any chance her daughter had forgotten to hand in some Voodoo object to the *curé*. The mother began by assuring everyone she had got rid of everything that might have the slightest connection with the worship of *loa*, but when further questions were urged upon her she admitted there was a sacred tree still standing near the house. The *curé* ordered his sacristan to saddle his mule straight away and go and cut the fetish down. On the way, when this delegate was crossing a dangerous stone-drain, his mount gave a leap which all but unseated its rider. The latter, familiar with the animal's wariness, let the incident pass without thought. Having reached the farm he cut down the sacred tree and returned to the chapel to give an account of his mission. The girl, still possessed, cried out when she saw him: 'My friend, you've had a stroke of luck. For two pins I'd have broken your neck.' It was not, of course, the girl speaking but the *loa* inside her. These were his last words. Having spoken them he fled out of her, leaving her exhausted and unconscious. He never came back, but the young woman never quite recovered her sanity.

A few peasants saw in the *renonce* the unhoped-for opportunity of ridding themselves forever of the werewolves which infested their country, or at least of breaking their occult power. Women accused of being 'child-eaters' were dragged in front of Father X. He questioned them and sent away those he thought were innocent. The rest he took to the sacristy where he exorcized them. One of my informers, directress of a Catholic mission station, was convinced that the *curé* exposed werewolves by placing the Gospels on their chests. Those who really belonged to this terrible sisterhood let out screams and waved their arms about as though to fly away, but sooner or later they collapsed, conquered by the power of the holy book. Once convinced the demon had fled, he sent them home after making them promise never to revert to their former ways.

The clergy ordained that all the big crosses in family burial places should be rooted up since they knew well that the peasants regarded them as the symbol of Baron-Samedi, King of the Dead. At the very moment when one great heap of these crosses was about to be fired a crowd of women who had come to watch were possessed by Baron-Samedi, Baron-la-Croix, and other members of the Guédé family. The spirits of the dead, expressing themselves through these women, are said to have uttered the following threats: 'Do you really think you can get rid of us like this? All you are burning is wood. Us, you will never burn. Today you throw these crosses into the fire but soon you will see another kind of fire burning in this valley.' Attempts were made to silence them by spattering them with holy water, but they mocked it and went on prophesying catastrophes and abusing the *curé*. The drought which hit the people of Marbial so hard in the following years was naturally put down to the wrath of the *loa*. Hence the person who provided the account ended with the following words: 'The *loa* spoke the truth, it's quite a fire they have lighted in Marbial. The sun burns so hot our gardens will no longer grow even millet. The sun burns our harvest and the rain falls no more. Drought is wiping us out.'

The reaction of the population of Marbial to the anti-super-stition campaign was not everywhere the same. Apart from its more or less openly declared opponents, there were quite a few families who 'rejected' enthusiastically and joined forces with the *curé* against their fellow citizens. Some were acting in a spirit of revolt against the bondage of Voodoo, others to gain favour with the *curé*, still others, under the influence of city life, thought that to practise Voodoo relegated them to the ranks of the ignorant and simple-minded peasantry. And then with many converts economic considerations weighed heavily. Even when they could have returned to the Voodoo fold some people remained faithful to their oath and freely admitted they were glad never again to have to be always paying out small sums of money for *manger-loas*. True, some complained of the new expenses now imposed on them by the Church. Their tirades on the subject of the occasional fees of the Church were sometimes bitter and showed a secret resentment.

It remains to be seen to what extent Catholicism triumphed in the Marbial valley. On this question I have some information which seems to me significant. First, the sincerity of the 're-jectors' became suspect when they were converted. A woman who described herself as a good Catholic and went regularly to Mass told me she had not deserted the *loa* 'who are good spirits and protect us from the devil'. (She said her own *loa* had never done any harm.) They watched over her and she knew well that if ever she fell ill she must get in touch with them rather than the *curé*. She had noticed a serious deterioration in her private circum-stances after she had 'renounced', and a marked improvement only when she had celebrated a costly service to the *loa*.

Another informant, who told me without a qualm that she not only believed in the *loa*, but also served them, had yet openly forsworn them so that her child could be baptized. Further-more; she was convinced that her *loa* would not hold this against her for 'they are immortal, invisible and everywhere'.

I shall not soon forget the awed and heart-stricken tones of the peasant who, having declared that his family had always revered the *loa* of Africa, cried out, 'No, no, my *loa* are not devils. They have never eaten anyone. On the contrary it is they who protect me against evil spirits and werewolves. I shall never be ungrateful to them. It is not I who created them but God Himself. How could He have made them if they were not good?'

There can be no doubt that many Voodooists basked in the hope that the *loa* would prove understanding and would not hold against them the hostile acts of violence for which they were not responsible, nor for an apostasy imposed on them from without and which was repugnant to them. Once the first impact of surprise had worn off many told themselves that after all the *loa* were too intelligent and powerful to take umbrage for what had happened to their material symbols. A certain Salis, who prided himself on the possession of a pot in which lived a captive spirit, was made to bring it to the presbytery where it went to join musical instruments, sacred pictures and crockery on the pyre. A few days later the spirit in the pot came and told his *protégé* not to worry about this loss as he was keeping very fit himself and the destruction of his dwelling-place made no difference to him. He even counselled his servant to recant and take communion in the Church, if he thought wise, as this would make no difference to their relationship. Another peasant, on whose ground a tree dedicated to Legba had been cut down, told me that the god had not left his home but had merely moved to another tree.

Among the obstinately loyal who refused to 'reject', there was a *hungan* who explained to me why he had never wished to abandon the cult of his ancestors. 'Better the man,' he told me, 'who openly says he does not wish to "reject" because he does not believe his *loa* are devils, than the Catholic or Protestant who practises witchcraft in secret. I am a *hungan* who serves the *loa* and I say as much to anyone who wants to hear it. During the anti-superstition campaign "rejectors" came to me, threatened me, abused me and called me a werewolf. They accused me of eating little children. I knew that one day I would expose them. I said to them: "I have only one master, that is Almighty God. Is the *curé* my master? I'm grown up, not a child." Those who had "rejected" gave up greeting me.'

For many Voodooists the 'renunciation' became a genuine dilemma of conscience which some solved in a rather subtle way. One of these was Sylvestre who, having sworn never to serve the *loa* again, identified them 'in spirit' with the saints, whose pictures he had retained. He no longer went to the *hungan*, but he did say Mass which 'in spirit' was always addressed to the *loa*. He put tasty dishes near the pictures of the saints to round the ceremony off. Cynically he admitted: 'That's how we fix things, so the *curé* serves the *loa*.'

Certain members of the clergy were anxious to use the confusion created by the anti-superstition campaign as an opportunity for fighting Protestantism. Using the well-known amalgam procedure, they tried to bracket Protestants with impenitent Voodooists. The bands of zealots who overran the countryside stopped at the houses of notorious Protestants and tried by threats to draw them into the bosom of the Church. Hymns composed by the *curés* for the special hearing of the 'rejectors' mix violent denunciation of Voodoo with verses proclaiming: ' "Protestant" is the religion of Satan—doesn't lead to Heaven.'

VOODOO AND PROTESTANTISM

In the various Protestant sects which abound in Haiti (Baptists, Methodists, Anglicans, Adventists, Pentecostists and others) Voodoo found even more formidable and tenacious adversaries than in Roman Catholicism. For 'paganism', of whatever kind, is always equated by the various Protestant denominations with 'satanism', and treated with total intransigence. Whereas so many Catholics practise Voodoo more or less openly, Protestants must break, not only with the cult itself, but with all that might in any way recall it to their thoughts. One preacher I knew flew into a rage whenever the members of a *combite* work group stopped in front of his house with their musical instruments. Music and Voodoo were so closely associated in his mind that the mere sight of a trumpet drove him to distraction. It is precisely this refusal to compromise, this naïve purism which has attracted so many conversions. Many Voodooists have become Protestants (*entré dans le Protestant*) not because Voodoo failed to supply their need for a purer, loftier religion, but on the contrary, because they felt themselves to be the target of angry *loa* and saw in Protestantism a refuge. Hence Protestantism beckons as though it were a shelter, or more precisely a magic circle, where people cannot be got at by *loa* and demons. Conversion, far from being the result of a *crise de conscience*, is often no more than the expression of an exaggerated fear of spirits. The rôle of Protestantism among Voodooists was well defined to me in a saying which I heard in Marbial and quote here word for word: 'If you want the *loa* to leave you in peace—become a Protestant.' This same conviction was reported in 1896, in the north of Haiti, by Monseigneur Kersuzan.[6]

No doubt it is the challenging attitude adopted by Protestants towards the *loa* which has finally convinced the peasants that this religion confers upon its adepts a sort of supernatural immunity. Conversions are usually inspired by illness, since illness is the commonest manifestation of a *loa*'s ill-will or anger. When all the resources of Voodoo—services, baths, infusions, driving out of *morts*—have been exhausted, a really fundamental remedy—conversion to a Protestant sect—is tried as a last resort. Sometimes it is the *hungan* himself who realizes the ineffectiveness of the cure prescribed and advises the patient or his family to abandon the *loa* and 'try Protestantism'.

Illness figures in most of the conversion cases which I heard of. A few examples will suffice to underline this fact. When I knew Mme L she was a Catholic who secretly served the *loa*. She told me that a few years earlier she had lost four children straight off, one after the other. She was left with one daughter who soon, also, fell seriously ill. Her husband and she moved heaven and earth to save her, but the treatment prescribed by the *hungan* was as little use as its predecessors. From day to day the condition of the child deteriorated. In desperation the parents decided to turn Protestant. As a token of their determination they cut down the sacred trees which grew round their house, destroyed all their cult objects and got some Baptists they knew to come and sing songs round the little patient. Encouraged by a perceptible improvement in the child's health they asked to be admitted to the Baptist community in Jacmel. They conducted themselves—

even for quite a time—as good Protestants, but when they were sure their daughter was out of danger they decided to return to the fold of Catholicism so as to be able to serve the *loa* again. However, before taking this decision they had made their daughter promise always 'to eat her bread' with the Protestants. They explained to her that owing her life, as she did, to Protestantism she would be taking a great risk if she gave up the Baptist Church to deal with *loa*. The girl remained a Protestant and married a Catechist.

Conversion can be an act of revolt or aggression against *loa* who have let you down. This is the burden of the following story told me by a Baptist peasant: 'I had three children called Nereus, Ducius and Daniel. The first cried all night, screamed and struggled as though trying to escape from a supernatural being. Sometimes trembling all over, he shouted, "Leave me, leave me alone, leave me alone."

'I went to a *hungan* who was a friend of mine. He summoned *loa* so that I might question them and he told my fortune with cards. Thus I learned my son was being "ridden" by a werewolf. The *hungan* calmed my fears: he told me it was not serious and that he would give up his calling and throw away his "points" if he failed to cure my child. I sold two oxen to pay for the treatment. But Nereus died.

'Ducius, my second son, suffered from a painful suppurating abscess. We didn't know what to do. I went to see the *hungan* Makeli Desir because my wife had seen him in a dream. He had me celebrate a service to soothe the anger of Damballah-wèdo who, he assured me, was at the root of my son's illness. I paid him generously from the revenues of my land. One morning at dawn I found my son dead.

'Three weeks later—I'm damned if Daniel didn't go down with raging fever. My wife says, "It's possible that the sacrifice was not to Damballah's taste." I say: "What do you want me to do? I've sold all my cattle." She implored me to go back to the *hungan* Makeli. On the way I was overtaken by a horseman who told me Daniel was dead.

'When I got home I was seized with violent anger. I smashed the *marassa* dishes, tore up the pictures of the saints, and said,

"No more *loa* for me, no more *boko*, it's all rubbish." Immediately after the funeral my wife and I became Protestant. I then had five more children and thanks be to Christ they are all alive.'

The hostility of spirits often takes the form of persistent bad luck. In this eventuality too, conversion to Protestantism can also be the only way out. I was told of a *hungan* who became a Protestant because he could no longer satisfy the demands of his *loa*. They came in dreams and demanded offerings and sacrifices which ate up his revenues. Nevertheless, he managed to fob them off up to the moment when, following a bad run of business, he was ruined and incapable of satisfying his *loa*'s whims. Out of spite they made his children die. At a loss how to bring his run of misfortune to an end the *hungan* gave up his profession and became a Protestant. Judging from what I heard, this step did not bring him the change he hoped. His bad luck dogged him and at last drove him to suicide. The Voodooists, of course, concluded that in this case the *loa* had proved themselves stronger than Protestants.

I have heard a peasant of Marbial admit, without a qualm, that he had been taken to the Baptist Church because he had lost— one after the other—his chickens, his pigs, his horses, and finally a son! He went to a *hungan* who began by getting quite a lot of money out of him on one pretext or another, but could give him no other advice than to offer a 'grand service' to the *loa*. The priest's rapacity made the man sceptical. Rather than lose the little that remained to him he determined to turn Protestant. God certainly accepted him, for since then he has no longer been troubled by *loa* nor has he been dogged by bad luck. 'If only I had thought of turning Protestant earlier,' he said to me with a sigh, 'by now I would have had enough money to buy land.'

Protestants who are ex-Voodooists are regarded as the sworn foes of their previous religion. Their intransigence towards it takes the form of obsessive scruples. But we may wonder whether the rigidity and intolerance of their attitude may not spring at heart from fear of back-sliding. Such a thing could be. A certain Prudence was seized during a Protestant service at Marbial with an attack of nerves which was noticeable for its phase of 'possession'. He was quickly taken home where his condition was regarded as so serious that his son, who still practised Voodoo, was sent for. A *hungan* was called in and a propitiatory service organized. A few days later Prudence had quite recovered. He did not think it necessary to give up Protestantism, but every year he gave his son a sum of money with which to make offerings to the *loa*.

A young woman, at the very moment she was being baptized, had an attack of possession which lasted a good quarter of an hour during which time she kept protesting against the commitment she was about to undertake.

The *loa*, it is said, do not like people returning to them in a grudging spirit or with mental reservations. A Protestant woman who became a convert to please the man she was living with, returned to Catholicism and the service of *loa* when he died. She hoped her daughter would follow her example, but the girl wanted to remain a good Protestant. Finally, however, the girl gave in to her mother's threats. A week later she was possessed by the god Ogu with such violence that she appeared to have lost her reason. She broke everything in reach, and called her mother a sorceress and werewolf. Certain words she let drop during this crisis suggested she was terrified of becoming a werewolf herself. It seemed that to punish her for her resistance the spirits were driving her to a criminal course which filled her with horror.

Sometimes, too, those who become converts to find shelter from the *loa* are disappointed to discover that their new religion does not shield them from misfortune. They then regret their decision and try, at first secretly and then openly, to reingratiate themselves with the *loa*. A peasant woman who became a Baptist to please her husband told me that a few weeks later a whole series of catastrophes burst upon her household. 'It was a veritable epidemic of troubles,' she said, 'our money affairs went badly, our holding produced practically nothing, our chickens fell ill, our cattle died one after the other, the least little wound we got turned septic and became infested with maggots. We became very poor and lost two children. It was all because we had abandoned the *loa* and because the *loa* had abandoned us.' After this series of disasters the couple decided to go back to

serving the *loa*. They went to the *curé* to forswear their Protestantism, received their certificate as rejectors and hurried off
to offer sacrifices to their family *loa*. For 'you must be a Catholic
to serve the *loa*' . . .

The same lack of sincerity seems to have characterized the
conversion of the peasant who, in order to get 'quick rich', frequented *boko* and *humfo*. His dealings with sorcerers and wicked
spirits received their punishment: his wife, whom he loved
dearly, went mad. To cure her he got hold of a well-known
hungan who ruined him with costly ceremonies without in return
effecting the least improvement in her condition. Impoverished
and desperate, our friend decided to convert to Protestantism,
himself and all his family too. His wife recovered her sanity, but
this miracle 'made no difference to him, did not open his eyes to
the error of his ways'. One day he was surprised in the act of
performing a ceremony for the spirits. He fell ill soon after and
confessed on his death bed that he had never given up his cult
of *loa*.

It would be unjust to explain the success of Protestant sects
entirely in terms of superstitious calculation. Other factors come
into play, particularly in urban districts where Protestantism
gets most of its recruits. I will mention a few in brief. The
personal influence of certain missionaries is difficult to assess,
but no one can question that the general service these men have
rendered the rural population, in creating schools and taking
pains with adult education, has often disposed people to Protestantism. Family solidarity and the influence of prominent
people also play a part in many cases of conversion.

We should not forget, while we are enumerating the motives
for changes of religion, those trivial causes such as quarrels with
curés or wounded susceptibilities—all of which have led several
Marbial families to turn Protestant.

There is an economic aspect, too, which is not without importance. The austere life of many Protestant families has resulted in
a certain prosperity which many like to regard as no more than
the reward of a just Providence. Their neighbours, who have
remained faithful to the traditional way of life and are therefore
less sober, less prudent, are sometimes tempted to believe that

they have only to become Protestant to improve their lot. Furthermore the Protestant sects, in particular the Baptists, make fewer financial demands on their members than do Catholicism and Voodoo. Money is so short and rural economy so precarious that many peasants find themselves in difficulty when the time comes to pay the *casuels* (occasional fees), however small, or to offer a big *manger* to the family spirits. Life without the help of religion is as inconceivable for a Haitian peasant today as it would have been for a French peasant of the thirteenth century, and so the prospect of getting into God's good books for a pittance has doubtless wrestled more than one conscience towards Protestantism. One Protestant woman who had listed all the spiritual satisfactions which she owed to her conversion, did not forget to mention the temporal advantages which it had also brought: 'Protestants don't have to spend much. On Sundays after the service you just give what you can—and that's not very much. We have no ceremonies to pay for. If one of us falls ill the whole community bears the expense.' This last phrase is an allusion to the *esprit de corps* which is characteristic of all religious minorities and which among Haitian Protestants takes an extreme form. From it springs a sense of security which appeals strongly to those who feel lonely or threatened.

Certain Protestant sects—Pentecostists or Shakers—who cultivate religious enthusiasm to the point of mystical trance, exert a strong pull on many Voodooists who for one reason or another wish to become Protestants. In the gatherings of these bodies they find an atmosphere something like that of the Voodoo sanctuaries.

A Pentecostal preacher describing his feelings when 'the spirit was upon him', listed to me exactly the same symptoms as those which I had heard from the mouths of people who have been possessed by *loa*. Between mystical trance and the classic 'attack of *loa*', the difference is probably slight. The fundamental attitude of the original religion clearly crops up again, in another key as it were, in the adopted religion. The same phenomenon occurred in the New World where the African slaves were converted to Protestantism. Undeniably the ecstasy which breaks out in the ceremonies of certain Protestant sects in the south of the United States reflects a survival, if not of rites, then at least of religious behaviour. In Haiti—to take but one example—the affinities of Shakers with Voodooists throw this phenomenon into relief.

Conclusion

The cults and practices described in this work are regarded by many Haitians as a scourge with which an unjust fate has been pleased to afflict their country. They are irritated—understandably—by the label 'Voodoo-land' which travel agencies have stuck on their home. Yet Haiti is far from being the only country in the New World where African cults continue to flourish. Today those cults still have millions of adepts in Cuba, Trinidad and above all in Brazil. Bahia, town of all Saints, is also the town of all West African gods. In Rio de Janeiro African cults are practised, in São Paulo and even in the depths of Brazil, in towns on the Amazon. Thus the *labrys*—the double-axe of Asia Minor and Crete, symbol of the thunder-god—having passed from the Mediterranean to Nigeria, draws closer year by year to the barrier of the Andes. From a scientific viewpoint a systematic comparison of Haitian Voodoo with the other black religions which have developed on American soil would be a work of enormous theoretical scope. But first and foremost it would reveal to us what have been the hardiest, most vigorous aspects of African religions, and the psychological patterns which have determined the borrowings from Catholicism. Whoever, for instance, has visited the sanctuaries of Haiti and Bahia can but have marvelled at the parallelism of cultural development in groups which, though common in origin, have been separated in space and time.

Compared to the *candomblés* of Bahia and the sanctuaries of Havana, the *humfo* of Port-au-Prince cut a sorry figure. The great poverty of the Haitian peasant has naturally affected his religion. He cannot devote as much money to his cult as his Cuban or Brazilian brothers. A Voodoo ceremony, at even the best *humfo*, cannot compare with a service celebrated in even the poorer quarters of Bahia. Moreover the African cults of Brazil and Cuba are much nearer their African source than those of Haiti. This is not surprising since slaves from the Coast were imported to these two countries right up to the second half of

359

the nineteenth century. The last Africans to be taken to Haiti were the Dahomeans of the police-force of King Christophe, a hundred and fifty years ago. Therefore, compared to the other religions (*candomblés* and *santeria*) Voodoo seems a decadent and rather bastardized African religion, but one which shows the origins of various different African elements all integrated in a new religion. By comparative research we could trace the contribution to Voodoo of the Fon, the Ewe, the Yoruba, the Congo tribes and doubtless many other ethnic groups. Such a work could only be undertaken by a scholar who was familiar not only with the other modern African religions, but also with the historic sources of the seventeenth and eighteenth centuries, with descriptions of the Africa from which the ancestors of present-day Haitians were uprooted. The main concern of such a work would be to show us the changes in the various conceptions of the gods and the evolutions of ritual; and in so doing the inquiry would save itself from being a mere display of erudition.

The comparison of Voodoo with the African religions from which it sprang, does not fall within the scope of the present work. A few examples will serve to throw into relief the kind of transformation which has occurred in the personalities and attributes of those gods who have been incorporated in Voodoo. Roger Bastide[1] has already told us of the vicissitudes of Legba (or Exu) in Brazil. Let us see what this same Legba has become in Haiti. In Fon mythology Legba, as interpreter to the gods, fulfils a function of primordial importance in the whole system of religion. He alone can deliver the messages of the gods in human language and interpret their will. He is also the god of destiny, he who presides over divination with palm-nuts or shells. As intermediary between human beings and the divine pantheon he is honoured first at every ceremony and receives the first offerings. He is also a phallic god, represented in front of every house by a little mound of earth out of which sprouts a phallus made of iron or wood. Out of this most potent of gods the Voodooists have made an impotent old man who walks on crutches. Recalling vaguely his rôle as divine messenger they have made a sort of doorman out of him, the supernatural guardian of the 'barriers' who must be invoked first of all *loa*. He has also remained the guardian of houses and to an even greater extent of roads, paths and crossroads. Since any intersection of ways is a hot-spot for magic, Legba-carrefour has become an important magician and presides over the ceremonies of sorcerers. Legba has lost much of his majesty but in exchange he has acquired new functions. As Roger Bastide deftly points out 'there has taken place a prolongation and intensification and not a diminution of an African trait'.

In Haiti, Damballah-wèdo is a benevolent snake spirit who haunts the springs and climbs on trees, whereas in Dahomey he is described by the clergy as one of the many manifestations of Dā, who is less a divine person than a force. Dā 'controls all life and motion'. While Mawu, the supreme god, is Thought, Dā is Life. He manifests himself 'in the world in a number of ways; it is said that there are many Dā, or rather manifestations of Dā, but the chief of them is Dā Ayido Hwedo (in Haiti Damballah-aida-wèdo), most commonly seen as the rainbow'. He is a being with a dual nature, both male and female. Coiled in a spiral round the earth, he sustains the world and prevents its disintegration. As he revolves around the earth, he sets in motion the heavenly bodies. Because his nature is motion, he is also water. 'He may still be recognized today in standing pools which recall the memory of the primordial waters: he is seen cleaving the waters like a flash of light.' Dā is the creator of mountains and also the excreter of metals. In the latter capacity, he partakes of the nature of the sun. Dā was born long before the other *vodû*.[2]

This brief and sketchy *aperçu* of the metaphysical speculations which the notion of Dā has provoked, put alongside the ideas which Haitian Voodooists have of Damballah-wèdo and Aida-wèdo, gives us the measure of the degradation suffered by the religions imported from West Africa to Haiti.

In Dahomey, however, there exist profound differences between the conception held by priests of a divinity and the practice and belief of the profane. It is this latter, popular religion which perpetuated itself among the descendants of the slaves. The priests who were among the captives sold in the West Indian markets could not set up as teachers of theology. Life in plantations was obviously not conducive to metaphysical speculations.

Amazing it is to find in Voodoo even those vestiges of Dahomean cults which there are.

The case of the *loa* Aizan provides another example of the way in which Voodooists have distorted Dahomean mythology. In Haiti Aizan is a divinity who is represented as an old woman, and who, as Legba's wife, protects markets, public places, doors and barriers. She is said to be the oldest of all the divinities and is therefore entitled to the first offerings. She is invoked immediately after her husband Legba. In Dahomey, Aizan is the name given to spirits older than the mythical founders of the tribes. In fact they watch over the latter, as also, over houses and markets. They are symbolized by mounds of earth which are sprinkled with oil and surrounded with *azan*—fringes of palm leaves. The memory of the connection between Aizan and the *azan* is kept up in Haiti where the palm leaf fringes, believed to be full of purifying and healing virtues, are called *aizan*. The sacred tree of the *loa* Aizan is the palm, and people possessed by him dress in white and carry a fringe of palm leaves stripped down into a 'tasselled' kerchief.

So it is we find in Voodoo undeniable traces of Dahomean mythology and its rich tradition, but they are traces grown faint, impoverished to the extent of being unrecognizable. Of the functions and attributes of the great Dahomean gods there remain only insignificant vestiges. The *vodû* have become genies and spirits, no longer august. The ritual of Voodoo, on the other hand, has suffered less from being transplanted than its system of beliefs. Take but one example: the initiation of the *kanzo* possesses a great number of archaic characteristics and still follows the scheme of its Dahomean prototype. The baptism with blood, the 'banking' of hair and nails in pots, the hand-clapping, the term of begging-duty, in short a thousand details faithfully reproduce the initiation stages of the famous Dahomean 'convents'. Yet these rites are not regarded as a form of personal death and resurrection; or, more exactly, that particular aspect of the initiation has become blurred and survives only in rites of which the significance has been lost. Voodooists do not know why parents and friends sob wretchedly when the novices are led blindfolded into the initiation room. Their exit, dressed in wind-

ing sheets, does not strike them as a procession of corpses about
to be recalled to life.

Very pertinently, Herskovits observes, *à propos* Voodoo and
other Afro-American religions, that beneath Christian manners
and customs they often conceal practices and attitudes which are
obviously African. As an example he cites the worship of ancestors
which in Haiti often takes place under cover of funeral rites, and
in the dances and meals which go with memorial services.

Does Voodoo serve a useful purpose in Haitian society, or is it, as
is too often said, no more than a pitiless exploitation of the poor
by smart-alecks and charlatans? We have already mentioned the
considerable sums which peasants have to pay out for treatments
which are almost entirely magical. Many Marbial families complain of having 'lost their foothold' (been ruined) because of *hungan*. I remember hearing the good and honest Lorgina demand 17
gourdes and 17 centimes from a wretched woman who had come
to beg her help against a werewolf who was sucking her child's
blood. White magic, just like black magic, often involves those
who resort to it in considerable expense. Therefore, from a
strictly economic point of view it is undeniable that Voodoo
heavily burdens the resources of the peasant population. Those
who denounce superstition as the shackle on the material
advancement of the peasants, are not entirely wrong. If better
food, decent clothing and more comfortable accommodation
constituted the sole needs of the Haitian rural masses, then without hesitation one could join the ranks of those who are working
for the destruction of Voodoo. But the inner man himself also
needs security; it is precisely because he is so poor and always in
danger of want or illness that the peasant is strongly attached to
Voodoo.

Without *loa* or *boko* how would he get any assurance that his
business will get better, that his own, or his dear ones' illness is
curable? Have those who inveigh against *hungan* and *boko*, ever
thought of the agony of a woman who, when her child is ill, cannot reach a doctor? As long as there is no organized medical
service in Haiti, Voodoo will go on.

No society, if it is to preserve its mental health, can do without
entertainment. The faithful find in Voodoo not only a com-

munion with the supernatural, but also an opportunity of amusing themselves. The songs and dances are sacred, but they afford those who indulge in them an altogether profane pleasure. You have only to watch the leapings and twistings of the dancers in front of their partners to measure the intensity of the pleasure which they derive therefrom. The social utility of Voodoo is easily illustrated. Ceremonies in honour of *loa-racines* help to increase family solidarity since such ceremonies require the co-operation and unity of all members in the collective fulfilment of obligations to *loa*.

The reader will wonder whether Voodoo is a moral or immoral religion. The question should not be framed in these terms since Voodoo is not a religious system with a well defined body of doctrine; nevertheless, the spirits, being conceived in the image of men, do act in conformity with the moral laws which rule Haitian society. The 'good *loa*' cannot approve crime and the 'bad *loa*' can only look for assistance to shady characters. The *loa* are friends who intercede in private life and who often act as interpreters of public opinion. A *loa* can quite easily reproach his 'horse' for behaviour which his neighbours regard as reprehensible and reprimand him for something which he thinks nobody knows about. It is in this sense the *loa* have a claim to be regarded as the guardians of public morality.

The useful and productive rôle of Voodoo in the domain of art is there for all to see. In music and dancing it has allowed the Haitian peasantry to maintain and develop its African heritage—and develop it to a high level of excellence. A well-conducted Voodoo ceremony is something worth seeing: drummers and dancers are often virtuosos of their craft. I do not hesitate to say that Voodoo gives to the traditional culture of Haiti its sole originality. How sad, how empty would be the rural Haitian scene without the artistic activities of which Voodoo is, at one and the same time, cause and essence! By the intimate union of religious and artistic feeling it brings dignity into lives which would otherwise be brutalized and crushed by poverty and the back-breaking labour of the fields. Voodoo gives its adepts an escape from a reality which is too often sordid. Within the framework of a Western-type civilization, it is a many-sided institution suited to various uses—but an institution, above all, in which a man can participate with his whole being.

Voodoo as a religious system has lost none of its creative force. In the anthropologist's sense, it 'functions'. Not only is it the object of a profound faith but its adepts continually enrich it with fresh contributions both to its mythology and to its liturgy. The rôle played by the Haitian *humfo* and that of certain sanctuaries in ancient Greece—of Dionysos or Demeter for instance—have certainly much in common. Those early societies which specialized in orgiastic dances have been compared with the *zar* sects of Abyssinia and Egypt, but even more aptly could they be compared to the Voodoo cult-groups.

There is, however, an important difference between Voodoo and the cults just mentioned. It is too often forgotten that Voodoo, for all its African heritage, belongs to the modern world and is part of our own civilization. The rites and beliefs which have been described in this book may have given a slightly distorted picture of Haitian society, since they have been necessarily somewhat isolated for the purpose of examination. For a true picture it is essential to remember that although the religion of the black peasant is still, to a large extent, African, the institutions of Haiti, its political ideals, its notion of progress, are those of a Western state. Voodoo gods, in spite of their African names and lore, are under the influence of their environment. Man has always made his gods in his own image and this is strikingly true of Haiti: the *loa* have the tastes of modern man, his morality and his ambitions. They are no longer the gods of an African tribe, exotic and remote, but deities who act and think in the industrialized world of today. This is why they are as familiar and as close to us as the gods of ancient Greece were to the people who worshipped them. The westernization of an African religion has brought to light all the features which it shares with the religions of the ancient world, so that anyone acquainted with the classical universe can easily enter the mysterious world of Voodoo. He feels as though he were among gods who speak his language and behave in a way he can understand.

Voodoo is a paganism of the West. We discover it with joy or horror, according to our temperament or our background. Many of us go to Haiti in search of our classical heritage, and find in Voodoo the charm of fairy tales. Without compelling us to give up our habits and our ties with the present, it takes us into a magic realm.

Notes

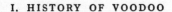

I. HISTORY OF VOODOO

1 LEYBURN, *The Haitian People*, pp. 131–42.

2 MOREAU DE SAINT-MÉRY, *Description topographique*, v. 1, pp. 26–34; and DESCOURTILZ, *Voyage d'un naturaliste*, pp. 116–79.

3 HERSKOVITS, *The Myth of the African Past*, pp. 33–53.

4 HERSKOVITS, *Dahomey*, v. 1, pp. 63–4.

5 On African survivals in Voodoo's religious vocabulary, consult COMHAIRE-SYLVAIN, *A propos du vocabulaire des croyances paysannes* and *Survivances africaines dans le vocabulaire religieux d'Haïti.*

6 *Description topographique*, v. 1, p. 46.

7 *Voyages d'un Suisse*, p. 131.

8 MOREAU DE SAINT-MÉRY, *Loix et constitutions des colonies françaises*, v. 4, p. 384, 829; v. 5, p. 234.

9 VAISSIÈRE, *La Société et la vie Créole*, p. 213.

10 Ibid, p. 213.

11 PEYRAUD, *L'Esclavage aux Antilles françaises*, p. 181.

12 MOREAU DE SAINT-MÉRY, *Loix et constitutions*, v. 4, p. 384

13 *Nouveau voyage aux îles de l'Amérique*, v. 4, p. 132.

14 *La Société et la vie Créole*, p. 204.

15 V. 1, pp. 46–51.

16 *Voyage d'un naturaliste*, v. 3, p. 181.

17 *Description topographique*, v. 1, pp. 210–11.

18 *Voyage d'un naturaliste*, v. 3, p. 181.

19 *Histoire du peuple haïtien*, p. 59.

20 *Manuel d'histoire d'Haïti*, pp. 66–7.

21 Consult HAZOUMÉ, *Sur le pacte du sang au Dahomey.*

22 MADIOU, *Histoire d'Haïti*, v. 1, pp. 72–3, 97; v. 3, p. 33.

23 *Des colonies et particulièrement de celle de Saint-Domingue*, pp. 217–20.

24 *Le Messianisme chez les noirs du Brésil.*

25 MORFAU DE SAINT-MÉRY, *Description topographique*, v. 1, pp. 651–3.

26 MADIOU, *Histoire d'Haïti*, v. 1, p. 97.
27 *Des colonies et particulièrement de Saint-Domingue*, pp. 18–19.
28 *Voyage d'un naturaliste*, v. 3, p. 186.
29 *Histoire d'Haïti*, v. 2, p. 91.
30 *Voyage d'un naturaliste*, v. 3, p. 28.
31 DESCOURTILZ, *Voyage d'un naturaliste*, v. 3, pp. 383–4.
32 *L'Evolution stadiale du vaudou*, pp. 28–32.
33 *Histoire d'Haïti*, v. 2, p. 91.
34 *Colonies étrangères et Haïti*, v. 1, pp. 292–3.
35 ALAUX, *Soulouque et son empire*, pp. 61, 71 and 173.
36 *Haiti or the Black Republic*, p. 183.
37 Ibid, pp. 197–204.
38 Ibid, p. 201.
39 *The Magic Island*, pp. 118–19.
40 Ibid, pp. 121–3.
41 *En Haïti*, p. 56.
42 Consult COMHAIRE, *The Haitian Schism*, on the 'great Haitian schism'.

II. THE SOCIAL FRAMEWORK OF VOODOO

1 *The Haitian People*, pp. 3–13.
2 Further information on Voodoo confraternities and clergy will be found in HERSKOVITS'S *Life in a Haitian Valley*, passim; DEREN, *Divine Horsemen*, pp. 151–85; and RIGAUD, *La Tradition vaudoo*, pp. 71–6.

III. THE SUPERNATURAL WORLD

1 Almost everyone who has written on Voodoo has provided a list, more or less extensive, of the different *loa*. The most complete is that in RIGAUD'S *La Tradition vaudoo*, pp. 141–6. DEREN (*Divine Horsemen*, pp. 82–3) has brought together in tabular form all the principal *loa*, giving each its 'family', its functions and its symbolic colour.
2 For the classification of the Congo *loa*, see MENNESSON-RIGAUD and DENIS, *Cérémonie en l'honneur de Marinette*, pp. 13–14.
3 *Cérémonie en l'honneur de Marinette*.
4 *La Tradition vaudoo*, pp. 221–3.

5 The phenomenon of possession in Haitian Voodoo has already been the subject of several studies. I would quote, in particular, the many publications of DR MARS, who has specialized in study of the mystic trance (see the Bibliography). Pages 146–9 and 186–9 of HERSKOVITS's *Life in a Haitian Valley* define the problem as a whole in an extremely pertinent manner. MAYA DEREN (*Divine Horsemen*, Chap. VII) has described in great detail the impressions she experienced when 'mounted' by the goddess Ezili.

There are close analogies between possession among Voodooists and among the black population of Brazil. It is therefore worth-while to consult BASTIDE, *Cavalos dos santos* (in *Estudos afro-brasileiros*, 3a, pp. 29–60)

6 *Sociologie et psychanalyse*, p. 252.

7 *Magie et médecine*, pp. 36–37.

8 The rôle of the dream in Voodoo is the subject of a study by BOURGUIGNON, *Dreams and Dream Interpretation*. On the symbolism of dreams, see MÉTRAUX, *Croyances et pratiques magiques dans la vallée de Marbial*, pp. 165–70.

9 Marie-Noël's dream has been published by MENNESSON-RIGAUD and DENIS, *Quelques notes sur la vie mystique de Marie-Noël*.

10 Many details concerning the cult of twins have been taken from ODETTE MENNESSON-RIGAUD's excellent study of the subject (*Etude sur le culte des marassa en Haïti*). PRICE-MARS and HERSKOVITS may also be consulted with profit: *Culte des marassa* and *Life in a Haitian Valley*, pp. 201–5.

11 *Life in a Haitian Valley*, p. 204.

IV. RITUAL

1 All works on Voodoo include descriptions of rites, but there exist few systematic studies of the ritual as a whole. It is, however, well worth consulting DENIS and DUVALIER, *L'Evolution stadiale du vaudou*, and RIGAUD, *La Tradition vaudoo*.

2 *La Religion populaire*, pp. 18–19.

3 *Le Sacrifice du tambour assoto(r)*, p. 18.

4 *Sacrifice d'un taureau*, pp. 33–34.

5 There are many descriptions of the musical instruments used in Voodoo. Among the most notable are COURLANDER, *Musical Instruments of Haiti*; DENIS and PAUL, *Essai d'organographie haïtienne*; and COMHAIRE-SYLVAIN, *La chanson haïtienne*.

6 *La Tradition vaudoo*, p. 387.

7 HERSKOVITS, *In a Haitian Valley*, pp. 273–76.

8 *Le Sacrifice du tambour assoto(r)*, pp. 10–11; 58–59.

9 *Divine Horsemen*, p. 236.

10 Sources for this chapter are quoted in MÉTRAUX, *Les Rites d'initiation dans le vaudou haïtien*.

11 For mystical marriage in Voodoo, see also MENNESSON-RIGAUD, *Notes on Two Marriages with Voodoo Loa* in DEREN, *Divine Horsemen*, pp. 263–70.

12 These ceremonies have been described in greater detail by MÉTRAUX, *Le Noël vaudou en Haïti*. Madame ODETTE MENNESSON-RIGAUD has also given a good description of Christmas celebrations in the country, in an article entitled *Noël vaudou en Haïti*.

13 For the cult of the dead in Haiti, see DENIS, *Le Cimetière*; DEREN, *Divine Horsemen*, pp. 41–46; HERSKOVITS, *Life in a Haitian Valley*, pp. 205–18; MARCELIN, *Coûtumes funéraires*; MÉTRAUX, *Rites funéraires des paysans haïtiens*; ODDON, *Une cérémonie funéraire haïtienne*; ROUSSEAU, *Un enterrement à la campagne*. Much information on this theme will also be found in SIMPSON's articles on Voodoo in the north of Haiti.

14 *Le Service des loa*, pp. 71–75.

V. MAGIC AND SORCERY

1 Magic and witchcraft have held the attention of most writers who have dealt with Voodoo. There is an excellent exposition of the question in HERSKOVITS, *Life in a Haitian Valley*, pp. 219–48, and in SIMPSON, *Magical Practices in Northern Haiti*.

2 HERSKOVITS, *Life in a Haitian Valley*, p. 222.

3 Quoted by MARCELIN, *Les Grands dieux du vaudou haïtien*, p. 122.

4 *Mythologie vaudou*, v. 2, p. 166.

5 The same ceremony is described by RIGAUD, *La Tradition vaudoo*, pp. 167–204.

6 *Voodoo Gods*, pp. 184–5.

7 *Magic Island*, pp. 92–103.

8 *Rituel observé en vue de la protection du nouveau-né.*

9 *Le Vaudou haïtien*, p. 186.

VI. VOODOO AND CHRISTIANITY

1 LEIRIS, *Note sur l'usage de chromolithographies*, p. 207.

2 *The Belief System of Haitian Vodun*, pp. 36–37.

3 *Life in a Haitian Valley*, p. 281.

4 *Nouveau voyage aux îles de l'Amérique*, v. 6, pp. 330–31.

5 *Description topographique*, v. 1, p. 35.

6 This subject has been dealt with more fully by MÉTRAUX, *Vaudou et protestantisme*.

CONCLUSION

1 *Immigration et métamorphose d'un dieu.*

2 On the idea of Dā in Dahomey, see MERCIER, *The Fon of Dahomey*, pp. 220–22.

Voodoo Glossary

Abobo Ritual acclamation which punctuates the end of *rada* songs. Uttered, too, during ceremonies as a sign of personal satisfaction. The exclamation is sometimes accompanied by the noise produced by striking the mouth with the fingers.

Acassan A much appreciated beverage made of manioc starch. Drunk with milk and sugar.

Agida A small bow used for beating the 'second' drum in a *rada batterie* (drum group—see below).

Ago Ritual exclamation meaning 'Attention!'.

Aizan Fringe made with fibres of palm (*Oreodoxia regia*). Has the power of keeping away evil. That is why the *aizan* is worn by initiates when they emerge from their period of retreat. The *aizan* is often hung on the lintel of *humfo* doors, on the *poteau-mitan* or on other sacred objects. Sometimes it is used to cover offerings.

Aizan Chiré The ritualistic stripping into fringes of palms; occurs at the beginning of ceremonies. The operation is accompanied by songs, and ends with the ritual baptism of the talisman.

Akra *Beignet* made of manioc or malanga flour.

Arrêt or **Arrestation** Magic charm to stop the effects of witchcraft or the hostility of bad spirits.

Assein Iron rod topped with a little round platform. It is kept before the altar for holding candles. In Dahomey the *asê* are important cult accessories. They represent the ancestors.

Asson Rattle of *hungan* and *mambo*, made of calabash covered with a net in which are enmeshed beads or snake vertebrae.

Assoto Large, tall drum struck by several drummers who dance round it. Regarded as sacred; construction marked by long ceremonies. Inhabited by a *loa* and on this account often dressed in clothes.

Atutu Ball of hot flour which initiates squeeze in their hands at the end of the *bulé-zin*; brings to an end period of retreat.

Awessan Silk scarf worn by the *kanzo hunsi*.

BAGI Sanctuary room containing the altar to the *loa*.

BAKA Evil spirit. Supernatural agent of sorcerers.

BANDA A lascivious dance which is performed by the Guédé *loa*.

BATTERIE The Haitian word for the ensemble of drums in an orchestra.

BOHUN Funeral rite which consists of hitting calabashes, set over a bowl of water, with sticks.

BOKO This word derived from the Fon word *bokono* (priest) is generally applied to *hungan* who practise black magic, but is often used for a Voodoo priest. The *boko* is also a healer.

BORNER To restrain or 'limit', to stop an evil *loa* from doing any harm to a person or a group of persons.

BULAYER Drummer who beats the *boula*.

BULÉ-ZIN Ceremony in which earthenware pots in which offerings have been cooked, are coated with oil and heated until the oil catches fire. The *bulé-zin* is a multivalent ceremony, forming part of initiation, consecration and funeral ritual. The fire is supposed to heat the *loa* and give them more power. The sacralia, too, are exposed to the flames of the *zin*.

BOSAL From the Spanish *bosal* which means 'savage, untamed'. This word is used of *loa* who appear for the first time in a person, or of *hunsi* who have not yet finished their initiation.

BULA The smallest of the *rada* drums.

CANARI Large pot which is consecrated and broken at funeral rites. *Canari* debris are scattered at cross-roads. The *casser-canari* rites are widespread, particularly in the north of Haiti.

CAPRELATA Magic charm.

CAPRELATEUR Magician who makes *caprelata*.

CASSAVA Manioc girdle-cake.

CAYE Creole word for house.

CAYE-MYSTÈRE House of spirits or *loa*. Synonym for *humfo* or sanctuary.

CHANSI Rattle made of tin.

CHUAL Creole form of *cheval* (horse). Person possessed by a *loa*.

CLAIRIN Cheap white rum.

COMBITE Group of peasants working together to the sound of music.

CONNAISSANCE Knowledge of sacred lore which gives power to the *hungan* or the *mambo*.

CREOLE Native to the country.

CROISIGNIN Literally: *croix-signer*—to '*cross-sign*'. To trace, with flour or any other substance, a cross on any ritual object or person.

DAHOMEY-Z-ÉPAULES Rapid dance performed with the top part of the body upright and shoulders rotating in time to drum rhythms.

DIVINO Seer. *Hungan* who is a specialist of divination.

DJÈVO Initiation room.

DOSSU Child born after twins.

DYOK Evil eye.

EAU-SIROP Mixture made with *sirop de batterie* (syrup made from sugar cane) and water.

ENGAGEMENT Pact which binds a person to a wicked spirit.

ENVOI MORTS Sending of dead against a person in order to make him ill or cause his death. This form of witchcraft is also called *expedition*.

ESCORTE Group of *loa* accompanying important *loa*. This word sometimes means a *loa* 'family'.

GANMELLE Wooden trestle used for the preparation of 'baths', or to hold food for *loa*.

GARDE Protective charm.

GOURDE Unit of Haitian currency. The gourde is worth $0.20. or 1s.

GOVI Pitcher into which *loa* are brought down and which contain spirits.

GROS-BON-ANGE One of the two souls which everyone carries inside himself.

HABITANT Peasant.

HUNGAN Voodoo priest.

HUNGENIKON Choir-master in a Voodoo society. The man or woman (also called *reine chanterelle*) who 'launches' (*envoie*) the songs and stops them. She helps the priest and takes his place when he is possessed or when for one reason or another he cannot conduct the whole ceremony.

HUNSI Man or woman who has passed through initiation and who helps the *hungan* or *mambo*.

HUNSI-KANZO *Hunsi* who has passed through the initiation rites.

HUNTO A drum spirit and also the biggest drum in the *rada batterie*.

LA-PLACE Title in a Voodoo society for the master of ceremonies. Armed with a sword or matchet he leads processions, presents arms, pays homage to the *loa* and helps the officiant.

LOA Supernatural being in Voodoo. This word is usually translated by 'god', 'divinity'. In fact a *loa* is more a genie, demon or spirit.

LOA-RACINE Inherited ancestral spirit of a family.

MACOUTE Satchel made of leaves of the Bourbon palm; part of a peasant's everyday equipment.

MANGER-DYò Offering used in consecration rites. Consists of sweet potatoes, yams, malangas, cassava, ground maize, the whole mixed together and sprinkled with acassan and syrup. Used also for consecration are maize, grilled peanuts and lumps of cassava.

MANGER-GUININ Food offered to the *rada-loa*. The *manger-guinin* seems to be no different from the *manger-dyò*.

MANGER-LOA Ceremony intended to feed the *loa* in which animals and various foods are offered.

MANMAN The biggest drum in the *rada batterie*.

MARASSA Divine twins.

MASISI Pervert, homosexual.

MONTER This verb is used of a *loa* coming down into someone, and possessing him.

NAGO Fon name for the Yoruba.

NOM VAILLANT Ritual name for a *hungan* or *mambo* bestowed at the end of his or her initiation.

OGAN Iron bell with external striker. The *ogan* can be a bit of metal which is beaten with a metal rod.

PAQUETT In French, *paquet*, a package. This is a sacred bundle containing various magical ingredients, used in the treatment of the sick.

Pè Brickwork altar in a sanctuary. On it are kept sacred pitchers, stones belonging to spirits, attributes of gods and accessories of *hungan* and *mambo*. Offerings for divinities are put on the *pè*.

PÉRISTYLE *Humfo* annexe which looks like a big shed, open at the sides. The scene of nearly all Voodoo ceremonies and dances.

PETRO Group of Voodoo gods and spirits.

PITTIT-FEY *Petite-feuille*—little leaf—member of a Voodoo society.

PLACAGE Union between a man and a woman recognized by public opinion, but not by law.

PLACÉE Common-law wife.

PLACER-NAM Ceremony in which an object, notably a drum, is consecrated.

PÈRE-SAVANE Bush priest.

POINT Magico-religious term signifying 'supernatural power', 'magic power', 'mystical effluvia'. The *point* can be a charm and a spirit which executes the will of a sorcerer.

POTEAU-MITAN Post in the centre of the peristyle regarded as the thoroughfare of the spirits. It is an outstandingly sacred object.

POT-TÊTE Pot containing hairs, body hair and nail-parings of an initiate.

RADA Name derived from the town of Arada in Dahomey. Family of *loa* and the ritual carried out for that family.

REJETER The act of abjuring Voodoo practices or an abjurer of Voodoo.

REPOSOIR Tree or any other place where a *loa* is supposed to live.

ROUMBLER The calling of *loa* by beating drums.

SEGOND Middle drum of the *rada batterie*.

SERVICE Ceremony in honour of Voodoo divinities.

TI-BON-ANGE One of the two souls which everyone possesses.

TRAITEMENT Cure undertaken with herbs and magic charms.

VENTAILLER Ritual act by which birds are whirled round at arms' length.

VÈVÈ Symbolic design representing the attribute of a *loa* traced on the ground with maize flour, ash, coffee grounds or brick dust.

WANGA Evil charm.

YANVALOU Dance which is carried out with the body sloping forward, hands on knees, and shoulders rolling.

ZOBOP Member of a secret society of sorcerers.

ZOMBI Person from whom a sorcerer has extracted the soul and whom he has thus reduced to slavery. A *zombi* is to a certain extent a living corpse.

Bibliography

ACHILLE (Aristide). Les Croyances des masses haïtiennes (*Optique*, Port-au-Prince, n. 32, Oct. 1956, pp. 59–64).

ALAUX (Gustave d'). *L'Empereur Soulouque et son empire*. Paris, Michel Lévy, 1856.

ARMAND (Maurice). Grossesse gémellaire et tréponèmes en Haïti (*Les Griots*, Port-au-Prince, v. 3, n. 3, Jan–Mar. 1939, pp. 404–409).

AUBIN (Eugène). *En Haïti*. Planteurs d'autrefois, nègres d'aujourd'hui. Paris, Armand Colin, 1910.

AUBOURG (Michel). La Divination dans le vodou (*Bulletin du Bureau d'Ethnologie*, Port-au-Prince, 2nd. ser., n. 12, 1955, pp. 36–46).

BACH (Marcus). *Vaudou*. Religion, sorcellerie, magie. Paris, Hachette, 1955.

BASCOM (William R.). The Focus of Cuban Santeria (*Southwestern Journal of Anthropology*, Albuquerque, N.M., v. 6, n. 1, 1950, pp. 64–68).

BASTIDE (Roger). Structures sociales et religions afro-brésiliennes (*Renaissance*, New York, v. 2 and 3, 1945, pp. 13–29).

— *Introduction à l'étude des interpénétrations des civilisations*. Paris, 1949 (mimeographed text).

— Le Messianisme chez les noirs du Brésil (*Le Monde non chrétien*, Paris, n. ser., n. 15, July–Sept. 1950, pp. 300–8).

— Dans les Amériques noires: Afrique ou Europe? (*Annales, Economies, Sociétés, Civilisations*, Paris, 1948, pp. 17–34) (reproduced in *Cahier des Annales*).

— *Sociologie et psychanalyse*. Paris, Presses Universitaires, 1950.

— Medicina e magia nos candomblés (*Boletim bibliografico*, São Paulo, n. 16, 1950, pp. 7–34).

— Contribution à l'étude de la participation (*Cahiers internationaux de Sociologie*, Paris, v. 14, 1953, pp. 30–44).

— Le 'château intérieur' de l'homme noir (in *Éventail de l'histoire vivante. Hommage à M. Lucien Febvre*, I, Paris, 1953, pp. 255–60).

— Estudos Afro-Brasileiros (*Boletim 154 da Facultade de Filosofia, Ciências e letras da Universidade de S. Paulo*, 3rd. ser., 1953).

— Contribution à l'étude de la participation (*Cahiers internationaux de Sociologie*, Paris, v. 14, 1953, pp. 130–40).

— Immigration et métamorphose d'un dieu (*Cahiers internationaux de Sociologie*, Paris, v. 20, 1956, pp. 45–60).

BASTIEN (Rémy). *Anthologie du folklore haïtien*. Mexico, 1946 (*Acta anthropologica*, I, 4).

BASTIEN (Rémy). *La Familia rural haitiana*. Mexico, Libra, 1951.

BELLEGARDE (Dantes). *Histoire du peuple haïtien* (1492–1952). Port-au-Prince, 1953 (Collection du cent-cinquantenaire de l'indépendance d'Haïti).

BERBAIN (Simone). *Étude sur la traite des Noirs au golfe de Guinée. Le comptoir français de Juda (Ouidah) au XVIIIᵉ siècle*. Paris, Larose, 1942 (*Mémoires de l'Institut francais d'Afrique noire*, n. 3).

BERNARD (Regnor C.). Hommage à Marie-Noël (*Bulletin du Bureau d'Ethnologie*, Port-au-Prince, Mar. 1947, pp. 27–29).

BONSAL (Stephen). *The American Mediterranean*. New York, Moffard, Yard & Co., 1912.

BOURGUIGNON (Erika E.). Dreams and Dream Interpretation (*American Anthropologist*, Menasha, Wis., v. 56, n. 2, part I, 1954, pp. 262–8).

CABON (P. A.). *Notes sur l'histoire religieuse d'Haïti. De la révolution au concordat* (1789–1860). Port-au-Prince, Petit séminaire, collège Saint-Martial, 1933.

Campagne antisuperstitieuse. Documentation. Impr. du Progrès Almonacy. Le Cap, 1941.

CAPLAIN (Jules). *La France en Haïti. Catholicisme, vaudoux, maçonnerie*. Paris (n. d.).

CARR (Andreio T.). A Rada Community in Trinidad (*Caribbean Quarterly*, Trinidad, B.W.I, v. 3, n. 1 (n. d.), pp. 35–54).

COMHAIRE (Jean L.). The Haitian Schism: 1804–1860 (*Anthropological Quarterly*, Washington, D.C., v. 29 (new ser., v. 4), n. 1, 1956, pp. 1–10).

COMHAIRE-SYLVAIN (Suzanne). *A propos du vocabulaire des croyances paysannes*. Port-au-Prince (*s. n.*), 1938.

— La Chanson haïtienne (in *Haïti. Poètes noirs*. Présence africaine, Paris, v. 12, 1951, pp. 61–87).

— (Suzanne and Jean). Loisirs et divertissements dans la région de Kenscoff, Haïti (*Revue de l'Institut de Sociologie*, Brussels, 18th year, n. 2, 1938) (t. to p. 25 p.).

— Survivances africaines dans le vocabulaire religieux d'Haïti (*Études dahoméennes*, Institut francais d'Afrique noire, Porto Novo, n. 10, 1955, pp. 8–20).

Considérations sur l'état présent de la colonie française de Saint-Domingue. A political and legislative work presented to the Ministry of Naval Affairs by M. H. D. Paris, Grangé impr., 1776–1777, 2 v.

COURLANDER (Harold). *Haiti Singing*. Chapel Hill, University of North Carolina Press, 1939.

— Musical Instruments of Haiti (*The Musical Quarterly*, New York, v. 37, n. 3, July 1941, pp. 171–83).

— Gods of Haiti (*Tomorrow*, New York, v. 3, n. 1, 1954, pp. 53–60).

COURLANDER (Harold). The Loa of Haiti: New World African Deities (in *Miscelanea de estudios dedicados a Fernando Ortiz por sus discipulos, colegas y amigos*. La Havana, 1, 1955, pp. 142–443).

CRAIGE (John Houston). *Black Bagdad*. New York, Minton, Balch & Co., 1933.

DANNESKJOLD-SAMSŒ (Axel). *Der Schlangenkult in Oberguinea und auf Haiti*. Inaugural Dissertation . . . of The University of Leipzig. Weida i. Th., 1907.

DENIS (Lorimer). Rapport de la Section d'Ethnographie afro-haïtienne (*Bulletin du Bureau d'Ethnologie*, Port-au-Prince, Dec. 1946).

—   La Religion populaire (*Bulletin du Bureau d'Ethnologie*, Port-au-Prince, Dec. 1946, pp. 16–40).

—   Baptême de feu dans le culte vodouesque (*Bulletin du Bureau d'Ethnologie*, Port-au-Prince, Mar. 1947, pp. 1–4).

—   Rituel observé en vue de la protection du nouveau-né contre les maléfices des sorciers, le mauvais œil ou maldiocre, les mauvais-airs ou loup-garous (*Bulletin du Bureau d'Ethnologie*, Port-au-Prince, 2nd. ser., n. 2, Mar. 1947, pp. 5–6).

—   *Quelques aspects de notre folklore musical*. Port-au-Prince, 1950 (Published by the Bureau d'Ethnologie de la République d'Haïti, 2nd ser., n. 7).

—   Origine des *loas* (in Les Afro-Américains, *Mémoires de l'Institut française d'Afrique noire*, Dakar, n. 27, 1953, pp. 195–9).

—   Le cimitière (*Bulletin du Bureau d'Ethnologie*, Port-au-Prince, 2nd. ser., n. 13, 1956, pp. 1–16).

DENIS (Lorimer) and DUVALIER (François). Une cérémonie du culte Petro (*Les Griots*, Port-au-Prince, v. 2, n. 2, Oct.–Nov.–Dec. 1938, 1st year).

—   Une cérémonie en l'honneur de Damballah (*Les Griots*, Port-au-Prince, v. 3, n. 3, Jan.–Feb.–Mar. 1939, 1st year, pp. 316–19).

—   Une cérémonie d'initiation. Le 'laver-tête' dans le culte vodouesque (*Les Griots*, Port-au-Prince, v. 2 and 3, n. 2 and 3, Oct.–Nov.–Dec. 1939; Jan.–Feb.–Mar. 1940, 2nd year, pp. 657–69).

—   L'Évolution stadiale du vodou (*Bulletin du Bureau d'Ethnologie*, Port-au-Prince, n. 3, Feb. 1944, pp. 9–32).

—   La Culture populaire de la poésie, du chant et des danses dans l'esthétique (*Bulletin du Bureau d'Ethnologie*, Port-au-Prince, 2nd ser., n. 12, 1955, pp. 1–29).

DENIS (Lorimer) and PAUL (C.-Emmanuel). *Essai d'organographie haïtienne*. Port-au-Prince (n. d.) (Published by the Bureau d'Ethnologie de la République d'Haïti).

DEREN (Maya). Social and Ritual Dances of Haiti (*Dance*, New York, 1949).

DEREN (Maya). *Divine Horsemen. The Living Gods of Haiti.* London, New York, Thames & Hudson, 1953.

— Religion and Magic (*Tomorrow*, New York, v. 3, n. 1, 1954, pp. 21–51).

DESCOURTILZ (M.-E.). *Voyages d'un naturaliste et ses observations faites sur les trois règnes de la Nature, dans plusieurs ports de mer français, en Espagne, au continent de l'Amérique septentrionale, à Saint-Yago de Cuba et à Saint-Domingue, ou l'auteur, devenu le prisonnier de 40.000 Noirs révoltés, et par suite mis en liberté par une colonne de l'armeé française, donne les détails circonstanciés sur l'expédition du général Leclerc.* Paris, Defart, 1809, 3 v.

DORSAINVIL (J.-C.). *Une explication philologique du vodou.* Paper read to the Société d'histoire et de géographie d'Haïti. Port-au-Prince, Impr. V. Pierre-Noël, 1924.

— *Vodou et névroses.* Port-au-Prince, Impr. 'La Presse', 1931.

— *Psychologie haïtienne. Voudou et magie.* Port-au-Prince, 1937.

DORSAINVIL (J.-C.) and FRERES DE L'INSTRUCTION CHRÉTIENNE. *Manuel d'histoire d'Haïti.* Port-au-Prince, Procure des Frères de l'Instruction chrétienne, 1949.

DUCŒURJOLLY (S.-J.). *Manuel des habitans de Saint-Domingue.* Paris, Lenoir, 1802, 2 v.

DUNHAM (Katherine). *Las Danzas de Haiti.* Versiones en español e inglés. Mexico, 1947 (*Acta anthropologica*, II, 4).

EDDAH. Le Vaudoux (*Le Nouvelliste*, Port-au-Prince, 12, 28 Sept., 16 Oct., 9 Nov. 1905).

FERMOR (Patrick Leigh). *The Traveller's Tree.* London, John Murray, 1951.

FILIOZAT (Jean). *Magie et médecine.* Paris, Presses Universitaires, 1943.

FOISSET (J.). Quelques considérations générales sur les superstitions (*La Phalange*, Port-au-Prince, 25 Feb. 1942).

FOUCHARD (Jean). *Les Marrons du syllabaire.* Port-au-Prince, Éd. Henri Deschamps, 1953.

FRANCK (Harry A.). *Roaming through the West Indies.* New York, The Century Co., 1920.

FROUDE (James Anthony). *The English in the West Indies, or the Bow of Ulysses.* New York, Charles Scribner's Son, 1888.

GASTON-MARTIN. *Histoire de l'esclavage dans les colonies françaises.* Paris, Presses Universitaires de France, 1948.

GIROD-CHANTRANS (J.). *Voyages d'un Suisse dans différentes colonies d'Amérique pendant la dernière guerre.* Neuchâtel, 1785.

HALL (R. A.). The Genetic Relationships of Haitian Creole (*Ricerche linguistiche. Bolletino dell'Istituto di Glottologia dell'Università di Roma*, v. 1, 1951).

HALL (R. B.). The Société Congo of the Ile à Gonave (*American Anthropologist*, Menasha, Wis., v. 31, 1929, pp. 685–700).

HANNA (Rev. S. W.). *Notes of a Visit to Some Parts of Haiti.* London, Jan.–Feb. 1835–36.

HAZARD (Samuel). *Santo Domingo, past and present, with a glance at Hayti.* New York, Harper & Brothers, 1873.

HAZOUMÉ (Paul). *Le Pacte du sang au Dahomey.* Paris, Institut d'Ethnologie, 1937 (*Travaux et mémoires de l'Institut d'Ethnologie*, v. 25).

HERSKOVITS (Melville J.). *Life in a Haitian Valley.* New York, A. A. Knopf, 1937.

— African Gods and Catholic Saints in New World Negro Belief (*American Anthropologist*, Menasha, Wis., v. 39, n. 4, 1937, pp. 635–43.).

— *Dahomey, an Ancient West-African Kingdom.* New York, J. J. Augustin, 1938, 2 v.

— Drums and Drummers in Afro-Brazilian Cult Life (*The Musical Quarterly*, New York, v. 30, n. 4, 1934, pp. 477–92).

— *The Myth of the Negro Past.* New York, London, Harper & Brothers, 1941.

— The Contribution of Afroamerican Studies to Africanist Research (*American Anthropologist*, Menasha, Wis., v. 50, n. 1, 1948, pp. 2–10).

HOLLY (Arthur). *Les Daimons du culte vodou.* Port-au-Prince, Edmond Chenet, 1918.

HONORAT (Michel Lamartinière). *Les Danses folkloriques haïtiennes.* Port-au-Prince, 1955 (Published by the Bureau d'Ethnologie de la République d'Haïti, 2nd. ser., n. 11).

HOUSTON (Zora). *Voodoo Gods. An inquiry into native myths and magic in Jamaica and Haiti.* London, J. M. Dent, 1939.

HYPPOLITE (Michelson-Paul). *Contes dramatiques haïtiens.* Port-au-Prince, 1951 and 1952, 2 v.

— Le carnaval. Instruments et danses (*Optique*, Port-au-Prince, n. 1, Mar. 1954, pp. 33–39).

— *Une étude sur le folklore haïtien.* Port-au-Prince, 1954 (Collection du cent-cinquantenaire de l'indépendance d'Haïti).

KERGOZ (Jean). *L'Expulsion des Vaudoux.* Paris, Librairie générale catholique Arthur Savaete, ed., 1921.

KERSUZAN (François-Marie). *Conférence populaire sur le vaudoux donnée par Monseigneur l'Évêque du Cap-haïtien le 2 aout 1896.* Port-au-Prince, Impr. H. Amblard, 1896, 27 pp.

— *Allocution synodale de Monseigneur... prononcée le 13 février 1898 sur la nécessité sociale d'observer les commandements de Dieu, et allocution à la réunion contre le vaudoux le même jour.* Cap-Haïtien, Impr. du Progrès, 1898, 21 pp.

LABAT (Le P. Jean-Baptiste). *Nouveau Voyage aux Isles de l'Amérique.* Paris, G. Cavelier, 1722, 6 v.

LACHATANERE (Romula). La Santeria (*Bulletin du Bureau d'Ethnologie,* Port-au-Prince, n. 2, 1943, pp. 28–30).

LEAF (Earl). *Isles of Rhythm.* New York, A. S. Barnes & Company, 1948.

LÉGITIME (Général). *La Vérité sur le vaudoux.* Port-au-Prince, (n. d.), 67 pp.

LE HERISSÉ (A.). *L'Ancien Royaume du Dahomey. Mœurs, religion, histoire.* Paris, E. Larose, 1911.

LEIRIS (Michel). Martinique, Guadeloupe, Haïti (*Les Temps modernes,* Paris, n. 52, Feb. 1950, pp. 1355–68).

—   Sacrifice d'un taureau chez le houngan Jo Pierre Gilles (in *Haïti. Poètes noirs,* Présence africaine, v. 12, 1951, pp. 22–36).

—   Note sur l'usage de chromolithographies par les vodouisants d'Haïti (in Les Afro-Américains, *Mémoires de l'Institut français d'Afrique noire,* Dakar, n. 27, 1953, pp. 201–7).

LEYBURN (James G.). *The Haitian People.* New Haven, Yale University Press, 1945.

LOEDERER (Richard A.). *Vodoo Fire in Haiti.* New York, Doubleday, 1936.

MABILLE (Pierre). Pierres tonnerre, pierres à feu (in Les Afro-Américains, *Mémoires de l'Institut français d'Afrique noire,* Dakar, n. 27, 1953, pp. 209–11).

MADIOU (Thomas). *Histoire d'Haïti.* Port-au-Prince, Impr. J. Courtois, 1847–48, 3 v., v. 4, 1904.

MALENFANT (Colonel). *Des colonies et particulièrement celle de Saint-Domingue.* Paris, Audibert, 1814.

MARCELIN (Milo). Les Grands dieux du vodou haïtien (*Journal de la Société des Américanistes de Paris,* n. ser., v. 36, 1947, pp. 51–135).

—   *Mythologie vodou.* Port-au-Prince, Les Éditions haïtiennes, v. 1: rite arada, 1949; v. 2: rite arada, 1950.

—   Folklore Haitiano. Creencias y supersticiones (*Archives. venezolanos de folklore,* Caracas, 1st year, n. 2, July–Dec. 1952).

—   Cents croyances et superstitions (*Optique,* Port-au-Prince, n. 7, Sept. 1954, pp. 48–56).

—   Le Vodou: religion populaire (*Optique,* Port-au-Prince, n. 14, Apr., pp. 37–44; n. 17, July, pp. 45–51; n. 19, Sept. pp. 47–50, 1955).

—   Coutumes funéraires (*Optique,* Port-au-Prince, n. 11, Jan. 1955, pp. 45–59).

—   Danses et chants vodou (*Optique,* Port-au-Prince, n. 12, Feb. 1955, pp. 29–37).

—   Les Fêtes en Haïti (*Optique,* n. 16, June 1955, pp. 33–45).

—   Écrivains étrangers et le vodou (*Optique,* Port-au-Prince, n. 32, Oct. 1956, pp. 53–57).

MARCELIN (Philippe Thoby) and MARCELIN (Pierre). *Le Crayon de Dieu.* Paris, La Table ronde, 1952.

MARS (Louis). *La Crise de possession dans le vaudou.* Essai de psychiatrie comparée. Port-au-Prince, Impr. de l'État, 1946.

— La Crise de possession dans le vaudou (*La Vie médicale*, Paris, Noël 1952, pp. 81-88).

— La psychopathologie du vaudou (*Psyché*, Paris, Sept.-Oct. 1948, pp. 1063-88).

— Nouvelle contribution à l'étude de la crise de possession (*Psyché*, Paris, n. 60, Oct. 1951, pp. 3-32).

— Nouvelle contribution à l'étude de la crise de possession (in Les Afro-Américains, *Mémoires de l'Institut francais d'Afrique noire*, Dakar, n. 27, 1953, pp. 213-31).

— Phenomena of 'possession' (in *Tomorrow*, New York, v. 3, n. 1, 1954, pp. 61-73).

MARS (Louis) and DEVEREUX (Georges). Haitian Voodoo and the Ritualization of the Nightmare (*Psychoanalytic Review*, v. 38, n. 4, Oct. 1951, pp. 334-42).

MAXIMILIEN (Louis). *Le Vodou haïtien. Rite radas-canzo.* Port-au-Prince, Impr. de l'État, 1945.

— Voodoo, Gnosis, Catholicism (*Tomorrow*, New York, v. 3, n. 1, 1954, pp. 85-90).

MENNESSON-RIGAUD (Odette). The Feasting of the Gods in Haitian Vodu (*Primitive Man*, Washington, D. C., v. 19, n. 1-2, Jan. & Apr. 1946, pp. 1-58).

— Noël vodou en Haïti (in *Haïti. Poètes noirs*, Présence africaine, 12, Paris, 1951, pp. 37-60).

— Étude sur le culte des marassas en Haïti (*Zaïre*, Brussels, n. 6, June 1952, pp. 597-621).

— Vodou haïtien. Quelques notes sur les réminiscences africaines (in Les Afro-Américains, *Mémoires de l'Institut français d'Afrique noire*, Dakar, n. 27, 1953, pp. 235-58).

— Une vieille coutume haïtienne (*Conjonction*, Port-au-Prince, n. 48, pp. 46-49).

MENNESSON-RIGAUD (Odette) and DENIS (Lorimer). Quelques notes sur la vie mystique de Marie-Noël (*Bulletin du Bureau d'Ethnologie*, Port-au-Prince, Mar. 1947, pp. 30-34).

— Cérémonie en l'honneur de Marinette (*Bulletin du Bureau d'Ethnologie*, Port-au-Prince, 2nd ser., n. 3, July 1947, pp. 13-21).

MERCIER (P.). La Possession comme fait social (*La Revue internationale*, Paris, n. 3, 1946, pp. 287-98).

— The Fon of Dahomey in African worlds, *Studies in the cosmological ideas and social values of African peoples*, London-Toronto, Oxford University Press, 1954, pp. 210-34).

MERWIN (Bruce W.). A Voodoo Drum from Hayti (*University of Pennsylvania Museum Journal*, Philadelphia, Pen., v. 8, n. 2, 1917, pp. 123-5).

MÉTRAUX (Alfred). The Concept of Soul in Haitian Vodu (*Southwestern Journal of Anthropology*, Albuquerque, N. M., v. 2, n. 1, 1946, pp. 84–92).

— Chants vodou (*Les Temps modernes*, Paris, n. 52, Feb. 1950, pp. 1386–93).

— Les Paysans haïtiens (in *Haïti, Poètes noirs*, Présence africaine, Paris, v. 12, 1951, pp. 112–35).

— Médecine et vodou en Haïti (*Acta tropica*, Bâle, v. 10, n. 1, 1953, pp. 28–68).

— Le Culte vodou en Haïti (*La Revue de Paris*, 60th year, Aug. 1953, pp. 119–29).

— Croyances et pratiques magiques dans la vallée de Marbial (Haïti) (*Journal de la Société des Américanistes de Paris*, n. ser., v. 42, 1953, pp. 135–98).

— Réactions psychologiques à la christianisation de la vallée de Marbial (Haïti) (*Revue de psychologie des peuples*, Le Havre, 8th year, n. 3, 1953, pp. 250–267).

— Les Croyances animistes dans le vodou haïtien (in Les Afro-Americains, *Mémoires de l'Institut français d'Afrique noire*, Draker, n. 27, 1953, pp. 239–44).

— Le Noël vodou en Haïti (*Bulletin de la Société neuchâteloise de Géographie*, Neuchâtel, v. 51, part 5, 1954–55, pp. 95–118).

— Rites funéraires des paysans haïtiens (*Arts et traditions populaires*, Paris, n. 4, Oct.–Dec., 1954, pp. 289–306).

— Vodou et protestantisme (*Revue d'histoire des religions*, Paris, v. 144, 1953, pp. 198–216).

— Divinités et cultes vodou dans la vallée de Marbial (Haïti) (*Zaïre*, Louvain, n. 7, July 1954, pp. 675–707).

— Les Rites d'initiation dans le vodou haïtien (*Tribus*, Linden Museum, Stuttgart, New ser., v. 4–5, 1954–55, pp. 177–98).

— Les Dieux et les esprits dans le vodou haïtien (*Société suisse des Américanistes*, Geneva, Bulletin, n. 10, Sept. 1955, pp. 2–16; n. 11, Mar. 1956, pp. 1–9).

— Le Mariage mystique dans le vodou (*Cahiers du Sud*, Marseilles, 43rd year, n. 337, 1956, p. 420).

— Le Culte du vodou à Haïti (in *Le Monde religieux. L'Afrique païenne et juive*. Lezay, v. 26, 1956–1957, pp. 148–158).

— Les Rites de naissance dans le vodou haïtien (in *Mélanges Pittard*, Brive (Corrèze), 1957, pp. 229–33).

— Histoire du vodou depuis la guerre de l'indépendance jusqu'à nos jours (*Présence africaine*, Paris, n. 16, Oct.–Nov. 1957, pp. 135–150).

— Le Vodou et le christianisme (*Les Temps modernes*, Paris, 12th year, n. 136, June 1957, pp. 1848–83).

MÉTRAUX (Rhoda). Affiliations through Work in Marbial (Haïti)

(*Primitive man*, Washington, D.C., v. 25, n. 1 and 2, Jan. & Apr. 1952, pp. 1–22).

METZGER (E.). Haïti. III. Vaudoux Verehrung und Kannibalismus (*Globus*, Brunswick, v. 47, 1885, pp. 252–3).

MOREAU DE SAINT-MÉRY (Louis-Élie). *Description topographique, physique, civile, politique et historique de la partie française de l'île de Saint-Domingue.* (*Avec des observations générales sur sa population, sur le caractère et les mœurs de ses divers habitans; sur son climat, sa culture, ses productions, son administration, etc.*) Philadelphia, 1797, 2 v.

— *Loix et constitutions des colonies françoises de l'Amérique sous le vent.* Paris, 1780, 5 v.

MORTEL (Roger). *La Mythomanie sociale en Haïti.* Essais de psychologie. Port-au-Prince, Impr. du collège Vertières, 1947.

NEWELL (William W.). Myths of Voodoo Worship and Child Sacrifice in Haiti (*Journal of American folklore*, Boston, New York, v. 1, 1888, pp. 16–30).

NILES (Blair). *Black Hayti: a Biography of Africa's Eldest Daughter.* New York, 1926.

ODDON (Yvonne). Une Cérémonie funéraire haïtienne (in Les Afro-Américains, *Mémoires de l'Institut français d'Afrique noire*, Dakar, v. 27, 1953, pp. 245–53).

PARSONS (Elsie Claws). Spirit cult in Hayti (*Journal de la Société des Américanistes de Paris*, n. ser., v. 20, 1928, pp. 157–79).

PAUL (Emmanuel-Casséus). *Notes sur le folklore d'Haïti. Proverbes et chansons.* Port-au-Prince, 1946.

— *Nos chansons folkloriques et la possibilité de leur exploitation pédagogique.* Port-au-Prince, 1951 (Collection 'Notre Terre').

— *La 'Gaguère' ou le combat de coqs.* Port-au-Prince, 1952.

— *Considérations sur le dogme du vodou.* Paper on Voodoo read to the Table Ronde Session of Jan. 31, 1954. (Roneoed text from the Haitian National Commission for Cooperation with UNESCO).

— Folklore du militarisme (*Optique*, Port-au-Prince, n. 6, Aug. 1954, pp. 24–27).

— Les Chansons folkloriques haïtiennes (*Optique*, Port-au-Prince, n. 8, Oct. 1954, pp. 28–35).

— Bilan spirituel du Boyérisme (*Revue de la Société haïtienne d'histoire, de géographie et de géologie*, Port-au-Prince, v. 23, n. 87, 1952, pp. 1–15; v. 24, n. 90, pp. 30–38; n. 89, pp. 37–47; n. 91, pp. 43–49, 1953).

— Représentations religieuses dans le vodou (*Bulletin du Bureau d'Ethnologie*, Port-au-Prince, 2nd ser., n. 12, 1955, pp. 47–54).

— La Notion de Mana dans la culture haïtienne (*Optique*, Port-au-Prince, n. 30, Aug. 1956, pp. 49–52).

PETERS (Carl Edward). *Lumière sur le houmfort*. Port-au-Prince, Cheraquit, imprimeur-éditeur, 1941.
— *Le Service des 'loas'*. Port-au-Prince, Impr. Telhomme, 1956, 108 pp.
PEYTRAUD (Lucien). *L'Esclavage aux Antilles françaises avant 1789*. Paris, Hachette, 1897.
PIDOUX (Charles). Les États de possession rituelle chez les Mélano-Africains. Eléments d'une étude psychosociologique de leurs manifestations (*L'Évolution psychiatrique*, year 1955, part 2, Apr.–June, p. 271).
Pour servir au ministère apostolique. Réflexions et documents. Port-au-Prince, Impr. La Phalange, 1950.
PRADINES (Emerante de). Instruments of Rhythm (*Tomorrow*, New York, v. 3, n. 1, 1954, pp. 123–6).
PRADO (J. F. de ALMEIDA-). A Bahia e as suas relacoes com o Daomé (in Instituto historico e geografico brasileiro. *IV Congresso de historia nacional*, 21–28 *avril de* 1949, v. 5, Rio de Janeiro, 1950, pp. 377–439).
PRESSOIR (C.). *Le Protestantisme haïtien*. Port-au-Prince, v. 1, parts 1 and 2, Impr. de la Société biblique et des livres religieux d'Haïti, 1945.
PRICE-MARS (Jean). *Le Sentiment et le phénomène religieux chez les nègres de Saint-Domingue*. Port-au-Prince, 1928.
— *Ainsi parla l'oncle* . . . Paris, Impr. de Compiègne, 1928 (Bibliothèque haïtienne).
— Lemba-petro. Un culte secret (in *Revue de la Société d'histoire et de géographie d'Haïti*, Port-au-Prince, v. 9, n. 28, 1938, pp. 12–31).
— Les Survivances africaines dans la communauté haïtienne (*Études dahoméennes*, Institut francais d'Afrique noire, Porto Novo, v. 6, pp. 5–10).
— Culte des marassas (*Afroamerica*, Mexico, v. 1, n. 1, 2, Jan. and June, 1945, pp. 41–49).
— Africa in the Americas (*Tomorrow*, New York, v. 3, n. 1, 1954, pp. 75–84).
— *Une étape de l'évolution haïtienne*. Port-au-Prince.
PRICHARD (Hesketh). *Where Black rules Whites: A Journey across and about Hayti*. London and New York, 1910.
RAMOS (Arthur). A possessâo fetichista na Bahia (*Archivos do Instituto Nina Rodrigues*, Bahia, 1st year, 1932).
— *As culturas negras no Novo Mundo*. Rio de Janeiro, Companhia editora nacional, 1946 (*Brasiliana*, 5th ser., v. 249).
REBOUX (Paul). *Blancs et Noirs*. Paris, Flammarion, 1919.
Réflexions et documents pour servir au ministère apostolique. Port-au-Prince, Impr. La Phalange, 1950.

RIGAUD (Milo). *La Tradition vaudoo et le vaudoo haïtien.* Son temple, ses mystères, sa magie. Photographs by Odette Mennesson-Rigaud. Paris, Niclaus, 1953.

RIGAUD (Odette-M.), see MENNESSON-RIGAUD.

ROUMAIN (Jaques). *A propos de la campagne 'antisuperstitieuse'.* Port-au-Prince, Impr. de l'État, 1942.

— *Le Sacrifice du tambour-assotor.* Port-au-Prince, Impr. de l'État, 1943 (Publications du Bureau d'Ethnologie de la République d'Haïti, n. 1).

— *Gouverneurs de la rosée.* Port-au-Prince, 1944 (Collection indigène).

ROUSSEAU (Alfred). Un enterrement à la campagne (*Le Soir*, Port-au-Prince, 4 May 1907).

ROY (Louis). Quelques aspects de la biotypologie haïtienne (*Bulletin du Bureau d'Ethnologie*, Port-au-Prince, n. 2, 1943, pp. 7-21).

SAVINE (Albert). *Saint-Domingue à la veille de la révolution.* Souvenirs du baron de Wimpffen, annotés d'après les documents d'archives et les mémoires. Paris, L. Michaud, 1911.

SCHOELCHER (Victor). *Colonies étrangères et Haïti.* Résultats de l'émancipation anglaise. Paris, Pagnerre, 1843.

SEABROOK (W. B.). *The Magic Island.* New York, The Literary Guild of America, 1929.

SEPILLI (Tulio). Il sincretismo religioso afro-cattolico in Brasile (*Studi e materiali di storia delle religioni*, Bologna, v. 24-25, 1953-4, pp. 1-49).

— *Il sincretismo religioso afro-cattolico in Brasile, II* (note aggiuntive). Roma, Istituto di antropologia dell'Università, 1955.

SIMPSON (George Eaton). The Vodun Service in Northern Haïti (*American Anthropologist*, Menasha, Wis., v. 42, n. 2, 1940, pp. 236-54).

— Peasant Songs and Dances of Northern Haiti (*The Journal of Negro History*, Washington, D.C., v. 25, n. 2, 1940, pp. 203-15).

— Haiti's Social Structure (*American Sociological Review*, Menasha, Wis., v. 6, n. 5, 1941, pp. 640-9).

— Loup-garou and Loa Tales from Northern Haiti (*Journal of American Folklore*, Philadelphia, v. 55, n. 218, 1942, pp. 219-27).

— Traditional Tales from Northern Haiti (*Journal of American Folklore*, Philadelphia, v. 56, n. 222, 1943, pp. 255-65).

— Four Vodun Ceremonies (*Journal of American Folklore*, Philadelphia, v. 59, n. 231, 1946, pp. 154-67).

— The Belief System of Haitian Vodun (*American Anthropologist*, Menasha, Wis., v. 47, n. 1, 1945, pp. 35-59).

SIMPSON (George Eaton). Two Vodun-Related Ceremonies (*Journal of American Folklore*, Philadelphia, v. 61, n. 239, 1948, pp. 49–52).

— Acculturation in Northern Haiti (*Journal of American Folklore*, Philadelphia, v. 54, n. 254, 1951, pp. 397–403).

— Magical Practices in Northern Haiti (*Journal of American Folklore*, Philadelphia, v. 67, n. 266, 1954, pp. 395–403).

— Peasant Children's Games in Northern Haiti (*Folklore*, London, v. 65, n. 2, 1954, pp. 67–73).

ST.-JOHN (Spencer). *Hayti or the Black Republic*. London, Smith, Elder & Co., 1884.

STERLIN (Philippe). *Vèvès vodou*, 1st and 2nd ser. Port-au-Prince, ed. Philippe Sterlin, 1954.

SYLVAIN (Georges). *Un Grand Haïtien témoigne. Dieu et liberté*. Port-au-Prince, La Phalange, 10 Mar. 1942.

SYLVAIN (Jeanne G.). L'Enfance paysanne en Haïti (in *Haïti. Poètes noirs*, Présence africaine, Paris, v. 12, 1951, pp. 88–111).

TAFT (Edna). *A Puritan in Voodoo-Land*. Philadelphia, Penn. Co., 1938.

TIPPENHAUER (L. Gentil). *Die Insel Haïti*. Leipzig, 1893.

TROUILLOT (D.). *Esquisse ethnographique. Le Vodoun. Aperçu historique et évolutions*. Port-au-Prince, Impr. R. Ethéart, 1885.

UNESCO. *L'Expérience-témoin d'Haïti*. Première phase: 1947–1949. Paris, 1951 (Monographie sur l'éducation de base).

VAISSIERE (Pierre de). *Saint-Domingue* (1629–1789). *La Société et la vie créole sous l'ancien régime*. Paris, Perrin, 1909.

VIAUD (Léonce). Le Houmfor (*Bulletin du Bureau d'Ethnologie*, Port-au-Prince, 2nd ser., n. 12, 1955, pp. 30–35).

(Anonymous) The Whistle and the Whip (*Tomorrow*, New York, v. 3, n. 1, 1954, pp. 91–94).

WILLIAMS (Joseph J.). *Voodoos and Obeahs*. Phases of West Indian witchcraft. New York, London, Allen, 1932.

WILSON (Edmund). Voodoo in Literature (*Tomorrow*, New York, v. 3, n. 1, 1954, pp. 95–102).

WIRKUS (F.) and DUDLEY (T.). *Le Roi blanc de la Gonave*. Le culte du vaudou en Haïti, 1915–1929. Paris, Payot, 1932.

WOLFF (S.). Notes on the Vodoun Religion in Haiti with reference to its social and psycho-dynamics (*Revue internationale d'ethnopsychologie normale et pathologique*, Tangier, v. 1, n. 2, 1956, pp. 209–40).

Index

391